CLASS AND REFORM

CLASS AND REFORM

School and Society in Chicago,

1880-1930

David John Hogan

UNIVERSITY OF PENNSYLVANIA PRESS

Philadelphia

Portions of the material in chapter 3 were previously published in
History of Education Quarterly and are reprinted here with permission.

Library of Congress Cataloging in Publication Data

Hogan, David John, 1946–
    Class and reform.

    Bibliography: p.
    Includes index.
    1. Education—Political aspects—Illinois—Chicago—History—
Case studies.   2. Politics and education—History—Case studies.
3. Chicago (Ill.)—Politics and government—To 1950.   4. Child
welfare—Illinois—Chicago—History—Case studies.   5. Vocational
education—Illinois—Chicago—History—Case studies.   I. Title.
LC90.I3H63   1985   370.19′09773′11   84–17222
ISBN 0-8122-7934-4

Printed in the United States of America

To my parents, William Cecil and Margaret Anne
Hogan, to my brothers, Terry, Alan, and Michael, and
to my sister, Katherine, in love and gratitude.

CONTENTS

Acknowledgments ix

Preface xi

1. SOCIAL ORDER AND PROGRESSIVE REFORM IN CHICAGO,
   1877–1912 1

   Class Relationships in the Gilded Age, 4. Années Terrible,
   17. Progressive Reform in Chicago, 25. Progressive Reform
   and the Liberal Moment, 46.

2. THE IRONIES OF PROGRESSIVE CHILD-SAVING 51

   Child Labor and Compulsory Education Legislation, 52. The
   Juvenile Court and Probation, 60. Reforming the Urban
   Environment, 66. Kindergartens, 79. Child-Centered
   Pedagogy, 82. Child-Saving and the Market Revolution, 93.

3. THE LIMITS OF REFORM: CHILD LABOR, COMPULSORY
   EDUCATION AND THE REMAKING OF THE CHICAGO
   WORKING CLASS 96

   Labor and Educational Politics, 1874–1903, 97. Child Labor
   and the Domestic Economy of the Chicago Working Class,
   101. The Political Economy of Home Ownership, 114.
   School Attendance and Class Formation, 123. Progressive
   Reform and the Remaking of the Chicago Working Class,
   136.

4. THE TRIUMPH OF VOCATIONALISM   138

The Origins of Vocational Education: The Transformation
of Work, 139. The Politics of Practical Education, 152. The
Institutionalization of Vocationalism, 167. The Cooley Bill,
175. Vocational Guidance, 181. Mental Testing and Junior
High Schools, 185. Vocational Education and the Market
Revolution, 192.

5. CENTRALIZATION AND THE TRANSFORMATION OF PUBLIC
EDUCATION (coauthored with Marjorie Murphy)   194

The Politics of Centralization, 196. Centralization, Business,
and Progressive Politics, 214.

6. CONCLUSION: PROGRESSIVE REFORM AND THE MARKET
REVOLUTION   228

Notes   237

Index   319

ACKNOWLEDGMENTS

This book started as a Ph.D. dissertation at the University of Illinois. There, Paul Violas, Frederick Jaher, Randy McGowen, Jim Farrell, and Clarence Karier, particularly, provided support and encouragement. Sam Bowles, Ian Davey, Michael Frisch, Michael Katz, David Labaree, Bruce Laurie, Walter Licht, Marje Murphy, Mark Stern, and David Tyack read subsequent drafts and made valuable suggestions. Marje Murphy, especially, gave the manuscript such a close reading that I needed to rewrite most of it from scratch. Michael Frisch wrote a critical review that went way beyond the call of duty. Lori Rubenstein struggled through the Preface with me time and again, while Michael Hogan offered valuable help with chapter 1. Michael Katz and Dean Dell Hymes of the Graduate School of Education at the University of Pennsylvania created an institutional home that made possible the completion of the manuscript. A Spencer Fellowship from the National Academy of Education and a grant from the University of Pennsylvania Research Foundation supplied financial support. Liz Welsh typed—and retyped—the manuscript with untiring good humor and expertise. Tom Seals, Rosemary Blogg, Lori Rubenstein, Gary Lande, Jim Larkin, Marje Murphy, Randy McGowen, David Labaree, Robert Shreefter, and Patrick Manning provided friendship and stood by me in moments of travail. Lori Rubenstein, particularly, bore with me as I completed the last draft, and for that she is due special thanks. The editors of the *History of Education Quarterly* gave permission to republish material in chapter 3 from the Fall 1978 issue, as did the City Club of Chicago for the diagram in chapter 4. My brother Terry undertook the thankless job of completing the index. Finally, I'd like to express my appreciation to the staff of the University of Pennsylvania Press, particularly to Jo Mugnolo, Ingalill Hjelm, and the late Maurice English, for their support and help.

PREFACE

In the last year of the nineteenth century, John Dewey, then a professor of philosophy, psychology, and education at the University of Chicago, completed a short monograph that he entitled *The School and Society*. He wrote that the book represented an "effort to conceive what roughly may be termed the 'New Education' in the light of larger changes in society." "The change," he claimed, "that overshadows and even controls all others, is the industrial one—the application of science resulting in the great inventions that have utilized the forces of nature on a vast and inexpensive scale: the growth of a world-wide market as the object of production, of vast manufacturing centers to supply this market, of cheap and rapid means of communication and distribution between all its parts." Dewey believed that there had been no "revolution in all history so rapid, so extensive, so complete." This revolution had made "the face of the earth over, even as its physical forms; political boundaries are wiped out and moved about, . . . population is hurriedly gathered into cities from the ends of the earth; habits of living are altered with startling abruptness and thoroughness; the search for the truths of nature is infinitely stimulated and facilitated, and their application of life made not only practicable, but commercially necessary." He concluded: "Even our moral and religious ideas and interests, the most conservative because the deepest-lying things in our nature, are profoundly affected. That this revolution should not affect education in some other than a formal and superficial fashion is inconceivable."[1]

Twenty-nine years later, George S. Counts published *School and Society in Chicago*, a study of "the play of social forces upon the school" during the reign of Mayor "Big Bill" Thompson in the 1920s. Taking issue with those who divorced the school from society, Counts sought to document the impact of organized groups and larger "social forces" upon education.

criteria differentiate classes from each other: not an inequality matrix but the system of class relations. Thus, in traditional Marxist approaches to class, classes are differentiated by their relation to the system of wage labor: a capitalist class that purchases labor power in the labor market, a working class that sells labor power in the labor market.[9] In the second kind of categorical definition, the focus is less upon the individuals or groups who occupy particular positions in the social structure or who "bear" social relations than upon the positions or the social relations themselves.

In certain kinds of studies—for example, in studies of changes in the systems of stratification, "opportunity structures," or patterns of voting behavior, or when attempting to specify the class character of social relations—categorical conceptions of class are necessary and appropriate. Which set of characteristics is used to differentiate classes, or to specify the nature of social relations, is a theoretical, not a conceptual, issue. For example, whether income and occupation or class position are used to measure differences in social behavior reflects a choice between two alternative categorical conceptions of class derived from two competing theoretical traditions, not a choice between a categorical and a noncategorical conception of class. Although categorical conceptions of class are necessary and desirable in certain kinds of analyses, these conceptions, irrespective of the theoretical tradition from which they are derived, have one serious limitation: They are not intrinsically historical concepts that elucidate historical processes. At best, categorical conceptions of class allow the historian to impose, a priori, a social grid upon social life. They do not themselves describe or explain historical process or change.

No one has made this point more forcefully than E. P. Thompson. Thompson insists that the concept of class denotes neither groups of people sharing common "life chances" nor categories of people occupying common positions within a status hierarchy. Rather, he argues, class is a certain kind of historical phenomenon, an "event." Class "happens." "By class," he wrote, "I understand a historical phenomenon unifying a number of disparate and seemingly unconnected events, both in the raw material of experience and in consciousness. I emphasize that it is a historical phenomenon. I do not see class as a 'structure,' nor even as a 'category,' but as something which in fact happens (and can be shown to have happened) in human relationships."[10] In another essay he drew the distinction between a categorical conception of class and a historical conception thus:

Sociologists . . . have stopped the time machine and, with a good deal of conceptual huffing and puffing, have gone to the engine room to look and tell us that nowhere at all have they been able to locate and classify a class. They can only find a multitude of people with different occupations, incomes, status-hierarchies, and the rest. Of course they are right, since class is not this or that part of the machine, but the way the machine works once it is set in motion—not this and that interest, but the friction of interests—the movement itself, the heat, the thundering noise. Class is a social and cultural formation (often finding institutional expression) which cannot be defined abstractly, or in isolation, but only in terms of relationship with other classes; and ultimately, the definition can only be made in the medium of time—that is, action and reaction, change and conflict."

What Thompson in effect proposes is that historians view class from two closely related perspectives: either as a special kind of historical "event," or as a special type of historical "process." To view class as an "event" is to focus on class relationships—the interactions, the conflicts, the negotiations, the accommodations between members of social classes—at different points in time. To view class as a process is to focus attention upon class formation, the manner in which class relationships generate the development of distinctive and antagonistic social groupings. Classes form through and as a consequence of their class relationships. Classes do not "precede" but "arise" out of "struggle," he wrote, "and develop only in relationship to each other." "We cannot have two distinct classes," he continued, "each with an independent being, and then bring them into relationship with each other."[12] For Thompson, then, "class conflict" and "hegemony," for example, are particular kinds of events or "situations" in history, the first involving overt conflict between classes and the second a relatively stable arrangement of subordination and superordination between classes.[13] However, situations of class conflict are not just ordinary events. They are particularly privileged ones, in that they generate fundamental changes in the nature of social organizations and provide the context and dynamic of the process of class formation.

Thompson's approach to class—his focus upon class as an event and as a process, upon class relationships and class formation—has wrought a revolution in labor and working class history, both in the United States and the United Kingdom. Yet his account of the nature of class analysis is not without its difficulties.[14] The first difficulty centers on Thompson's point-blank rejection of any kind of categorical definition and his argument that class be defined in terms of class consciousness. "Class happens," he writes, "when some men, as a result of common experiences, feel and articulate the identity of their interests as between themselves, and as against other men whose interests are different from (and usually opposed to) theirs."[15] But to define class in this way poses two serious difficulties. To begin with, it simply runs counter to historical evidence. As Perry

Anderson suggests, "Classes have frequently existed whose members did not identify their antagonistic interests in any process of common classification or struggle. Indeed, it is possible that for most of historical time this was the rule rather than the exception."[16] The English working class did not disappear when it failed to exhibit a consciousness of itself as a class. In an American context such a criticism carries even more weight, for in the United States class conflict has been pervasive and persistent yet only episodically articulated and experienced in class-conscious terms. Ethnicity, race, and even sex and geography have been critical modalities of the cultural experience of the American working class, easily as significant as expressions of class consciousness, and important axes along which the process of class formation has taken place. In other words, Thompson unacceptably subordinates the process of class formation to a teleology—the development of class consciousness. Whether class consciousness, or political mobilization, occurs is essentially a contingent matter, a function of the brittleness of class relationships and the level of class conflict. Again, Thompson's account of class formation is rigidly linear and unable, therefore, to account for the fact that classes are not merely made but also unmade and remade, indeed, made, unmade and remade in a continuous process of class formation, decomposition and reformation.[17] And finally, Thompson's definition of class in terms of class consciousness neglects the fundamental and prior sense in which, as Cohen writes, "a person's class is established by nothing but his objective place in the network of ownership relations. . . . His consciousness, culture and politics are issues intrinsic to the process of class formation, as Thompson rightly insists, but they do not constitute the defining criteria of class."[18]

Thompson intended his definition of class in terms of class consciousness to avoid the chief difficulty confronting categorical definitions of class that defined class either in terms of groups of individuals sharing common locations in the social structure or in terms of the structure of class positions themselves—their inability to explain social practice in general and collective action and class mobilization in particular. Yet it is quite possible to provide a conceptual link between the categorical aspects of class (class positions, groups of individuals) on the one hand and collective action on the other without relying on teleological and linear conceptions of class formation and without ignoring the importance of the structural aspects of class. Two concepts are required to forge this link: a notion of class practice and a nonteleological and nonlinear conception of class formation. Bob Connell in particular has emphasized the importance of this strategy, the one to focus our attention on what people who share a common fate do, and the second to highlight the importance of the continual process of development, decomposition, and reconstitution of distinctive class-based forms of organization, intellectual traditions and sensibilities, and patterns of social behavior—in a word, class practices. "It is not what people are," he writes, "or even what they own, so much as what they do with their resources and their relationships, that is central. . . . Classes are not abstract categories but real-life groupings, which, like heavily-travelled roads, are constantly under construction: getting organized, divided, broken down, remade."[19]

The second major difficulty of Thompson's approach to class analysis centers on his failure to distinguish between two closely related but analytically distinct notions—the concepts of class relations and class relationships, or in generic terms, between social relations and social relationships. A class relation is a particular kind of social relation—wage labor. Class relationships are the interpersonal relationships between members of two classes—capitalists and workers, for instance. The first presupposes the second; the structural logically precedes the interpersonal. Class conflict and hegemony are not class relations but particular kinds of class relationships, the one involving overt conflict and the other a relatively stable pattern of superordination and subordination between the members of two classes. In his substantive historical writings, Thompson focuses exclusively on the interpersonal, on social relationships. While social relations are never entirely absent, they remain for the most part mute, invisible, covert, implicit in the character of the interpersonal. We have to infer the history of social relations from the history of social relationships. It is certainly true that one way in which historians can describe the character and effects of changes in social relations is by examining their impact on social (or class) relationships, but the first cannot be reduced to the second—they are analytically distinct notions related in a complex dialectic mediated by social practices: social relations shape or "structure" social relationships, social relations and relationships shape social practices, and social relationships and practices in turn reconstitute and transform social relations in a continual process of cultural production.[20]

This distinction between social relations and social relationships permits a further modification to Thompson's theory of class formation. Given Thompson's nominalistic preoccupation with class relationships, he can provide no more than a partial and incomplete account of the process of class formation. His conception allows us at best to merely describe the efforts of subordinate classes to limit or shape the behavior of working class people, and the resistance and accommodations, the "autonomy" or "agency" of the working class, in the face of such efforts. It is not fully possible in his account to grasp the way in which working class behaviors—their class practices—are also "structured" by social relations and institutional arrangements. As we shall see, working class educational behavior in Chicago, for example, was not only influenced by the activities of middle-class reformers in securing compulsory attendance and child labor legislation but also by the system of social relations that promoted extensive investment by parents in their children's human capital. Thompson's conclusion then that "the working class made itself as much as it was made" misleads in the insistence that only capitalists or middle-class reformers shape working class behavior, and needs, therefore, to be recast in terms that include structural as well as interpersonal processes.[21]

The utility of the notion of structuration is not limited, however, to the contribution it can make to our understanding of the process of class formation. It also provides a means for conceptualizing the manner in which the class relation characteristic of capitalist societies, namely, markets in labor, is able to effect a gradual transformation, through its impact on the organization of social practices, in social relations generally—political, ideological and sexual—and the institutional arrangements associated with them. In fact it is exactly such a transformation that Progressive reformers engineered in Chicago in public education, in the family, in childhood, and in the state during the Progressive Era. In introducing vocational education and practical pedagogies, for example, reformers in Chicago succeeded in transforming public education into what Karl Polanyi would call an "adjunct" of the market economy. In the long run, Polanyi argued in *The Great Transformation,* a market economy functionally requires, and creates, a society organized in such a way that it operates "as an adjunct to the market":

Instead of economy being embedded in social relations, social relations are embedded in the economic system. The vital importance of the economic factor to the existence of society precluded any other result. For once the economic system is organized in separate institutions, based on specific motives and conferring a special status, society must be shaped in such a manner as to allow that system to function according to its own laws. This is the meaning of the familiar assertion that a market economy can function only in a market society.

Although Polanyi's formulation has a decidedly functionalist quality to it, it does capture a fundamental historical development characteristic of market societies—the progressive "structuration" of social relations and institutional arrangements around what Anthony Giddens calls "the class principle" or what Connell and Irving describe as the process through which "class relations come to dominate other patterns of relationship as an aspect of the process of carving out a distinct region for the operation of class relationships, the process of *creating* a social 'space' of a certain kind." In effect, class does not merely delimit categories of individuals; it is above all a structuring process, continually organizing and reorganizing social relations, institutional arrangements, and cultural formations through time.[22]

One further conceptual matter remains to be considered: the nature of class politics. The orthodox procedure for distinguishing class from nonclass politics involves a particular application of a categorical conception of class, classifying a particular political activity or outcome—voting behavior, membership in a political organization, ideological commitments—on the basis of differences in the social background of the relevant political actors or subjects or on the presence or absence of class rhetoric. Thus, for example, George Mowry and Richard Hofstadter identify the Progressives as "middle class" on the basis of a collective biography of Progressive reformers. (They failed, however, to demonstrate that opponents of Progressive reform were not "middle class.") Richard Jensen, John Allswang, and Paul Kleppner, after detailed investigations of the relative salience of "class" or "economic" versus "ethno-religious" or "ethnocultural" characteristics of voters in the Midwest, proclaim that midwestern politics in the late nineteenth century divided along ethno-religious rather than class lines. Julia Wrigley, in a recent study of "class politics" in Chicago, proposes to specify "the conditions under which education is treated as a class issue" but then goes on to classify educational politics in Chicago as a form of "class politics" because leading actors in educational politics in Chicago came from organized labor and organized capital and because the former often had recourse to class rhetoric in their battles with the latter.[23]

For certain kinds of purposes, categorical approaches to the analysis of class politics, whether of the social characteristics of political actors or the presence or absence of class rhetoric, are desirable and useful. They could be made even more useful if researchers employing categorical approaches to class politics incorporated within their analyses an account of the nature of the political problematics within which political actors act politically and not merely an analysis of the relative significance of different aspects of the social background of political actors. Three distinct political problematics can be distinguished: social-structural, distributional, and cultural. The first centers on social relationships or political conflicts that directly involve the structure of social relations (including, obviously, class relations) and the pattern of institutional arrangements surrounding and supporting them. Distributional politics include activities designed to gain power, increase income or wealth, or to enhance status or prestige within the existing structural and institutional arrange-ments of the society. Cultural politics center on questions of group iden-tity or cohesion. Of course, any one particular political conflict might involve more than one problematic, and political conflicts of one particular kind (say, social-structural) can and usually do have extensive distribu-tional and cultural consequences. Moreover, on occasion what might ap-pear at first glance to be one kind of politics often turns out on closer inspection to be simply a displaced form of another kind. Cultural politics, for example, are often symbolic expressions of social-structural or distri-butional politics.

This expanded categorical approach to the analysis of class politics has much to recommend it, but it does have, in common with all categor-ical conceptions of class, one important limitation. Categorical concep-tions of class, as noted earlier, do not describe or constitute historical processes. Rather, they merely classify groups of individuals according to a particular set of criteria. Categorical conceptions of class politics share the same difficulty—they do not describe or represent historical processes. To do that requires a conception of class politics as a political process. One way to accomplish this is to locate political behavior and political events—conflicts over the structure of social relations and institutional arrangements, conflicts over the distribution of wealth or power, and political mobilization, for example—in the broader contexts of processes of structuration and class formation.

Class analysis, particularly the notions of structuration and class for-mation, rather than social control theory provides the conceptual building blocks of the following study of the relationship between the school and society in Chicago. At a theoretical level, I have framed the study as an analysis of the Great Transformation and the years between 1893 and 1912, a particularly important moment, a "liberal moment" to paraphrase J.G.A. Pocock, in America's Great Transformation.[24] Sometimes out of a desire to end "social justice," sometimes to secure a "social democracy," sometimes to promote "social efficiency," sometimes all three at once, reformers endeavored to end the abuses of the market revolution, "adjust" the family, government, schooling and even childhood itself to the logic of the market economy, and created a wholly new set of institutional mechanisms to regulate social relationships. The significant processes that characterized the Great Transformation were not, however, those of elite imposition or social control, pluralist competition, or even class conflict (although examples of each can be found) but processes of structuration and class formation, for it is in these two processes that the creation of a market society and the key to Progressive reform can be located.

America's Great Transformation did not, of course, begin in the nineteenth century, let alone during the Progressive Era, but dates at least from the end of the seventeenth century.[25] And it involved a lot more than a mere revolution in social arrangements. It also included an intellectual revolution, the triumph of a highly idiosyncratic form of liberalism, one deeply influenced by eighteenth-century republican thought. From the time of the Stamp Act crisis in the mid-1760s through the end of the nineteenth century, Americans blended the classical republicanism or "civic humanism" of Machiavelli and the eighteenth-century English "commonwealth" or "Whig" tradition on the one hand and Lockean liberalism on the other.[26] Republicanism extolled "virtue" over "self-interest," feared "commerce," "corruption," "dependency" and interest-group politics, and favored social hierarchy and periodic moral reformations of the people.[27] Lockean liberalism by contrast recognized the legitimacy of self-interest, urged the creation of a natural economic order based on free labor, contractual relations, and a self-regulating market, favored economic growth, approved of individual self-improvement and the distribution of wealth on the basis of individual achievement and merit, and claimed that individuals were endowed with natural rights.

Although neo-Whig historians—Bernard Bailyn, Gordon Wood, J.G.A. Pocock, and others—argue that republicanism rather than liberalism dominated Revolutionary political thought, others, particularly Joan Appleby, Morton White, and Isaac Kramnick, have persuasively argued that liberal assumptions pervaded the political language of the 1760s and 1770s.[28] Tensions and contradictions, of course, abounded: between power and liberty, progress and decay, self-interest and public virtue, independence and deference, social hierarchy and natural rights, court and country, and above all, as J.G.A. Pocock suggests, between commerce and virtue. Leading political figures—Jefferson, Paine, Madison, Hamilton—brewed their own particular blends of republican and liberal thought, each resolving or ignoring the tensions between liberalism and republicanism in his own distinctive way.[29] Later still, Jacksonian Democrats, Whigs, equal rights republicans, and Lincoln's Republican party concocted their own particular visions.[30] Gradually, over the course of the nineteenth century, a distinctive intellectual tradition emerged, neither Lockean nor Machiavellian, neither court nor country, neither purely liberal nor entirely republican, but one fundamentally liberal in character with important evangelical, Scottish Enlightenment and republican components—a millennial and republican liberalism that provided the conceptual structure and political language of Progressive reform at the end of the nineteenth century.[31]

The character of this idiosyncratic blend of republican and liberal thought was quite apparent by the 1820s. On the one hand, an ascendent liberalism celebrated natural rights, an economic order based on free labor and a self-regulating market, self-improvement and character development, western expansion, and economic development, self-interest, equal opportunity, individual achievement, a "classless" society free of artificial privileges and social hierarchy and factionalized interest-group party politics. But on the other hand, Jacksonian Democrats and Whigs were forever uncovering "conspiracies" against liberty, forever obsessed with "corruption," forever promoting moral reformation, and, Whigs especially, forever tormented by a tension between commerce and virtue. In a recent review of the historiography of Jacksonian America, Sean Wilentz concluded that "politicians and lawmakers of all persuasions . . . were becoming increasingly enamored of liberal concepts of property, the market, and (in the North) wage labor." "Between the Revolution and 1850," he goes on, "changing class and social relations led to recurring reinterpretations of republicanism and battles over what the republican legacy meant. During that period, some groups of Americans . . . came increasingly to interpret the republican framework as one or another form of liberal capitalist polity and economy. They did not reject republicanism in favor of liberalism; they associated one with the other."[32]

And so it went throughout the nineteenth century. Liberalism triumphed, but it was not a pure form of Lockean liberalism that evolved. Republican motifs penetrated and deeply influenced American liberalism—above all a "recurrent tension" between "commerce" and "virtue" identified by Pocock in late eighteenth-century American political thought. Nineteenth-century Americans redefined commerce and virtue in important ways, industrializing commerce and commercializing virtue, for example, but at a conceptual level the tension between commerce and virtue continued to define the internal problematic of American politics and set the ideological limits of political debate and social reform throughout the nineteenth century.[33] If nineteenth-century political debate, at least until the advent of socialist thought in the late nineteenth century, had an unremittingly intramural character to it, the reason is not that Americans shared a Lockean or republican consensus but that the antinomies of commerce and virtue allowed of no intermural competition. This is not to deny the fierceness and the apocalyptic dimensions of the competition— witness only Jackson's veto of the Second Bank of the United States and the Civil War—but merely to characterize its underlying logic. Pocock goes much too far in describing America as a nation of "tormented saints" rather than "pragmatic Lockeans," but the notion does capture something of the pervasive, haunting fear of corruption and decay, the immanent ambivalence toward commerce and the persistent quest for moral regeneration and virtue of nineteenth-century America.[34]

But while eighteenth- and nineteenth-century Americans internalized a political problematic cathected around the conceptual antinomies of commerce and virtue, they also found and institutionalized ways to reconcile, deny, sublimate, or repress the intellectual tension between commerce and virtue. Thomas Paine and Alexander Hamilton, two very unlikely bedfellows, denied that a tension existed at all, although for very different reasons. Paine believed that corrupt governments and aristocratic privilege rather than economic relations were the source of inequality and injustice, and he simply refused to believe that a nation of independent small producers would stray from the path of republican virtue and social harmony.[35] Hamilton, following Hume, was not in the least ambivalent about self-interest and commerce, denied the possibility of creating a classical republic of virtuous citizens, particularly in a society already extensively commercialized, and argued that economic development, particularly manufacturing, would train citizens in habits of industry, frugality, self-control, and order. Self-interest and commerce did not contradict but promoted civic virtue and the public good.[36] Jefferson and Madison, on the other hand, unlike Paine and Hamilton, recognized a tension between commerce and virtue but assumed that the tension could be contained. Jefferson placed his faith in western expansion, an independent yeomanry, enlightened rule by a natural aristocracy in a society of civic equals, and a return of the Spirit of '76.[37] Madison shared Jefferson's agrarianism and policy of western expansion, but he also favored a system of constitutional checks and balances to preserve social order in a commercialized society of restless and ambitious individuals given to factional political squabbles.[38] Jacksonian Democrats were possessive individualists to their hickory boots, but feared, as Paine and Jefferson had feared, government-sponsored privilege and economic power and "aristocratic" conspiracies against the "liberty" and "equality" of the citizenry.[39] Whigs feared conspiracies and corruption as much as Jeffersonians and Jacksonian Democrats but located them not among Federalists or supporters of the Bank of the United States but in the inflamed "passions" of undisciplined demagogues, lazy workingmen, Catholic immigrants, and factional party politicians. At the same time they believed that a policy of economic development and western expansion joined to equal opportunity and to the moral improvement of the individual would reconceive commerce and virtue.[40] The Jacksonian labor movement, and later the Knights of Labor and Populists, attacked "monopoly," "class privilege," and other violations

Chapter 1

SOCIAL ORDER AND PROGRESSIVE REFORM IN CHICAGO, 1877–1912

In the century or so following the ratification of the Constitution, an economic revolution, based on the expansion of markets in goods, capital, land, and labor, transformed the face and character of American life. Settlers opened up new land for commercial exploitation. Farmers produced and sold ever larger amounts of agricultural products to merchants in exchange for the manufactured products of the factories of the Northeast. Canals and railroads formed regional commodity markets. Bankers expanded existing capital markets and created new ones. Success, entrepreneurial ambition, and the ingenuity of accountants stimulated new organizational structures in commerce, manufacturing, and transportation. Lawyers, judges, and legislators invented new law or bent the old law to meet the exigencies of a contractual society. Markets in labor grew and multiplied, absorbing in turn indentured servants, independent commodity producers, and immigrants. Seeking profits, manufacturers transformed the labor process through mechanization and specialization. Pedagogues, evangelical Protestants, and charity workers struggled to inculcate the axioms of bourgeois piety and probity into the hearts of the young, the ungodly, and the poor. Cities grew as immigrants poured into them by the millions. And new concentrations of wealth and power, new social classes, and new forms of social conflict made their ominous entrance into American history.[1]

Perhaps more than any other city in America, Chicago exemplified and symbolized the market revolution. Where the Protestant Ethic triumphed in Boston, at least for a time, from Chicago's fledgling beginnings, the Spirit of Capitalism ruled. In little more than half a century, Chicago firmly established itself as the center of an economic empire that sprawled from the Ohio Valley in the east clear across the Mississippi Valley to the Rockies in the west. At least it seemed so to novelist Frank Norris:

The Great Gray City, brooking no rival, imposing its dominion upon a reach of country larger than many a kingdom of the Old World. For thousands of miles beyond its confines was its influence felt. Out, far out, far away in the snow and shadow of northern Wisconsin forests, axes and saws bit the bark of century old trees, stimulated by this city's driving energy. Just as far to the southward pick and drill leaped to the assault of veins of anthracite, moved by her central power. Her force runted the wheels of harvester and seeder a thousand miles distant in Iowa and Kansas. Her force spurs the screws of . . . innumerable squadrons of lake steamers crowding the Sault Sainte Marie. For her and because of her all the Central States, all the Great Northwest, roared with traffic and industry; sawmills screamed; factories . . . clashed and flowed; cog gripped cog; beltings clasped the drums of mammoth wheels; and converters of forges belched into the clouded air their tempest breath of molten steel.[2]

Chicago's extraordinary economic growth depended on its strategic geographical location. Located at the heel of Lake Michigan and at the heart of vast and rich farmlands, it soon became the transportation hub of the nation and the entrepôt of the Midwest. But from the time of the Civil War, Chicago's burgeoning industries pushed it rapidly toward preeminence as an industrial center as well. By 1890 Chicago had become the national center of the meat slaughtering and packing industry, an important national center in the printing and publishing industry (second only to New York), in the iron and steel industry (third largest in the country), clothing, boots and shoes (largest center outside Philadelphia and New England), lumber and wood products, railroad cars (Pullman), foundry and machine shop goods, coffee, leather and tanning, flour milling, copper, tin, sheet iron, and a hundred others.[3]

Along with transportation, commerce, and industry, the city's population exploded in the decades after 1840. From 4,500 in 1840, the population leapfrogged to 100,000 in 1860, 300,000 in 1870, 500,000 in 1880, 1.7 million in 1900, and 2.2 million in 1910. So, too, the size of the labor force: from almost 170,000 in 1880 to 1.3 million by 1930, a jump of over 600 percent. Between 1880 and 1930, over 637,000 immigrants, the great majority of them from southern, eastern, and central

Europe, settled in Chicago. Thus, immigration dramatically altered the ethnic composition of the city. Whereas in 1880 the first countries of birth in Chicago's foreign-born population were Germany, Ireland, Canada, England, and Sweden, by 1910 they were Germany, Poland, Russia, Austria, and Ireland. Germans, who constituted about 34 percent of the city's population in 1900, accounted for only 1 percent in 1930. Indeed, even by 1920, Poles and Russian Jews outnumbered Germans among Chicago's foreign-born, and the Irish were soon eclipsed by the Italians. In 1900 foreign-born individuals or children of immigrants accounted for fully 77 percent of Chicago's population. Even by 1930 the foreign-born or second-generation immigrants represented 65 percent of the population (25 percent and 40 percent respectively). In that year, Chicago had the largest Scandinavian, Polish, Czech, Slovak, and Negro populations of any city in the world, and the third largest Italian. Only two cities in Poland had more Poles than Chicago in 1930, and only two cities in Ireland had more Irish. In addition, Chicago was the third largest Swedish city in the world, the third largest Bohemian, and the third largest Jewish.[4]

But, as impressive as Chicago's economic and population growth appeared to the city's civic boosters, on occasion they noted with shock that it also had its share of social traumas and unpleasant consequences. During the railroad strikes of July 1877, the editors of the *Chicago Tribune* admitted, to their dismay, that "dangerous classes" and "social disorders" pervaded Chicago. Most Americans thought such developments only possible in Old World societies. Classes were not supposed to develop in the New World. But, reasoned the *Tribune*'s editors, "We, too, have our crowded tenement houses, and our entire streets and neighborhoods occupied by paupers and thieves. We now have the communists on our soil. Thus, too, we have rough brutal classes of laborers, soldiers, miners, and railroad strikers. Finally, the extremes of wealth and poverty are not to be seen here as abroad; the rich growing richer and the poor poorer—a fact to tempt disorder."[5]

Rarely in the next quarter century did the *Chicago Tribune* demonstrate greater prescience. But then the signs of incipient disorder could hardly be ignored. The gap between rich and poor, the growing separation of classes, and conflicts between labor and capital intimated a crisis of serious proportions. Middle-class fear and anxiety grew increasingly acute and nourished a flurry of law and order campaigns and moral reform movements in the 1870s and 1880s. Finally in the mid-1890s, a new generation of reformers appeared intent upon reconciling the classes, eliminating social injustice, and recalibrating institutional arrangements.

CLASS RELATIONSHIPS IN THE GILDED AGE

In 1847 workers at a factory in Chicago downed their tools and went out on strike. While the first recorded strike in Chicago's history, it was by no means the last: Several thousand more followed by the turn of the century. Between 1881 and 1900 workingmen walked out on strike 20,783 times in Illinois. In the six-year period between 1881 and 1886, capital locked labor out 3,511 times. Five times between 1877 and 1919—in 1877, 1886, 1894, 1904–05, and 1919—major "civil disorders" rocked Chicago and threatened the social order. Hostile and antagonistic organizations developed: trade unions, radical political parties, open-shop employers associations, and business "watchdog" committees. Strikers destroyed property and physically intimidated strike breakers; employers successfully enrolled the help of police, the state militia, the courts, and private agencies in their cause. Clearly, the relations between labor and capital fell far short of the natural harmony envisaged by the apostles of a market society.[6]

Invariably, Chicago's businessmen responded to outbreaks of labor unrest with a "law and order" campaign. But they occasionally responded in other ways. Some businessmen, strongly committed to strategies of individual moral rehabilitation, emphasized sobriety, industry, thrift, and righteousness. One of them, George Pullman, pursued industrial peace through industrial paternalism; others, along with a sizable group of middle-class reformers, looked to temperance, Sunday schools, the YMCA, evangelical revivals, and charity reform. The apparent failure of Gilded Age reform in the midst of a severe economic and political crisis during the first half of the 1890s opened the way for a new generation of reformers with decidedly different views.

Three issues dominated the conflict between labor and capital in the latter part of the nineteenth century: conditions of employment (particularly with respect to wages and hours of work), autonomy within the workplace, and the structure of social relations. Politically, the last exceeded the second in importance, and the second the first, although numerically the first and second far outnumbered the third. Of the 20,783 strikes in Illinois between 1881 and 1900, 6,431 (30.9 percent) involved wages and hours; 8,336 (40.1 percent) were control strikes concerned with issues of union recognition and the closed shop, enforcement of union rules, and strikes against the introduction of machinery; 6,015 (28.5 percent) involved various combinations of the two. Issues concerned with control of the workplace were thus numerically more important, and apparently, for employers, far more significant. For the six years, between 1881 and 1886, 67.3 percent of the strikes for increased wages were successful, and 37.2 percent of the strikes against reduction of wages were successful. But only 29 percent of other control strikes were successful. The Illinois Bureau of Labor Statistics concluded that the "percentages of successful strikes" were smallest "among those strikes inaugurated to enforce a recognition of unions, and matters connected with them in any other class."[7] Control strikes were thus both more frequent than wage strikes and most strongly resisted by employers.

Politically, however, the most significant conflicts between labor and capital involved the legitimacy of the evolving structure of social relations. During the 1850s, sixties, and seventies, labor drew upon the artisanal language of radical republicanism and the producer ideology to protest not only their poverty and declining control over the labor process but their diminished opportunities for proprietorship, the increasing concentration of economic and political power, the growing crystallization of society into classes, and the "tyranny" of "wage slavery." When Andrew Cameron, a Scottish immigrant printer and editor of the *Workingmans Advocate,* wrote editorials in the 1860s condemning the erosion of craft skills and tradition, the "tyranny" of "wage slavery," and the "greedy capitalists" who were withholding a "fair share" of the fruits of production from the "producing classes," he used the language of "manly independence" and "self-improvement."[8] In the 1860s, during the growth of the eight-hour movement, the character of labor's resistance began to change. Labor spokesmen wrote less and less of recreating a society of "self-made men" and more and more of the incompatible "interests" of labor and capital and of the need to create a "cooperative commonwealth." Although they continued to speak in the language of the producer ideology, they did so less, as they gradually adopted the language of "working" and "capitalist" classes and excluded "capitalists" and "manufacturers" from the "producing" classes (as well as those traditionally excluded—bankers, gamblers, lawyers, liquor merchants). During the 1870s, 1880s, and 1890s, the transition from an artisanal politics to a working-class politics accelerated. Three times before the end of the Gilded Age—in 1877, 1885–86, and in 1894—workers openly challenged capitalism, the last time on a scale approaching, in the eyes of many contemporaries, a civil war.

The Great Upheaval in Chicago in 1877 began when railroad switchmen went on strike in response to a threatened pay cut by the Michigan Central Railroad. By the next day, workers at the stockyards, the packing houses, the lake vessels, the streetcars, wagons, tanneries, stoveworks, clothing factories, lumber yards, brick yards, furniture factories, and a

parties appeared to compete for the loyalties of the working class. The Workingman's party, which staged a political convention in October 1877, changed its name to the Socialist Labor Party (SLP) and, while not eschewing trade union activity entirely, concentrated its energies on local election campaigns. In the fall elections of 1878, the party won more than 10 percent of the vote and elected four members to the state legislature. In the elections of the spring of 1879, the SLP polled 12 to 14 percent of the votes and elected four aldermen.[13] In the early 1880s a "social revolutionary" movement appeared, combining an idiosyncratic blend of anarchist, syndicalist, and socialist elements. Between 1883 and 1886 the movement grew rapidly. By the end of 1884, six groups in the city had affiliated with the International Working Peoples Association (IWPA); six months later the number had jumped to seventeen.[14] In 1884 an Internationalist-led union, the Progressive Cigar Union No. 15, took the lead in establishing a citywide trade union confederation, the Central Trade Union (CTU), to challenge the Chicago Trades and Labor Assembly (CTLA), founded in 1887 and dominated by moderate American and Irish skilled workers with strong ties to the Democratic party. Although it grew slowly at first, by the end of 1885, the CTU could count 13 unions under its umbrella, compared with the 19 of the CTLA. By April 1886, the number of unions in the CTU had risen to 22, including the 11 largest in the city.[15]

At the same time, the Knights of Labor and the Eight-Hour Movement in 1884 and 1885 grew rapidly. Founded in the aftermath of the 1877 revolt, the Knights had briefly flourished in Chicago and then atrophied; by July 1885 District Assembly No. 24 could count only 13 locals and a total membership of 551. A year later, however, DA No. 24 had 88 locals with 14,019 members. DA No. 57 grew in the same period from 6 locals with 1,355 members to 40 odd locals and 7,734 members. By September 1886 the Knights could claim a membership of 164 locals in Chicago with "at least 45,000 members."[16] The IBLS concluded that only 17 percent of the membership of the Knights of Labor also belonged to trade unions, and that "this remarkable revival of labor organization among all classes engaged in manual industry, must be regarded as one of the most significant movements which has developed in recent times."[17]

Unlike the narrow craft-based unions, the Knights opened membership to all members of the "producing classes," regardless of skill. "The body of the order," reported the IBLS in 1886, "is composed of the industrial classes proper, mechanics, artisans, operators, clerks, miners, laborers, and those everywhere who work for wages." It noted that the Knights "accepts and seeks its membership from all classes, regardless of race, creed, color, sex, or occupation, and its aim is to unite them not by trade affinities or any narrow . . . interests, but in a brotherhood which shall make the cause of any one the common cause of all." The Knights believed that the general inclusion of all workers represented a coming to terms "with the whole issue between all capital and all labor, and with the social and economic conditions of the great mass of the employed," in particular, with the "general introduction of machinery" that had revolutionized the methods of industry, practically destroyed the trades, and made trade unions "obsolete." The times demanded a classwide organization and not narrow trade union exclusiveness; the trade unions had failed "to meet the issues and fill the needs of the present day."[18]

The growth of the Knights in 1885 and 1886 reflected, in part, the sudden resurgence of the Eight-Hour Movement in the first four months of 1886. In 1886 some eight hundred studies occurred in Chicago, most of them in the first four or five months; almost half of them were concerned with the eight-hour day. According to the IBLS, "There were, in round numbers, about 100,000 engaged in the movement, or nearly one-third of the total number participating in the entire country."[19]

The Eight-Hour Movement mobilized the Chicago working class as no other issue had done before. And it did so around a platform that stressed emancipation from industrial slavery rather than the resuscitation of entrepreneurial independence, as the Eight-Hour Movement of the 1860s had done.[20] John R. Commons characterized the period thus:

All the peculiar characteristics of the dramatic events of 1886 and 1887, the highly feverish pace at which organizations grew, the nation-wide wave of strikes . . . the wide use of the boycott, the obliteration, apparently complete, of all lines that divided the laboring class, whether geographic or trade, the violence and turbulence which accompanied the movement—all of these were signs of a great movement by the class of the unskilled, which had finally risen in rebellion. . . . The movement bore in every way, the aspects of social war. A frenzied hatred of labor for capital was shown in every important strike. . . . Extreme bitterness toward capital manifested itself in all the actions of the Knights of Labor, and wherever the leaders undertook to hold it within bound they were generally discarded by their followers. . . .[21]

In Chicago the Eight-Hour Movement climaxed in early May 1886. Following a series of large mass demonstrations (upward of 25,000 people) during April, by the end of April it appeared that around 62,000 workers, including 35,000 packing yard employees, were prepared to strike if their demand for the eight-hour day was not granted on May 1, when a nationwide general strike, the first such strike in the history of the American labor movement, was scheduled to take place. Another 25,000 workers had requested the eight-hour day but had not threatened to strike. Businessmen implacably opposed the movement; the police prepared for massive "civil disorders"; the middle classes feared social revolution. On May 1 some 30,000 workers struck, two-thirds of them demanding ten hours' pay for eight hours' work.[22] Some employers gave in to the strikes, but others started a lockout. Labor and capital dug in for a long and protracted battle, but two days later, on May 3, at a demonstration in Haymarket Square to protest the shooting of a striker outside the McCormick plant the day before, someone threw a bomb at a police contingent attempting to break up the lawful and peaceful assembly.[23]

Six policemen died of wounds caused by the explosion. A determined law and order campaign immediately followed. The police arrested more than one hundred individuals on mere suspicion that they held radical views. Despite the absence of a shred of evidence linking the bomb to the leaders of the IWPA, the state attorney general proceeded to prosecute them. "Law is on trial," he told the court. "Anarchy is on trial. These men have been selected, picked out by the grand jury and indicted because they are the leaders. They are no more guilty than the thousands who follow them. Gentlemen of the Jury, convict these men, make examples of them, hang them and save our institutions, our society."[24] The jury convicted them, the presiding judge sentenced them, and the following year the state hanged them.

Meanwhile, the Union League and the Commercial Club led a funding drive to build a National Guard Armory at Fort Sheridan in anticipation of the coming apocalypse. Employers organized against the Knights through an intensive open-shop campaign involving lockouts and arbitrary wage reductions (the most important of which was the lockout of twenty-thousand packing yard workers and the cutting of their wages by 20 percent), "yellow dog" contracts, blacklists, physical intimidation, and lobbying for repressive conspiracy laws. In the spring of 1887 the Illinois legislature pushed through a conspiracy law (the Merritt Conspiracy Law) in an effort to incorporate into statue law the theory of conspiracy used by the court to condemn the leaders of the IWPA—namely, that the prosecution had only to show that "revolutionary" beliefs were expressed in a public manner in order to successfully prosecute the speakers for crimes committed by someone else. In June 1887 the legislature also passed an antiboycott law making boycotting a conspiracy punishable by five years' imprisonment, a two-thousand-dollar fine, or both.[25]

Law and order campaigns provided the first line of defense against radicalism. But they were not the only defense. Some middle-class reformers and businessmen hoped that less coercive forms of social control would persuade the working class to abandon the folly of trade unionism, strikes, and attacks on the established order. Throughout the Gilded Age, advocates of temperance, Sunday schools, the YMCA, evangelical revivals, and charity reform urged the working class to sobriety, industry, piety, and thrift in the expectation that moral uplift would eliminate the sources of social protest—and the need for coercive social control.[26]

Temperance advocates first made their mark in Chicago in 1874.[27] Unlike the temperance movement of the Federalist era, the leaders of the Gilded Age temperance movement sought not to reestablish control over the common man through refurbishing a deferential society but, like the temperance movement of the 1830s and 1840s, to couple self-improvement and self-reliance with moral virtue and temperance, and both with salvation and social order. Temperance organizations blamed the riots of 1877 on "idle and vicious young men" corrupted by alcohol. After the Haymarket affair, C. C. Bonney of the Citizen League for Law and Order suggested that "the present war on the institutions of society began years ago in attacks on religion, on the observance of Sunday as a sacred day, and in laws requiring the closing of saloons."[28] Social disorder resulted from poverty caused by wages squandered on liquor. In 1883 Joseph Medill, editor-publisher of the *Chicago Tribune,* directly linked poverty and radicalism to drink. "I have never known a workman," he argued, "no matter what might be his wages, who freely indulged his appetite for liquor and nicotine, that never made much headway." Liquor was the "chief cause of the impecunious conditions of millions of the wage classes of this country." Instead of a steady job, hard work, frugality, they spend "their earnings on intoxicating drinks," while they complain incessantly "of their bad luck, denounce the tyranny of capital, and allege that they . . . [are] cheated in the division of the profits produced by capital and labor."[29] A minister of Chicago's Methodist Episcopal Church linked "imbecility, ignorance and wickedness" to drink. "The care of these and other classes of sufferers impose unjust burdens on good citizens. Our present liberty is threatened, our homes and very existence is rendered unsafe." The Citizens League for the Suppression of the Sale of Liquors to Minors, created in 1877 by leading businessmen and others, blamed saloonkeepers for "educating our boys in all departments of crime and fitting them, for the jail, the penitentiary, the almshouse, the insane asylum, and in many cases, the gallows."[30] Still other temperance advocates sought out the immigrant whose drinking habits they believed posed a dire threat to Protestant and Republican institutions.[31]

Where some reformers sought to implant bourgeois piety and Protestant rectitude through temperance, others looked to a Protestant holy war against sin, idleness, aetheism, popery, and subversion. With the aid of God's will, prayers, itinerant revivalist ministers, and the dollars and organizational genius of big business, evangelicals would drive the heathen back, save souls, eradicate poverty and vice, and restore godliness, self-reliance, order, and prosperity to the land.

The unchurched masses and the Catholic immigrants worried the reformers the most. "What is to be done with, and for, our foreign population," worried the Chicago Baptist Association in 1882, "is fast becoming one of the foremost of the tremendous problems which Americans, and American Christians, must solve."[32] The Chicago Missionary Society shared similar fears. Immigration "is unfavorable to the maintenance of piety and religious restraints." Unless the immigrants were exposed to the word of God, anarchy would result. "There is no force which has power in restraining the possessions of men from running riot," it declared, "as those sanctions which come from a gospel which preaches Christ."[33] But the righteous did not merely fear the unchurched foreign masses, they feared the unchurched masses, period. In 1883, after returning from one of his long evangelical trips to the United Kingdom, Dwight Moody warned his audience of Christian workers, ministers, and laymen of the damages of allowing American working men to become like the unchurched working men of England, "hard-hearted and hard-headed men" who "gathered in their sops on Sunday, or some place else, and talk communism or infidelity." Protestants must, he concluded, convert "the lower classes of people here in Chicago" to prevent an apocalypse. "I say to the rich men of Chicago, their money will not be worth much if communism and infidelity sweep the land."[34]

The apprehension of Protestant ministers and evangelicals for the unchurched masses grew particularly after the railroad riots in 1877 and the Haymarket incident of 1886, veritible "earthquakes" that convinced men of property and men of God that the masses must be "christianized."[35] "These laboring men," declared one minister in 1877, "so narrow and selfish in their proceedings, these tramps, and bummers, and thieves, the very sight of whom is a disgust, are . . . members of the same communities with us. In some sense we are responsible for their souls; responsible, at least, to do all we can to raise them out of ignorance and woe."[36] The events of 1886 appeared equally cataclysmic. Shortly before Haymarket, Moody bluntly warned that "either these people are to be evangelized or the leaven of communism will assume such enormous proportions that it will break out in a reign of terror such as this country has never known. You can hear the mutterings of the coming convulsion even now, if you open your ears and eyes."[37]

Evangelicals threw themselves wholeheartedly into the fray. Led by Methodists, Baptists, and Congregationalists, Chicago's Protestant churches engaged in a vigorous home missionary movement. Within a year of the railroad riots, the Methodists were busy saving souls and the country. In 1882 the Baptists capped their years of home missionary work by establishing the city Mission Society, and in 1884 the Congregationalists created the Chicago City Missionary Society. In the mid-1880s the "nonsectarian" Armour Mission opened.[38] Protestants also established Sunday schools throughout the city: during the 1857–58 revival, they opened fourteen schools. By the mid-1860s the churches had opened thirty-one schools.[39] Methodist Sunday schools were the most numerous, followed by the Baptists, Lutherans, Presbyterians, and Protestant Episcopalians. During the 1870s and 1880s, enrollments and the number of Sunday schools continued to mushroom. Between 1884 and 1892 enrollments increased from 74,975 to 138,183. By 1889 the churches operated some 750 Sunday schools enrolling approximately 170,000 students.[40]

City missions and Sunday schools did not exhaust the agency or inventiveness of the evangelicals. In 1883 Dwight Moody outlined plans for a "training school" to bridge the gap between the church and the working classes. The school would train "a band of men and women" who would "stand in the gap" between the working classes and the church. He failed, however, to interest businessmen in the enterprise until the rise of the Knights of Labor in the mid-1880s, the rash of eight-hour strikes in 1886, and the Haymarket affair. When Moody approached the subject again in 1886, men of wealth were more receptive. He told a meeting of businessmen in January 1886, assembled to raise money for the school, that he hoped the school would provide a "training school for Christian workers" whom he called "gapmen," "irregulars" or "law makers." These "gapmen" would learn "how to reach the masses." Armed with the Gospels, they would "go into the shops and meet those bareheaded infidels and skeptics." "One great purpose we have in view in the Bible Institute," Moody declared, "is to raise up men and women who will be willing to lay their lives alongside of the laboring classes and the poor and bring the gospel to bear upon their lives."[41] In February 1887 Moody's supporters organized the Chicago Evangelization Society to carry forward the planning and building of the institute. Two and a half years later, the Chicago Bible Institute opened. By the year of Moody's death (1899), what he called the "West Point Christian Service" had graduated 1,153 "gapmen" or "irregulars" into the army of bourgeois piety.[42]

In addition to missions and Sunday schools, evangelicals also relied upon a traditional evangelical device, the revival, to undo Satan's work.

After a period of revivalist lassitude following "The Great Revival" of
1857–58, good old-fashioned revivalism returned during the mid-
1870s—and with a vengeance, peaking in Moody's campaigns of the late
1870s and early 1880s. In the revival the soldiers of Christ could do their
missionary work on a scale that befitted the seriousness of the task. "Revival," declared Moody in the year of his death, "is the only hope for our
republic, for I don't believe that a republican form of government can last
without righteousness."[43]

The revivals, which would last anywhere from one week to a month,
attracted large crowds night after night. Impatient with theological subtle-
ties, revivalists liked their theology straight and simple, devoid of Calvinist
theories of limited atonement and damnation. Laced with the comely
nostrums, simple homilies, and sentimental moralisms of Horatio Alger,
Victorian sentimentality, and middle-class piety, the sermons of revivalists
provided spiritual solace, promised material success, and guaranteed social
order if only sinners would "Take Jesus." Salvation, like economic success,
was not a matter of "foreordination," "justification," and "sanctification"
but an individual act of will, "T-A-K-I-N-G Jesus."[44] But, for the most
part, the revivals failed to convert the unchurched or the working class. It
seems, rather, that they appealed to the already converted and to the
transplanted and aspiring middle-class youth from small-town and rural
Midwest America, small businessmen, white collar workers, some skilled
tradesmen, and the newly successful and wealthy.[45] The unchurched and
unconverted masses remained out of reach of God's word. The Moody
Mission among Chicago's Italians, for example, remained an abysmal failure. In the twenty-four years following its establishment in 1910, 130
souls joined the mission. Moody himself admitted in St. Louis that it was
"principally the middling class" that had come under his influence.[46] And
why not? Had not Moody announced that "the back-bone and sinew of
any city or community is the middle class, the honest, industrious toiling
thousands to whom government must look in every emergency for support and for the maintenance of law and order?"[47] Had not Samuel Jones
assured them that heaven was to be inhabited exclusively by the middle
class?[48] Even Chicago's churchmen despaired in the 1880s and 1890s of
the continued failure of the Protestant churches to reach the working man
and the unchurched masses. "Have the working classes fallen away from
the churches or have the churches fallen away from the working classes?"
asked the Reverend C. F. Goss of the Chicago Avenue Church. He feared
that "there is no place in the average Chicago church for the poor man, . . .
surrounded by individuals who not only regard poverty as a disgrace, but
by their vulgar display endeavor to perpetually remind the poor man of

his poverty."[49] Prohibitive pew rents, antagonistic clergy, and the concentration of Protestant churches in middle-class neighborhoods did not tempt the working class into Protestant churches. Of the twenty-nine Episcopalian, Presbyterian, and Congregational churches in the city in 1885, for example, twenty were located in sections of the city inhabited by wealthy or middle-class citizens. In areas of the city where immigrants lived, only two could be found. The Methodists and Baptists did somewhat better, although they too located a majority of their churches in middle-class neighborhoods.[50]

Charity reform provided the last major device that moral reformers of the Gilded Age employed to inculcate the maxims of bourgeois piety and to preserve the society of "free labor." After the Great Fire of 1871, the Cook County Board of Supervisors (CCBS) and the Chicago Relief and Aid Society (CR&AS) exercised primary responsibility for welfare in Chicago, although they did so according to very different principles.[51] The CCBS distributed various forms of indoor and outdoor relief to the destitute on a relatively pragmatic basis; the CR&AS, on the other hand, opposed in principle the outdoor relief policy of the board of supervisors and the practice of "indiscriminate alms giving." Outdoor relief "demoralized" the poor; its effects were "pernicious." An immediate end should be made to "blind giving," soup houses, and "indiscriminate alms without investigation." Such practices only engendered "indolence and beggery." Alms should be given only after "careful inquiry" to those "in whom the habits of temperance, industry, and thrift, give promise to permanent benefit from the alms furnished. . . ." In effect, aid should be limited "to that class of worthy and industrious poor, who, by reason of sickness, accident, loss of employment or poverty, have fallen temporarily behind, and to rescue them from permanent pauperism by timely assistance."[52]

Supervised by a corporation lawyer and a clothing manufacturer, administered by a Christian evangelical minister, C. G. Trusdale, and with a board of directors composed of "among the most prominent of the business and professional men of the city," the society wished to ensure the unhampered operation of free market laws to aid the worthy poor. "Great providence should be an exercise of charitable work," the society advised its middle-class supporters in 1884, "lest through its agency barriers be erected against the operation of wholesome and material laws, and people be sheltered from the punishment which the welfare of the community requires shall be visited upon idlers and criminals." To prevent the demoralization of the poor and to ensure "self-sufficiency," the society warned again and again against "indiscriminate alms giving." Such aid, it said, "is always a crime against society and an injury to the individual."[53]

In 1883 the CR&AS found itself faced with "an interloper," the Charity Organization Society (COS) of Chicago. First established in Buffalo by the Reverend Stephen Hymphreys Gurteen in 1877, the COS soon became known as an advocate of a "new" or "scientific" charity.[54] Within two years, according to the second secretary of the COS, Alexander Johnson, "despite the strenuous opposition of the old society," the COS "had a firm footing in the city and a substantial body of subscribers."[55] The new organization had three principal objectives: to coordinate and streamline existing charity work, to eliminate the twin evils of public outdoor relief and indiscriminate alms giving, and to do something about "the growing separation of classes." The first two objectives of the COS were identical to the objectives of the CR&AS: Like the CR&AS, the founders of the COS wanted charity to foster self-reliant, self-supporting individuals, capable of individual success in a market society, not foster dependency. The COS differed from the CR&AS in the concern, almost a preoccupation, of its leadership with class relationships. Convinced that the "niggardly dole relief" policies of the CR&AS and the bureaucratic and impersonal character of outdoor relief exacerbated already tense class relationships and did nothing to facilitate the direct personal contact necessary to bridge the yawning chasm between the classes, the COS recommended urgent reform. "The 'Social Gulf' between the rich and the poor," wrote Alexander Johnson, "is widening rapidly; classes are growing apart; all the evils that afflict the old cities of Europe have their antitypes, although not so deeply entrenched and developed." The question of pauperism, he went on, was "not one of alms, nor of redistribution of wealth, but of genuine neighborhood." Unless charity workers reestablished "relations of friendship between rich and poor, cultured and ignorant," America would cease to be "one people" and break into "two hostile camps."[56] Charles Henderson, a Baptist minister, University of Chicago sociology professor, and COS official, agreed.[57] "Public outdoor relief tends to separate society into classes," he told the National Conference of Charities and Corrections in 1891.

It aggravates a peril which is already great. It accentuates the difference of rich and poor. It makes the only bond between the prosperous and the broken that of the officials who dole relief from a treasury. When those who give to the poor visit them in their homes, there is a personal tie of humanity; but when the State interferes to do this work, that tie snaps. Prejudices are increased, bitter feelings are fastened in the unfortunate and forgotten.[58]

The concern expressed by Johnson and Henderson with the growing separation of classes reflects a process that Gareth Stedman Jones, following Marcell Mauss, calls "the deformation of the gift." Jones argues that charity or alms giving is a gift with specific social qualities: "A gift is a relationship between persons." "If it is depersonalized," Jones concludes, "the gift loses its defining features: the elements of voluntary sacrifice, prestige, subordination, and obligation."[59] Where separation of classes takes place, for whatever reason (residential segregation by class, the destruction of close personal ties between employer and employee, outdoor relief), a breakdown of social relationships and traditional methods of "social contact" occurs.[60] This seems to have been the reason that leaders of the COS in Chicago, as in London and elsewhere in America, urged the adoption of a system of "friendly visiting" in order to facilitate direct contact between the classes. Through friendly visiting, the causes of social discontent and class friction might be eliminated, as Dr. Frederick Wines, secretary of the Illinois State Board of Charities, argued in 1892:

Charity organization seeks to bring the rich and the poor together believing that the Lord is the maker of them both. It encourages individuals to seek out individuals and to supply their individual necessities, in the spirit of brotherhood. It believes that by such personal contact, the hearts of the rich and poor will alike be made better, and that the gulf which separates social classes and which, with the increases of wealth, yawns wider and wider, can be partially bridged.[61]

The preoccupation of the COS with class relationships represented a significant departure from the traditional problematic of Gilded Age charity reform: individual character and mobility through inculation of the maxims of piety and thrift.[62] The COS did not abandon the moral reformers' concern with individual character and mobility, and it certainly did not question the structure of social relations underlying the growing separation of classes, but it did place a wholly new emphasis upon class relationships, upon the separation of classes and their reconciliation. In 1888 the COS and CR&AS merged, but a number of Protestant ministers in the city identified with the Social Gospel movement, and residents of a settlement house established on the west side in 1889 continued to voice similar fears about "the growing separation of classes," particularly during the economic, industrial, and political crisis that swept Chicago, and America generally, in the mid-1890s.[63]

ANNEES TERRIBLE[64]

In 1885 prices for farm products began to fall. Five years later, populists associated with the National Farmers Alliance won control of twelve state legislatures, six governorships, three United States Senate seats, and fifty-two seats in the House of Representatives.[65] During 1891 and 1892 prices continued to fall, and support for the creation of a new political party grew. In February 1892 delegates from the National Farmers Alliance, the Knights of Labor, the Patrons of Industry, and other farm and labor organizations established the Peoples party. Four months later, on July 4, the party convened in Omaha to announce its platform:

We meet in the midst of a nation brought to the verge of moral, political, and material ruin. Corruption dominates the ballot-box, the legislatures, the Congress, and touches even the ermine of the bench. The people are demoralized, . . . public opinion silenced, . . . labor impoverished, . . . and the land concentrating in the hands of capitalists. The urban workmen are denied the right of organization for self-protection, . . . the fruits of the toil of millions are boldly stolen to build up colossal fortunes for a few, unprecedented in the history of mankind. . . . From the same prolific womb of governmental injustice we breed the two great classes—tramps and millionaires.

The platform went on to label the financial policy of the national government which funded gold-backed bonds and limited the coinage of silver "a vast conspiracy against mankind," denounced "capitalists, corporations, national banks, rings, trusts," argued that "wealth belongs to him who creates it," declared the necessity of restoring "the government of the Republic to the hands of the plain people" and establishing "equal rights and equal privileges . . . for all the men and women of this country," and demanded that the government "own and operate the railroads in the interest of the people," expand the "circulating medium," initiate the "free and unlimited coinage of silver and gold at the present legal ratios of sixteen to one," a "graduated income tax" to limit the concentration of wealth, and prohibit the "alien ownership of land." "If not met and overthrown at once," the platform stated, the "vast conspiracy against mankind . . . forebodes terrible social convulsions, the destruction of civilization, or the establishment of an absolute despotism."[66]

The Omaha platform expressed the anger, fears, and aspirations of "the producing classes" of rural America in the language of producerism, radical republicanism, and antimonopoly—the language of corruption, privilege, and equal rights. In its identification of the common interests of all producers of wealth, in its hostility to special privilege and the aggregation of economic and political power, in its fear of the corruption of republican institutions and the creation of a class society, the Omaha platform reasserted the principles of Jacksonian reform, but in at least two respects the Omaha platform was not a simple facsimile of Jacksonian

antimonopoly. Although the party proposed to decentralize banking, it
did not advocate linking the money supply to some inflexible metallic
standard, and it did not propose to restore laissez-faire competition to all
sectors of the economy. Instead, the party proposed to nationalize railroads and communications and to prohibit absentee ownership of land.
In revising Jacksonian antimonopoly, the Populists attempted to come to
terms with the profound economic transformation of American life since
Jackson's day, but they did so in a manner intellectually grounded in the
traditions of equal rights and republicanism. Populist antimonopolism
provided a creedal basis for radical but nonsocialist political reform for
the next four years and created the opportunity for the formation
of a political alliance between the producing classes of rural and urban
America.[67]

In the election of 1892 the Populist candidate, General Weaver, secured over one million votes and twenty-two electoral college votes. With
the single exception of the Republican party in 1856, no third party had
ever done so well in its first appearance in national politics. In Illinois
voters elected a Democrat sympathetic to Populist concerns, John Peter
Altgeld, governor of the state, on a platform of antimonopoly, industrial
arbitration, penal reform, factory legislation, civil liberties, repeal of an
1889 compulsory education law (the Edwards Act) requiring instruction
in English, and tax reform.[68] The following year, 1893, leaders of the
Populist movement in Illinois and organized labor began to canvass the
possibility of creating a Labor-Populist alliance. Although the Omaha
platform, as Henry Demarest Lloyd put it, had failed "to say a word of
any value for the workingman's movement—nothing in favor of trade
unions or the Eight-Hour Day," Lloyd and several prominent labor leaders in Illinois, particularly Tommy Morgan, a member of the Socialist
Labor party in Chicago and a founder of the Chicago Trades and Labor
Assembly, determined to forge a Labor-Populist alliance in Illinois.[69] In
October 1893 the Galseburg convention of the Illinois State Federation
of Labor passed an amendment to its constitution emphasizing the "necessity for independent political action on the part of producers" and
called for a conference of all labor and farm organizations of Illinois within
six months in order to secure "unity of action and singleness of purpose."[70]
Lloyd, meanwhile, completed his impassioned antimonopoly tract *Wealth
Against Commonwealth,* denouncing the "barbarians from above" who had
assumed "seats of power kings do not know" and whose "greed" and
"rapacity" threatened "private enterprise, public morals, judicial honor,
legislative faith, gifts of nature," "political brotherhood," and "democracy."[71] In December Lloyd appeared before the annual convention of the

American Federation of Labor in Chicago declaring the need for a "new conscience" and a "new democracy of human welfare" in the light of the "irrepressible conflict" between capitalists and the people and extensive unemployment. At the urging of Tommy Morgan, the convention recommended publication of 20,000 copies of Lloyd's address and that all member unions of the AFL hold referendums endorsing independent political action on behalf of welfare legislation, initiative and referendum, municipalization of utilities, nationalization of communications, railroads and mines, and "the collective ownership by the people of all means of production and distribution."[72]

Meanwhile, in New York on May 5, 1893, a major corporation, the National Cordage Company, declared bankruptcy. The market collapsed abruptly; by Christmas, some 500 banks and almost 16,000 businesses had declared bankruptcy, including a number of leading railroads. Investment dropped precipitously, and unemployment climbed to between 17 and 20 percent of the labor force. In Illinois the number of business failures increased 50 percent between 1892 and 1893, while the increase in the value of liabilities involved jumped from $2.6 million to $18.7 million. In 1894, 717 businesses failed, with liabilities of $8 million; in 1895, 856 businesses with assets of $14.2 million; and in 1896, 1,130 businesses failed with liabilities valued at $22.2 million.[73]

Estimates of the number of unemployed in Chicago during the fall of 1893 indicated a catastrophe of unprecedented proportions. The carpenters' union reported in September that upward of 80 percent of its members were unemployed. A police census of a sample of manufacturing establishments the same month estimated a 40.3 percent unemployment rate overall. At some factories only a fraction of the workforce remained: at Illinois Steel, only 225 out of 3,600 men; at Pullman Palace Car, 1,670 out of 4,348; at McCormick, 440 out of 2,200; at Deering, 600 out of 3,000. In the railroad freight yards and the meat packing industry, the situation was not as bad, but even then 20 percent and 25 percent of their employees, respectively, had been laid off. Settlement workers estimated a rate of unemployment in many neighborhoods of between 35 and 40 percent. The mayor estimated that 200,000 were out of work. Wage reductions averaged between 10 and 20 percent.[74] The Populist editor of the Chicago *Searchlight* found, on the night of August 2, over 500 unemployed men sleeping under the open sky on the north pier and about 250 on the floors of a building on the excursion dock, "honest toilers suffering from intolerable legislative and monopolistic wrongs." Tens of thousands more slept in alleys, city hall, police stations, vacant lots, deserted buildings, wagons, and viaducts.[75] Ray Stannard Baker, a reporter for the *Chi-*

cago Record, exclaimed, "What a spectacle! What a human downfall after the magnificence and prodigality of the World's Fair which has recently closed its doors! Heights of splendor, pride, exaltation in one month; depths of wretchedness, suffering, hunger, cold in the next."[76] Large demonstrations on the lake front and in the Loop passed resolutions attacking "wage-slavery" and denounced government by lawyers and millionaires.[77] "Huge demonstrations of the poor, the unemployed, and the hungry" reminded Jane Addams of "the London gatherings in Trafalgar Square."[78] Graham Taylor roamed Chicago's neighborhoods, deeply anguished by the poverty and distress he saw everywhere. How, he wondered, did these people "keep soul and body together?" Many years later, he recalled, the army of "upturned faces and calloused hands" was a "transforming experience" and "in ineffaceable memory."[79] One civic agency described the situation as simply "appalling":

Chicago saw an army of unemployed men wandering about its streets all day and sleeping on the floors of the city hall and police stations at night. The city government was without money and confessed itself unable to care for the hungry and homeless men who sought the shelter of its public buildings at night. The country relief offices were thronged by crowds of men and women clamoring for food and fuel. The poor house was full to overcrowding: thousands lay down at night in cold, darkness and hunger, dreading the morning; unable to pay rent, they saw nothing before them but the prospects of being turned into the streets. Evictions were common. The distress had become appalling.[80]

On top of this economic catastrophe, a bloody confrontation between labor and capital threatened the city, and the nation, with a new civil war. During the fall of 1893 and the winter of 1894, George Pullman cut the wages of his workers an average of 25 percent but as much as 50 percent in some cases while refusing to reduce the rents the workers had to pay for their company-owned housing.[81] In desperation, workers joined the American Railroad Union, an industrial union formed in 1892 by Eugene Debs, and sent a grievance committee to confer with the management. Rather than negotiate, however, the management fired the members of the grievance committee.[82] On May 11 over 90 percent of the workers at Pullman walked out on strike. In June the striking employees petitioned the ARU to declare a boycott—a sympathy strike—on all railroads using Pullman cars. The ARU at first hesitated, but when Pullman repeatedly refused to arbitrate, it declared a boycott on June 26. Within a few days, all twenty-six railroads out of Chicago were shut down, the strike had extended to twenty-seven states and territories, and an estimated 260,000 railroad workers had joined the strike. Early in June organized labor in Chicago decided to call a general strike in sympathy with the railroad workers, and the AFL debated whether to call a nationwide general strike.[83]

At the beginning, Debs viewed the strike as a "fight . . . between the American Railroad Union and the Pullman Company." Later, as the conflict widened and deepened, he began to see it as "a contest between the producing classes and the money power of the country, . . . between the railroad corporations united solidly upon the one hand and the labor forces on the other. . . ."[84] But even at the end of the strike Debs had not yet been converted to the socialist view positing the inevitable separation of classes and class struggle in a capitalist society—his intellectual commitments were still very much to the antimonopolism and equal rights of radical republicanism. Indeed, he voted for the Peoples party in the 1894 elections.[85] Moreover, while the Pullman strike mobilized the Chicago, and much of the national, working class around a class-conscious ideology that threatened a good deal more than George Pullman's 6 percent profit on his company housing, and culminated almost a half-century of class formation, the Pullman strikers mobilized around an antimonopoly rather than socialist ideology. Still the radical, even revolutionary, character of the strike cannot be ignored: It represented a deliberate, disciplined, union-led, classwide confrontation with monopoly control over corporate control of the workplace. "The Pullman strike," wrote Selig Perlman, "marks an era in the American labor movement because it was the only attempt ever made in America of a revolutionary strike on the continental European model. The strikers tried to throw against the associated railways and indeed against the entire existing social order the full force of a revolutionary labor solidarity embracing the entire American wage earning class brought to the point of exasperation by unemployment, wage reductions and misery. . . ."[86]

Certainly capital, the federal government, the press, and the respectable classes looked upon the strike—what they called "Debs Rebellion"—in apocalyptic terms. The vice president of the Pullman Company argued that the strike represented a conflict not about wages or rents but about the "control" of "business," a point of view shared by the General Managers Association (GMA).[87] The *New York Times* described the strike as "the greatest battle between labor and capital that has ever been inaugurated in the United States." On July 3 the *Chicago Tribune* called the strike a revolutionary "insurrection."[88] "If the strike would be successful," editorialized another newspaper, the *Chicago Herald*, "the owners of the railroad property would have to surrender its future control to the class of labor agitators and strike conspirators who have formed the Debs Railway

Union."[89] Richard Olney, Grover Cleveland's attorney general, appointed Edwin Walker, a member of the GMA's legal committee and general counsel for one of the railroads involved in the strike, a special federal attorney in Chicago to defend corporate property and "interstate commerce." On instructions from Olney (also a railroad lawyer and director of a railroad involved in the boycott), Walker took out a court injunction forbidding all strike activity.[90] When the injunction failed to end the strike, President Cleveland decided, on July 4, Independence Day, to end the "reign of terror in Chicago" by sending in federal troops without first obtaining the permission of Governor Altgeld as required by the Constitution. When Altgeld protested, Cleveland responded "that in this hour of danger and public distress, discussion may well give way to active efforts on the part of all authority to restore obedience and law and to protect life and property."[91]

The combined weight of federal troops, court injunctions, the intransigence of Pullman and the General Managers Association, and desperate poverty finally broke the strike. But not without considerable political cost to the Democratic party, for in the meantime, the Depression, the Pullman strike, and Cleveland's action spurred the creation of a Labor-Populist alliance in Illinois and convinced Altgeld to wrest control of the Democratic party from "Clevelandism."

Illinois Populists tried to tempt labor into this alliance with them as the Depression deepened during the winter of 1893–94 and the prospects of "independent political action" by labor grew. During April and May 1894 a series of exploratory conferences between representatives from the Cook County Farmers Alliance, the Peoples party, the Chicago Central Labor Union, the Chicago Socialist Labor party, Bellamy nationalists, Knights of Labor, single taxers, prohibitionists, and free silver organizations agreed to "unite the farmers with the city laborers in one invincible political party" based on the Omaha platform of the Peoples party and the AFL political program, excepting Plank 10, adopted by the AFL in December 1893.[92] At a Populist-sponsored conference in Springfield on May 28 of "all labor and farm organizations," including the Illinois State Federation of Labor and the Socialist Labor party, the delegates adopted a platform pledging the union of "urban industrialists and agriculturalists in one harmonious political party," approved the Omaha platform, and recommended that the Peoples party adopt the AFL's political program at its meeting the next day. The Populists accepted all of the AFL's program, but refused to accept Plank 10—"the collective ownership by the people of all means of production and distribution."[93] The conference broke up without creating a Labor-Populist alliance, although at a second meeting, during the Illinois State Federation of Labor convention in early July, the attempt succeeded, after Henry D. Lloyd introduced a modified version of Plank 10: All members of the organizations represented at the conference would "vote for those candidates of the Peoples Party at the coming election who will pledge themselves to the principle of the collective ownership by the people of all such means of production and distribution as the people elect to operate for the commonwealth."[94] The conference had succeeded in creating not only a coalition of rural and urban "producers" but a coalition that went beyond the antimonopolism of the Omaha platform to a Fabian socialist program.[95]

Altgeld's outrage at Cleveland's role in the Pullman strike, plus the poor showing of the Democratic party in the 1894 elections, convinced Altgeld of the necessity to check the domination of the Democratic party by "Clevelandism" and "the monied interests." Within three months of the end of the Pullman strike, Altgeld began to support anti-Cleveland elements within the Democratic party in New York.[96] In April 1895 he secured a declaration from a special convention of the Illinois Democratic Party in favor of free silver. He gave speeches wherever he could, denouncing "vast concentrations of capital" that corrupted "everything it touches with a moral leprosy" and threatened "republican institutions."[97] The following year, the Illinois delegation to the national convention of the Democratic party in Chicago chose Altgeld as chairman of the Illinois delegation. At the convention Altgeld outwitted Cleveland's supporters and gained control of the platform committee.[98] The platform repudiated Cleveland's "policy of gold monometallism" and, referring to the events of 1894, denounced the "arbitrary interference by Federal authorities in local affairs as a violation of the Constitution of the United States" and "government by injunction." The party declared itself in favor of vigorous enforcement of the Sherman Act, enlargement of the powers of the Interstate Commerce Commission, limited tariffs, abolition of national bank notes, an income tax, industrial arbitration, and above all, free coinage of silver.[99] In the debate over the platform, William Jennings Bryan addressed the convention concerning the "paramount issue":

Mr. Carlisle said in 1878 that this was a struggle between "the idle holders of the capital" and "the struggling masses, who produce the wealth and pay the taxes of the country": and, my friends, the question we are to decide is: Upon which side will the Democratic Party fight; upon the side of "the idle holders of idle capital" or upon the side of "the struggling masses"? . . .

If they [defenders of the gold standard] dare to come out in the open field and defend the gold standard as a good thing, we will fight them to the uttermost.

Having behind us the producing masses of this nation and the world, supported by the commercial interests, the laboring interests and the toilers everywhere, we will answer their demand for a gold standard by saying to them: You shall not press down upon the brow of labor this crown of thorns, you shall not crucify mankind upon a cross of gold.[100]

Bryan's speech thrust him to the forefront of the Democratic party presidential candidates. Altgeld, plagued by serious reservations about Bryan's intellectual competence and his understanding of the silver issue, preferred to nominate Senator Bland of Missouri but eventually endorsed Bryan.[101] Bryan's nomination dismayed and terrified the respectable classes, mobilized capital on behalf of his Republican opponent, McKinley, and reportedly moved Theodore Roosevelt to remark that Bryan and Altgeld were "plotting a social revolution and the subversion of the American Republic." He went on to intimate that civil war could follow and that he himself might have to confront Altgeld on the field of battle.[102]

Roosevelt need not have worried. Bryan's nomination by the People's party in July split the Peoples party wide apart, provoking antimonopolists like Lloyd to desert the party.[103] Both Bryan and Altgeld were defeated in November and with them any possibility of radical reform, whether the producerist petty bourgeois and pietistic democratic variety of Bryan or the antimonopolism of the Populists and Altgeld.[104] President McKinley and Governor Tanner did not consider themselves reformers of any kind. But in Chicago a new and very different reform movement, still in its infancy, thrived.

PROGRESSIVE REFORM IN CHICAGO

On March 8, 1889, the *Chicago Tribune* reported that two young college-educated women were soon to embark on "A Project to Bring the Rich and Poor Together."[105] Six months later, the two women, Jane Addams and Ellen Gates Starr, opened a "settlement house" at the corner of Polk and South Halstead on the near West Side in the middle of an immigrant working-class neighborhood. By 1909 eighteen more had opened.[106] In explaining the origins of the settlement house movement, Jane Addams emphasized two considerations: the "subjective necessity" and the "solution of . . . social and industrial problems." "We have in America," she wrote concerning the former, "a fast-growing number of cultivated young people who have no recognized outlet for their active faculties. They hear constantly of the great social maladjustment, but no way is provided for them to change it, and their uselessness hangs about them heavily." Settlements provided them an opportunity to give "tangible expression" to their "notions of human brotherhood" and the "democratic ideal," to participate in "a renaissance of . . . early Christian humanitarianism" among those who wished "to share the lives of the poor, the desire to make social service . . . express the spirit of Christ."[107]

Settlement houses, however, were not only an expression of subjective necessity, they were also the product of objective need. Addams insisted that the "breakdown" of representative government in the wards, the alienation and poverty of immigrants in the neighborhoods, sweatshop conditions, child labor, commercialized vice and amusements, bitter clashes between labor and capital, and, above all, the division of the city "into two nations . . . broken up into classes" required that reformers replace the traditional emphasis of Gilded Age reform upon individual moral rehabilitation with one that stressed "social morality" and "social democracy."[108] "To attain individual morality in an age demanding social morality, to pride one's self on the results of personal effort when the time demands social adjustment," Addams insisted in *Democracy and Social Ethics*, "is utterly to fail to apprehend the situation." "The highest moralists," she argued elsewhere, "have taught that without the advance and improvement of the whole, no man can hope for any lasting improvement in his own moral or material individual condition."[109] In opening Hull House, she and Ellen Gates Starr intended to provide "a center for a higher civic and social life; to institute and maintain educational and philanthropic enterprises, and to investigate and improve the conditions in the industrial districts of Chicago," to be, in short, "an experimental effort to aid in the solution of the social and industrial problems that are engendered by the modern conditions of life in a great city." What America needed, she insisted, was a moral reformation that recognized "that the dependence of classes on each other is reciprocal; and that as the social relation is essentially a reciprocal relation, it gives a form of expression that has peculiar value." Residents of settlements hoped "to make social intercourse express the growing sense of . . . economic unity and to add to the social functions of democracy," "to make the entire social organism democratic."[110]

From almost the day Jane Addams and Ellen Gates Starr opened Hull House, they set about the task of educating middle- and upper-class Americans about immigrants and educating immigrants in the ways of middle-class America. Addams and other settlement workers insisted that settlement houses were not charitable institutions, that residents of settlement houses were not "friendly visitors" but genuine "residents" of immigrant neighborhoods. Addams stressed that settlement residents assumed the responsibility of "interpreting" the immigrant working classes to the middle and upper classes of Chicago. "Whatever other services the settlement may have endeavored to perform for its community," she wrote, "there is no doubt that it has come to regard that of interpreting the foreign colonies to the rest of the city in the light of a professional obligation." Mary McDowell, for a time a Hull House resident and later a founder of a settlement in the stockyards district, claimed that settlements provided the "chance to work with the least skilled workers . . . not for them as a missionary, but with them as a neighbor and seeker after truth."[111] As soon as settlement houses opened, residents began "to investigate . . . the conditions in the industrial districts in Chicago" and to educate and agitate for reform. They investigated housing conditions, municipal services, factory conditions, sweatshops, child labor, "commercialized" vice and amusements, wages and family budgets, civic corruption, juvenile delinquency, child mortality, municipal services, saloons, truancy, epidemics, illiteracy, industrial accidents, strikes, unemployment, poverty, and neighborhood life. And having investigated, they proselytized and organized for reform. Urging abandonment of the voluntarism of the Gilded Age, they proposed using the powers of the state to correct injustice and advance the cause of social democracy: protective legislation for working women, child labor and compulsory education legislation, legislation to regulate factory and sweatshop conditions, unemployment insurance, mother's pensions, worker's compensation, improved municipal services, creation of a juvenile court and a probation system, vocational guidance offices, playgrounds, parks, vocational and "socialized" education, women's suffrage, kindergartens, a federal children's bureau, federally funded health care systems for mothers and children, civic reform, and the election of honest aldermen. In nearly every instance they succeeded, to one degree or another, and in doing so established the foundations of the welfare state that Franklin D. Roosevelt expanded (rather than invented) during the 1930s.[112]

In addition to the investigation and interpretation of immigrant life, settlement workers also devoted themselves to the task of educating the immigrant working class to life in America. Settlement house workers might have described themselves as genuine "residents" of immigrant neighborhoods, but there can be no mistaking the irreducibly pedagogical character of the relationship between residents and the immigrant poor. Soon after they moved into Hull House, Addams and Starr decided "to share the race life and to bring as much as possible of social energy and the accumulation of civilization to those portions of the race which have little. . . ." Within two weeks of opening Hull House, "Mrs. Starr started a reading party in George Eliot's *Romala*." They covered the walls of Hull House with reproductions collected in Europe of paintings that combined "an elevated tone with technical excellence." These provided, Addams believed, "a strong impulse toward the heroic and the historic." Art classes and exhibitions and a library of prints for neighborhood residents to borrow provided a medium of cultural expression and social communion—an "enduring form of social life"—to "free . . . social expression" and bind neighbors together "through common intercourse."[113] They opened a kindergarten for young children (whose teacher vainly but good humoredly endeavored to impress temperance principles upon the children's mothers) and organized groups for boys and girls that "were not quite classes and not quite clubs" in which girls were taught cooking, dressmaking, and millinery, boys taught industrial skills in a variety of trades, and both given the opportunity "for initiative and for independent social relationships." A Woman's Club taught mothers proper principles of child care, hygiene, nutrition, moral development, and appreciation of the value of school attendance for their children.[114]

Over the course of time, settlement house workers increasingly viewed their activities as a kind of "municipal housekeeping," applying the special qualities associated with women's role in the home—compassion, sympathy, benevolence, moral rectitude, and the skills of household management—to the world at large.[115] Women should have the vote, for example, not so much because they laid claim to civic autonomy and equality of citizenship but because of the special qualities and skills that women could bring to the task of "social amelioration" and to creating a "world nearer to their hearts desire—a better world for their children to live in." Women did not need the vote, or protective legislation, for their own sake but "for their children's sake." Domesticity, moreover, imposed a moral duty upon women to participate in "municipal housekeeping." "Many women today are failing properly to discharge their duties to their own families and households," Addams wrote, "simply because they fail to see that as society grows more complicated," it is necessary that women shall extend their sense of responsibility to many things outside of the home, "if only in order to preserve the home in its entirety." Hull House residents tried repeatedly to convince neighborhood women "that if it were a womanly task to go about in tenement homes in order to nurse the sick, it might be quite as womanly to go through the same district in order to prevent the breeding of so-called 'filth diseases.' " It was just as feminine and just as important for a woman to work for social reform—and to be able to vote in order to advance the cause of reform—as it was for her to mother her children and manage her home:

Women who live in the country sweep their own yards and may either feed the refuse of the table to a flock of chickens or allow it innocently to decay in the open air and sunshine. In a crowded city quarter, however, if the street is not cleaned by the city authorities, no amount of private sweeping will keep the tenement free from grime; if the garbage is not properly collected and destroyed, a tenement house mother may see her children sicken and die of diseases from which she alone is powerless to shield them; if woman would keep on with her old business of caring for her house and rearing her children, she will have to have some conscience in regard to public affairs lying quite outside of her immediate household. The individual conscience and devotion are no longer effective.[116]

Although women and settlement house residents should vote and participate in social reform movements, Addams argued that they should participate in a particular kind of way. Hull House, she claimed, "from its very nature" could "stand for no particular social propaganda" or "for marching and carrying banners, for stating general principles and making a demonstration." Social settlements could have nothing to do with any kind of political or industrial activity that represented, or was likely to provoke, class conflict. Rather, settlement houses must stand "for uncovering the situation and for providing the legal measures and the civic organization through which new social hopes might make themselves felt" and then use the "newly moralized issue" as a means "to educate the entire community by a wonderful unification of effort."[117] Through a combination of investigation, organization, education, "social ethics," and "enlarged" or "municipal housekeeping," women generally, and settlement house residents particularly, could remake the world in the image of the home. Together they could create an urban and even national family with all the peace and harmony characteristic of domestic tranquility—a "social democracy" free of injustice and the separation of classes.

After 1900, settlement workers increasingly gave of their time, energy, and moral authority to national progressive causes: the National Consumers League, the National Child Labor Committee, the National Woman's Trade Union League, the National American Woman Suffrage Association, the National Playground Association, the National Conference of Charities and Corrections, the National Association of City Planning, the NAACP, the National Education Association, the National Housing Association, and others.[118] Their efforts climaxed in 1912 when settlement workers merged their causes in a nationwide political crusade to elect Theodore Roosevelt, the candidate of the newly born Progressive party, president of the United States of America. Jane Addams, who seconded the nomination of Roosevelt at the August convention of the Progressive party in Chicago, explained that social workers "had increasingly felt the need for a new party which should represent 'the action and passion of the times,' which should make social reform a political issue of national dimensions, which should inaugurate an educational campaign advocating its measures to the remotest parts of the country. . . ." Convinced "that the nexus between citizens could be more scientific and durable and at the same time more understanding and heartfelt" and that "the very sentiments of compassion and desire for social justice were futile unless they could at last find expression as an integral part of corporate government," the members of the convention approved a platform that "expressed the social hopes so long ignored by the politicians," above all "measures of amelioration," "social justice," and "remedial legislation . . . essential to the nation's welfare."[119]

In the months that followed, Addams and other social workers exploited "the wonderful opportunity for education . . . on the social justice planks in the platform" that the campaign provided. Addams campaigned throughout the country, wrote six articles explaining the platform of the Progressive party, and took an active role in the affairs of the National Progressive Committee, the Illinois State Progressive Committee (IPC), and the Cook County Progressive Committee. Raymond Robins, until 1907 head resident of the Northwestern University settlement, joined the IPC and acted as chair of the Cook County Progressive convention. Margaret Robins, president of the National Women's Trade Union League, and Mary McDowell, head resident of the University of Chicago settlement, were both members of the executive committee of the IPC. Graham Taylor supported the Progressive party through his editorials in the *Chicago Daily News*. Despite their best efforts, Roosevelt lost the election, but social workers did not assume that his defeat doomed the Progressive quest for social justice and social democracy. The work of investigation, education, organization, and reform would go on. And in the form of the National Progressive Service, it did.[120]

The opening of Hull House in 1889 dates the first expression of Progressive reform in Chicago. Thorstein Veblen might dismiss the "solicitude" of settlement workers for the immigrant poor as a mere device "to enhance the industrial efficiency of the poor and to teach them the more adequate utilization of the means at hand" and to inculcate, "by precept and example . . . certain punctilios of upper class propriety in manners and customs," but to others Hull House represented the most significant effort

of the period to reconcile the classes.[121] "If Christ Came to Chicago,"
William T. Stead, an English social gospel minister, wrote in 1894, "there
are few objects that would more command His sympathy and secure His
help than efforts to restore the sense of brotherhood to man and to reconstitute the human family on a basis adjusted to modern life" than settlement houses. Hull House was, he insisted, "one of the best institutions in
Chicago" because it endeavored "to help the people by the redeeming
grace of good neighborliness":

What the monastery of St. Bernard was to the Astercians, what the original Brotherhood of St. Francis was to the Franciscan Order, so Hull House will be to the
brotherhoods and sisterhoods of helpers and neighbours, who in increasing numbers will take up their residence in the midst of the crowded and desolate quarters
of our over-crowded cities. Only by this means can we hope to reconstruct the
human family and restore something approaching to a microcosm of a healthy
organization in every precinct in the city. Mere propinquity counts for a great deal
in human affairs.[122]

But as impressed with Hull House as he was, Stead did not believe
that settlement houses alone could resolve the pressing social problems,
above all the growing separation of classes that confronted Chicago.[123] At
a meeting at the Central Music Hall in November 1893 that Stead called
to consider ways of dealing with the severe depression that had devastated
the economy of the city since the summer, Stead warned the audience of
civic leaders and interested citizens that settlement houses alone could not
solve Chicago's pressing social problems. "If Christ Came to Chicago . . .
He would not find Christian sympathy and a flouishing republic but
callous indifference, myopic complacency, widespread misery, a growing
separation of classes, and the ominous spectre of violent class conflict."
Chicago required, he declared, a "Civic Revival" by "a body of men and
women . . . dedicated to the redemption of the municipal and social system." Other speakers echoed the same sentiment. Tommy Morgan described the "social conditions" in the city and reminded his audience that
"if the pleadings of editor Stead, in the name of Christ and for justice,
cannot shake you out, someone may blow you out with dynamite." As
might be expected in the city that had witnessed the Haymarket affair only
seven years previously, pandamonium broke out.[124]

Stead's admonition and Morgan's warning galvanized a group of
citizens, including Jane Addams, to establish an organization, the Chicago
Civic Federation, to deal with the emergency and develop a broad program of civic and social reform.[125] Led by Lyman Gage, president of the
First National Bank (in later years, Theodore Roosevelt's secretary of the

treasury) and Ralph Easley (later the first secretary of the National Civic Federation) and a governing council of one hundred prominent citizens, the federation would "serve as a medium of acquaintance and sympathy between persons who reside in the different parts of the city, who pursue different vocations, who are by birth of different nationalities, who profess different creeds, . . . who, for all these reasons, are unknown to each other" and "to gather together . . . all the forces for good, public and private, which are at work in Chicago." This could be accomplished, the charter went on, through

the quickening of the public conscience, the arousing of the citizens to their duties and rights as citizens, the harmonizing of public and private agencies for good, the encouragement of wise and judicious legislation, the upholding of law and order, peace and justice, the promotion of fair dealing between man and man in the industrial world, the forwarding of humane and enlightened views and practices in dealings with the unfortunate, the vicious and the defective, the advancement of the education of the masses, the ultimate separation of municipal affairs from party politics, security and honesty in elections, systematic and intelligent charity organizations, and securing of capable and interested public officials.[126]

One of the clauses of the charter of the Civic Federation urged its members to develop "systematic and intelligent charity organizations." Shortly after the November 1893 Central Music Hall meeting, the fledging federation conducted an extensive survey of the extent of distress, decided to oppose the dole and to provide an extensive system of work relief to be administered by a new organization, the Central Relief Association. In the late spring of 1894, the CRA terminated most of its relief work, assuming that the worst of the crisis was over. In the meantime, the CRA firmly established charity in Chicago along the lines laid down by the charity organization movement: an elaborate system to monitor and coordinate all relief activities in the city, reduction of outdoor relief to the barest minimum, and an extensive program of friendly visiting. The CRA (and its successors, the Chicago Bureau of Charities and the Chicago Bureau of Associated Charities) divided the city into districts, each of which instituted friendly visiting programs between the poor and the well-to-do "to furnish an avenue for helpful and friendly communication between them." (District boundaries were drawn in such a manner as to include within each district members of the well-to-do classes.) By the end of 1897, the association employed some eight hundred friendly visitors, supervising sixteen hundred families.[127]

Several prominent reformers, however, expressed deep ambivalence or outright opposition to the new arrangements.[128] In 1895 Charles

Henderson, for example, praised the effort of the charity organization movement to establish charity on a scientific basis but argued that the growing separation of classes in America could not be halted by recourse to paternalism and deference. The social psychology of the charity relation, Henderson insisted, must take cognizance of the political and ideological realities of the "New World":

> The old charity spirit, the patronage of feudalism is doomed. In the new charity none can serve with advantage who do not sincerely accept Burns' doctrine that a man is a man. A mere verbal, insincere lip-service of humanity, with the absolute caste feeling crouching in the background, is an anachronism. Modern democracy is sensitive to discern and feel; it is quick to resent. Masks are torn off without mercy. . . . Nothing but absolutely sincere fellowship will even begin to touch the heart of the people. And the chasm is already so wide that nothing but the sacrifice of many devoted citizens will, as in the old Roman legend, cause the threatening abyss to close.[129]

Several years later, Jane Addams, like Henderson, a leading member of the Civic Federation, developed a similar but more detailed critique of the "charity relation." For Addams, the charity relation contradicted America's "democratic" tradition. While aware of the changes taking place in the charity relation, Jane Addams concluded that "there is no point of contact in our modern experience which reveals more clearly the lack of equality which democracy implies." Despite progress in charity work, the paternalism of philanthropy could not be denied, nor could its undemocratic "unconscious division of the world into the philanthropists and those to be helped." This "assumption of two classes," the persistence of "two ethical standards," violated democratic social ethics, and nowhere more so than in the practice of friendly visiting or the "charity relation." Although she analyzed the ambiguities and nuances of the charity relation and its effects on the friendly visitor and the poor, she primarily focused on the social misunderstanding created by the dual "ethical standards" and the disparate experiences separating the classes. Friendly visiting, she insisted, was undemocratic and unlikely to bridge the gap between the classes; if anything, it accentuated the separation of classes. America did not so much need more charity but social justice, and above all, a system of social insurance.[130]

Over the course of the next decade, a coalition of reformers, some motivated by humanitarian and social justice considerations, others by the desire to improve "social efficiency," attempted to secure the beginnings of a system of social insurance.[131] In 1911 they succeeded in gaining two bills—one a worker's compensation bill and the other a mother's pension bill—despite the hostility of many businessmen to the first and the COS to the second.[132] The significance of these acts, however, resides not only in the combination of social justice and social efficiency considerations that secured them but also in the fact that their passage reflected a breach, even if narrow, in the protective wall of bourgeois ideology of self-reliance and voluntary charity and the traditional institutional arrangements connecting the family, the state, and the structure of social relations. With the decline of property as the basis of the domestic economy of American family life and its replacement by a system of wage labor, reformers began to recognize all the possibilities of economic insecurity and dependency associated with the shift. Self-reliance and voluntary charity were well and good in a society of yeoman farmers, self-supporting craftsmen, and entrepreneurs, but in a society of wage earners they did not prevent misery and discontent.[133] Time and time again the advocates of social insurance referred to the "anxieties," "insecurities," and "fears" of the "wage earner" confronted by the very real possibility of sickness, injury, unemployment, and the certainty of old age, if they lived long enough. Charles Henderson, for example, in supporting workmen's compensation, noted that wage earners had no protection against the crippling economic consequences of serious industrial accidents. "No statistics which can be gathered," he wrote, "that can visualize the conditions of constant dread of suffering and pauperism which are the hourly torment of thoughtful workmen. . . . The aim of social insurance is not only to keep the wolf from the door, but to keep him so far away that he cannot destroy sheep with his howls."[134]

In 1911, then, reformers had succeeded in creating a binary system of social insurance (worker's compensation) and social welfare (mother's pensions) to replace the older system of voluntarism and private charity and adjusting the domestic economy of the working class family to the market revolution.[135] Social insurance and social welfare did not contradict the market revolution, they confirmed and advanced it. Where the moral reformers of the Gilded Age denied the existence of a class society and focused upon promoting social mobility through individual moral rehabilitation, social insurance and social welfare presupposed a class society and sought to help the family adjust to the vicissitudes of a family economy based on wage labor.[136]

In the years that followed passage of the worker's compensation and mother's pensions bills in 1911, professional case workers rather than settlement house residents took over responsibility for the administration of the services. By 1930, professional case workers exercised a virtual monopoly.[137] The *Social Science Director* for Chicago in 1930 listed more than seven hundred agencies "directly concerned with the proper functioning of social work in the community." Four agencies alone—the United Charities, the Jewish Social Service Bureau, the Field Service Division of the Cook County Bureau of Public Welfare, and the Unemployed Relief System—employed, in 1935, 1,120 social workers and case work aides. A 1937 study estimated that almost 1,400 professional case workers were employed in Chicago, in addition to settlement workers, parole officers, workers in social work publicity and propaganda, and research workers.[138] Friendly visiting, moreover, rather than settlement work, provided the prototype or model of professional case work.[139] In a sense, professional case work came to constitute a mechanism for institutionalizing personal influence and supervising family life under the mantle of scientific expertise at a time when the growth of large social work bureaucracies and "social distance" exacerbated the "deformation of the gift" and "the separation of classes."[140]

In addition to their efforts to alleviate distress and to adjust the family to the market revolution, Progressive reformers, with the Civic Federation again taking the lead, also endeavored to create mechanisms to prevent conflicts between labor and capital from deteriorating into class warfare. During the Pullman strike, the federation created a special committee, chaired by Jane Addams, to arbitrate between the General Managers Association and the American Railroad Union. Pullman summarily rebuffed the offer, but after the strike, the federation sponsored a Congress on Industrial Conciliation and Arbitration in November 1894 and appointed Jane Addams secretary of the organizing committee. The congress, wishing to protect the "public interest" and to lessen the chances that future strikes would assume the apocalyptic proportions of the Pullman conflict, recommended passage by the state legislature of a bill establishing a system of arbitration and drafted a prototype.[141] The U.S. Strike Commission, following its own investigation of the strike, recommended the creation of a five-man "United States Board of Conciliation and Arbitration" for the mediation of interstate disputes and the creation of state boards for intrastate disputes.[142] John Peter Altgeld, already convinced by Henry Demarest Lloyd's *A Country Without Strikes* and the increasing bitterness of the clashes between labor and capital that the state should enforce arbitration "to prevent industrial strife, and in fact, a civil war," called for a special session of the state legislature for August 1895 and secured passage, aided by the lobbying efforts of the federation, of an act creating the Illinois State Board of Arbitration, composed of a representative from organized labor, a representative of capital, and a third "independent" member.[143] The arrangement faithfully mirrored the growing awareness

10

and acceptance of the deep social divisions within American society and the desire of reformers to construct bureaucratic mechanisms for regulating class relationships. If conflict between labor and capital could not be prevented, it at least need not lead to class warfare.

Meanwhile, settlement house residents took it upon themselves to educate labor and capital in their respective responsibilities. Strikes, Jane Addams informed trade unionists, were a "social waste" that violated principles of "fraternity" and "universal brotherhood" and produced nothing but "class bitterness and strife." Union leaders should repudiate all theories that "divide all men so sharply into capitalists and proletarians." Instead, they should adopt the "social point of view" and a "larger conception of citizenship."[144] Similarly, Graham Taylor argued that unions should restrict themselves to the education of workers in social consciousness rather than class consciousness. "If the labor union would become more of a school," he wrote, "its usefulness would be vastly increased."[145] Although some settlement residents openly identified with workers in a number of highly publicized strikes (Pullman in 1894, Hart, Shaffner, and Marx in 1910), Jane Addams and Graham Taylor generally refused to publicly commit themselves to either the cause of labor or capital, and this was as true of the 1900 building trades strike, the 1903 International Harvester strike, the 1904 stockyards strike, and the Hart, Shaffner, and Marx strike in 1910 as it was true of the Pullman strike in 1894.[146] Addams and Taylor preferred to arbitrate strikes, to mediate between labor and capital, to prevent, as Jane Addams put it, conflicts between labor and capital "from becoming in any sense a class warfare." During "all those dark days of the Pullman strike" that made obvious "the growth of class consciousness," for example, Addams tried to maintain "avenues of intercourse with both sides" and served as the secretary of the committee set up by the Civic Federation to arbitrate the strike. In an address before the Chicago Women's Club, later published in *The Survey*, Addams criticized George Pullman's paternalism and intransigence. The strike, she argued, reflected a growing conflict "between the democratic ideal which urges the workmen to demand representation in the administration of industry and the accepted position, that the man who owns the capital and takes the risks has the exclusive right of management, . . . a clash between individual or aristocratic management, and corporate or democratic government." In a pointed comparison with Shakespeare's tragic anti-hero King Lear, Addams suggested that Pullman's misguided paternalism was out of touch with the needs of "social morality" and "social ethics" and had brought in its train not filial affection and social harmony but "the growth of class bitterness" and "division along class lines."[147]

After the strike, Addams played a key role in the effort of the Civic Federation to create the Illinois State Board of Arbitration, and sixteen years later, in 1911–12, joined with other leading settlement workers, including Florence Kelley, Graham Taylor, and Mary McDowell, and the National Civic Federation in the successful campaign to persuade President Taft and Congress to create a federal industrial relations commission "with as great scientific competence, staff resources and power to compel testimony as the Interstate Commerce Commission" charged with the responsibility of investigating and uncovering the causes of strikes and union violence, thereby providing an adequate factual basis for arbitration and reconciliation.[148] In August 1912 Congress passed and Taft signed a bill establishing the U.S. Industrial Relations Commission.[149]

Progressive reformers pursued political reform at the local level with as much energy, although in the long run much less successfully, as they did social reform. Jane Addams and Graham Taylor, beginning in 1895, both endeavored to replace local aldermen not to their liking, but the Civic Federation and its offspring, the Municipal Voters League, remained the agency primarily responsible for political reform in Chicago, at least during the second half of the 1890s.[150] The charter of the Civic Federation indicated the broad objectives of its political program: "the ultimate separation of municipal affairs from party politics, security and honesty in elections, . . . and securing capable and interested public officials."[151] Initially, the federation seemed content to hire detectives and lawyers to supervise elections, hold ward meetings, endorse honest candidates, and support reformers like Graham Taylor in their efforts to unseat machine politicians at the ward level.[152] Events in Springfield and Chicago in 1895, 1896, and 1897, however, led the federation's leadership to pay much closer attention to municipal politics and to the relation between municipal politics and business. It did so not because Lyman Gage, Ralph Easley, and other business leaders of the federation were suddenly converted to the "equal rights" republicanism of Eugene Debs, Tommy Morgan, Henry Demarest Lloyd, the Labor-Populist alliance, or even John Peter Altgeld, but because the business practices of the utility magnates and civic corruption undermined public confidence in business and businessmen, spawned "tax influences," hampered the creation of stable and orderly business environments, and violated the axioms of "good government."[153] In their fear of political corruption and in their desire to replace politics with administration, political reformers combined a neoclassical fear of corruption and factional politics with a neo-Federalist commitment to centralized government by an administrative elite.[154] But although hostile to the corruption of politicians by businessmen, the reformers were not hostile to business as such. They assumed, as Albion Small suggested, "the fundamental necessity of basing social prosperity of all sorts upon a secure foundation of business principles."[155] They wished merely to redesign the relationship between local government and business and place city government on a businesslike basis, or as Franklin MacVeagh put it, secure conditions "most favorable to the introduction of business methods": "executive independence," "executive responsibility," "the restriction of the powers" of the city council, "civil service reform—the merit system," "home rule," and "a paid, professional, expert city government."[156]

During 1895 the Chicago City Council brazenly "boodled" nine utility franchises, the two most important of which involved the Cosmopolitan Electric Company and the Ogden Gas Company. The boodle so outraged the press, sections of the business community, and the leadership of the Civic Federation that the federation held a mass meeting on March 3 to protest the boodle and petitioned Mayor Hopkins to veto the bills. (Hopkins refused.)[157] In May the Ogden Gas Company and Charles T. Yerkes, a Chicago traction magnate, secured extension of their respective monopolies from the Illinois legislature, but Governor Altgeld vetoed the bills, declaring that they represented "a flagrant attempt to increase the riches of some men at the expense of others by means of legislation."[158] The following January, however, the reformers were again faced with another traction boodle, this time engineered by Alderman "Bathhouse John" Coughlin. When Coughlin managed to override Mayor Swift's veto and openly taunted the civic reformers, the Civic Federation decided to take its gloves off. The federation sent out invitations to representatives of the Union League Club, the Citizens Association, the Commercial Club, the Board of Trade, and several other business and civic organizations to attend a municipal reform conference to discuss the situation and "do something." Initially, sentiment favored the creation of a reform third party, but Lyman Gage and Graham Taylor persuaded civic reformers to create a "reform machine," the Municipal Voters League (MVL), to do battle with the "grey wolves" that dominated city council and to undo the "unholy alliance" between corrupt councilmen and rapacious capitalists by promoting "the nomination and election of aggressively honest and capable men to public office, to investigate and publish for the information of voters the records of candidates for offices, to secure the separation of the municipal business of Chicago and Cook County from national politics, and to aid in the strict enforcement of civil service laws." The federation selected George Cole, a Chicago businessman, to be the first "boss" of the MVL.[159]

Over the course of the next three years, the Civic Federation and the MVL secured the election of candidates hostile to boodlering in Chicago and defeated legislation in Chicago and Springfield supported by the utility companies and the boodlers.[160] In the elections of 1896, Chicago voters elected 24 league candidates or ones acceptable to the MVL (out of a possible 34); in 1897, 14 of 34, in 1898, 23 of 34, in 1899, 25 of 34, and in 1900, 19 of 34. In the 1899 elections only 3 of the 36 men elected to the council were known boodlers. By 1900, "honest" men formed a dominant and overwhelming plurality in the city council. Only seven members of the old gang were left in office.[161] In 1903, when Lincoln Steffens returned to Chicago to examine the results of the municipal reform movement, he found that while three of the worst "bosses" still held their seats (Johnny Powers, Coughlin, and "Hinky Dink" Kenna), the rest had been driven from their lair. "The good people of Chicago," he concluded, "have beaten boodling." Chicago was "Half Free and Fighting On."[162]

Beating the boodlers, electing honest politicians, and securing "representative government" constituted only the first of the objectives of the political Progressives. Their second objective focused on the transformation of municipal administration in Chicago. The reformers, as Lincoln Steffens wrote, were not content with mere honesty. They wanted "honesty and efficiency, too."[163] Within a month of receiving its state charter in February 1894, the Civic Federation began to search for ways to secure "good government" by redesigning the structure and operating principles of municipal government in Chicago. In March 1894 the federation undertook an investigation of civil service laws and eventually drafted, with the help of the Chicago Civil Service Reform League, a civil service bill designed to limit the spoils system and patronage, the lifeblood of machine politics. The following March, after intense lobbying by the federation, Governor Altgeld, the Reform League, and a number of other Chicago and Illinois business and civic organizations, the Illinois legislature passed "An Act to Regulate the Civil Service of Cities."[164] Within two weeks of its passage, voters in Chicago adopted the act through a local options clause, created the Chicago Civil Service Commission and gave it power to classify offices under merit rules, to select candidates for appointive posts through a competitive examination system, and to remove civil service employees for incompetence. Through a variety of loopholes, however, patronage politics continued only slightly hobbled until Mayor Harrison, his fingers burnt by an acrimonious patronage battle in the police department, appointed a committed civil service advocate, John Ela, to the Civil Service Commission in 1900. Ela expanded the use of "promotion examinations" and introduced a system of "efficiency ratings" to determine promotions. Harrison also reduced the number of "provisional" appointments; by the time he left office in 1905, examinations were held for every office in the classified civil service. Civic reformers were well satisfied with the results of their work: William Kent boasted to Lincoln Steffens in 1904 that the merit system was "here to stay."[165]

Political Progressives also attempted to alter the city's charter. In 1894 a committee of the Civic Federation proposed a state constitutional amendment granting Chicago a new city charter. A Northwestern University professor, John H. Gray, became chairman of the federation's committee on charter revision and began work to propagate "the latest accepted theories of municipal government." In particular, the federation desired to concentrate and centralize power in the mayor's office and eliminate politics from municipal government, "which, of all our governmental agencies, is the most distinctly administrative, and therefore nonpolitical" and in need of "as great ability and as much expert knowledge as the management of any large private industry."[166] In 1902 the federation, along with representatives of twenty-two other civic organizations, including the Citizens Association, the MVL, the Chicago Bar Association, and the settlement house movement, met to draw up a revised city charter. In 1903 the state legislature approved the charter, and in 1904 the Illinois voters approved the creation of a charter convention for Chicago. In June 1904 the Chicago Charter Convention convened for the first time.[167]

For the next two years, the work of charter revision limped along sporadically, but in late 1906, the pace quickened considerably. Delegates to the convention stressed time and again the desirability of home rule, the consolidation of Chicago's highly decentralized structure of government, fiscal and tax reform, further civil service reform, the centralization of executive power in the mayor's office, election of the mayor by the council rather than the electorate at large, and the necessity of scientific, nonpartisan administration. Delegates from the Merchants Club successfully sponsored a series of proposals to centralize the authority of the school superintendent, reduce the size of the school board, oppose popular election of school board members, and institute a system of "merit pay." One delegate to the convention, Charles Merriam, a University of Chicago professor of political science and charter member of the City Club, undertook a study of Chicago's finances (published in January 1906 as the *Report on an Investigation of the Municipal Revenues of Chicago*) and recommended the consolidation and centralization of taxing authority and collection to enhance "efficiency" and "growth." Like the majority of delegates to the convention, Merriam believed that the "greatest troubles in city government have been: 1) the lack of adequate power, and 2) the lack of unity and responsibility in government" and that the "function of the mayor is the same function as the president of the railroad."[168]

Despite the best efforts of the Civic Federation, the City Club, and the Citizens Association, opposition from the Chicago Federation of Labor, the Chicago Teachers Federation, United Societies for Local Self-Government (an umbrella organization of immigrant societies opposed to Sunday closings), and the Democratic party defeated the new charter in a citywide referendum in September 1907.[169] But while discouraged, the apostles of what Merriam called "administrative efficiency" did not intend to give up.[170] In 1908 Merriam secured his appointment as secretary of the Chicago Harbor Commission about to investigate harbor facilities in Chicago. Merriam convinced the commission to hire someone with "special knowledge and training" to prepare a "concise report on the commercial advantages" of new harbor facilities and their relationship to other commercial and transportation requirements, and then hired a colleague of his at the University of Chicago to undertake the research.[171] The next year, 1909, Merriam successfully ran for alderman. He soon established himself as the leading representative of "good government" and convinced the council to create a Commission on City Expenditures (with himself as chairman) to investigate budget procedures, the letting of contracts, and city payrolls. Employing "capable experts" to undertake "investigations as a means of securing administrative efficiency," Merriam and the commission created a "scientific and up-to-date" budgetary process that centralized fiscal accountability in the controller's office in order to prevent "administrative inefficiency," "graft," and "collusion with contractors." The commission also investigated "the practical operations of the merit system" and persuaded the mayor to create an "Efficiency Division" within the Civil Service Commission as a further obstacle to patronage and favoritism, to streamline organizational and accounting procedures within city government, and develop a uniform salary scale based upon "efficiency ratings." Summarizing the work of the commission in a 1910 address to the City Club of Philadelphia, Merriam suggested that the commission was "merely trying to carry on in a scientific way the same sort of work for a large city corporation which any large business organization does for itself every year."[172]

Meanwhile, in 1910, Merriam established, under the auspices of the City Club, the Chicago Bureau of Public Efficiency to act as a watchdog over the city's finances, to exercise a "rigid scrutiny of all the complicated schemes of local government," and to serve as a guardian of "administrative efficiency" by promoting consolidation of municipal functions and centralization of administrative authority.[173] But in spite of the successes of the Commission on City Expenditures and the Bureau of Public Efficiency, Merriam remained convinced that the promise of political progressivism had yet to be fully realized. In 1911 he decided to run as a Republican for the mayor's office on a platform that stressed the end of "graft, crime, lawlessness, sloth, waste and extravagance" and promised "honest, efficient administration" devoid of patronage and party politics. Despite the strong support of settlement house workers, the Chicago Chamber of Commerce, the City Club, the Civic Federation, the Chicago Bureau of Public Efficiency, and the money of Charles Crane, Cyrus McCormick, Harold McCormick, and Julius Rosenwald, Merriam lost the election to Carter Harrison, although only by a slender margin.[174]

Political Progressives also hoped to redesign the relationship between municipal government and business. Boodlerism revealed not only the corruption of city aldermen but the rapacious greed and the unbridled monopolistic powers of the utility companies. The activities of Yerkes and his ilk undermined the public image of business, threatened the legitimacy of businessmen as community leaders, and inhibited the creation of a stable, orderly, "tax efficient" business environment. Defeat of the boodlers at the voting booth, however, represented only one part of the Progressives' strategy to refashion the relationship between business and government. A second involved a determined campaign to redeem businessmen, clean up business practices, and restore the legitimacy of business. Shortly after the establishment of the MVL, two of its members, William Kent and John Harlan, attended a meeting of the Commercial Club, a powerful organization of business magnates, and sharply criticized businessmen for their involvement in boodlerism and shady business deals. "It is not the silver craze alone," Kent argued, "which is ruining the credit of the country abroad, but the sharp tricks of 'businessmen' who are running a close race between millions and the penitentiary."[175] Walter Fisher, third "boss" of the MVL, informed Lincoln Steffens that the MVL hoped to reform the business class and business practices as much as it wished to defeat the boodlers. Steffens commented:

The city council had been bought and owned by Yerkes, the street railway magnate and other businessmen who wanted franchises, extensions, and privileges generally. Fisher and the Chicago reformers were forcing the aldermen to stand for the city, and in dealing with businessmen to represent the public interest in making bargains. They were fighting first the corruption of their own class, letting the police evils of the lawless wait; they were reforming the good, not the bad.[176]

Many businessmen found arguments of this kind convincing, even a number from the old school, like Marshall Field. Yerkes was beyond the pale. "He shocked me," Field once exclaimed to a banker after a meeting with Yerkes. "He is not safe."[177]

But this was not all. The Civic Federation undertook a variety of "investigations" of business practices and the "tax inefficiencies" of traction companies in Chicago. In a series of reports on traction companies published in 1898 and 1901, the federation charged that the common stock of the companies had been severely watered down and that their operations were not "tax efficient." The federation declined to draw the inference, however, that municipal ownership of the traction companies constituted an acceptable solution to the problem, as Tommy Morgan, John Peter Altgeld, and Henry Demarest Lloyd had proposed. The federation would have nothing to do with the republican and populist antimonopolism of Morgan, Altgeld, and Lloyd. Instead, it recommended that the capital stock of the companies be properly valued, that the companies reduce fares from a nickel to four cents or return 20 percent of their income to the city, and that they pay a 6 percent dividend on their capital.[178] The federation assumed a similar hands-off posture toward trusts as well. In 1899, responding to widespread concern over the rise of trusts and the apparent failure of the Sherman Anti-Trust Act, the federation sponsored a national convention on trusts in Chicago; but rather than endorse any proposal that had even the vaguest whiff of anti-trust sentiment, the federation supported, as the National Civic Federation and Theodore Roosevelt would later do, the right of the government to inspect corporations and exercise a moderate degree of supervision of trusts.[179] And finally, the federation played an active role in the city charter reform movement. In particular, the federation sought adoption of uniform tax standards, the elimination of tax fraud, and an increase in the city's bonding and taxing powers.[180]

The charter failed to pass in part because of the opposition of a large section of the Chicago business community.[181] Like the failure of the Merriam mayoral race several years later, the defeat of charter reform reflected the refusal of much of Chicago's business community to accept the sharp boundaries between municipal government and capital accumulation proposed by political Progressives and the rejection of the kind of business environment desired by bankers like Lyman Gage of the Civic Federation.[182] Indeed, as early as 1903, prominent businessmen in Chicago complained to Lincoln Steffens that reform was nothing more than "anarchy" and "socialism," and that it had "hurt business." They "regretted the passing of the boodle regime." Steffens reported that capital had decided to "boycott" reform and "give it a bad name"; businessmen hoped for "a government that understands and is just to business."[183] Whereas the reformers had tried to run local government on a businesslike basis, businessmen wanted "good government." In the 1911 mayoral race, businessmen again opposed reform. The biographer of one of Merriam's staunchest supporters, Julius Rosenwald, noted that while "the civic reformers and some enlightened businessmen were of Merriam's side . . . many of the big business interests preferred Carter Harrison."[184]

Although the Progressives delivered Chicago to Theodore Roosevelt in 1912, the defeat of Merriam in 1911 intimated the demise of political progressivism in Chicago. When William Hale Thompson won the mayoral race in 1915, and held the office until 1931 with the exception of one term between 1923 and 1927, "the spoils system," wrote Merriam, "swept over the city like a noxious blight, and the city hall became a symbol for corruption and incompetence."[185] "Thompsonianism," wrote Harold Gosnell, "came to be a symbol for spoils politics, police scandals, school board scandals, padded payrolls, gangster alliances, betrayal of the public trust, grotesque campaign methods, and buffoonery in public office."[186] Both parties became "the handmaidens of the business interests."[187] When the Democrats, led by Anton Cermak, swept the Republicans aside in 1931, some of this changed, but not all of it. Away went the open protection of organized crime and the worst manifestations of political corruption and graft. But in most other respects, the triumphs of the Democratic machine represented little more than a changing of the guard, one "more willing," as Gosnell observed, "than Mayor Thompson to meet the demands of the tax machinery and drastic economy in local government." Despite the dislocations of the Depression, Gosnell found that the "economic set up of the city was altered in details but not in its general pattern. The self-made politicians understood the self-made businessman, as they talked the same language. . . . They said, in effect, to the businessmen: 'You leave us alone, and we will leave you alone.' "[188] This live-and-let-live attitude was entirely satisfactory to business. It did not need to govern in order to rule, or to profit. Nor even did it need to rule continuously in order that its essential interests be protected. While "the business group dominates when it will," wrote Charles Merriam, "it does not will to rule continuously as a responsible class might commonly be presumed to do." The reason, he concluded, was because "the government is at its beck and call."[189]

In effect, after 1931 businessmen and machine politicians forged a new relationship between business and municipal government in Chicago.

It was not the kind of relationship envisaged by the political Progressives, but an urban version of what Gabriel Kolko called "political capitalism." "It is business control over politics," Kolko wrote, "rather than political regulation of the economy that is the significant phenomenon of the Progressive Era. Such domination was direct and indirect, but significant only insofar as it provided means for achieving a greater end—political capitalism." Political capitalism, he concluded, "is the utilization of political outlets to attain conditions of stability, predictability, and security—to attain rationalization—in the economy."[190] In 1931 in Chicago, corporate capital and machine politics covenanted an urban version of political capitalism, a doctrine of separate spheres for the political economy. This doctrine committed one party to pay its taxes, not engage in overt corruption or seriously embarrass the city administration, invest in the city to provide employment opportunities, and refrain from political campaigns that weakened or destroyed the Democratic party political machine, while the other party supplied "tax efficient" city services, administered local government in a businesslike manner, provided a centralized and accessible system of decision making, and finally, contained radical impulses. In the political hothouse of the 1930s, with the structure of social relations placed under severe strain by the Depression, this was no small achievement, as Harold Gosnell concluded:

What is the balance sheet of machine politics in an urban center such as Chicago during a period of economic crisis? On the credit side of the ledger should be placed the success of the bosses in softening class conflicts. By granting petty favors to various nationalistic and local groups, by taking advantage of the subsidies offered by the national government, by keeping the attention of the voters distracted by factional quarrels and sham disputes, the party machines have kept minor party movements from gaining any headway. From the standpoint of the business leaders, this function . . . has been very useful. Some of the submerged groups may not be so appreciative; but the fact remains that during years 1930–1936 the city was comparatively free from labor disputes, hunger riots, and class warfare. The decentralized, chaotic and inadequate character of the government organization of the city has discouraged far reaching demands upon local authorities.[191]

Initially, political Progressives secured a measure of success in replacing "dishonest" politicians in the city council, reorganizing the administrative structure and operating procedures of city government, and altering the relationship between local government and business in Chicago. In the long run, however, they failed to destroy machine politics and the "invisible government" of business. By 1911, machine politicians had regained control of the city council and the mayor's office, and after 1915,

indulged in civic corruption at a level that easily matched that of the 1880s
and 1890s, rolled back many of the administrative reforms of the political
Progressives, and encouraged a loose and nebulous distinction between
capitalist economics and democratic politics. Not all of the efforts of the
reformers proved futile, but the reformers' neo-Federalist vision of local
government did not prevail.

Progressive Reform and the Liberal Moment

Perhaps more than any other city in the country, Chicago exemplified and
symbolized the market revolution of the nineteenth century. By the mid
1890s, however, a chronic social crisis threatened to disrupt, even over-
throw, the market revolution: A severe economic depression threw hundreds of thousands out of work and onto charity; labor and capital
challenged each other in apocalyptic confrontations; trusts and monopolies limited economic competition and opportunity and corrupted local
and state government; political machines undermined the integrity of republican government; rampant vice, illiteracy, crime, delinquency, and
dependency threatened the social fabric; children and women toiled in
mines and factories; the "growing separation of classes" and an insurgent
socialist movement blocked the creation of a stable and harmonious community united by common values, institutions, and purposes; law and
order campaigns seemed impotent, and the efforts of the purveyors of
industrial paternalism, evangelical Protestantism, temperance, and charity
reform seemed futile.

In response to the market revolution of the nineteenth century and
its excesses wrought by capitalists and a threatened counter-revolution by
a hungry and politically conscious working class, a mixed group of the
citizens of Chicago mounted not so much a counter-revolution of their
own but a reformation—a reformation of the market revolution—and a
counter-counter-revolution against radical and socialist politics.[192] In
1893–94, "many representative citizens" of Chicago recognized for the
first time "the organic" character of society, wrote Albion Small, "and that
social peace depends upon something more like a balance between property and poverty." "Prudential reason," the belief that "society must pick
up its own chips or the chips will clog the wheels," spurred reformers into
action.[193] Within a remarkably short time they founded settlement houses,
the Chicago Civic Federation, the Municipal Voters League, the Chicago
Relief Association, the Immigrants Protective League, the City Club, the
Committee of Fifteen, the Chicago Housing Association, the Committee

on Social Legislation, the Public Education Association, and dozens of others in a concerted effort to reduce social injustice, eliminate corruption, extend equal opportunity, reconcile the classes, and recalibrate institutional arrangements in the face of the need for "social adjustment."

Invariably, the reformers were relatively young, highly educated, from middle-class families, Protestant and Republican. Bankers, businessmen, settlement house workers, clergymen, women's club executives, journalists, and academics predominated. Of the settlement house workers, for example, nearly all came from old stock middle-class families; 90 percent had attended college.[194] Businessmen, bankers, professionals, churchmen, settlement residents, and women's club executives joined the Civic Federation. Businessmen dominated its leadership: three of its first ten presidents were prestigious bankers, one was a president of the Board of Trade, and the others presidents or directors of large manufacturing or insurance companies. The membership of the MVL drew upon members of the Civic Federation, the Union League, the Citizens Association, the Commercial Club, the Board of Trade, the Marquette, Iroquois, and Hamilton clubs, academics, and settlement workers. In a sample of fifty MVL leaders between 1896 and 1920, Joan Miller found that thirty were professionals with lawyers predominating, while the other twenty were businessmen. She found no blue or white collar employees; almost all were wealthy or mingled socially with the rich; over 50 percent were natural-born Protestants with a college education or better; there were no Catholics; over 70 percent belonged to the Republican party.[195]

Other Progressive organizations exhibited similar profiles. The membership of the Chicago Vice Commission (to be discussed in the following chapter) was mainline Progressive: physicians, lawyers, clerics, academics, a university president, a former national president of the General Foundation of Womens Clubs, and businessmen.[196] The leadership of the Committee of Fifteen by 1915 (again, to be discussed in chapter 2) included five clergymen (including Graham Taylor), nine philanthropists or social workers, three educators, four lawyers, one doctor, and thirty-four businessmen.[197] Academics (22.5 percent), businessmen (22.5 percent), lawyers (20.0 percent), social workers (12.5 percent), and journalists (10.0 percent) accounted for nearly all of the membership of the Illinois Immigrants Protection League in 1907–08. Exactly one-third had earned doctorates; 64.6 percent had acquired a college degree at least.[198] Businessmen (50 percent), lawyers (19.4 percent), architects and engineers (9.6 percent), and academics (6.9 percent)—including G. H. Mead and Charles Merriam—dominated the membership of the City Club.[199] Of the fifty-six directors of the Chicago COS between 1886 and 1908, fourteen were merchants, ten bankers, seven lawyers, four manufacturers, three educators, three settlement workers, three managers, and two each of physicians, ministers, and real estate dealers. Six were miscellaneous. Of the forty-five for whom information on education is known, only ten had no college education, thirty-three had attained a degree, and twelve had received an advanced degree.[200]

Apart from the membership of individual organizations, comprehensive data on the social characteristics of 2,500 men and women who participated in at least one of approximately seventy reform groups and agencies in the city between 1892 and 1919 has been collected by Stephen Diner. Diner reports that of the 2,500 Progressives, 215 were involved in three or more reform organizations, and of these 215, the overwhelming majority were middle or upper middle class. Occupationally, a third were businessmen, a quarter were lawyers or judges, 14.4 percent were university professors, and the remainder professionals in other fields.[201] Almost 90 percent of the reformers were Protestants, and almost 80 percent had completed some form of higher education (approximately 50 percent had completed both undergraduate and professional or graduate school).[202] Some 32 percent lived within a three-quarter-mile rectangle surrounding the University of Chicago in Hyde Park, while a further 21 percent lived in the Gold Coast area. Some 113 of the 169 men belonged to the City Club, 55 belonged to the Union League Club, 45 to the Chicago Club, and 36 to the Commercial Club. Among the 46 women, 35 belonged to the Women's City Club, and 22 belonged to the Chicago Women's Club. Of the 67 for whom data on party affiliations was available in 1917, 57 were Republican, 12 Democratic, and 2 Independent.[203]

Progressive reformers in Chicago thus appear to belong to two social groups: members of the business and upper middle classes. The reformers do not approximate anything like the profile of a declining middle class—the sons and daughters of an old mugwump elite—suggested by Richard Hofstadter.[204] But neither do they resemble, at least not essentially, Robert Wiebe's "new middle class" of rising professionals.[205] Rather, on the whole, Progressive reformers in Chicago more closely approximate the business and upper-middle-class reformers of the kind described by Samuel P. Hays.[206] Wiebe's approach is helpful in that he drew a connection between Progressive reform and the process of class formation. Unhappily, however, he mischaracterizes both the class involved and the nature of the link between class formation and Progressive reform. Wiebe proposes that Progressive reform resulted in part from the decline of "community" and the growth of a "distended society," and in part from a "search for order" by an ascendant "new middle class" seeking to institu-

tionalize a "bureaucratic revolution" based on the values of "continuity
and regularity, functionality and rationality, administration and management." "The heart of Progressivism," he concluded, "was the ambition of
the new middle class to fulfill its destiny through bureaucratic means."[207]
Apart from the fact that the business and upper middle class rather than
the "new middle class" dominated reform in Chicago, the growth of a
"distended" society is far too abstract and removed from the social conflicts and passions of the 1880s and 1890s to capture the pervasive sense
of social crisis of that time. Wiebe's argument implies a teleological and
class-conscious link between Progressive reform and class formation—that
Progressive reform resulted from "the ambition of the new middle class to
fulfill its destiny through bureaucratic means." The direction of the linkage
should be reversed and its nature altered. The "making" of the business
and middle classes did not cause Progressive reform, although the development of a working class and the growing separation of classes certainly
were part of the casual matrix that produced it. Progressive reform did
not provide a manufactured pretext for the making of the business or
middle classes. Rather, the social crisis and the class conflicts of the 1880s
and 1890s provoked the political mobilization of the upper middle and
business classes, out of which grew Progressive reform. Jane Addams did
not reduce the settlement movement to the "subjective necessity" of settlements but located the rise of settlements in the context of the "objective"
needs for reform. Lyman Gage, likewise, in his presidential address to the
Civic Federation in early 1895, emphasized that the Civic Federation "was
not an invention, the result of an ingenious mind studying to provide
some new form of public activity for restless persons hungry for notori-
ety." Rather, he observed, "it was a crystallization of sentiment slowly
formed through long periods against civil and social abuses no longer
bearable."[208]

Neither Progressive reform nor processes of business- and middle-
class formation can thus be separated from the social crisis that generated
the former and occasioned the latter. Clearly, however, the critical causal
relationship is between the social crisis of the 1880s and 1890s and Progressive reform. Yet to pose the causal argument in these bold terms is
not entirely satisfactory. It gets us only so far and no more, for it does not
enable us to understand why Progressives intellectually construed the social developments of the 1880s and 1890s as a social crisis, why they
employed the language they did, and why they adopted the particular
objectives they adopted. "Civil and social abuses" were "no longer bearable" to Progressives because they represented incontrovertible evidence
of widespread "conspiracy" and "corruption" that if not checked por-

tended the veritable collapse of the republic. In effect, the events of the 1880s and 1890s represented an apocryphal moment, not so much a republican or "Machiavellian moment" as a "liberal" moment in which "virtue" stood compromised by unrestrained "commerce" and its consequences.

But although the 1880s and 1890s constitute a liberal moment, the late nineteenth century was hardly a simple Lockean moment. Over the course of the late eighteenth century, Americans had brewed a distinctive American ideology that combined liberal propositions about economic order, social relations, and political rights with republican maxims concerning balanced government, moral reformation, and millennial visions of America's destiny. Republican liberalism, not liberalism and not republicanism, posed the political problematic of Progressive reform. Monopolists, socialists, and anarchists conspired against the nation; utility magnates and political bosses corrupted democratic government; child labor, illiteracy, prisons, commercialized vice and amusements corrupted the young; the growing separation of classes and class conflict mocked their vision of social order and social harmony; social injustice and inequalities of opportunity contradicted the promise of equality and blocked the redemption of America.[209] These were distinctive republican liberal constructions of the social tensions and conflicts generated by a market society, the growing pains of a class society passing through its adolescence. We might think of the Progressives as the pediatricians of the Great Transformation, nurturing the growth of a reformed and moralized capitalism, balancing the humors of the body politic, proscribing quack nostrums like socialism and equal rights republicanism, and prescribing generous doses of moral regeneration, reconciliation of the classes, regulation of trusts and factory conditions, elimination of child labor, commercialized amusements and vice, suppression of machine politics, "adjustment" of social institutions to the market economy, "social efficiency," and extension of equal opportunity. Collectively these responses constitute the Progressives' contribution to America's Great Transformation and the immediate context of the child-saving and educational reforms of late nineteenth- and early twentieth-century Chicago.

Chapter 2

THE IRONIES OF PROGRESSIVE CHILD-SAVING

Confronted with a growing tension between the equal rights tradition of republican thought and increasing inequality, between republican independence and wage labor, and between republican virtue and social conflict, Whig reformers in the 1830s and 1840s resuscitated and expanded the common school system.[1] Common schools would provide equal opportunity, nurture industrious and disciplined characters, create a "classless" society, and guarantee social order. "Education, then, beyond all other devices of human origin," wrote Horace Mann in 1848, "is the great equalizer of the conditions of men—the balance wheel of the social machinery. . . . It does better than to disarm the poor of their hostility towards the rich; it prevents being poor. . . . [I]f this education should be universal and complete, it would do more than all things else to obliterate factitious distinctions in society."[2]

By the early 1890s, it seemed to some Americans at least that few of the hopes of that first generation of educational reformers had been fulfilled.[3] Social inequality and injustice had not disappeared but increased as the market revolution advanced. "Factitious distinctions in society" had not been obliterated. The poor were hostile to the rich. The "growing separation of classes" threatened the survival of the republic. Children remained the innocent victims of inadequate schooling, poor housing, demoralizing reformatories, indifferent parents, steely-eyed employers, commercial vice and vicious amusements. In sum, injustice, inequality of opportunity, and social conflict had compromised the moral legitimacy of American society and undermined social order. The balance wheel had failed to balance; the social machinery had broken down. In fact, it seemed as if the social machinery needed a redesigned balance wheel, additional flywheels, an oil change, recalibration, and a new generation of social engineers to run it.

For the next two decades, Progressive reformers in Chicago came back again and again to tinker with the balance wheel and the social machinery, indeed so much so that child-saving became a leading idiom of Progressive social criticism and the chief icon of the redeemer nation.[4] In eliminating the abuse and misuse of children, in extending educational opportunity, in the proper socialization of children, social justice could be secured and a social democracy established. As with so many other Progressive reforms, child-savers employed the political language of commerce and virtue rather than of social control: on the one hand, the "corruption" of children and youth by child labor, commercialized vice and amusements, poor housing, adult prisons, city streets, and poor schooling, and on the other hand, the "necessity," as Jane Addams put it, of "social and individual salvation."[5] In saving its children, America itself could be saved. In the attempt, however, reformers created a ubiquitous tutelary apparatus to supervise and control the socialization of children and transform childhood itself into an adjunct of the market.

CHILD LABOR AND COMPULSORY EDUCATION LEGISLATION

"Our very first Christmas at Hull House," wrote Jane Addams, "when we as yet knew nothing of child labor, a number of little girls refused the candy which was offered them as part of the Christmas good cheer, saying simply that they 'worked in a candy factory and could not bear the sight of it.' " On investigation, Addams and Starr "discovered that for six weeks they had worked from seven in the morning until nine at night, and they were exhausted as well as satiated. The sharp consciousness of stern economic conditions was thus thrust upon us in the midst of the season of good will."[6]

Nothing engaged the moral outrage of Progressives as much as child labor. When three boys from a Hull House club the same winter "were injured at one machine in a neighborhood factory for lack of a guard which would have cost but a few dollars," resulting in the death of one of the boys, Addams and Starr felt prostrated with "horror and remorse." When they realized that the factory owner did not share their horror and remorse and would do nothing to prevent a further tragedy, and that even "incredibly small children" worked in factories and sweatshops through-

out the neighborhood, Addams and Starr began "carefully" to collect
information on child labor in the areas surrounding Hull House.[7] Meanwhile, in late 1891, Florence Kelley took up residence at Hull House. The
primary objection to child labor, she believed, is "the humane objection
that it makes childhood an object of exploitation, . . . yet it is safe to say
that this objection has never been a sufficient dynamic power in this
country."[8] In the hullabaloo that followed the release of an investigation
by the wife of Tommy Morgan of sweatshop conditions in the garment
industry, Kelley urged the Illinois State Bureau of Labor Statistics to
undertake a formal investigation of the sweating system in Chicago. The
bureau accepted her proposal and appointed her a special agent to carry
out the investigation. In the Nineteenth Ward, for example, with 7,000
children of school age (six to fourteen inclusive), Kelley found that the
schools had places for only 2,579 children. Most of the remaining children
were engaged "in child labor in most cruel forms."[9]

The following year, 1893, shortly after the inauguration of John
Peter Altgeld as governor, the General Assembly of Illinois appointed a
special commission to conduct a survey of sweatshop conditions in the
state. Florence Kelley and another Hull House resident, Mary Kenney,
offered to guide members of the commission through the neighborhood
surrounding Hull House. Kelley later wrote that

the Commission had been intended as a sop to labor and a sinecure, a protracted
junket to Chicago, for a number of rural legislators. Our overwhelming hospitality
and devotion to the thoroughness and success of the investigation by personally
conducted visits to sweatshops, though irksome in the extreme to the law givers,
ended in a report so compendious, so readable, so surprising that they presented
it with pride to the legislature. For the press, the sweating system was that winter
a sensation.[10]

Kelley added that "no one was yet blase" that the legislature would
pass a law banning child labor, although Jane Addams wrote that "on the
Sunday the members of the commission came to dine at Hull House, our
hopes ran high. . . ."[11] Illinois at that time had legislation, dating from
1872, and revised in 1879, 1883, and 1887, that prohibited child labor
in coal mines and occupations "injurious to health or dangerous to life
and limb" for children under thirteen. None of these acts, however, had
included provisions for the enforcement of the law. An act of 1891 had
made it unlawful for any person, firm, or corporation to employ a child
under thirteen years of age without a work certificate issued by the local
board of education. A board of education could issue such a certificate if
the labor of the child was required by an indigent family and if the child

had attended school for at least eight weeks in the current year. The act did not require proof of age, however, and, like earlier child legislation, made no provision for the enforcement of the act.

The deficiencies of the act, and the pervasive evidence of extensive child labor in Chicago, prompted a committee of the Chicago Board of Education in 1892 to recommend that all children under thirteen attend school for the complete year, not just sixteen weeks a year. It also recommended enforceable penalties for parents who infringed the letter of the law.[12] When the commission proposed a comprehensive factory act regulating sweatshops and prohibiting all child labor under thirteen, residents of Hull House, led by Florence Kelley, and members of the Trades and Labor Assembly (forerunner of the Chicago Federation of Labor) began intensive lobbying efforts (for the residents of Hull House, their first venture into lobbying) to secure passage of a new law. They also urged the legislature to include a clause, as Jane Addams put it, "limiting the hours of all women working in factories or workshops to eight hours a day, or forty-eight a week" in order that they might perform "the household duties which crowd upon her." To their surprise, they succeeded in securing an act that regulated sanitary conditions in sweatshops, prohibited the employment of all children under thirteen in factories, workshops, and sweatshops, limited the employment of women to eight hours a day, and provided for the enforcement of the act by creating a department of factory inspection. Governor Altgeld appointed Florence Kelley the first chief factory inspector of Illinois when Henry Demarest Lloyd turned down the offer.[13]

The annual reports of the factory inspectors suggest that from the very beginning Kelley and her staff were less interested in the control of the garment trades and sweatshop conditions than in enforcing the child labor provisions of the 1893 act and using their findings as a factual basis from which to urge further reform of the child labor and compulsory education laws. During the first five months, officers of the factory inspectors department inspected 2,452 places of employment within which 6,575 children aged between fourteen and sixteen worked, or 9.7 percent of the employment of these firms. Among these children, the inspectors found "a deplorable amount of illiteracy." In the next two reports, Kelley reported similar findings and urged reform of the child labor law.[14] When the General Assembly failed in 1895 to pass new child labor legislation that Kelley had helped draw up, Kelley prevailed upon the mayor of Chicago, Carter Harrison, to appoint a commission of nine representatives "to investigate the question of child labor." With the support of the industrial committee of the Civic Federation of Chicago, the new committee investigated the employment of children in the dry goods stores of the city. The following year the committee argued that such employment "demoralized" the children, added only very little to the family budget, and recommended the prohibition of employment of children under fourteen years of age in mercantile occupations. Through Mrs. Kelley's persistent agitation and the report of the investigative committee, the legislature passed a new child labor act in 1897, extending the scope of the law to include mercantile institutions, stores, offices, and laundries, and made the enforcement of child labor legislation more practicable by stipulating that the presence of children under sixteen on a work place constituted prima facie evidence of employment. Two months later, 2,000 additional children between fourteen and sixteen employed in mercantile establishments were brought under the purview of the act.[15]

Despite its distinct improvements over the earlier laws, the act of 1897 failed to satisfy child-savers. The provision that caused the greatest concern permitted children to be employed under the affidavit of their parents, a provision that seemed to encourage perjury rather than discourage child labor. In 1901 E. T. Davies, chief factory inspector, estimated that in the previous twelve months, 5,000 children worked in Chicago, of whom 3,000 were employed on false affidavits. Davies inaugurated a practice of making "numerous crusades by day and night" in an effort to enforce the act and arouse public interest in a new law. This had "a most salutary effect," for through "the combined efforts of the women's clubs, social settlement workers, labor organizations, the press, the clergy, State Factory Inspectors Department, and the Child Saving League of Chicago," a special committee, including Jane Addams, Lester Bodine, Edwin Cooley (then superintendent of schools), and Davies himself, drafted a bill drawing upon the desirable features found in the child labor laws of other states. When introduced into the General Assembly in 1903, the bill was "seriously and openly opposed by the glass bottle manufacturing interests of the state and secretly opposed by certain other commercial influences." Despite the opposition, the legislature passed the bill with few amendments, the credit for which Davies gave to "Miss Jane Addams of Hull House, and her co-workers, and the members of the industrial committee of the State Federation of Women's Clubs, who made several trips to Springfield at the time the bill was under consideration by the Legislature."[16]

Although Florence Kelley had misgivings about the adequacy of the child labor law in Illinois, she conceded that the reforms secured between 1893 and 1904 amounted "to a revolution." Between 1902 and 1908, the percentage of working children in the state declined from 3.7 to 1.3

percent.[17] But passage of child labor laws and the zealous work of factory inspectors alone cannot account for the decline in child labor.[18] Four other factors were also involved: a decline in the demand for child labor, passage of effective compulsory education laws, enforcement of the laws by local boards of education, and changes in the educational aspirations of Chicago's immigrant working class. The first three will be considered below, and the fourth in the following chapter.

With a number of notable exceptions, most employers supported child labor legislation, or did not actively oppose it. The Chicago Board of Education reported as early as 1890 that after canvassing the opinion of businessmen toward child labor legislation, of some 300 responses, a few employers expressed disapproval of the 1889 compulsory education and child labor laws, but the great majority not only assured the superintendent of education of their willingness to obey the law but also declared their approval of the law.[19] A 1915 study of 152 manufacturing establishments by the Illinois Department of Factory Inspection turned up strong support for child labor legislation among employers. Despite the intense opposition of John M. Glenn, president of the Illinois Manufacturers Association, to child labor legislation, 80.9 percent of the firms answering the question "Do you find employees fourteen to sixteen years of age deficient in education and general usefulness?" answered yes. Of employers answering the question "Do you prefer to employ children over sixteen years of age?" 96.6 percent answered yes.[20]

The relatively widespread acceptance of child labor legislation among businessmen did not necessarily express magnanimity. Most employers probably found it simply unnecessary or unprofitable to employ children. Technology, as much as humanitarianism, removed children from the workforce. In the bookbinding trade, for example, Florence Kelley noted that the "folding machine is replacing the smaller girls in all the best equipped industries."[21] The tobacco industry introduced automatic cigarette-making machines in the 1890s, drastically reducing the demand for children's labor: whereas 11.7 percent of the work force in Illinois making cigars was under sixteen in 1894, it had dropped to 5 percent in 1896 and 1.1 percent in 1906.[22] This cut occurred without the benefit of any legislation forbidding the employment of children between fourteen and sixteen. In the communications industry, the introduction of the telephone in the downtown business area eliminated the need for messenger boys; by 1908, Chicago Telephone (employing 60 percent of the work force in the industry) employed only twelve children under sixteen.[23] The adoption of the pneumatic tube in the department stores during the first decade of the twentieth century made the small army of cash boys and girls redundant: Between 1902 and 1904 Marshall Field let go all its cash boys. Among the seven largest department stores in Chicago, the percentage of their work force under sixteen dropped from 14 percent in 1897 to 8.6 percent in 1900 and 3.5 percent in 1908. Plainly, by the end of the first decade of the twentieth century, the few jobs remaining for children were "dead end jobs."[24]

Two further factors responsible for the decline in child labor included the success of the child-savers in persuading the state legislature to pass meaningful compulsory education laws and persuading local school boards to enforce the law. Florence Kelley had no doubts that "the key to the child labor question is the enforcement of school attendance to the age of sixteen." "Children under fourteen years," she wrote, "can never be wholly kept out of the factories and workshops until they are kept in school," and she recommended "that the legislature make the prosecution of derelict parents not as it now is, merely discretionary with the local school boards, but mandatory upon them."[25] Superintendents Howland and Lane held similar views, but the board remained committed to a policy of "moral suasion" of recalcitrant parents and refused to prosecute offending parents. In part, the policy of the board reflected the state of the law: as Superintendent Lane pointed out in 1895, "the law is ineffective because no penalty can be enforced."[26] A law of 1883 had required all children between eight and fourteen to attend school for a period of not less than twelve weeks annually, but as a special committee of the board of education concluded in 1888, the law was "practically incapable of enforcement."[27] A new act in 1889, known as Edwards' Law, altered the age of compulsory education from seven to fourteen, increased the period of attendance to sixteen weeks annually, and provided for the appointment of at least one truant officer to apprehend children and to prosecute offending parents. Unhappily for child-savers, the Edwards Law also contained provisions requiring children, if they attended private rather than public schools, to be taught in the English language for the common branches of learning and gave local school boards the power to certify private schools in their respective school districts.[28] These latter two provisions provoked a storm of protest from Lutheran and Catholic groups that resulted in severe Republican electoral losses in 1890 and 1892 and the repeal of the Edwards Law in 1893.[29]

The repeal of the Edwards Law left the Chicago school board uncertain as to its power to enforce attendance at school through the courts. Some members of the board remained committed in principle to the use of moral suasion rather than recourse to the courts and favored abolishing the compulsory education department.[30] In 1897, however, a new compulsory education law made enforcement through the courts easier, and the board of education gave the go-ahead to the new superintendent of compulsory education, T. J. Bluthardt, to enforce it. After he successfully prosecuted his first case under the new law, Bluthardt declared, "We certainly should not permit a reckless and indifferent part of our population to rear their children in ignorance to become a criminal and lawless class within our community." The education department "should rightfully have the power to arrest all these little beggars, loafers and vagabonds that infest our city, take them off the streets and place them in schools where they are compelled to receive education and learn moral principles."[31] Bluthardt did not make idle threats. A corps of fifteen truant officers in 1898 reached forty officers within ten years, and fifty-three six years later in 1914.[32]

The lasting significance of the 1897 act is that it considerably diminished parental prerogatives over children and established the principle that the state could exercise its authority, even at the expense of parental rights, over children in order to end a humanitarian abuse, secure equal opportunity, and instill citizenship. The idea that compulsory education could promote equal opportunity and citizenship had been widely accepted for many years, but prior to the compulsory education act of 1897, the law did not allow and the board of education did not encourage any serious infringement upon parental rights. The superintendent of compulsory education reported in 1890, for instance, that although the department had investigated some 17,400 cases of nonattendance in 1889–90, "no arrests have been made; the work has been accomplished by kind moral suasion, not a single instance of interference with parental authority, no prosecution or persecution."[33] The act of 1897, plus the pressure that the child-savers placed on the board of education to prosecute wayward parents, transformed the relationship between parents and the school board as the agent of the state. Henceforth, "parental authority" would have to give way to the requirements of equal opportunity and citizenship.

The successes of the child-savers in engineering this recalibration of the social machinery can be traced to two factors. First, the unambiguous evidence of extensive child labor collected by the child-savers deeply shocked respectable middle-class sentiment in the city both for its cruelty and for its denial of educational opportunity to children. Humanitarian sentiment had no sympathy for the right of employers to hire children or for the right of parents to send their children to work. Moreover, the reformer's arguments that "indifferent parents," "poor family life," or "bad home conditions" were responsible for nonattendance seemed to make recourse to the courts both necessary and palatable. Abbott and Breckinridge, for example, argued that the problem of nonattendance did not really constitute a problem of truancy in "the well-to-do sections of the city, where the question of attendance . . . is not a social problem of importance as it is in the poor and congested neighborhoods." In poor neighborhoods, they argued, "the home and the parents, not the child and the school," caused nonattendance. They concluded, therefore, that it was "useless to talk about the waywardness of the child or the shortcomings of the schools or the teachers" until the family background of nonattenders had been reformed. "All the conditions of family life need to be changed," they argued, "and nothing short of thorough-going family rehabilitation will bring the home up to the level of cooperation with the school." Child-savers were not so much hostile to the family as to the family that failed to properly educate its children.[34]

Second, conflicts between labor and capital, the growing separation of classes and the influx of European immigrants in the 1890s and early 1900s multiplied and deepened the demands for compulsory education and citizenship training. The railroad strike of 1877, Haymarket in 1886, Pullman in 1894, and immigration in the 1890s provided the immediate backdrop to the passage of compulsory education acts in 1883, 1889, and 1897. In view of the problems of "communism and the relations of labor and capital," declared the Citizens Association of Chicago in 1881, "our school system must, to a great extent, fail in its usefulness to the state" unless it preoccupies itself with "*direct* moral and religious training." The *Chicago Tribune* concurred. "Education is the sole guardian of property," it declared in 1882. Compulsory education eliminated illiteracy and therefore "communism." In 1885 it asserted that "communistic agitation, labor riots, and debauched municipal politics show already . . . the dangers of citizenship lacking in intelligence and self-respect." In 1886 the *Tribune* claimed that "it ought to be the first function of the public schools to teach loyalty, love of country, and devotion to American principles and institutions." A few days later, alluding to the Haymarket, the paper called for "Americanism in the Public Schools." In 1890 the *Tribune* editorialized that Chicago's increasingly "heterogeneous" population necessitated compulsory education.[35]

Chicago's public school officials responded affirmatively to these demands. "The public school," declared Superintendent Josiah Pickard in 1877, "as an institution of the State, bases its claim for existence upon the fact of its essential service to the States. This service consists in the preparation of the citizen for the performance of duties inseparable from his citizenship." "The public school should be regarded as a department of the government to properly prepare the children for citizenship," wrote

Superintendent Albert Lane in 1892. Two years later, the year of the
Pullman strike, the board expanded the teaching of American history in
the fourth, fifth, and sixth grades. The new course of studies, reported
Superintendent Lane, "greatly enlarged the scope of historical study, and
cultivated patriotism and a high regard for American institutions." "Educate or perish," warned Daniel Cameron, president of the board in 1896.
Inundated by a vast immigrant population "whose habit of thought, political training and belief" were "antagonistic" to American institutions,
the public schools provided "our social and political safeguards." The
following year, the president urged "the propriety of increasing the instruction in civics in our schools" so that children, "having ascertained
their duties as related to the community," would acquire "permanent
admiration and loyalty" for the country.[36]

In sum, although the demands of the child-savers centered upon
ending the abuse and misuse of children by parents and employers, their
demands resonated with the demands of businessmen, civic organizations,
and the press for the schools to play a larger role in the protection of
American social relations and the aspirations of education officials to regulate social relationships through citizenship training. The confluence of
middle-class sentiment, the activities of the child-savers, the fears of businessmen, and the hopes of education officials resulted in a series of legislative actions and board of education policy changes that in the name of
humanitarianism, equal opportunity, and citizenship training effected a
significant enlargement of the powers of the state over the education and
socialization of the children of Chicago.

THE JUVENILE COURT AND PROBATION

In his speech of the Central Music Hall in 1893, William T. Stead described Chicago as "very near the bottom" in protecting its juvenile offenders from the contamination of adult offenders. "There is very little
reverence for children in Chicago," he asserted. Indeed, "messenger boys
not more than fourteen years of age, go in and out of the police cells every
hour of the night gaining an intimacy with the drunken and debased
classes, which can hardly be said to tend towards edification."[37]

Stead's voice was not the first and certainly not the last to be raised
against the condition of juvenile care in Chicago. But to those concerned
with care and treatment of juveniles in Illinois, it seemed, as Carl Kelsey
of the Illinois Childrens Home and Aid Society suggested, that "Illinois
had been slow to appreciate the advances made by many of her sister states

in the case of children."[38] They were particularly concerned with the fate of those juveniles detained in the Chicago House of Corrections and the Cook County jail. When the Board of Public Charities visited the two institutions in 1890, its members found nine children under sixteen in the Cook County jail and forty-five in the Chicago House of Corrections. "What a shame," they wrote, "to place these boys in such a school of vice."[39]

Child-savers refused to tolerate these conditions. In 1891 Timothy Hurley, president of the Visitation and Aid Society (a Catholic church organization), unsuccessfully sponsored a bill in the Illinois legislature authorizing corporations "to manage, care and provide for children who may be abandoned, neglected, destitute or subjected to perverted training."[40] Two years later, in 1893, the year Stead pricked the conscience—and the fears—of his Chicago audience, the Chicago Women's Club began to lobby for a school for juveniles in the city jail. Two years later the city opened a reformatory, later named the John Worthy School.[41] Simultaneously, the Chicago Women's Club and the Board of Public Charities pressed for legislation to create a juvenile court so that children "might be saved from contamination of association with older criminals."[42]

And so it went throughout the nineties. Child-savers conducted surveys, made speeches, established contacts, formed committees, wrote papers, and staged conferences. Organizers of the 1898 meeting of the Illinois State Conference of Charities devoted the entire program to "the children of the state." The 1898 report of the Board of the State Commissioners of Public Charities expressed the general objectives of the reformers thus:

There are at the present moment in the State of Illinois, especially in the city of Chicago, thousands of children in need of active intervention for their preservation from physical, mental and moral destruction. Such intervention is demanded, not only by sympathetic consideration for their well being, but also in the name of the commonwealth, for the preservation of the State. If the child is the material out of which men and women are made, the neglected child is the material out of which paupers and criminals are made.

The report also described how the reformers thought their objectives might be obtained:

We make criminals out of children who are not criminals by treating them as if they were criminals. That ought to be stopped. What we should have in our system of criminal jurisprudence is an entirely separate system of courts for children in large cities who commit offenses which would be criminal in adults. We ought to have a "children's court" in Chicago, and we ought to have a "children's judge" who should attend to no other business. We want some place of detention for those children other than a prison. . . . A thing we want to borrow from the State of Massachusetts is its system of probation. No child ought to be tried unless he has a friend in court to look after his real interest.[43]

Child-savers did not mobilize in vain. In the closing months of 1898, the Chicago Association appointed a committee to draft a bill to establish a juvenile court, including Judge Harvey B. Hurd as chairman, Lucy L. Flower of the Chicago Women's Club, Julia Lathrop of the State Board of Charities and Hull House, and Timothy Hurley. Within a few months, the committee and the Chicago Bar Association had prepared a bill and secured sponsors within the Illinois House of Representatives. On July 1, 1899, the Juvenile Court Act—"An act to regulate the treatment and control of dependent, neglected and delinquent children"—became law.[44]

Contemporaries regarded the new law as the single most significant legislative act pertaining to delinquent and dependent children in the nineteenth century, symbolizing the end of a basically penal approach to delinquency and the beginning of "preventive" criminology.[45] Reflecting the reformers objectives, the act included a very broad definition of juvenile delinquency, provided for separate hearing of children's cases in a court of chancery (a noncriminal court of equity in which the normal protections of due process did not apply) rather than a criminal court, detention of children apart from adult offenders, and creation of a probationary staff for the care of delinquent children. The law made no provision, however, for funding the salaries of the probationary staff.[46]

The most striking feature of the act is the shift it represented away from a criminology stressing punishment to one emphasizing prevention, education, and rehabilitation. Reformers rationalized this shift, and the expansion of the power of the state vis-à-vis the family that it involved, by recourse to the ancient English equity doctrine of *parens patriae*. *Parens patriae* sanctioned the right of the state to act as parent to children whose physical or moral welfare was threatened by their natural parents or guardians. "We know," noted Chicago juvenile court judge Julian Mack, "that for over two centuries the Court of Chancery in England has exercised jurisdiction for the protection of the unfortunate child. . . ."[47] Another Chicago judge, Victor Arnold, in surveying the juvenile movement, concurred. "The juvenile court laws," he wrote, "are usually so broad that the State, in its capacity of *parens patriae* . . . will take jurisdiction over practically every significant situation where it appears it should do so in the interests of the child."[48] It followed, therefore, that the normal constitutional protections of due process were no longer necessary in juvenile courts. Indeed, such protections impeded the educational and rehabilitative purpose of the court.[49]

While the adoption of the doctrine of *parens patriae* significantly expanded the power of the state to directly intervene in family life, reformers were not hostile to the family per se. Rather, the act gave the state the authority to intervene in the unhealthy family in order that it might relocate the child in a healthy one. The last section of the act, for instance, stated: "This act shall be liberally construed to the end that its purpose may be carried out, to wit: That the care, custody and discipline of a child shall approximate as nearly as may be that which should be given by its parents, and in all cases where it can properly be done with the child placed in an improved family home and become a member of the family by legal adoption or otherwise."[50] Furthermore, promoters of the juvenile court hoped to make institutions that were responsible for the care of the delinquent child as familylike as possible. Shortly after assuming his responsibilities, Judge Tuthill complained about the "prison like" atmosphere of the John Worthy School. Tuthill proposed that the state build an institution in the countryside away from the vices and temptations of the city, and that the institution teach basic classroom skills and provide vocational education.[51] Within five years, the state built and opened the Illinois State School at St. Charles.

Finally, the Juvenile Reform Bill enjoined the court to use probation as an alternative to the institutionalization or incarceration of the delinquent child. Certainly the court did not shy away from incarcerating the intractable delinquent if necessary. Far better for the delinquent to be incarcerated in an institution, Judge Tuthill argued, "where he can be taught even against his own will the primary duty of obedience to authority," than to be left in a "disorganized" family with its "vicious habits and demoralizing associates."[52] But in principle the court preferred to use probation as a means of educating and rehabilitating the delinquent child and his family. Incarceration remained a last resort after all else had failed.

The introduction of the probation system reflected a major intellectual reorientation of juvenile social policy. In part, adoption of probation expressed a retreat from hereditarian thought and a wider acceptance of environmentalist theories of deviant behavior. In part, it reaffirmed the anti-institutionalist sensibilities of noted child-savers Charles Loring Brace and Samuel Gridley Howe. But above all, the creation of the probation system reflected a new appreciation of the importance of the home and family life in preventing, and not merely causing, delinquency.[53] To Jane Addams "nothing is more impressive than the strength, the continuity, the varied and powerful manifestation, of family affection."[54] Abbot and Breckinridge agreed. While they located the source of delinquency in the "demoralized" family, the "poor home," the "degraded home," and the "crowded home," they also believed that the family, if healthy and properly "organized," could prevent delinquency.[55] But since, as Carl Kelsey put it, the "lessons of home life and individual responsibility cannot well be taught to children *en masse*," probation provided a means of doing so on a family-by-family basis. Probation could serve a tutelary or educational function for the families of delinquent children. Called "visiting teachers," and obviously modeled upon the "friendly visitors" of the COS, probation officers employed a pedagogy of moral suasion, emulation, and, if necessary, coercion, to educate and uplift the family and rehabilitate the delinquent. "With the great right arm and force of the law," wrote Judge Tuthill, "the probation officer can go into the home and demand to know the cause of the dependency or the delinquency of the child." A probation officer could become "practically a member of the family," teaching "them lessons of cleanliness and decency, of truth and integrity." Even if "threats may be necessary, in some instances, to enforce the learning of the lessons he teaches," the outcome makes it worthwhile, for by his teaching the probation officer "transforms the entire family into individuals which the state need never again hesitate to own as citizens."[56]

Court procedures accurately reflected the rehabilitative and educational objectives of the child-savers. Since the court desired reformation and education, not retribution and punishment, the "trial" of the delinquent resembled the proceedings of a court of chancery rather than a normal criminal trial. In particular, due process and rules of evidence applicable in criminal trials were suspended and diagnostic and "preventive" proceedings introduced into the court. Henry Thurston, for a while the chief probation officer of the Chicago juvenile court, described the intent of the law as to "set the judge face-to-face with neglected and delinquent children of all kinds, free to disregard the technicalities of criminal court procedure and to ask simply the question, 'What, in view of all the circumstances surrounding this child's life, is it best to do for him?' "[57] For Judge Tuthill the purpose of the juvenile court's proceedings was "not to find out whether he [the delinquent] has done an act which in an adult would be a crime, and to punish him for that; such facts are considered merely as evidence tending to show whether the boy is in a condition of delinquency, so that the state ought to enter upon the exercise of its parental care over the child."[58] For Judge Julian Mack the court's procedure individualized punishment: It tailored the punishment to the needs of the child, not to the nature of the crime. "The problem to be determined," he wrote, "is not, 'Has this boy or girl committed a specific wrong?', but, 'What is he, how has he become what he is, and what would best be done in his interest, and in the interest of the state, to save him from a downward career?' "[59]

Although the judges of the juvenile court were not averse to committing delinquents to institutions if the offense was serious enough, or if the delinquent was particularly intractable, they preferred to use the probation system if possible. Between July 1, 1899, and June 30, 1909, Breckinridge and Abbott report, the court placed 59.3 percent of the boys and 37.5 percent of the girls brought before it on probation; the court committed 21.3 percent of the boys and 51.1 percent of the girls to institutions.[60] For the years 1915–19, the court placed 34.9 percent of boys and 31.1 percent of girls on probation; the court institutionalized 22.1 percent of boys and 39.9 percent of girls, an intriguing gender difference.[61] Finally, data reported in the *Illinois Crime Survey* of "an unselected group" of 1,000 boys and 500 girls for the years 1920–26 indicates that probation remained the most important method employed by the court in its disposition of delinquency cases.[62]

The remarkable popularity of probation in the decades after 1899, the suspension of due process, and the exceptionally broad definition of delinquent behavior in the act support the conclusion that the act of 1899 profoundly altered the relationship between the family and the state and invented wholly new state machinery to supervise the socialization of delinquent children. Yet it is a mistake to argue, as Platt does, that the child-savers of the Progressive Era made "a social fact out of the norm of adolescence," or that the objectives of the child-savers can be described as mere "social control" or that they were hostile to the family.[63] Progressive reformers did not "invent" delinquency: the act of 1899 culminated a movement going back at least to the Jacksonian era.[64] In focusing on the families of the immigrant poor, the court did not intend to establish a coercive regime of social control over the immigrant working class or to undermine the working class family. The act of 1899 intended, the procedures of the court reflected, and the pedagogy of probation exemplified a policy of individual moral rehabilitation through proper socialization within the family, albeit supervised by officers of the court.[65] Institutionalization generally remained a procedure of last resort, and even that, child-savers hoped, would accomplish what the family had failed to do: morally rehabilitate the delinquent and prepare him for entrance into the marketplace and the responsible exercise of his duties as a citizen.

Reforming the Urban Environment

In 1892 the U.S. Labor Department requested Florence Kelley to direct an investigation of slum conditions in Chicago as part of a larger comparative study of slums in major American cities. For ten weeks the investigators checked every room in every flat on every floor in every building on every street and alley in the area surrounding Hull House. What they found dismayed and horrified them. "Rear tenements and alleys form the core of the district," wrote one of the investigators, "and it is there that the densest crowds of the most wretched and destitute congregate. Little idea can be given of the filthy and rotten tenements, the dingy courts and tumble-down sheds, the foul stables and dilapidated outhouses, the broken sewer pipes, the piles of garbage fairly alive with diseased odors. . . ." In such a brutal physical environment, what hope was there for the swarms of children "filling every nook, working and playing in every room, eating and sleeping in every room, pouring in and out of every door and seeming literally to pave every scrap of 'yard.' "[66]

It seemed self-evident to the residents of Hull House that such conditions rendered impossible the adequate moral development of the children of the city. Jacksonian and Gilded Age reformers had relied on direct, personal contact and emulation to promote individual character development, but to the reformers of the 1890s the vices, temptations, size, anonymity, corruptions, and poverty of the city rendered traditional pre-urban methods of character development insufficient. Moral development required a moral environment, and not merely direct person-to-person contact. But Chicago, rather than providing a fit moral environment for the young to grow up in tempted the young into delinquency, crime, dissipation, gambling, and vice. The year after Florence Kelley began her investigation of slum conditions, W. T. Stead pronounced Chicago "the *cloaco maxima* of the world." But, Stead insisted, Chicago could yet become "the ideal city in the world" if only those "helpers" dedicated to "civic revival" and "the redemption of the municipal and social system" could beautify the city, pave streets, eliminate saloons and brothels, provide adequate playgrounds "for the service of children" and gymnasiums for adults, build parks and recreation grounds, and conduct pageants and processions.[67] Jane Addams exhorted reformers to seek "to know the modern city in its weaknesses and wickedness, and then seek to rectify and purify it until it shall be free at least from the grosser temptations which now beset the young people who are living in its tenement houses and working in its factories." And Charles Henderson exclaimed that the records of . . . [juvenile] courts and the stories of . . . probation officers must soon arouse the administrators of cities, of school and park boards, of churches, of philanthropists and patriotic men of wealth to a supreme and prolonged effort to transform the environment: to make the houses and streets clean and wholesome; to provide playgrounds; to see that the natural energies of youth are turned from destructive to constructive activities; and that the mind and soul are everywhere surrounded by pure, delightful and inspiring suggestions.[68]

The street trades and commercial amusements in particular provoked the ire of child-savers. Throughout the late nineteenth and early twentieth centuries, boys by the thousands worked the streets of Chicago as peddlers, delivery boys, newsboys, bootblacks, and errand boys. They evaded school, gambled, formed gangs, jackrolled drunks, thieved, slept in doorways and back alleys, and indulged in the vices of the flesh.[69] In 1906 the Chicago Women's Club established the Juvenile Protection League—later renamed the Juvenile Protection Association—to expose the street life of Chicago's young. It also applied pressure on city hall to ban or regulate a wide variety of commercial amusements available to the young, nickelodeans and dance halls especially.[70] But it was Jane Addams who provided the most influential reformist account of street life and youth culture in Chicago. What hope, she asked in *The Spirit of Youth and the City Streets,* could there be for the youth of the city constantly exposed to the corruptions of the "gin-palaces," "huge dance halls" whose "coarse and illicit merry-makings" confuse "joy with lust and gaity with debauchery," to "the most blatant and vulgar songs," to "all that is gaudy and sensual, . . . the highly colored theater posters, the trashy love stories, the featured hats, the cheap heroics of the revolvers displayed in the pawn shop windows," enticed by "the house of dreams" and surrounded by "vice deliberately disguised as pleasure." Possessing "a spirit of adventure," prized for their "labor power" in meaningless and boring work rather than for their "innocence" and "tender beauty," the youth of the city could not but be seduced into a life of delinquency, cheap thrills, gambling, dissipation, and vice.[71] To prevent such a tragedy, Addams recommended a three-part strategy.

First, parents should not so much attempt to repress the "sex impulse" or "the spirit of adventure" of the young but instead endeavor to "diffuse and utilize this fundamental instinct of sex through the imagination" in its "higher capacities." Adults should help the young to "substitute the love of beauty for mere desire, to place the mind above the senses," to replace "psychic impulsion for the driving force of blind appetite." The "wrecked foundations of domesticity" could only be overcome, she argued, if sensitive mothers, "through their sympathy and adaptability, substitute keen present interests and activity for solemn warnings and restraint, self-expression for repression." There was but one path open to America: "freedom for the young people made safe only through their own self-control."[72]

Second, Addams implored reformers to "purify" the urban environment of its "grosser temptations," to "make safe the street in which the majority of our young people find their recreation and form their permanent relationships." Traditional rural modes of moral development had been rendered "totally unsuited to modern city conditions." To "intelligently foster social morality" and self-control, reformers needed to "secure innocent recreation and better social organization." The city had to take "over the function of making provision for pleasure," to replace commercial amusements—the five-cent theater, dance halls, saloons, gambling, vice—with parks, playgrounds, recreation centers, festivals, street processions, bands of marching musicians, orchestral music in public squares. Such innovations, she reasoned, would not only promote individual moral development but a social morality as well, drawing people together across the barriers of class, ethnicity, and age. Anything less she believed "intolerable" and a serious threat to the promise of compulsory education and the juvenile court.[73]

And third, Addams argued that schools should serve a dual function: protect children from the corruptions of temptations of the world while at the same time prepare them for it. "Each generation of moralists and educators find themselves facing an inevitable dilemma," she wrote, "first to keep the young committed to their charge 'unspotted from the world,' and second, to connect the young with the ruthless and materialistic world all about them in such wise that they may make it the area for their spiritual endeavor." "Education," she argued, "alone has the power of organizing a child's activities with some reference to the life he will later lead and of giving him a clue as to what to select and what to eliminate when he comes into contact with contemporary social and industrial conditions." A "socialized education" would both enhance "social morality" and prepare the young for the world of work. Schooling "must be planned so seriously and definitely for those two years between fourteen and sixteen that it will be actual trade training so far as it goes . . . but at the same time . . . the implications, the connections, the relations to the industrial world, will be made clear."[74]

Jane Addams did not like and could never be accused of arm-chair theorizing, and here, as in other matters, she wrote about her first-hand experience. Some sixteen years before publishing *The Spirit of Youth,* she had opened a playground, the first in Chicago, at Hull House. Her efforts had proved contagious. In the years that followed, nearly all of Chicago's settlement houses established playgrounds on the assumption that playgrounds would lower truancy and delinquency. In the spring of 1896, the Chicago Women's Club decided to promote playgrounds in "congested" areas; within three years, with the help of a one-thousand-dollar subsidy from the city council, the club had opened six playgrounds. The following year, the Associated Charities of Chicago opened the first of its playgrounds. The Harper Commission, a blue-ribbon investigation of public education in Chicago, recommended in 1899 that the board of education build playgrounds in selected areas of the city. The board accepted the recommendation: between 1899 and 1909 it opened thirty playgrounds and recreation centers in largely immigrant sections of the city at a cost of some $15 million.[75]

The extension of Chicago's park system followed along similar lines. Although Chicago possessed a large park system as early as 1880—indeed, Chicago's boosters claimed that Chicago's parks were second to none in intelligence of design, arcadian beauty, and subliminal social value[76]—by the mid- to late 1890s worried settlement house workers in the tenement house districts in the southern and western sections of the city anxiously noted the "alarming" decline in the ratio of park space to population.[77] Others expressed similar fears. Guests at a banquet of the Chicago Real Estate Board in October 1897 heard Congressman Henry Boutel plea for parks and playgrounds in the poor sections of the city. Jacob Riis spoke at a special meeting of the Municipal Science Club at Hull House in the spring of 1899, and a few days later, addressed a special meeting of the Merchants Club. After the address, in which Riis stressed the ability of parks to promote proper citizenship, the club voted to financially support a small parks program.[78]

Later that year, 1899, Mayor Harrison appointed a Special Parks Commission to investigate the city park and playground needs. In the year that followed, the commission opened five small parks and assumed the upkeep of a sixth. By the end of 1904, through the combined efforts of the commission and philanthropists, the commission operated nine parks drawing over a million children per year. The following year the commission published a *Plea for Playgrounds* and successfully lobbied for an amendment to the state laws allowing park boards to acquire property adjacent to existing facilities, and to buy and sell land where small parks were most needed.[79] Within a year, the South Park Board purchased sites for a dozen parks in the stockyards district, Englewood, and Calumet. Its president, Henry Foreman, explained why:

The South Park Commissioners were the first to act. In the crowded quarters they found hordes of dirty and poorly clothed children swarming in the public ways, their playground. They found mothers with no green spot near by to refresh them and their little ones. They found young men and women in many localities with no neighborhood centers where they could meet and enjoy beautiful uplifting pastimes. They found men weary from hard labor, with few places for beneficial recreation to break the monotony of their lives, but with avenues of disastrous amusements on every side.[80]

By 1916 the city of Chicago had fifty-five playgrounds or playground parks under municipal administration. During that year a lively debate developed concerning the desirability of integrating playgrounds and schoolyards. The "fusionists" won the debate; by the end of the year the South Park Commissioners had established forty playgrounds in public schoolyards. Five years later, the board of education took over administrative control of the playgrounds.[81]

Supporters of the playground and park movement wished to accomplish two objectives: get children off dirty, busy streets heavy with disease and traffic and improve the moral environment of the young. By removing children from the vices and temptations of the city's streets, and placing them in properly designed and supervised environments, children could be taught "morals," "social consciousness," and "citizenship." A Chicago playground handbook instructed playground leaders to match the nature of games with the age and capacities of the children and to promote social morality. The playground leader "should praise every tendency of a boy or girl to sacrifice himself or herself for the good of the team" and in this way lay "the foundation of cooperation, politeness and good morals." For Clarence Rainwater, for a while the director of playgrounds in Chicago, the playground provided an opportunity not only to develop character in children but to gain "control of the remaining 80 percent of the population during the sixty-four hours per week in which even the laboring element is at leisure." For Jane Addams, parks and playgrounds promoted "social morality" among immigrant children and their families. Graham Taylor informed five thousand delegates at the first annual convention of the Playground Association of America, meeting in Chicago in 1907, that "the city which has made its reputation by killing hogs, has awakened to the fact that manufacturing good and sturdy citizenship is even more important." Edgar Bancroft of the Merchants Club warmly endorsed playgrounds. "This is not anarchy, not the preaching of a new course of municipal action," he declared, "but it is common sense applied to actual conditions." Chicago's newspapers shared the sentiment. Small parks, editorialized one, are a work of expediency rather than philanthropy. The city is asked to do something not out of the goodness of its heart, but out of the soundness of its head. To let air and sunlight into these packed quarters, to introduce sanitary conditions, to give the children open space to play is a matter of business, of sound economics, of self protection.[82]

Finally, for Henry Curtis, the first secretary-treasurer of the Playground Association of America, playgrounds provided an opportunity "to keep children away from temptation and to give them right motives and habits," a device to prevent juvenile delinquency and a form of "social insurance" against political disorder from "discontented workers." "We are sitting on the lid of an industrial volcano, that might in almost any decade rend our commercial world in sunder and bring forth destructive strikes, anarchy or French Revolutions," declared Curtis. Playgrounds, apparently, could save not only American children but America itself.[83] Curtis and Addams undoubtedly approved of a 1913 Labor Day pageant at a playground in Chicago's Palmer Park that included a representation of Labor and Capital joining hands to symbolize industrial peace and social harmony.[84]

Advocates of civic planning shared a similar vision. At the time of the World's Fair and for a decade afterward, reformers nurtured a vision of the city beautiful, orderly, and moral in which children would grow up right and adults live in peace and harmony. Although he had been appalled by the spatial separation of classes, the physical squalor, and the moral decay of Chicago, W. T. Stead nonetheless dreamed that "the great impulse born of the World's Fair" would lead the citizens of Chicago to transform the city "according to the best thought of the greatest thinkers." Charles Zueblin of the University of Chicago and one time president of the American League for Civic Improvement exclaimed ten years later "that the Chicago World's Fair was a miniature of the ideal city," a "symbol of regeneration," inspired "by a common aim working for the common good" in which the "individual was great but the collectivity was greater." "The making of the new city will mean the making of a new citizen," Zueblin predicted. The same year, C. W. Robinson recalled the great "White City" as "a dream city" but a dream that "has outlived all else." William Rainsford remembered "that city of the ideal" in which "order remained everywhere, . . . no boisterousness, no unseemly merriment" whose "beauty . . . brought gentleness, happiness, and self-respect to its visitors." Joseph Lee of the playground movement directly linked child saving and city planning. "The child should be helped to carry his city and his country with him in imagination." "To this end," he concluded, "we must make much use of symbols. . . . We must preserve and dignify our monuments, erect our public buildings in a spirit of revenue for the Commonwealth."[85]

In 1906 the Merchants Club (later that year to merge with the Commercial Club) decided to retain Daniel Burnham, principal architect of the World's Fair, to prepare a comprehensive planning document for the city of Chicago. Three years later, on July 4, 1909, the Commercial Club published *The Plan of Chicago*. "Chicago, in common with other great cities," Burnham wrote, "realizes that the time has come to bring order out of the chaos incident to rapid growth, and . . . the influx of people of many nationalities without common traditions or habits of life." Rampant "disorder, vice, and disease" and "the frequent outbreaks against law and order which result from narrow and pleasureless lives" threatened "the moral and physical health" of the city. "Broad thoroughfares through the unwholesome district," the enlargement of the park system, "impressive groupings of public buildings," the development of the lakefront and the towering dome of the city hall that Burnham compared to St. Peters in Rome would establish the majesty and the authority of the public and thereby create "civic unity" and "the good order . . . essential to material advancement." Shortly after the release of the plan, Mayor Busse appointed a 328-member Chicago Plan Commission (mostly businessmen, with a sprinkling of educators, social workers, architects, and politicians). The commission eventually produced an eight-page manual summarizing the plan and the Chicago Board of Education bought 15,000 copies as the text for a civics course on "Right Citizenship and City Planning."[86]

Three years after the Commercial Club published the *Plan of Chicago* and Jane Addams completed *The Spirit of Youth and the City Streets*, Jane Addams also completed *A New Conscience and an Ancient Evil*, a study of white slavery and prostitution. A society that had repudiated "slavery and class struggle" and "commercial aggression and lawlessness" surely had to reject white slavery, purify the urban environment of commercialized sex and promote the development of a "new conscience." The new morality, she argued, could not be secured through "the forced submission that characterized the older forms of social constraint" but would have to be "based upon the voluntary cooperation of self-directed individuals" and repudiation of the double standard. In a manner analogous to *The Spirit of Youth*, *A New Conscience* protested the commercialization of sex, recommended sublimation rather than repression, adopted a thoroughgoing environmentalism, and urged the kind of moral development that would create "self-directed individuals" and enhance "social morality."[87]

Jane Addams wrote *A New Conscience and an Ancient Evil* in the middle of a campaign against white slavery, commercialized vice, and the liquor interests in Chicago that had started following a muckraking article in 1907 by George Kibbe Turner, "The City of Chicago: A Study of the Great Immoralities" for *McClure's Magazine*.[88] In cities like Chicago, Turner argued, "the sale of dissipation" had become "a great business" whose "methods and motives are the methods and motives of pure business and must be considered as such." Turner estimated that Chicago had about 7,300 licensed liquor outlets—most of them owned by "the liquor interests," or an average of 1 to every 285 people, and a further 1,000 unlicensed outlets, also owned by the breweries. On average, every man, woman, and child in Chicago drank, in 1906, 70 gallons of beer alone, about 3½ times the national average. He also claimed that saloons were centers of gambling, the commercialization of democratic politics—"the business of ward politics"—drug trafficking, corruption of the police force, and important centers, along with brothels, dance halls, "criminal hotels," and the Levee district, "of the second great business of dissipation—prostitution." In Chicago "dealers in women" had organized prostitution "from the supplying of young girls to the drugging of the older and less salable women out of existence—with all the nicety of modern industry. As in the stockyards, not one shred of flesh is wasted."[89]

The same year that Turner's article appeared, an assistant state attorney in Chicago, Clifford Roe, prosecuted several white slavers. Roe's superiors transferred him to another division. A group of prominent businessmen and professionals belonging, as the *Chicago Tribune* put it, to "leading organizations of wealth and progressive inclinations" (including the Commercial Club) formed a Joint Club Committee to financially support Roe if he would continue his investigations of the white slave trade and work toward the closure of the three major segregated areas of concentrated vice in the city, particularly the Levee, south of the Loop. The committee, according to the Reverend E. A. Bell, had "no illusions about the speedy annihilation of vice, however desirable such annihilation undoubtedly is. What these businessmen do seek is to expose and as far as possible destroy the commercial exploitation of youth of both sexes to their destruction."[90] In 1909 Roe resigned from the state attorney's office and began working for the Joint Club Committee. His investigations led him to the conclusion, he later wrote, that "most large cities are in fact market places where girls are sold and bought."

An America commercialized has commercialized its daughters. Who would have ever prophesized a century ago that today, like hardware and groceries, the daughters of the people would be bought and sold? But to such a day as this our greed for money has brought us. How low have we sunk when now we make commerce of virtue and market the sanctity of the home?[91]

The extension of the market revolution to sex revealed by Turner and Roe prompted the citywide Illinois Vigilance Association, dozens of neighborhood associations led in the main by clergymen, the Chicago Society for Social Hygiene, the Juvenile Protective Association, the Chicago Law and Order League, the Immigrants Protective League, evangelical red-light "rescue missionaries," the Women's Christian Temperance Union, several Chicago newspapers, and the Church Federation (an umbrella organization representing 600 Protestant congregations) to mount a campaign to expose the evils of the white slave trade and commercialized vice and close the segregated vice districts.[92] In January 1910 Busse appointed the Chicago Vice Commission; in May the commission set to work.[93] A year later, the commission released its *Report* under the heading "Constant and Persistent Repression of Prostitution the Immediate Method: Absolute Annihilation the Ultimate Ideal."

The report of the Chicago Vice Commission contained three major conclusions, all quintessentially Progressive in character. "The first truth the Commission desires to impress upon its citizens of Chicago," the commission noted, "is the fact that prostitution in this city is a *Commercialized Business* of large proportions with tremendous profits of more than Fifteen Million Dollars per year, controlled largely by men, not women."[94] The commission argued that if "the male exploiter" could be separated from the problem, the city could "minimize its extent and abate its flagrant outward expression" and, in addition, "check an artificial stimulus which has been given the *business* so that the larger profits may be made by the men exploiters." The commission assumed that "so long as there is lust in the hearts of men [the social evil] will seek out some method of expression," but that the commercialization of sex on the supply side—the infrastructure of saloon proprietors, hotel managers, dance hall owners, pimps, procurers, and madams—"artificially" stimulated the demand for sex. In effect, the commission adhered to a supply-side sexology: supply created the demand. Eliminate the supply, and the demand would fall.[95]

Second, the commission argued that prostitutes, wives, and children were all the innocent victims of prostitution. It dismissed as "naive" the view that young women entered prostitution because of character flaws. Rather, poverty, poor environment, lack of recreation, "ignorance of hygiene," low wages, "broken promises," "craving for excitement," or the false and fraudulent enticements of the procurer propelled or trapped young girls and women into prostitution. "Some well-meaning persons

declare that [prostitutes] should be left to their fate; that they are criminals, and should be treated as such." The commission did not share this
view, nor did it "feel that this is an answer to the problem." Moreover,
prostitution victimized innocent children as well. Both humanitarianism
and the physical welfare of the nation required that each and every brothel
in the city be designated as a "house of contagious disease."[96]

Finally, the commission recommended a series of reforms designed
to destroy commercialized vice and improve the moral environment of the
city: closure of the segregated vice districts, the appointment of a permanent "morals commission" to continue the fight against vice, the creation
of a morals court, the establishment of properly supervised municipal
dance halls, vocational education for girls fourteen to sixteen years of age,
sex education courses in the school, housing reform ("better housing
conditions should be studied and applied. . . . Aside from the dangers
resulting from insanitary conditions, bad housing breeds vice and crime"),
destruction of the nexus between commercialized vice and the saloon,
minimum wages for women and girls, the moral rehabilitation of prostitutes, and "adequate protection" for the thousands of innocent young
immigrant women who arrived in Chicago alone without kin, friends, or
protection.[97]

A month after publication of the report, the members of the Joint
Club Committee who had supported Clifford Roe formed the nucleus of
a new organization, the Committee of Fifteen, to apply pressure on the
mayor and city council to act on the recommendations of the Vice Commission.[98] The committee intended, it declared, to direct "its full force
against commercialized prostitution." It succeeded, supported by the Juvenile Protective Association, in securing the closure of the segregated
vice districts, the creation of a morals court, and the appointment of a
morals commission. Other organizations also worked to restrict commercialized vice. The Immigrants Protective League directed by Grace Abbott
expanded its efforts to protect hapless immigrant girls from white slavers
and procurers and to secure regular employment for girls. The Chicago
Society for Social Hygiene devoted its energies to the suppression of
commercialized vice, ending of the double standard, and sex education for
the young. In 1916 the Illinois legislature passed a minimum wage law
for women following the Illinois senate's report on vice.[99] Efforts to secure
housing reform proved less successful: Sophonisba Breckinridge and
Edith Abbott completed yet another investigation of housing conditions
in Chicago and emphasized "the demoralizing lack of privacy," but the
Chicago Real Estate Board successfully blocked any efforts to introduce
reforms that violated either the principles of the "business creed" or the

"color line." Even the bloody race riots of 1919 failed to generate meaningful housing reform.[100]

The battle against the saloon proved more successful, although it took
a constitutional amendment to secure success. In the late 1890s and early
1900s, several publications had stressed the evils of the saloon: Saloons
supplied the rum that enslaved the will, corrupted youth, spawned idleness, sloth, and poverty, demoralized families, and supported commercialized vice, gambling, civic corruption, and machine politics. A number of
commentators recognized that saloons also provided important social
"functions" in working-class neighborhoods and recommended the development of "substitutes" for the saloon: parks, playgrounds, "temperance
saloons," and municipal theaters. In 1903 reformers persuaded the city
council to pass an ordinance prohibiting the sale of liquor to minors; three
years later, they convinced the council to pass an ordinance raising the
annual license fee for saloons from $600 to $1,000 and forbidding the
issuance of any new licenses until the ratio of saloons in the city was
reduced to 1 for every 500 persons. Between 1906 and 1916, the number
of saloons dropped from 8,097 to 7,094. In the inner city areas, however,
the ratio remained far lower. In the First Ward, for example, 675 licensed
saloons existed in 1916, or 1 for every 77 persons.[101]

But success continued to come in other areas. Although the wets
defeated a proposed constitutional amendment (the Gaumer Proposal) in
1907 providing for statewide Prohibition, the drys managed to win a
town-option bill. The Illinois Anti-Saloon League went to work. Organized along precinct and ward levels, the league mobilized a small army of
25,000 workers, mostly volunteers, to establish a committee in each precinct in Illinois. In Chicago they formed a committee in each ward. The
league recruited clergymen as "precinct whips"; it successfully manipu-
lated the direct primary to win promises of support from party politicians;
it carefully and systematically gathered support from women suffragists,
employer and taxpayer groups. Above all, it adroitly exploited the local
option to win over precincts or wards. By the end of 1907, 160 precincts
in Chicago had lined up on the dry side, thereby closing 199 saloons. By
the end of the following year, nearly half of Chicago was without a
saloon.[102]

In 1908–09, however, the Prohibition movement came to a dead
stop in Chicago. An organization founded in 1906, the United Societies
for Local Self-Government, led the opposition. By 1909, United Societies
reportedly included some 1,087 separate ethnic organizations with a
membership of 258,224, and constituted, as Allswang suggests, "the out-
standing inter-ethnic, or omni-ethic, organization of the city; it continued

to exist and derived its power from the fact that the overwhelming majority of Chicago's ethnics found the idea and then the actuality of Prohibition absolutely repugnant." Ethnic groups opposed Prohibition because they believed "that it was something willfully and maliciously foisted upon them by the Native-Americans." Buenker found that "ethnic newspapers denounced prohibition with invective seldom matched in the annals of journalism," while four times between 1919 and 1933 Chicago voters in referendums rejected Prohibition. In each of the referendums, Chicago voted between 72 percent and 83 percent "no" to Prohibition. So great was opposition to it that, as Charles Merriam observed, "almost no known dry has ever been elected mayor, prosecuting attorney or sheriff of Chicago or Cook County and many campaigns have turned chiefly upon the problem of comparative wetness."[103]

Although stymied in Chicago, the Prohibition movement went from success to success in Illinois at large. Relying on a strategy of piecemeal reform, Prohibitionists gained passage of laws banning drinking on trains, near state universities, old folks homes, soldiers and sailors homes, and naval training institutions. They narrowly failed to secure legislation for statewide Prohibition in 1917, but in January 1919, the Illinois legislature ratified the Eighteenth Amendment.[104]

Advocates of parks, playgrounds, tenement housing reform, city planning, anti-vice crusades and Prohibition shared one common objective: the creation of an urban environment conducive to the proper moral development of children. Moral development in turn would facilitate civic virtue—or what Jane Addams called "social morality"—and social harmony. But to secure moral development, civic virtue, and social harmony, Progressives abandoned the direct face-to-face encounters of Gilded Age reform and adopted, as Paul Boyer points out, two different kinds of environmentalist solutions. The first, "negative environmentalism," emphasized the use of "repressive" or "coercive measures to uproot vice and impose a higher standard of civic virtue," while the second, "positive environmentalism," emphasized a "subtler, less direct approach: that of remolding the city's physical environment as a means of elevating its moral tone." The anti-vice crusade and Prohibition exemplified negative environmentalism while the movements for parks, playgrounds, housing, and city planning reform expressed the philosophy of positive environmentalism. Boyer also argues that while "prohibition and anti-vice crusades energized the middle and lower middle classes in the drive to achieve urban moral homogeneity, positive environmentalism was the characteristic mode adopted by the commercial elites to achieve the same goal." Indeed, Boyer claims that the coercive crusades of the Progressive years reveal a downward social shift from where it had been in the 1870's and 1880's, when genteel, upper class ladies had volunteered as friendly visitors for their local charity organization societies. We are now dealing with the kind of socially marginal people who in these same years were being drawn into the fundamentalist churches, with their Biblical creeds and their rigid codes of personal morality. They were perhaps closest to the anonymous city dwellers who had volunteered as tract distributors and Sunday school teachers a century before.[105]

Boyer insists, however, that the popularity of positive environmentalism did not signal an end to social control but merely to a "blurring of the class realities" and the "social control" objectives of the urban reform movement. "In an earlier day," Boyer concluded, "urban moral reformers had often been quite candid in acknowledging that they sought to control or at least influence certain identifiable groups." Progressive environmental reformers "by contrast, rarely acknowledged such a mundane class dimension to their cause. They represented the 'civic ideal'—the collective stirring of the entire urban population toward a finer, purer collective life!"[106]

There can be no question about the popularity of environmentalist, particularly positive environmentalist, reform strategies during the Progressive Era, but Boyer's account needs to be qualified in several respects. First, Boyer ignores the ubiquity and salience of the rhetoric and logic of child-saving in both expressions of environmentalism.[107] He acknowledges that both forms of environmentalist reform converged on character formation, albeit from different directions, but seems unmindful of the fact that while urban reformers were certainly conscious of the capacity of a reformed urban environment to promote the moral rehabilitation of adults, in the main they focused on the moral development and civic training of children. Second, while it is possible to separate urban reform proposals into positive and negative environmentalism, it is not possible to divide the reformers along the same axis. Reformers who supported the building of parks and playgrounds also worked vigorously for the elimination of commercialized vice and the regulation of commercialized amusements, not to mention the juvenile court and probation. The principal figures involved in the crusade against commercialized vice, for example, do not fit Boyer's characterization of negative environmentalists. E. A. Brill and Rodney ("Gypsy") Smith, two prominent fundamentalist red-light "rescue missionaries," fit Boyer's characterization, but Graham Taylor and leaders of the Chicago Vice Commission kept them at arm's distance and on the margins of the anti-vice crusade.[108] Eric Anderson's investigation of the Committee of Fifteen revealed that most of the fifty-five members between 1913 and 1916 were Protestant Republicans or Progressives. None could be identified as a Democrat. Among the fifty-five members, Anderson counted nine philanthropists or social workers, five clergymen, three educators, four lawyers, one physician, and thirty-four businessmen. Anderson went on:

Many of the businessmen associated with the committee also supported religious and charitable organizations. . . . Five of the directors were trustees for major universities, and others were patrons of cultural institutions such as the Art Institute. Twenty-six of the 56 directors of the Committee between 1913 and April 1916 belonged to the Union League Club. The chief organizer and first president of the Committee, Clifford Barnes, described himself as an 'educator and capitalist' and had experience as a Hull House worker, pastor, University of Chicago instructor, and College president of the Legislative Voters League.[109]

Finally, to label the objectives of the reformers "social control" distorts the nature of reform ideology, obscures the logic of their behavior, and invites confusion between the use of social control as a term to characterize the intentions or objectives and as a theoretical term to denote the functional consequences of particular social arrangements. Reformers certainly felt free to use the coercive power of the state to manipulate the environment of the young, but they did so not because they wanted to impose an authoritarian apparatus of social domination over the immigrant working class but because they wanted to nurture individual moral development. Child-savers were less interested in social control than in individual and social redemption. When E. A. Ross suggested to his contemporaries in 1901 that the organic "living tissue" of Gemeinschaft had been superceded by "the rivets and screws of Gesellschaft with its huge and complex aggregates" and that "social control" in the future would have to be "artificial rather than natural," he wrote as a theoretician of social order and as a social mechanic of a bourgeois society, not as an apologist for an authoritarian society.[110]

KINDERGARTENS

Sometime between 1865 and 1867—the date is uncertain—disciples of the German pedagogical reformer Friedrich Froebel (1782–1852) opened a kindergarten in Chicago. The opening of the kindergarten, according to a historian of the kindergarten movement in Chicago, C. P. Dozier, had only "a local influence" and "did not inaugurate a movement." The kindergarten movement as such dates, she argues, from 1874, the year Alice

Putnam started a small study group to read and discuss "the precious gospel for all children" developed by Froebel.[111]

Out of Alice Putnam's study group grew, in 1878, a Froebel Society, whose president, Mrs. E. W. Blatchford, "saw at once the uplifting influence this system would have on the children of the poor, and volunteered the support of a free kindergarten." Soon after, the society opened a kindergarten in the church of another missionary to the poor, Dwight L. Moody. Inspired by evangelical zeal, "other philanthropic women took up the cause and kindergartens followed each other in rapid succession in churches and missions." The same year, the kindergarteners dissolved the Froebel Society and created, in its place, the Chicago Froebel Association charged with the responsibility of establishing a free training school for kindergarten teachers. The following year, Mrs. Putnam and several others interested in expanding the work of the "mission kindergartens" formed the Chicago Kindergarten Club. Four years later, after the appointment of Francis Parker as head of the Cook County Normal School, Parker invited Mrs. Putnam and the Chicago Froebel Association to make the Normal School its headquarters. By the mid-1880s, then, the kindergarten movement in Chicago was well established, but from that time on, the close association between the kindergarten and settlement movements transformed the leadership although not the character of the kindergarten movement in the city.[112]

When Hull House opened in 1889, the first organized activity that the residents started was a kindergarten, conducted and paid for by Jenny Dow. Jane Addams and Ellen Starr had some minor acquaintance with the ideas of Froebel, but they opened the kindergarten less out of a philosophical commitment to Froebel's ideas than in response to what they perceived as the needs of the children in the Hull House neighborhood: instructing children in elementary principles of hygiene and manners and the development of social instincts and inclinations through cooperative play and group activity. In this manner, Hull House residents hoped, the kindergarten, like the settlement, would act as an agency to socialize the surrounding community.[113]

Over time, the connection between the kindergarten movement and settlement houses tightened. In 1893 the Chicago Kindergarten Institute made the Hull House kindergarten the training center for kindergarten teachers. Mary McDowell, founder of the University of Chicago settlement in the stockyards district, trained as a kindergartner at Hull House, taught kindergarten, and established the mother's club there. Amalie Hoffer, and her sister, Bertha Hoffer Hegner, opened the Pestalozzi-Froebel

Kindergarten Training School in the basement of Chicago Commons in the fall of 1897. By 1911, 19 of 23 settlements had kindergartens.[114]

The close association between the settlement and the kindergarten movements in Chicago reinforced a social and political rather than educational conception of the purpose of the kindergarten. Most supporters of the kindergarten believed, like Elizabeth Harrison, that the "more apparent advantages" were the more important: for instance, the acquisition of "habits of punctuality, respect, reverence, cooperation and self-control in which the child is thus early trained before their opposites can be established by the street, the alley and the saloon." In her *A Study of Child Nature from the Kindergarten Standpoint* (1895)—a book that went to fifty editions—Harrison explicitly linked social feminism, child study, and the social function of the kindergarten. Froebel, she explained, invented "the science of motherhood," demonstrated the importance of "the understanding of little children in order that they may be properly trained," and established that "the destiny of the nations lies far more in the hands of women—the mothers—than in the hands of those who possess power." Those that rocked the cradle ruled the world.[115] Writing of the Chicago kindergarten movement in 1897, Nelli Vandewalker observed:

> The influence of the kindergarten upon the locality in which it is situated is a great factor in the recognition of its value by all classes alike. At present the problems of education are sociological rather than pedagogical. It is not more skillful teaching, not more perfect organization, not even a deeper insight into psychological principles . . . [rather] it is the relation of school and of education to the great social movements of the time. A new gospel of humanity is stirring the hearts of the people, and finding its expression in the social settlement and kindred movements. . . . [T]he public school needs the kindergarten as an entering wedge for that cooperation of social forces in a community which has so long been lacking.[116]

The board of education held a similar view, but it made no serious effort to open kindergartens until the year of the Pullman strike. As early as 1881, the board recognized the need for kindergartens to socialize the children of the poor. But despite the prodding of the *Chicago Tribune,* which believed kindergartens could help prevent strikes, the board acted slowly.[117] By late 1892, of the ninety-two kindergartens in the city, only ten of these were in rooms provided by the board, although they were located, as the board emphasized, in those "poor areas" of the city where the need to learn "character" and "self-discipline" was greatest.[118] In 1894, however, the board had a change of heart, deciding to increase the number of kindergartens in order to ensure proper "moral training." "Careful research into the history of pauperism and criminality seems to show that the child's bent is fixed before his seventh year," the board said. "If childhood is neglected, the child will mature lawless and uncontrolled and the final end will be the jail or the poorhouse. . . ."[119]

Over the course of the next year, the board opened 14 kindergartens. By the end of the 1898–99 school year the board conducted 63 schools established in "poor districts" where they were "most needed." Ten years later, the board ran 125 kindergartens, nearly all of them in "poor," "immigrant," or "manufacturing" districts.[120] The board continued to regard kindergartens as an agency of Americanization in which children of immigrant parents could be taught the English language, habits of "self-discipline" that would facilitate their progress through elementary school,"patriotic thought," and "good citizenship."[121]

CHILD-CENTERED PEDAGOGY

In a series of efforts to improve the motivation of Chicago's children to learn and to improve the effectiveness of Chicago's teachers, the Chicago Board of Education introduced object training in 1861, drawing in the early 1870s, and clay modeling and manual training in the 1880s.[122] We do not know how successful these experiments proved to be, but to at least one observer in the early 1890s, rote memorization, drill, recitation, and corporal punishment all but exhausted the pedagogical skills of Chicago's teachers. "In the public schools of Chicago," wrote Joseph Mayer Rice, "I found the instruction, in general, so unscientific that in judging them by the minimum requirement I should regard their standard as very low." In one school, children "had no opportunity to do any sight reading." A lesson on geography "was purely mechanical, consisting of nothing beyond a drill in cut and dried facts." In another geography class he found nothing but "drill in facts." In other classrooms in this school everything "was mechanical and unscientific." In another school, "nothing but purely memoriter work was attempted," although he did find the school pervaded by an atmosphere of "kindness." In one of Chicago's most famous schools, during a geography lesson examination the teacher bombarded pupils with the imperative, "Don't stop to think, but tell me what you know." And in a description of a reading class that he wrote about at great length, he detailed each and every "ridiculous" and "grotesque" movement that bewildered children were forced to make by their teacher using the "Delsarte system."[123]

An outraged and indignant press protested Rice's observations, but his words stung, and not without effect. A number of citizens—an interesting potpourri of settlement workers (Jane Addams), capitalists (Marshall Field), civic reformers (George Cole of the MVL), labor leaders (Tommy Morgan), ministers, rabbis, congressmen, jurists, and others—formed an ad hoc citizens school committee and called a mass meeting for late April of "all citizens who have at heart the interest and welfare of the public schools." The meeting decided to "inquire minutely into the workings of the public school system, because if the criticisms referred to are true there is grave cause for mortification and alarm."[124] Rice's criticisms and public pressure had their effect. The following year, Superintendent Lane introduced "learning from direct observation" pedagogies into Chicago's classrooms, particularly in nature study. Pedagogical methods were changed too, he noted, in geography and arithmetic, "to connect with the children's experience." Rice's plea for the improvement of teacher training also fell upon sympathetic ears. In 1896 the Chicago Board of Education voted to incorporate the Cook County Normal School into the Chicago school system as the Chicago Normal School. The board named the director of the Cook County Normal School since 1882 and advocate of the "new education," Colonel Francis Parker, the director of the new school.[125]

When he arrived in Chicago in 1882, Francis Parker had already established a reputation as an evangelist of the "new education." As superintendent of schools in Quincy, Massachusetts, he had abandoned the old fixed curriculum and introduced new subjects (music, drawing) and replaced rote memorization and recitation with object teaching and materials assembled by the teacher. He hoped, he had written in 1879, to establish a "science of education" based on the principles of child development. With mischievous irony and not a little dissimulation he insisted, "I am simply trying to apply well established principles to teaching, principles derived directly from the laws of the mind. The methods springing from them are found in the development of every child. They are used everywhere except the school."[126] The move to Chicago did not dim his evangelical fervor. Absolutely convinced of the righteousness of his cause, he talked and acted like a prophet, an American Moses leading the children of Chicago into the Promised Land of a child-centered classroom.

Parker had a simple educational credo: The child should be the center and inspiration of the school's activities and the school should pursue two objectives—character development and a democratic social order. "The child," he wrote in the very first page of *Talks on Pedagogics*, "is the climax and culmination of all God's creations, and to answer the question, 'what is the child,' is to approach nearer the still greater question, 'what is the

Creator and Giver of Life'?" The Creator had created the child in his own image; the "spontaneous tendencies of the child are the records of inborn divinity." "We are here, my fellow teachers," he preached, "for one purpose, and that purpose is to understand these tendencies and continue them in all directions, following nature." By following nature, "we can save *every* child."[127] Traditional methods ignored the child's natural curiosity of the world around him, the experimental basis of observation, description, and understanding, the importance of activity and learning-by-doing, and the necessity to provide for the child's needs for expression. The "science of education" required that subject matter be organized in a manner consistent with the process of children's mental development and the development of character. Otherwise, children were denied "mental nutrition" and the opportunity to exercise and develop "the principle of cooperation" and "the social motive."[128]

Only with a pedagogy based on the science of education, Parker insisted, could the school hope to develop character in children. "Our duty," he wrote, "is to know the child and supply the conditions for his highest growth and character." "The true test of the school," he insisted against those who would measure a school by grade averages, "is to be found in the development of character." Education should aim at the "proper cultivation of the naturally divine motives which every child possessed. These motives, unless blighted by formal teaching methods, made every child an artist, a searcher for and lover of truth, and an altruist." Consequently, Parker, like other child-centered pedagogues, and Horace Mann, a half-century earlier, opposed what he called "the systematic cultivation of selfishness through bribery by means of rewards and percents, and the improper stimulation by promotion" or the "list of rewards." The "whole system of rewards" and "emulation as incentives," he insisted, should be abolished and replaced with activity—"work, study, exercise, play"—the "daily bread of the school."[129] In effect, Parker did not merely reject traditional pedagogy; he repudiated the classroom culture of possessive individualism.

Parker's hostility to competitive emulative classroom strategies cannot be separated from his antagonism to "aristocracy" and "class education." Such education, he averred, rested on "the method of quantity teaching," and this in turn relied on "textbooks, pages, word-cramming, and word-recitation; of learning, believing and conforming; the method of pedantry; the method that limits the mental horizon; the method that keeps the mind from looking outside of a certain definite circle; the method of implicit belief." True education, on the other hand, was both "scientific" and "democratic" and utilized "the method of quality teaching." Indeed, the ideal school should be an embryonic democracy, "a form of community life necessary in training for good citizenship in a democracy." On a larger scale, the common school represented the only real hope for democracy in America, and, for that matter, the world. Traditional education produced "subject-peoples." The "new education" aimed at the creation of a "free people" and "universal salvation." Whereas Woodrow Wilson wished to make the world safe for democracy, Parker aspired to Americanize the world not with war and diplomacy but with school-room democracy. "God," he said, "made America the schoolhouse of the world."[130] For Parker then, pedagogy and politics were inseparable. In the last analysis, child-centered pedagogy and democratic social relations were different sides of the same coin.

John Dewey, professor of philosophy, psychology, and education at the University of Chicago, held similar views. When he arrived in Chicago in the summer of 1894 to take up his position at the University of Chicago, Dewey lauded Parker as "the father of progressive education."[131] Parker viewed Dewey no less enthusiastically. Shortly after arriving in Chicago, Dewey gave a series of lectures at the Chicago Normal School. After raptly listening to Dewey quietly expounding "those radical ideas which simply remove the bottom from all existing forms of educational effort," Parker rose to his feet to respond:

Ladies and Gentlemen, if what Dr. Dewey has been telling is true, the world is wrong. If what he says is true, the millions upon millions of dollars which are expended upon our public school system, is not only spent in the wrong way, but we are dulling bright intellects and doing incalculable harm to the future generations. Only when we seat (ourselves) at the feet of the child, will the millennium come.[132]

When not teaching at the University of Chicago or giving guest lectures at the Chicago Normal School, Dewey searched the school supply stores of Chicago looking for school desks and chairs suitable "to the needs of children." One dealer remarked to Dewey: "I am afraid we have not what you want. You want something at which the children may work: these are all for listening." Dewey commented: "That tells the story of the traditional education."[133] Dewey failed to find desks and chairs that he wanted, but he decided nonetheless to go ahead with his plan to open an "experimental" school in Chicago. In 1896, two years after his arrival in Chicago, the Laboratory School opened its doors to its first students. Within a short time the school became the foremost progressive institution in the country, and Dewey a leading figure in the progressive educational movement.[134]

For Dewey, the need for the "new education" grew out of the impact of the market revolution and especially the industrial revolution, upon traditional informal educational arrangements. Recent social and industrial changes, he argued, had made a casualty of the "household and neighborhood" system of production, thereby destroying traditional mechanisms of skill acquisition and "character building." "One, two or at the most three generations" ago when "the household was practically the center in which we carried on . . . all the typical forms of industrial occupation," children "were gradually initiated into the mysteries of the several processes. . . . We cannot over look the factors of discipline and of character building involved in this kind of life: training in habits of order and of industry, and in the idea of responsibility, of obligation to do something, to produce something, in the world."[135]

At bottom, Dewey wanted to restore, imitate or mimic as much as possible not so much the form as the texture and purpose of these older educational arrangements. He acknowledged that the household could no longer be the center of the education of the child, but a reconstituted school could. Dewey feared, however, that several barriers stood in the way of this happening, particularly a series of dualisms within educational theory between thought and action, work and play, learning and utility, the practical and the academic. Each dualism impeded the acquisition of skill, character development, and the creation of a democratic society. Despite the pedagogical innovations of Parker and others, pedagogy remained shackled to traditional presuppositions:

In spite of all the advances that have been made throughout the country, there is still one unsolved problem in elementary and secondary education. That is the question of duly adapting to each other the practical and utilitarian, the executive and the abstract, the tool and the book, the head and the hand. This is a problem of such vast scope that any systematic attempt to deal with it must have great influence upon the whole course of education everywhere.[136]

The Laboratory School Dewey opened in 1896 attempted an "experimental" resolution to this "vexed question." The school was never large—its maximum size was 140 students and twenty-three teachers (with ten assistants), and it lasted only eight years—but it is doubtful that any school in America's history has had as much influence on pedagogical theory. Two "cardinal principles" guided "the entire school's operation and organization, as a whole and in details," the first "psychological" in character, and the second, "social." In all educative relationships the starting point, Dewey argued, "is the impulse of the child to action, his desire responding to the surrounding stimuli and seeking its expression in concrete form." And second, "the educational process is to supply the materials and the positive and negative conditions—the let and hindrance—so that his expression, intellectually controlled, may take a normal direction that is social in both form and feeling." Together the two principles promoted the student's "growth" as a social being.[137]

Dewey believed that to make "the impulse of the child to action" the starting point of the educational process would prove nothing less than revolutionary. It represented, he said, a "shifting of the center of gravity. It is a change, a revolution, not unlike that introduced by Copernicus when the astronomical center shifted from the earth to the sun. In this case the child becomes the sun about which the appliances of education revolve; he is the center about which they are organized."[138] The programmatic implications of this Copernican revolution in pedagogy Dewey summarized in *My Pedagogic Creed*. "The problem of method," he declared, "is ultimately reducible to the question of the order of the child's powers and interests." The teacher had to take responsibility for understanding the child's developmental process, to recognize the child's "felt needs" or "interests," and through the creation of a socially meaningful educational environment make possible "that reconstruction or reorganization of experience which adds to the meaning of experience, and which increases the ability to direct the course of subsequent experience." Dewey defined this process as "development" or "growth."[139]

Dewey's definition of education as growth shaped not only the pedagogy and curricula of the Laboratory School but his pedagogical and curricula proposals generally. A combination of practical, learn-by-doing pedagogies and the study of "occupations," Dewey believed, enabled the teacher to transcend the traditional distinctions between the theoretical and the practical, and between thought and action, that dominated orthodox educational practice.[140] He argued that the study of occupations, for example, provided the "instrumentalities through which the school itself" became a "genuine form of community life, instead of a place set apart in which to learn lessons," and gave to teachers a means of resolving the pervasive problems of motivation and discipline that plagued traditional education.[141] In the traditional classroom, he wrote, "there is no obvious social motive for the acquirement of mere learning." Instead, "almost the only measure for success is a competitive one" with the consequence that "the mere absorption of facts and truths is so exclusively individual an affair that it tends very naturally to pass into selfishness." In the Laboratory School all this had been changed. Characterized by "a spirit of social cooperation and community life," the "whole conception of school discipline changes." The result was a "deeper and infinitely wider discipline."[142]

As regards the spirit of the school, the chief object is to secure a full and informal community life in which each child will feel that he has a share and his own work to do. This is made the chief motive towards what are ordinarily termed order and discipline. It is believed that the only *genuine* order and discipline are those which proceed from the child's own respect for the work which he has to do and his consciousness of the rights of others who are, with himself, taking part in this work. . . . [T]he emphasis in the school upon various forms of practical and con- structive activity gives ample opportunity for appealing to the child's social sense and to regard for thorough and honest work.[143]

Dewey drew few boundaries between the school and society. Activity pedagogies and curricula that integrated the academic and the practical promised to overcome, he argued, that "medieval conception of learning" associated with "the division into 'cultured' people and workers, the sep- aration of theory and practice." Progressive education would prevent the separation of classes generated by traditional education and advance the cause of "democracy" and "equal opportunity." "Obviously," Dewey wrote, "a society to which stratification into separate classes would be fatal must see to it that intellectual opportunities are accessible to all on equable and easy terms. A society marked off into classes need be specially attentive only to the education of its ruling elements. A society which is mobile, which is full of channels for the distribution of a change occurring any- where, must see to it that its members are educated to personal initiative and adaptability."[144] He insisted that the "old schools were not conducted to give equal opportunity to all, but for just the opposite purpose, to make more marked the line between classes, to give the leisure and moneyed classes something which everyone could not get, to cater to their desire for distinction." In a democratic society, however, where education should serve all, the curriculum needed to be useful, concrete, intellectually chal- lenging, and socially meaningful. Practical activities, in that they fused the practical and the theoretical, united rather than divided classes by building a common cultural heritage. Since the student participated in occupational tasks within the "miniature community" of the school, the student would be constantly exposed to social discipline, social cooperation, democratic values, and "saturated with the spirit of service." Schools could, in this way, prevent "class struggle" while at the same time draw "industrial democracy out of industrial feudalism."[145]

Finally, Dewey assumed, following Jane Addams, that practical activ- ities in the classroom would overcome not just the separation of classes but the alienation of the worker from work. Dewey believed—and the Laboratory School was an attempt to prove—that education could make work meaningful. Like Jane Addams, Dewey believed that the system of labor characteristic of America reduced workers to "mere appendages to the machines they operated." Workers had no opportunity to develop "imagination" and "sympathetic insight as to the social and scientific values" of their work. This situation posed a challenge to public schools. "The problem of general public instruction," he claimed, "is not to train workers for a trade but to make use of the work environment of the child in order to supply motive and meaning to work." Occupations satisfied this requirement nicely. Unlike trade training, the study of occupations maintained "a balance between the intellectual and the practical phases of experience."[146]

In sum, child-centered pedagogy expressed a desire to reform society, to usher in the millennium through the progressive school. Education, Dewey insisted, was "the fundamental method of social progress and reform." Every teacher should think of himself as "a social servant set apart for the maintenance of proper social order and the securing of the right social growth. In this way, the teacher always is the prophet of the true God and the usherer in of the true kingdom of God."[147]

The results of the efforts of Parker and Dewey hardly matched their aspirations. But they did help improve teacher training, advanced the cause of teacher professionalization, deeply influenced educational theory and, in part, classroom pedagogical practices.

First, child-centered pedagogy gave direct sanction to the improvement of teacher training and professionalization. Both Parker and Dewey advocated improved teacher education and professional autonomy. Parker particularly influenced Superintendents Howland and Lane, and the teachers of Chicago, many of whom he trained at the Cook County and later Chicago Normal School. An editorial by Margaret Haley, editor of the *Bulletin* of the Chicago Teachers Federation and a former student of Parker's, resonates with both the spirit of Parker and a demand for improved teacher training and increased autonomy for teachers:

The idea with the majority of people seems to be that education is something to be imposed. The pupil is given to the teacher and she must force something into him. People work on the plan that human nature is essentially wrong and will go wrong, if allowed to run its true course. They fail to see in the child anything like the flower which, if allowed to grow will bloom, and, if curbed and hampered, will become a stunted thing. It seems to me and it is the motive of our fight in Chicago, that the teachers must take the child and develop what is in him, and not force something into him which is perhaps contrary to his nature. System and iron clad cause laid down by persons who are not themselves in sympathy with the education of the masses curb these efforts. The teacher must take forty or sixty pupils and apply to everyone the same course of study, when in many cases an entirely different line of work is required.[148]

Dewey's direct influence on teachers and their demands for professional autonomy was not as great, but he did exercise considerable influence over Ella Flagg Young, superintendent of schools in Chicago between 1909 and 1915.[149] From the time she became principal of the Skinner Grammar School, Ella Flagg Young encouraged teachers to develop their own methods of teaching. Later, under the supervision of Dewey, she wrote a dissertation, "Isolation in the Schools," in which she proposed an end to the system of "close supervision" and the creation of a "democratic" structure of educational administration and decision making through the establishment of "teachers councils." For superintendents and principals alone to determine policy reflected "the reasoning of a member of the ruling class."[150] Only in a democratic system of control, together with improved teacher training, could the children of Chicago receive the kind of education they deserved, progressive pedagogy demanded, and democracy required:

In order that teachers may delight in awakening the spirits of children, they must themselves be awake. We have tried to free the teachers. Some day the system will be such that the child and teacher will go to school with ecstatic joy. At home in the evening the child will talk about the things done during the day and will talk with pride. I want to make the schools the great instrument of democracy.[151]

Second, child-centered pedagogy promoted a developmentalist perspective in educational theory. From this perspective, particular pedagogical methods and curricula materials should be related to the intellectual and social development of the children apprehended through the close scientific study of child development. First conceived by Locke in the seventeenth century, nurtured by Rousseau, Pestalozzi, and Froebel in the eighteenth and early nineteenth centuries, and by the advocates of Christian nurture during the Victorian era, the developmentalist perspective attained epistemological maturity and scientific stature in the writings of Dewey, G. Stanley Hall, and the child study movement.[152] Developmentalistism emphasized two notions: the necessity of basing education on "the laws of development," and character formation. Commenting in 1908 on the commitment of Colonel Parker and the "science of pedagogy" to prevent "the perversion of most of the natural tendencies to growth and development," William C. Payne, principal of the Harrison School, argued that the new pedagogy had done so "very largely by bringing our methods more into accord with the laws of development . . . and a great faith in the efficiency of the Divine Plan as discovered in the study of child life." He also noted, however, that the new pedagogy, following Colonel Parker's lead, sought "the development of character through the formation of ideals resulting from the use of knowledge in acts of judg-ment."[153]

By the end of the first decade of the new century, the pages of the *Educational Bi-Monthly,* the publication of the Chicago Normal School, were filled with details of lesson plans that utilized the "dynamic factor," the "laboratory method," or "activity methods" in the classroom, whether in music, geography, math, social studies, or nature studies.[154] Relying heavily on the "laboratory method" and "activity methods," respectively, the board introduced, in 1909 and again in 1915–16, new civics courses to ensure that students acquired the proper habits of self-discipline and self-control.[155] A committee of principals in 1914 explained that teachers pursued the moral education in Chicago "almost universally through in-direct means rather than through formal lesson." The committee ap-plauded this procedure and justified it in the terms of the new pedagogy. "It is obvious that the changing needs of the growing child, his varying instincts and tendencies as he passes through successive stages of devel-opment, should be considered in selecting and arranging suitable material for moral training." The committee concluded that the method of habit and imitation for the elementary child would lead into a more rational ethical conception in the minds of the young.[156] Finally, beginning in the late teens, following the publication of William Heard Kilpatrick's "The Project Method" in 1918, a steady stream of articles on the project method issued from the pages of *The Chicago Schools Journal* for the next ten years. In terms of day-to-day pedagogical practice, the project method appears to have been one of the major legacies of child-centered pedagogy.[157]

But although there can be no mistaking the impact of child-centered pedagogy on educational rhetoric in Chicago, its influence on classroom practice is another matter entirely. The 1932 *Survey of the Schools of Chicago* discovered some evidence of innovative pedagogy and progressive class-rooms, but, on the whole, it concluded,

this survey of the kindergarten-primary grades discloses the fact that Chicago's young children are spending their school hours attending to the demands of the school set up, to the neglect of their own necessities or interests. They are devoting their time to pleasing the teachers. They are taking practically no responsibility for themselves or others. They are making relatively few decisions for themselves and fewer for their classroom group. They are asking few questions and seldom ex-pressing any ideas of their own. In brief, they are spending their hours in school practicing techniques for which they see no use and memorizing and repeating ideas that are not their own and which they do not value.[158]

In part, no doubt, the persistence of traditional pedagogical practices reflected simple inertia. But two other factors had greater significance. First, child-centered pedagogy failed, despite its partial victory over traditional pedagogical methods, to make any headway against the conventional social organization of the classroom: competitive exams and grading, age-graded classroom, and fixed curricula. Although Parker and Dewey deplored the use of emulation and rewards and similar devices in the classroom, they both failed to intellectually confront the power exercised by competitive evaluation and grading over classroom processes and outcomes, and to directly challenge, therefore, the heart of bourgeois pedagogy.[159] And finally, the *Survey* staff also hinted at a third cause: the absence of any discretionary authority by teachers to design and implement innovative programs and methods. "The teachers of these children are, in general," concluded the *Survey*, "devoting their time to carrying out plans which they had no share in evolving. They, like the children, are making few decisions relative to the work which occupies their time for at least five hours a day. At their best, the majority of these teachers of young children are conforming pleasantly, courteously, and graciously to uniform demands for uniform products."[160]

The failure of Chicago's teachers to expand their professional autonomy primarily reflected their inability to contest successfully the centralization and bureaucratization of educational administration in Chicago. That failure severely limited their ability to resist the multiplicity of bureaucratic demands for standardized procedures, tests, texts, and courses of study imposed by the administrative hierarchy. In turn, the centralization of authority and the bureaucratization of pedagogy were the direct outcomes of objectives sought by a generation of administrative reformers pursuing the goal of social efficiency. In that pursuit, administrative reformers not only bureaucratized pedagogy but industrialized it as well in the form of practical vocational learn-by-doing pedagogies. Even child study did not escape the clutches of social efficiency and competitive grading. When the board of education founded the Department of Child Study in 1899, the board charged it with determining the relative value of various pedagogic methods. Some ten years later, however, the department was not so much concerned with evaluating alternative pedagogies as with the "anthropometric" study of the physical capacities, characteristics, and defects of children, "mental efficiency" and "mental hygiene," and "individual needs." "It is hoped," wrote President Schneider in his annual report in 1909, "that in the course of time [through the Child Study Department] still closer segregation of good, bad, and indifferent children can take place in the schools, so that they can receive their education more according to their individual capacity." He insisted, however, that "no one can escape being the anvil or the hammer. . . . The sooner this is impressed on the children of the school, the better; . . . individuality belongs only to the genius." Child study has become but a means for improving the social efficiency of the school and "subordinate to the one objective of giving the children the most practical education."[161]

By 1930, then, classroom pedagogy in Chicago combined an uneasy and often contradictory mix of older pedagogical practices centered upon competitive evaluation and grading and a hybrid of various progressive pedagogies—child-centered, bureaucratic, and industrial. Classroom pedagogical practices in 1930 emerged from disparate organizational and ideological conflicts within and outside the school: the efforts of child-centered reformers, increasingly sanctioned by professional norms, to motivate and discipline individual children in large urban classrooms; conflicts between contending conceptions of pedagogical authority and administrative power; conflicts between a conception of an activities pedagogy and an industrialized pedagogy; and conflicts between competing conceptions of the objectives of schooling and of the relationship between the school and the political economy. From these complex political and ideological processes it is possible to discern the forces shaping pedagogical practice in Chicago. Ironically, what had commenced with Parker and Dewey as an effort to expel the marketplace from the classroom ended as the scientific measurement of children and learn-by-doing pedagogies designed to improve the social efficiency of the school in a market economy.

CHILD-SAVING AND THE MARKET REVOLUTION

In large part, we can trace the origins of the child-saving movement in Chicago during the Progressive Era to the impact of the market revolution on the lives of children and to the commitment of Progressive reformers to the intellectual imperatives of republican liberalism. Outraged by the commercial exploitation of children's labor power, dismayed by the commercialization of amusements, vice, and pedagogy, appalled by the unmistakable evidence of poverty, illiteracy, and delinquency, and fearful of the growing separation of classes, child-savers set about improving the moral development and citizenship training of children, extending equal opportunity and eliminating social conflict and disorder. They campaigned to secure meaningful child labor and compulsory education legislation, legislation to create the juvenile court and the probation system, the elimination of segregated vice districts, the regulation of commercial amusements, the opening of parks, playgrounds, and kindergartens, and the reform of school pedagogy. With the exception of the last, by and large they succeeded.

But while Progressive reformers opposed the excesses of the market revolution, they did not repudiate the market revolution itself. Progressives protested when they suspected that markets maketh children, but they believed that it was entirely appropriate to maketh children for the market. Through a combination of moral development, the extension of educational opportunity, and school reform—particularly vocational education—the children of Chicago could simultaneously be saved from the market and prepared for it. If children were saved from the market revolution, childhood was not; instead, childhood became an adjunct of the market economy, a time when young people were properly socialized and trained for their eventual entry into the labor market. In a sense, child-saving allowed Progressive reformers to reconcile "commerce" and "virtue" in much the same manner that western expansion and the doctrine of separate spheres had done during the course of the nineteenth century. In doing so, Progressives elevated child-saving into the deus ex machina of republican liberal politics: in saving children, the market revolution could be promoted and America redeemed. At the very moment that Frederick Jackson Turner declared the frontier closed, Progressive reformers committed America to a fateful ménage a trois between child-saving, redeemer politics, and the market revolution.

The political ascendancy of child-saving had three significant effects. First, it deflected attention away from the structure of social relations and the transformation of opportunity structures and focused attention instead upon the regulation of social relationships through moral development, the extension of educational opportunity, and the strengthening of the ties between schooling and the economy. Second, while Progressives expanded the responsibility of the state for social welfare, they did so in a uniquely American way: They linked the provision of social services to the needs of children rather than to the universal entitlements of democratic citizenship. In part, this reflected the inability of working-class or populist movements to redefine or extend the rights of citizenship, but it also reflected the intellectual authority of child-saving within American politics and the persistence of the nineteenth-century charity distinction between the deserving poor and the undeserving poor. Progressives did not so much reject the distinction as alter it to a distinction, so crucial to the American social service system of the twentieth century, between needy children and unworthy adults. The effect, as Bruce Bellingham argues, has been to place the child rather than the citizen "at the center of the welfare state."[162]

And finally, child-saving legitimated an unparalleled expansion of the tutelary powers of the state, particularly through compulsory education, the juvenile court and probation, and kindergartens. Progressives did so not because they were committed to a paternalism of the state, or because they were hostile to the family, or even because they hoped to "fulfill their destiny through bureaucratic means," as Wiebe proposes, but because they saw no other way of preserving and legitimating a republican liberal society. Two hundred years earlier John Locke had argued that successful participation in the marketplace and moral order required parents and tutors to cultivate "reason" and "virtue" in children and to abhor the exercise of patriarchial power. What Locke failed to appreciate was the tendency, recognized by de Tocqueville in the 1830s, for Lockean preoccupations to promote Hobbesean solutions.[163]

Chapter 3

THE LIMITS OF REFORM

Child Labor, Compulsory Education and the
Remaking of the Chicago Working Class

In *The Jungle* Upton Sinclair narrates the tragic impact of work in the stockyards upon the family life of a Lithuanian immigrant laborer, Jurgis Rudkis, his wife, Ona, and their children. When they arrive in Chicago, Jurgis and Ona are full of high hopes: They intend to work hard, reside with kin, save, buy a house, send their children to school, and prosper. But under the pressure of unemployment, injury, disease, and illness, the kinship system disintegrates, swindlers rip them off, poverty grips the family, the older children leave school to work, two children die of disease, Ona prostitutes herself to get a job, and Jurgis is jailed for attacking the Irish foreman who seduced her. While Jurgis is incarcerated, Ona and the remaining children die of poverty-induced illness. After release from prison, Jurgis leaves the city a demoralized tramp. When he returns, years later, he is a member of the Industrial Workers of the World.[1]

In its suggestion of an incipient revolution by a radicalized proletariat, the story of the Rudkis family is a shade too apocryphal. But the struggles and misery depicted by Sinclair were real enough for the immigrant working class of the late nineteenth and early twentieth centuries. That they refused to accept passively their fate is fact rather than fiction, for in response to the vicissitudes of their daily lives—unemployment, illness, injury, hard work for 10, 12, or 14 hours a day six days a week, poor housing and food, and poverty—working-class people devised a variety of strategies of survival and accommodation. They sent their children to work, purchased homes, joined unions and voluntary associations, participated in machine politics, lived in ethnic enclaves, attended parochial churches, sent their children to school, sometimes, if possible to parochial schools, and they kept them in school, by the 1920s, way beyond the age they were required to do so by law.

Unraveling the logic of these responses—their relationship to one another, to the structure of social relations, and to Progressive reform—is far from a simple matter, and the analysis undertaken here is far from complete. While Progressive reforms, particularly child labor and compulsory education legislation, undoubtedly influenced working-class educational behavior, changes in working-class educational behavior also reflected the influence of complex structural and cultural processes associated with the "remaking" of the Chicago working class around a bifurcated politics of the workplace (pure and simple unionism) on the one hand and ethnically differentiated family and neighborhood life on the other centered on machine politics, school attendance, home ownership, saloons, churches and voluntary associations following the defeat of the Pullman strike in 1894.[2] In other words, changes in working-class educational behavior did not so much reflect a successful strategy of social control by Progressive reformers, as reflect and reinforce a process of class formation—the remaking of the Chicago working class.[3]

LABOR AND EDUCATIONAL POLITICS, 1874–1903

From its earliest days, organized labor in Illinois opposed child labor and supported compulsory education. In 1874, for example, at the very first meeting of the fledgling Workingmen's party of Illinois, the party's platform included a demand for the abolition of child labor for children under fourteen years of age in factories, and the compulsory education of all children. This demand, and the many that followed, expressed at least four concerns: a humanitarian revulsion to child labor; a desire to eliminate children from the labor market and so increase the number of jobs available to adult husbands and fathers; the belief that the future economic welfare of working class children depended on education; and, above all, a conviction that preserving a republican democracy required an educated citizenry.[4]

Three years after the inaugural meeting of the Workingmen's party of Illinois, the Chicago Labor League released a political platform including an eight-hour day and the prohibition of child labor of children under twelve years of age. The same year, the Council of Trade and Labor Unions of Chicago issued similar demands.[5] In 1884 the Illinois State Federation of Labor (ISFL) urged the prohibition of all child labor of children under fourteen in workshops and factories and adoption and enforcement of compulsory education legislation. One labor leader, P. H. McLogan, put the issue thus:

Another remedial measure that we believe in is compulsory education. We consider that all important. We consider that as the State requires certain duties of the citizen, so it owes him certain duties; that it cannot perform any better or more important service than that of instructing the future citizen in morality and in his duties as a citizen, and that there is no more effectual way of doing this than by a general compulsory education. That takes the children from the street and from the factory and from the workshop and places them in a position where they will acquire sufficient knowledge to become worthy citizens of the State when they come of age.[6]

Labor leaders of all political persuasions shared McLogan's sentiments in the decades that followed. The Chicago Federation of Labor averred in the early 1900s that educated workmen would not sit idly by and let social injustice flourish; they would support the quest for social reform and help guard the traditions of republicanism.[7] In his presidential address to the annual convention of the Illinois State Federation of Labor (ISFL) in 1924, John Walker challenged the basic assumptions of the ascendant meritocratic theory of education. "If this country is to become really and truly a democracy, if it is to survive as the home of the free, it must do so through the education of the masses, and not through the acute minds of a small but highly educated class." "If the children of workingmen," he went on, "are to be efficient, self-respecting citizens of a great country, education will help them. If they are not to be oppressed by avaricious exploiters, they must not be slaves to ignorance. If they are to be free, they must have knowledge."[8]

Of all the defenses of compulsory education made by the labor leaders, a socialist, Tommy Morgan, perhaps provided the most eloquent and impassioned. Morgan's educational views were grounded foursquare in radical republicanism and in the provisions of the federal and state constitutions requiring a common education for all Americans. The founding fathers, he argued, had recognized that the survival of a democratic government required "the widest, deepest, and best education of every member of the state and nation." The Ordinance of 1787 gave expression to this belief, since its basis was "to so educate future generations of Americans that they could think and act as the Revolutionists had, and be ready and competent as men to rule and govern themselves and to successfully resist all individual or class rulership from within and without and thereby preserve and develop the republican institutions which independent thought and manly courage had established." Unhappily, however, the schools of late nineteenth-century Chicago were "neither adequate, thorough nor efficient." "Those who passed through the public schools," he went on, "have but a vague conception of the principles of society, government or law and hence are ill-prepared for the duties of citizenship, and their economic knowledge is equally vague." The immediate result of this was a decline in "intellectual manhood" and "self-government." The long-term consequence, already apparent, was the growing ability of the "Railroad Kings, Merchant Princes and Factory and Mine Lords of this day" to force "the masses back into slavery." Only a truly public system of education, and an education for full citizenship, stood between a democratic republic and a new industrial serfdom.[9]

In addition to its commitment to compulsory education and child labor legislation, organized labor also supported free textbooks for all children and a variety of curricula and pedagogical innovations introduced by the board of education during the 1890s. Labor believed that free textbooks represented a natural corollary to compulsory education and child labor legislation. Of what use was it to force children out of workshops and into the schools if the children could not afford the textbooks? The ISFL first raised the issue in 1885 and continued to do so most years for the next three or four decades, invariably with the observation similar to the one it made in 1916: "To have a real democracy in our educational system, free textbooks should be furnished in all our public schools." The campaign of the ISFL was not devoid of self-interest and not without some success. Eventually, in 1919, it secured passage of a local option bill in the Illinois legislature.[10] Labor also actively supported a number of curricula and pedagogical innovations introduced during the 1890s: music, art, drawing, physical culture, paper-cutting and painting, German, clay modeling, and color work.[11] When the *Chicago Tribune* (a cost-conscious but tax-shy organization) and several others mounted a vigorous attack on what it called "fads and frills" during January and February 1893,[12] and apparently persuaded several members of the board of education to introduce a motion on March 1 to discontinue the fads, labor responded vigorously.[13] A few days later at a regular meeting of the Chicago Trades and Labor Assembly, a resolution introduced by Tommy Morgan condemned the attack upon special subjects and called for a special public meeting March 11.[14]

At the March 11 meeting, Colonel Francis Parker, Henry D. Lloyd, and Morgan spoke in favor of the special subjects.[15] Morgan defended special subjects in terms of the necessity of a broad liberal education for the children of workingmen in a republican democracy. Only 22 percent of workingmen's children went beyond fourth grade, he pointed out, so that unless working-class children were given the special subjects in the grade school, they would never gain the benefits of exposure to the rich and progressive educational experiences that the children of the better-off classes received in private schools. Unless working-class children were given an education that was more than the three R's and equal to the education of the well-to-do, a system of "class education" would condemn the children of the working class to perpetual serfdom and exacerbate the separation of classes. "What has art education to do with [the working] class except to 'unfit' it for its obedience and mechanical service required of it?" Morgan asked rhetorically. "Are not all the educational innovations mere fads? And are not the schools themselves a menace to that contest which ignorance gives to those born to be drawn in harness by their masters?"[16]

Although the board decided to limit the number of special subjects, it did not eliminate them entirely. The controversy continued to simmer throughout the remainder of the 1890s and into the early 1900s. The antagonists were much the same as in 1893: on one side, the *Chicago Tribune*, several other newspapers, employers and businessmen, and some members of the board of education; on the other side, organized labor and a number of educational officials. Angry at the continued attacks on special subjects, in 1902 the Chicago Federation of Labor authorized its legislative committee to investigate the matter thoroughly. The committee concluded that the special subjects and the new pedagogical methods were desirable on both educational and political grounds since they "motivated" children bored with the three R's and equipped "pupils for life by giving them control of their powers, to create an enjoyment in work which will lead to continued endeavor . . . and give play to social spirit which leads to the practice of virtue, thus making ethics and intelligence bear fruit in conduct." The attack of the rich and the "frothings of prejudiced critics" on "fads and frills" suggested mere hypocrisy. The rich sent their children to expensive private schools where they secured "immunity from the effects of gradgrind methods." What was good for the goose was good for the gander, admonished the committee, particularly in light of the fact that approximately 50 percent of all children between the ages of ten and twelve worked in factories or workshops rather than attended school. The committee concluded that this represented "the saddest of all commentaries that can be made upon our industrial system" and urged that the state legislature "should forever destroy the institution of child labor by passing and enforcing such laws as will keep in school every child until he has graduated from the highest grade."[17]

Long before Progressive reform arrived on the scene then, organized labor supported compulsory education and child labor legislation. Moreover, although Progressive reformers and organized labor both supported compulsory education because they believed good citizenship required education, their respective conceptions of citizenship drew upon radically different intellectual traditions. Labor's drew upon the radical republicanism of Tom Paine and the nineteenth-century labor movement. The conception of citizenship advanced by Progressive reformers drew on liberal and meritocratic sources and, later, social efficiency doctrines, as we shall see in chapter 4. Labor's attitudes reflected decades of bitter struggle with capital. The posture of the Progressive reformers expressed widespread middle-class anxiety with "the growing separation of classes." While organized labor enthusiastically joined forces with Progressive reformers to secure compulsory education and child labor legislation, labor's participation did not so much represent an ideological victory for Progressive reformers as reflect yet another effort to preserve a democratic republic in the face of the feudal power and sinister machinations of "Railroad Kings, Merchant Princes and Factory and Mine Lords."

In effect, while organized labor and Progressive reformers both supported child labor and compulsory education legislation, they did so for quite different reasons. Organized labor, however, represented but one component of the Chicago working class—numerically the most significant component was the unorganized and relatively unskilled, largely immigrant working class. Since immigrants rarely expressed their attitudes toward compulsory education and child labor in a manner that historians can document, assessing the impact of Progressive reform on the immigrant working class is more difficult, although not impossible.

CHILD LABOR AND THE DOMESTIC ECONOMY OF THE CHICAGO WORKING CLASS

To Chicago's working class, work invariably involved hard back-breaking labor for long hours at unskilled or semiskilled jobs with low wages, frequent unemployment, and the constant risk of industrial accident or work-related illness. For many families, poverty was as much a part of daily life as the foul air, overcrowded housing and adulterated food. For others it forever lurked behind the next layoff, the next accident, the next illness. For some the struggle ended in pauperism and despair.

Data on income levels for Chicago's working-class families is woefully sporadic and incomplete. Still, enough is available to give at least a hint of the difficulties confronting working-class families. An 1882 investigation by the Illinois Bureau of Labor Statistics of 470 of "the more intelligent, industrious and prosperous" of Chicago's workingmen found the average wage of the family head to be two dollars to ten dollars a day, although over 60 percent of those investigated earned less than that for a day's wages and worked fewer than the 281 days of those investigated. The bureau estimated that two to ten dollars a day was insufficient to maintain "minimal living standards" for a family of four. Almost half of the families were forced to live "hand to mouth."[18] Two years later, another study of the bureau estimated that for the state as a whole 24 percent of the families were in debt at the end of each year and a further 9 percent managed to make both ends meet; on the basis of skill, 20 percent of skilled workers and 35 percent of the unskilled could not pay all of their expenses. In Chicago 30.5 percent of the families could not pay their expenses, and a further 18.6 percent could just barely meet them. In short, almost 50 percent of Chicago's working-class families were in debt or constantly on the edge of debt.[19] Finally, in a study of Chicago's immigrant population in 1907, the Immigration Commission estimated that for males eighteen years and over, 73.1 percent of foreign-born males, 60.7 percent of native-born males of foreign fathers, and 57.1 percent of native-born males of native fathers earned less than $600, at a time when the minimum family income necessary for subsistence was estimated to be $780.[20]

Frequent unemployment and layoffs greatly exacerbated the economic difficulties of the working-class family economy. A study by the U.S. Department of Labor of Chicago's Italian immigrant community in 1895 discovered that 57 percent of the Italian wage earners were unemployed during the year of the study: The average length of unemployment was seven months.[21] John Mayer estimates that in Chicago in 1890 the male heads of 38,705 families (18.1 percent of the total number of families in Chicago) were unemployed for eight weeks or more. Ten years later, the figure rose to 64,848, although the relative percentage was similar (18.0 percent). Mayer further estimates that an additional 1,883 widows in 1890 and 3,068 widows in 1900 were laid off for eight weeks or longer.[22] Even workers with regular employment frequently experienced layoffs, as Charles Bushnell discovered in a 1900 study of employment in three packing plants in Chicago. Bushnell calculated that the average unskilled workman lost eight and one-quarter weeks of work a year; skilled workers lost an average of three and four-fifths weeks a year.[23] For workers without a "regular" job, the situation, of course, was even worse. In a related analysis, Bushnell reported that the average period of unemployment in 1896 for "fifty representative cases" in the records of the county agent in the stockyards district was three and a half months in the course of the year.[24] Little had changed by 1901. In a study of the stockyards district, J. C. Kennedy found that not only did wages of workers decrease in the slack period but that in "some departments the workers lose approximately one-third of their time through unemployment." Layoffs averaged 10.9 weeks per unemployed worker. Approximately 25 percent of the workers studied experienced unemployment in the course of the year.[25] Among the working-class families suffering these hardships, very few relied on charity. Almost everyone depended on the earnings of children, and some on the income from working mothers, from boarders and lodgers.[26]

Although statistics on the number of working children are difficult to come by or generate, there can be little doubt that child labor provided the most significant source of supplemental income, both for skilled and unskilled workers.[27] In 1883 P. H. McLogan, a Chicago printer, described the plight of the unskilled worker thus:

> I don't see how it is possible they could lay up anything. They don't receive enough wages. They have to seek assistance from their children to live. In most cases the children of these day laborers have to go out as bootblacks or newsboys, or to run errands, or something of that kind, in order to earn a little money, because the father is not able to earn enough to support his family. Instead of laying up any money or anything of that kind, they are not able to earn enough to support themselves and their families.[28]

For Chicago's skilled workers, the situation seems only marginally better. The 1882 study of Chicago working-class budgets by the Illinois Bureau of Labor Statistics (IBLS) estimated that 20 percent of Chicago's working-class families depended upon income from wives and children (among immigrant groups the figures were far higher). The children of these families provided, on average, 36 percent of the family income. The IBLS study is replete with families unable to survive without help from children. One family, for example, headed by a German-born baker and consisting of the two parents and three boys ages sixteen, thirteen, and eleven, could not meet its yearly expenses of $600 with the income provided by the father ($450). To make up the difference, the oldest boy worked: "If it were not for the assistance rendered by the oldest son, their expenses would exceed their earnings." But even the income provided by working children often failed to meet the shortfall between expenses and income. A Scandinavian laborer, for example, with a wife and four children—nine-year-old male twins, an eleven-year-old boy, and a seven-year-old girl—could not sustain his family on his income of $405. The oldest boy worked, earning $200 a year, but the joint income of father and son fell short of the year's expenses ($632) by $27: "Live in a rented house, containing four rooms for which $8 per month is paid. House is a frame structure, poorly furnished with no carpets. They overrun their income."[29]

Similar patterns were to be found among working-class families in the decades that followed. In 1890 Mayer estimates that 8.8 percent of the 39,705 families with family heads out of work eight or more weeks relied on income from wives; 45.6 percent relied on income from children; and 25.9 percent relied on income from boarders and lodgers. (The categories are not inclusive nor mutually exclusive.) Supplemental income was important especially when the family was large and young; for families with male heads between the ages of forty-five and fifty-four, 78 percent depended on child income and 48 percent on boarders and lodgers. Ten years later, the pattern had altered somewhat, particularly with respect to dependence on child labor, dropping to 21.9 percent, although the reliance of these families on children remained high (40.9 percent). (See Table 3.1.)

Working class families thus relied heavily on children for supplemental income, although the degree of dependency varied with the family

Table 3.1 Percentage of Families with Income from Various Sources, by Age Distribution of Male Heads, Chicago, 1890 and 1900

	20–34	35–44	45–54	55 +	Combined
% of families with income from wives					
1890	14.0	9.0	8.0	3.0	8.8
1900	9.5	6.1	5.4	2.0	6.0
% of families with income from children					
1890	22.5	52.0	78.0	3.0	45.6
1900	10.5	25.0	37.4	1.3	21.9
% of families with income from boarders and lodgers					
1890	17.0	23.0	48.0	19.0	25.9
1900	14.6	19.7	40.9	15.2	22.1

Source: I. J. Mayer, "Private Charities in Chicago from 1871 to 1915" (Ph.D. dissertation, University of Minnesota, 1978), p. 459.

cycle. The level of dependency varied, moreover, by place of birth. When U.S. Department of Labor investigators studied social conditions in Chicago's slums in 1894, they found that foreign-born children between the ages of five and fourteen were more than four times more likely to be at work than native-born children (9.19 percent versus 2.16 percent respectively). (See Table 3.2.) More than twice the percentage of foreign-born children between five and fourteen were at school and worked compared to native-born children (3.7 percent and 1.23 percent respectively). Approximately equal percentages of native- and foreign-born children between five and fourteen were at home—more than likely to perform household work in the absence of working parents. Unfortunately, the Department of Labor did not differentiate between native-born children of native parents and native-born children of foreign parents. U.S. Immigration Commission figures for 1907 do, however, and indicate a considerable equalization of percentages for those at work, at school, and at home by place of birth. In particular, a considerably higher percentage of foreign-born children worked and a lower percentage attended school than native-born children in 1894. In 1907 the percentages were almost identical. (See Table 3.3.)

Child labor easily constituted the most important source of supplemental income to the working-class family, but it did not constitute the only source. The Immigration Commission figures for 1907 indicate that while approximately 25 percent of all families (irrespective of nativity grouping) secured a supplemental income from their children, approximately 10 percent of all families (again, irrespective of nativity grouping) also secured an income from working wives; moreover, 8.3 percent of families with native-born heads of foreign-born fathers, 10.6 percent of

Table 3.2 Percentage of Native- and Foreign-born Children (5–14) at Work, at School, and at Work and School, Chicago, 1894

Condition	Native-born	Foreign-born
Children at Home	29.22	26.17
Children at Work	2.16	9.19
Children at School	67.39	60.94
Children at Work and School	1.23	3.70
Total	100.0	100.0

Source: U.S. Commissioner of Labor, *Seventh Special Report. The Slums* (Washington, D.C., 1895), p. 76.

Table 3.3 Percentage of Children 6–15 at Home, at School, and at Work by Nativity, Chicago, 1907

Status	Nativity		
	Native-born of Foreign Father	Native-born	Foreign-born
At Home	8.9	9.4	9.7
At School	85.8	85.2	83.6
At Work	5.5	5.4	6.5
Total	100.0	100.0	100.0
number	1491	1604	518

Source: U.S. Immigration Commission, *Reports* (Washington, D.C., 1911), vol 66: p. 313.

native-born, and 37.3 percent of families with foreign-born heads also relied on income from boarders and lodgers (Table 3.4). The far higher percentage of families with foreign-born heads relying on income from boarders and lodgers prompted the Immigration Commission to conclude that "the immigrant family is on the whole dependent for its income upon a greater variety of sources than is the native family."[30] Yet, these figures only measure the percentage of families relying on supplemental income sources (the figures are not exclusive); they do not measure the relative contributions of each income source to the family income. The figures in Table 3.5 do so. As a percentage of the family budget, child labor easily accounted for the largest proportion in all nativity groupings, although it accounted for a noticeably higher percentage of the family income among families with foreign-born heads of foreign-born fathers (22.1 percent) than it did for families with native-born heads with foreign fathers (17.6 percent) and families with native-born heads (19.9 percent). Working wives contributed much lower percentages to the family economy, but the percentages did not vary by nativity. Families with foreign-born heads, however, derived a much higher percentage of their income (9.3 percent) from boarders and lodgers than families with native-born heads with foreign-born fathers (1.7 percent) or families with native-born heads of native fathers (3.0 percent).

Although differences between nativity groups are thus apparent with regard to child labor and boarding and lodging, differences among first generation immigrant groups are even more startling. In particular, marked differences in the ratio of the percentage of family income derived from child labor on the one hand and boarders and lodgers on the other characterized first generation immigrant families. For example, while Bo-

Lodgers, and Other Sources, by General Nativity and Race of Head of Family, Chicago, 1907

General Nativity & Race of Head of Household	Number of Selected Families	Percent of Families Having an Income From:			Payments of Boarders or Lodgers	Other Sources
		Earnings of:				
		Husband	Wife	Children		
Native-born of native father, white	22	61.8	4.5	27.3	18.2	9.1
Native-born of foreign father, by race of father						
German	44	84.1	9.1	22.7	11.4	15.9
Irish	28	92.9	10.7	25.0	3.6	7.1
Foreign-born						
Bohemian and Moravian	146	80.1	18.5	37.0	17.1	8.9
German	125	80.0	8.0	44.0	9.6	38.4
Hebrew, Russian	91	76.9	7.7	29.7	38.5	17.6
Hebrew, Other	29	86.2	0.0	27.6	41.4	3.4
Irish	78	84.6	3.8	44.9	17.9	15.4
Italian, North	53	88.7	13.2	28.3	56.6	7.5
Italian, South	219	95.4	18.7	24.7	17.4	1.8
Lithuanian	117	95.7	2.6	9.4	79.5	6.8
Magyar	20	90.0	0.0	15.0	65.0	0.0
Polish	338	80.9	6.8	20.7	43.5	13.3
Slovak	65	96.9	4.6	3.1	76.9	1.5
Swedish	113	77.9	20.4	36.3	42.4	2.4
Grand Total	1,495	87.4	10.4	26.3	35.7	11.8
Total native-born of foreign father	72	87.5	9.7	23.6	8.3	12.5
Total native-born*	94	86.2	8.5	24.5	10.6	11.7
Total foreign-born*	1,401	87.4	10.5	26.8	37.3	11.8

*NOTE: This table includes only races with 20 or more families reporting. The totals, however, are for all races.
Source: U.S. Immigration Commission, Reports (Washington, D.C., 1911), vols 26–27: p. 321.

Table 3.5 Percent of Total Family Income Within the Year, From Husband, Wife, Children, Boarders or Lodgers, and Other Sources, by General Nativity and Race of Head of Family, Chicago, 1907

General Nativity and Race of Head of Family	No.*	*Percent of Total Income From:*					
		Hus-band	Wife	Chil-dren	B & L**	Other	Total
Native-born of native father, white	22	78.7	0.8	8.8	7.8	4.0	100.0
Native-born of foreign father, by race of father							
German	44	69.8	3.6	14.9	2.5	9.1	100.0
Irish	28	68.7	1.1	25.2	.4	1.6	100.0
Foreign-born							
Bohemian and Moravian	146	53.6	3.5	33.8	5.8	3.4	100.0
German	125	50.8	1.2	34.2	2.7	11.2	100.0
Hebrew, Russian	91	54.8	.8	22.3	6.0	16.1	100.0
Hebrew, Other	29	69.8	.0	22.9	7.1	.1	100.0
Irish	78	53.5	.8	35.7	5.9	4.1	100.0
Italian, North	53	52.2	4.5	13.8	27.7	1.9	100.0
Italian, South	219	67.9	4.7	19.7	4.2	3.6	100.0
Lithuanian	117	75.2	.8	7.2	12.9	3.9	100.0
Magyar	20	54.1	.0	11.9	34.0	.0	100.0
Polish	338	66.6	1.9	15.5	10.1	6.0	100.0
Slovak	65	68.0	1.9	1.2	28.9	.0ᵃ	100.0
Swedish	113	61.6	4.7	21.1	7.7	4.9	100.0
Grand Total	1,495	61.4	2.4	21.8	8.8	5.7	100.0
Total native-born of foreign father	72	69.4	2.7	19.9	1.7	6.3	100.0
Total native-born	94	71.3	2.3	17.6	3.0	5.8	100.0
Total foreign-born	1,401	60.6	2.4	22.1	9.3	5.7	100.0

*Number of selected families.
**Payments of boarders or lodgers.
ᵃLess than 0.5 percent.
Source: U.S. Immigration Commission, *Reports* (Washington, D.C., 1911), vols. 26–27: pp. 290–91.

hemians and Moravians derived 33.6 percent of their family income from their children's earnings and 5.8 percent from boarders and lodgers, North Italians derived 12.8 percent of their income from children and 27.7 percent from boarders and lodgers. Slovaks were far more partial to income from boarders and lodgers (28.9 percent) than Poles (10.1 percent). Conversely, Poles were far more partial to income from working children (15.5 percent of the family income) than Slovaks (1.2 percent).[31] In effect, income derived from child labor and boarders and lodgers constituted alternative (although not mutually exclusive) strategies of income supplementation.

There is no data after 1907 as comprehensive as that provided by the Immigration Commission that allows conclusions to be drawn concerning the relative significance of child labor as a source of supplemental income. Nevertheless, a number of studies suggest that child labor continued to provide an important source of supplemental income, and that child labor resulted primarily from poverty-related causes. In 1912 Ernest Talbert reported that poverty proved by far the single most important determinant of child labor of children between fourteen and sixteen in the stockyards district.[32] A year later, Louise Montgomery conducted an intensive investigation of the labor of fourteen- to sixteen-year-old girls from 900 families in the stockyards districts and found 65 percent sent their daughters out to work at age fourteen because of the "actual need of the child's wages to supplement the earnings of the father."[33] The same year, 1913, Helen Todd, in a study of 800 wage-earning children, found that in 318 cases, the child worked either because of the death, illness, or injury of the father. Todd estimated that the average healthy life expectancy of the father of the child worker was probably no more than forty or fifty years of age. "Coming here as an out-of-door peasant, unused to our climate, to our machinery, to our highly specialized and speeded up industries," she wrote, "his health is rapidly undermined by the long hours of labor and the extremes of heat and cold, the lack of any protection from occupational disease, combined with insanitary housing, insanitary factories, and insufficient and adulterated food." So it was that while he was young and strong, the father could "stand the pace set by the machine, and keep himself and his family above the poverty line while his children are little." The impact of such hard physical labor in such harsh conditions inexorably ruined the father's health, and the decline of the family from near-poverty to dire poverty began. "By the time the eldest is about 14, his only capital, his physical strength, begins to wane. Some day, when he leaves the foundry, after from 12 to 14 hours' work over red-hot sand pits, at sixteen cents an hour, an icy chill stabs through his lungs as he comes into the winter air. So the family goes over the poverty line; the man either dies or comes through broken and weakened; and the children fall into the struggling, suffering, tumultuous mass at the very foot of the ladder."[34] Consequently, when Todd asked her subjects the question "What does your father do?" she invariably received answers like "He's sick," "He's got the brass chills," "He's got consumption," "He's paralyzed," "He can't use his hands," "A rail fell on his foot, and it's smashed," "He's dead—he got killed." Todd concluded:

These stories, told in the soft voices of little children, are endless. To the question, "Did your mother get any money from the company?" the answer is almost invariably, "No," or a shake of the small head, the child not caring to take enough strength from its work even to speak; and when you ask, "How many children are there besides you?" the answers usually range from five to seven. And when you say, "How many are there of you who are working?" the answer is sometimes one, sometimes two, seldom more; and often, without looking up, the child answers: "My mother—she works, and me." "And how much does your mother make?" "She makes eighteen cents an hour scrubbing downtown." "And how much do you make?" "I make six cents a thousand pasting on cigar bands." "And can you and your mother earn enough money to take care of the family?" "Yes, ma'am," she answers, "we gotta."[35]

Two further studies underline the continued precariousness of the family economy of the Chicago working class, even into the 1920s. In a 1914 study of 2,263 working children in Chicago by the Illinois Bureau of Labor Statistics, the bureau concluded that 23.2 percent left school and went to work at the request of their parents; 50.4 percent to help support the family; 2.1 percent to help support themselves; and 0.2 percent to support themselves. The IBLS concluded that overall, 76.15 percent of all the children left school to earn money to help provide for themselves and families. Finally, nine years later, in 1923, a study conducted by F. L. McCluer of 2,623 wage-earning families in Chicago found that even with the help of child labor and working wives, almost 30 percent could not reach a family income above the bare subsistence level. Were it not for these supplementary incomes, only 45.5 percent of families could reach a "comfortable" budget.[36]

Poverty or poverty-related causes also appear to provide the principal explanation of nonattendance, very often a disguised or indirect form of child labor. Poverty and poverty-related causes, for example, accounted for 50.5 percent of the 76 percent of all cases of nonattendance not attributable to physical handicaps in 1892, and 51.4 percent of the 54 percent of the same cases in 1900, as reported in the *Annual Reports* of the board of education (Table 3.6). A 1906 study by G. H. Britton of eight hundred

Table 3.6 Causes of Truancy and Nonattendance,
Chicago, 1892, 1900. By Percentage.

Year (1)	"Poverty"* Labor (2)	Home (3)	Illness (4)	Indif- ference, Incorrigi- bility (5)	Other (Physically Left City) (6)	Total (7)	Total 2 + 3 + 4 (8)
1892	23.3	10.7	16.5	25.5	24.0	100.0	50.5
1900	10.0	23.2	18.2	2.9	45.4	100.0	51.4

*Includes "poverty," "working out," "working at home."
Source: Chicago Board of Education, *38th Annual Report, 1892*, pp. 231–32; *46th Annual Report*, pp. 151–58.

forms of child labor found that parents often kept their older children out of school to baby-sit a younger child while the parents worked or to nurse a sick parent or sibling: "Children were found at home engaged in all sorts of housework and also in gainful occupations, either because their parents were indifferent to their education and preferred the small contribution to the family comfort made by the child, or because the illness or death of one parent or the extreme poverty of the family made even the child's help at home indispensible."[37]

Of the many case studies reported by Britton, two from the Dante School, one of a once-only truant, and the other of a "repeater," provide jolting reminders of the consequences of poverty for working-class educational behavior:

Louis B.—This child of nine years, whose parents were dead, lived with his grandmother and grandfather, neither of whom could speak English. The grandfather, besides having lost an arm, was ill and unable to work; the grandmother helped the family by picking up coal and wood on the railroad tracks, and occasionally picking and selling dandelions. Though fairly strong, she was too unskilled to do any sort of profitable work. The boy, the only other member of the family, paid the rent and supported his grandparents by the sale of newspapers. This he did entirely outside of school hours, having been absent only one day during the whole year and this day he went with his grandmother to interpret for her while she was trying to get a job picking rags on Canal Street. Louis finishes the fourth grade this year. They lived in one rear room for which they paid two and one-half dollars a month, and which was in fairly sanitary condition. It was needless to say that all the members of the family were without sufficient clothing to keep them warm and clean. What clothes the boy had were always in good repair, being generously covered with patches of different colors. He wore nothing under his little coat, not even a shirt. In the more prosperous days, the family had owned a white tablecloth which was cut up into kerchiefs to be worn around the neck of the boy to conceal the absence of the shirt. This is not cited as a case of school neglect, as the boy is doing well in school and was anxious to keep on, his ambition being to finish the school. It is plain that such a household is on a most precarious footing and that the boy's education and future usefulness are threatened by the hard work, the insufficient food and clothing and general scantiness of his life. A school pension for the fatherless child should be obtained. In the meantime, an arrangement has been made by which the monthly expenses for rent and coal have been met. The effects of his unchildlike struggle with poverty were shown by the boy's attitude toward the new suit of clothes which was provided for him. It was a gray suit and he objected to the color, preferring a black one because it would save a new suit in case one of his grandparents should die, an event which he thought quite likely to happen, as they were both very old.

Edward G.—This child of Polish parents, is the eldest of seven children; three of them are in school and four at home, the two youngest being twins. The father died two months before the birth of these babies. They were extremely poor, but in spite of the fact that they live in three rear basement rooms, the home and the children are well cared for. The mother goes out to work two or three days in the week and her average earnings are four dollars a week. She pays only three dollars a month for rent, however, and receives the county supplies. Edward, who is nearly 12, was kept out of school for a day at a time to take care of the children while the mother went to work. She kept the children out alternately, so that no one of them would lose very much time. There is no day nursery for the children of working mothers in this part of the city.[38]

At other schools in the district, similar stories could be told. A random sample of truants at the Komensky School (in a largely Bohemian and Polish neighborhood) disclosed that in each case "the children had been kept at home to help in various money-making occupations or to take care of the children so that the mothers could work." At the Oliver Goldsmith School, a Jewish school in the Ninth Ward, "a neighborhood of bad housing conditions—basement dwellings, overcrowded tenements, dark rooms, dirty streets," truants "were for the most part kept from school by their parents to do work of various kinds, and were, therefore, of working age, between ten and thirteen years, most of them from the third and fourth grades. None of them were incorrigible."[39]

A study of truancy and nonattendance in two schools, one on the West Side and the other on the North Side, by those two inveterate child-savers, Abbott and Breckinridge, in 1916 found that 79 percent of the families of nonattending children were either "very poor" or "poor." Some 48 percent of the cases were due to sickness of the child, 7 percent to the sickness of a sibling or parent, 12 percent to work at home, 7 percent for lack of shoes or clothing, and 4 percent for "interpreting" or "running errands." "No study of the causes of non-attendance of the city," they

concluded, "can fail to emphasize the fact that poverty is only too frequently the real excuse for non-attendance. In many cases where the father
is a decent, industrious workman in regular work, but with a large family
and small wages, it is impossible in the winter to 'get ahead.' The week's
earnings barely provided for the week's regular expenses of rent, fuel, and
food, and there is never any leeway, never, for example, any ready savings
for the next pair of shoes. It is astonishing how important the shoe problem is as a factor in non-attendance."[40]

Generally then, the labor of children fourteen to sixteen and the
nonattendance of younger children supplemented family income, the first
directly and the second indirectly, and helped keep the working-class family fed, clothed, and sheltered. Throughout the period, relatively high
proportions of working-class families sent their children fourteen to sixteen to work rather than to school. Nonattendance often represented a
disguised form of sporadic child labor or resulted from poverty-induced
causes (sickness, etc.). The income derived from child labor represented a
significant proportion of the total income of the working-class family, and
for the great majority of immigrant groups it was the most important
source of supplemental income. Family poverty or economic necessity
provided the principal motive for sending children to work rather than
keeping them at school.

Of course, even if working-class parents primarily sent these children
to work for reasons of economic necessity, it is entirely possible that these
same parents were also, in addition, antagonistic to schooling or indifferent to their children's welfare, as Progressive reformers often charged. On
balance, however, the evidence, although sketchy and circumstantial, and
based on aggregate and cross-sectional data rather than on individual and
longitudinal data (in which family income and child labor are directly
linked), suggests that working class parents primarily sent their children
to work because they were economically compelled to do so. Child labor
was neither capricious, arbitrary, nor insignificant but systematically
linked to the efforts of working-class families to find ways to provide for
the exigencies of survival. Even William Bodine, superintendent of Compulsory Education, a vigorous exponent of compulsory education, could
not deny it. Writing to Victor Olander on December 27, 1926, about a
proposal by Anne S. Davis, director of the Employment Certificate Bureau, to increase the grade requirement from sixth to eighth grade in
addition to the fourteen-year-old age limit, Bodine said that "many minors
from improvident families, even at age 14, find it hard to finish sixth
grade. . . . If raised to eighth grade, it would create hardship and misery
among thousands of juveniles who would become depressives and it

would increase truancy and delinquency among juveniles between 14 and 16." He went on to inform Olander that the truant officers in Chicago were "solidly against Anne Davis' drastic proposal, because they know the poverty conditions in Chicago. They know that many widowed mothers, with large families, are forced to have older children work. . . . It is a serious problem."[41]

In effect, patterns of child labor and nonattendance reflected working class strategies of economic survival. These strategies varied from one nativity group to another, and among first generation immigrant families. Some immigrant groups preferred to send their children to work, others to take in boarders and lodgers. Small though variable percentages of households of immigrant backgrounds included working wives. These differences reflected the impact of immigrant cultural traditions—the importance attached to privacy, the role of children in the family economy—on the struggle to survive, although they hardly represent the triumph of ethnicity over class. They reflect, rather, the interaction of cultural traditions and accommodation to the vicissitudes of survival in an economy based on wage labor. Yet other strategies—home ownership and school attendance—do the same.

THE POLITICAL ECONOMY OF HOME OWNERSHIP

The triumph of free labor had one particularly ironic outcome: It rendered economic independence an impossibility for all but a few. But if wage labor engendered lifelong economic dependency for most workers, it escalated the economic importance of home ownership. "The selection of a home," commented the *Workingmans Advocate* in 1874, "is the most important event of a lifetime," necessary "for stability and success," a "place of safety," security during a strike, and "the first step towards improvement in the condition of men."[42] If the family provided a haven in a heartless world, home ownership provided a refuge from the cold logic of wage labor.[43]

Purchasing a home, however, proved much more difficult than aspiring to home ownership and recognizing its economic significance as a hedge against frequent layoffs, recession, injury, illness, and old age. Less than 13 percent of Chicago's "prosperous workers" investigated by the Illinois Bureau of Labor Statistics in 1882 owned homes.[44] The 1900 manuscript census included data on home ownership, but historians have yet to undertake individual level analyses of home ownership in Chicago. Still, recent research on Philadelphia presents a picture that is unlikely to be substantially different for Chicago. Among skilled workers in Philadelphia in 1900, only 14.7 percent owned their homes; 11.2 percent of semiskilled and 9.2 percent of unskilled workers owned theirs. By contrast, 39 percent of professionals, 25 percent of proprietors, 33 percent of manufacturers, and 25 percent of foremen owned homes. Clearly, class position strongly influenced patterns of home ownership. When the figures are broken down by nativity, clear differences separate native white, Irish- and German-born heads of households on the one hand and Italian- and Russian-born heads on the other; 21.76 percent of native white heads owned homes, as did 30.24 percent of Irish-born and 28.76 percent of German-born heads. Alternatively, only 10.75 percent of homes with Italian-born heads and 3.96 percent of homes with Russian-born heads owned homes. It is significant that of the Italians who owned homes, 48.13 percent were proprietors, although proprietors accounted for only 1.46 percent of all Italians. In effect, nativity mattered, but not as much as class.[45]

If we assume that the pattern in Chicago did not differ dramatically from Philadelphia, the available data after 1900 suggests that patterns of home ownership altered significantly. In particular, the importance of class seems to have declined while the relationship between nativity and home ownership changed dramatically. Despite the very high level of poverty among immigrant groups in 1907, levels of home ownership among families with foreign-born heads (16.2 percent) matched the levels of home ownership among families with native-born heads of foreign fathers (16.8 percent) and the level among families with native-born heads of native fathers (18.3 percent). (See Table 3.7.) Clearly, immigrant families appeared willing to make extraordinary efforts to purchase a home. Moreover, they apparently continued to do so over the course of the next two decades, purchasing homes at a far higher rate than families with native-born heads. Between 1907 and 1930 the percentage of first generation families owning their homes jumped from 16.2 percent to 41.3 percent, an increase of more than 150 percent. (See Table 3.8.) Among some immigrant groups, the increases were particularly large. In 1907 only 7.4 percent of South Italians and 10.7 percent of North Italians owned homes; by 1930, 39.6 percent of all Italian families owned homes. (See Table 3.9.) In 1907, 7.2 percent of Slovak and 17.7 percent of Bohemian families owned homes; in 1930, 53.9 percent of all Czechoslovakians did so. Among Poles, home ownership increased from 17.5 percent to 49.0 percent; among Lithuanians, from 11.4 percent to 44.8 percent. By contrast, the rate of home ownership among native families increased by less than 2 percent from 16.8 percent to 18.6 percent, while among second

Table 3.7 Number and Percent of Families Owning Home, by General Nativity and Race of Head of Family

Chicago: 1907		*Owning Home*	
General Nativity and Race of Head of Family	*Number Reporting Complete Data*	*Number*	*Percent*
Native-born of native father, white	27	3	11.1
Native-born of foreign father, by race of father			
Bohemian and Moravian	1	—	a
German	60	14	23.3
Irish	41	5	12.2
Polish	1	—	a
Swedish	1	—	a
Foreign-born			
Bohemian and Moravian	222	41	17.7
German	178	82	46.1
Hebrew, Russian	214	23	10.7
Hebrew, Other	51	2	3.9
Irish	104	26	25.0
Italian, North	88	9	10.2
Italian, South	376	28	7.4
Lithuanian	166	19	11.4
Magyar	30	3	10.0
Polish	439	77	17.5
Servian	13	—	b
Slovak	83	6	7.2
Swedish	144	28	10.4
Grand Total	2,249	366	16.3
Total native-born of foreign father	104	19	18.3
Total native-born	131	22	16.8
Total foreign-born	2,118	344	16.2

aNot computed, owing to small number involved.
**Payments of boarders or lodgers.
bLess than 0.5 percent.
Source: U.S. Immigration Commission, *Reports* (Washington, D.C., 1911), vol. 26–27: p. 302.

Table 3.8 Percentage of Homeowners and Tenants by Population Group, Chicago, 1930

Population Group	Owners	Tenants	Unknown
All Families	31.1	67.9	1.0
White	32.7	66.3	1.0
Native	24.9	74.1	1.1
Native Parentage	18.6	80.3	1.1
Foreign or Mixed Parentage	29.2	69.4	1.1
Foreign-born	41.8	57.3	0.9
Negro	10.5	88.1	1.4
Other Races	1.6	95.7	2.7

Source: U.S. Bureau of the Census, *15th Census of the United States, 1930. Population, Families* (Washington, D.C., 1933), 6: p. 354.

generation families (native-born heads of foreign parents), the level increased from 18.3 percent to 29.2 percent. (See Table 3.8.)

Purchasing a home required great sacrifices even from families headed by skilled workers. Among semiskilled and unskilled workers, the sacrifices required were even greater. Usually, purchasing a home required the combined incomes of several household members or sources: the wages of the household head were rarely high enough to permit the family to save the large deposit required and to pay the two or three mortgage payments each year. In 1913 Louise Montgomery described the efforts of immigrant families to purchase homes in the stockyards district thus:

The ambition of the immigrant to own property is one of his most striking characteristics. For he will make almost unbelievable sacrifices both of his own comfort and of that of his wife and children, since the heavily mortgaged house too often calls for the united wage earning power of the entire family. . . . The strength of this feeling is due in part to the natural desire for a home, which in the stockyards district is intensified by a constant fear of reaching an early old age in helpless penury. The possession of a house from which one may draw an income is the highest mark of prosperity, just as the inability to pay one's rent is the lowest degree of poverty.[46]

Immigrant families had three possible sources of supplemental income: working wives, boarders and lodgers, and the income from working children. Data reported by the Immigration Commission for 1907 indicate that of these three sources, child labor contributed by far the highest proportion for each nativity group: the income from working children

Table 3.9 Percentage of Homeowners and Tenants Among Foreign-born White Families, Chicago, 1930

Country of Birth	Owners	Tenants
All Countries	41.8	57.2
England	31.0	67.9
Irish Free State	49.6	49.5
Sweden	43.6	55.5
Netherlands	55.8	43.3
Belgium	26.6	72.7
Germany	48.6	50.2
Poland	49.0	50.3
Czechoslovakia	53.9	45.1
Austria	42.3	56.9
Hungary	39.9	58.8
Yugoslavia	40.6	58.6
Russia	22.1	76.9
Lithuania	44.8	54.2
Roumania	28.1	70.9
Greece	17.8	80.8
Italy	39.6	59.3
Spain	13.0	84.8
Mexico	7.8	90.4

Source: U.S. Bureau of the Census, *15th Census of the United States, 1930. Special Report on Foreign-born White Families by Country of Birth of Head* (Washington, D.C., 1933), p. 129.

provided 19.9 percent of the total family income of second generation immigrant families, 17.6 percent for native families, and 22.1 percent for first generation immigrant families. (See Table 3.5.) By contrast, income from working wives provided 2.7 percent, 2.3 percent, and 2.4 percent for each nativity group respectively, and income from boarders and lodgers 1.7 percent, 3.0 percent, and 9.3 percent respectively. Moreover, the reports of the Immigration Commission indicate that while boarding and lodging provided close to 10 percent of the family income of first generation immigrant families, only families that had been in the United States less than ten years tended to rely heavily on income from boarders and lodgers: 44.3 percent of all first generation immigrant families living in the United States less than five years and 45.6 percent of all first generation immigrant families living in the United States between five and nine years. Less than 21 percent of those in the United States ten or more years relied upon income from boarders and lodgers.[47] (See Table 3.10.)

Table 3.10 Number and Percent of Foreign Households Keeping Boarders or Lodgers, by Nativity of Head in the United States, Chicago, 1907

Race of Head of Household	Number Reporting Complete Data	In the United States Under 5 Years			In the United States 5 to 9 Years			In the United States 10 Years or Over		
		No.	Keeping Boarders or Lodgers No.	%	No.	Keeping Boarders or Lodgers No.	%	No.	Keeping Boarders or Lodgers No.	%
Bohemian and Moravian	225	43	12	27.9	43	7	16.3	139	13	9.4
German	117	10	1	(a)	12	2	(a)	155	15	9.7
Hebrew, Russian	209	54	21	38.9	46	17	37.0	100	17	15.6
Hebrew, Other	50	11	5	(a)	26	7	26.9	13	5	(a)
Irish	102	2		(a)	5	3	(a)	95	13	11.7
Italian, North	76	24	11	45.8	20	12	60.0	32	10	31.3
Italian, South	359	71	13	18.3	119	19	16.0	109	18	10.7
Lithuanian	164	27	19	70.4	65	58	89.2	72	43	59.7
Magyar	27	10	8	(a)	8	3	(a)	9	4	(a)
Polish	439	103	61	59.2	125	74	59.2	211	39	18.5
Servian	33	27	7	25.9	4	2	(a)	2		(a)
Slovak	79	24	22	91.7	34	28	82.4	21	9	42.9
Swedish	148	3	1	(a)	13	5	(a)	132	49	37.1
Total	2,088	409	181	44.3	520	237	45.6	1,159	235	20.3

(a) Not computed, owing to small number involved.
Source: U.S. Immigration Commission, *Reports* (Washington, D.C., 1911), vol. 26–27: p. 292.

Although these figures are aggregate-level data and thus liable to suggest spurious ecological relationships between income sources and home ownership, the data nevertheless suggest a possible relationship between child labor and home ownership, namely, that children were sent to work to help the family purchase a home, and that in 1907 at least, working children provided the bulk of the supplemental income necessary to do so. Recent findings by Joel Perlman and Michael Katz that home ownership and school attendance were positively and strongly related (in Providence, Rhode Island, and Philadelphia, respectively) in 1900 in no way contradict this argument, for the argument simply presumes that parents sent children to work in order to generate sufficient savings to place a deposit on a home, or that parents sent them to work periodically when mortgage payments were due. In all likelihood, once a family had saved enough money to place a deposit on a house, younger siblings were kept at school rather than sent out to work, thus explaining the association between home ownership and school attendance noted by Perlman and Katz, although periodically even younger siblings were possibly sent out to work for short periods of time. All this, of course, is conjecture, but it is consistent with the available data, and from the perspective of class formation, entirely predictable: Patterns of child labor and home ownership resulted from the efforts of working class families to devise strategies to cope with unemployment, illness, injury, poverty, and old age in an economy based on wage labor but devoid of a meaningful social service system until the 1930s.[48]

After 1907 the picture becomes more complicated. The percentage of families taking in boarders and lodgers continued to decline: In 1907, 37.3 percent of families with foreign-born heads took in boarders and lodgers; by 1930, only 11.5 percent did so.[49] Simultaneously, the percentage of working wives increased substantially: In 1920, 10.4 percent of married women in Chicago were "gainfully employed"; ten years later, 14.6 percent were gainfully employed.[50] Furthermore, the proportion of children ages fourteen and fifteen not at school from families with foreign-born heads plummeted from 45.1 percent in 1910 to 5.7 percent in 1930; among youth sixteen and seventeen years old from similar families, the percentage declined from 87.1 percent to 49.6 percent, with the bulk of the decline occurring during the 1920s. (See Table 3.11.) Without individual-level statistics it is impossible to determine the relationship between child labor and home ownership, but it appears likely that families who purchased homes by 1920 relied far less on income from working children while relying more on income from husbands and working wives.

Although the details of the financing of home ownership among

Table 3.11 School Attendance by Age Cohort and Population Group, Chicago, 1910–1930

	7–13			14 and 15			16 and 17			18, 19, 20		
	1910	1920	1930	1910	1920	1930	1910	1920	1930	1910	1920	1930
Native white of native parentage	56,460	88,747	138,946	13,182	17,014	33,826	7,010	8,006	21,956	4,202	5,074	12,540
% of total school population	69.8	63.0	74.0	16.3	12.0	13.6	8.6	6.1	8.8	5.1	3.6	5.0
% of age cohort	93.4	94.2	97.3	80.6	80.9	96.3	41.4	41.3	65.2	16.2	16.0	23.6
Native white, of foreign or mixed parentage	157,513	196,671	208,810	33,470	32,709	66,013	12,188	11,649	37,945	4,975	5,517	16,005
% of total school population	75.6	69.6	56.3	16.0	11.5	17.8	5.8	4.1	10.2	2.3	1.9	4.3
% of age cohort	89.4	90.4	96.8	54.9	62.9	94.3	12.9	20.9	50.4	3.6	6.3	15.0
Foreign-born, white	24,161	16,946	11,037	4,094	5,568	3,125	1,456	2,405	6,592	1,343	1,274	2,594
% of total school population	77.8	57.4	37.0	13.1	18.8	10.4	4.6	8.1	22.1	4.3	4.3	8.7
% of age cohort	89.4	90.4	97.2	80.1	82.5	93.1	38.9	38.7	56.9	7.6	6.3	15.0
Negro	2,680	7,798	20,831	729	1,961	4,863	365	946	3,203	152	435	1,673
% of total school population	68.4	60.2	56.3	18.6	15.1	13.1	9.3	7.3	8.6	3.8	3.3	4.5
% of age cohort	91.8	92.2	96.8	80.1	82.5	93.1	38.9	38.7	56.9	7.6	8.1	15.2
TOTAL	240,844	310,269	381,820	54,192	57,275	108,147	20,967	23,621	66,848	10,691	12,367	33,996
% of total school population	74.3	66.5	55.3	15.8	12.2	15.6	6.4	5.0	9.6	3.2	2.6	4.7
% of age cohort	91.8	93.6	97.4	80.1	72.6	94.6	38.9	29.1	57.8	7.6	9.8	18.2

Source: For 1910 and 1920, E. Burgess and C. Newcombe, eds., Census Data of the City of Chicago, 1920 (Chicago, 1931); for 1930, U.S. Bureau of the Census, 15th Census of the United States, 1930. Population, II: 1,143.

working-class families are thus not fully apparent, there can be little doubt about the commitment of the Chicago working class to home ownership, nor about the significance of home ownership to the remaking of the Chicago working class. The spread of home ownership among the Chicago working class represented both a strategy of survival and self-respect in a market society and an institutional rearrangement of working-class culture that reinforced and consolidated what was still, in 1900 or 1910, a relatively fragile bifurcation of working-class culture into a politics of the workplace, centered on the trade union, and a politics of the neighborhood, hitherto centered on the political machine, saloons, churches, and voluntary associations, but that thereafter also included home ownership and school attendance. But home ownership also contributed to the remaking of the Chicago working class in an additional way by reinforcing the ethnic and above all the racial homogeneity of working-class neighborhoods. Determined to protect the market value of the costly investments they had struggled so hard to make, and wanting to live among their own kind, working-class homeowners bitterly resisted the efforts of blacks to purchase homes or rent in white neighborhoods. Although competition in the labor market and conflict at the workplace contributed to the racial segmentation of the Chicago working class, home ownership proved no less potent.

How much so became apparent during and immediately after the "great migration" of blacks from the South in the mid to late teens, and in the events leading up to the race riots of late July–early August 1919. As blacks began to move into white neighborhoods, white homeowners formed property owners protective associations, as the Chicago Commission on Race Relations put it, "for the purpose of preserving property values," and engaged in systematic campaigns of intimidation, foreclosures, exclusions, terror, bombings, and even murder, although the homeowners associations denied responsibility for the bombings and the killings.[51] The Commission concluded that white fears (unfounded, according to the Commission) of declining property values as a result of the black "invasion" were a major underlying cause of the bloody riots—resulting in the death of thirty-one persons, mostly black—of July 1919.[52] Home ownership did not create a bifurcated working-class politics, but in addition to the triumph of pure and simple unionism and machine politics, and the ethnic and racial fragmentation of the Chicago working class, it helped consolidate the split within working-class politics that marked the remaking of the Chicago working class.

SCHOOL ATTENDANCE AND CLASS FORMATION

In 1913 when Helen Todd asked 500 working children in Chicago the question "If your father had a good job and you didn't have to work, which would you rather do—go to school or work in a factory?" 412 children replied that they would rather work in a factory. Many of the reasons had to do with the children's dislike of being in school, but Todd believed that most of the reasons were economic in nature—the children could clearly tell the economic difference between a report card and a pay envelope. "Once I worked in a night school in the Settlement, an' in the day school too," said one child. "Gee, I humped myself. I got three cards with 'excellent' on 'em. An' they never did me no good. My mother she kept 'em in the Bible, an' they never did her no good, neither. They ain't like a pay envelope."[53]

Yet most children did go to school, and not just those required to do so by the law. Between 1910 and 1930 the percentage of the fourteen-to-fifteen age cohort of native white children of native parentage increased from 80.6 percent to 96.3 percent; for native white children born of foreign or mixed parentage, from 66.3 to 94.4 percent; for white foreign-born children, from 54.9 to 94.3 percent; and for blacks, from 80.1 to 93.1 percent. The sixteen-to-seventeen age cohort exhibited an equally dramatic upward trend: for native white children of native parentage, school attendance increased from 41.4 percent in 1910 to 65.2 percent in 1930; for native white children of foreign or mixed parentage, the percentage increased from 22.6 to 54.7 percent; for white foreign-born children, from 12.9 to 50.4 percent; and for blacks, from 38.9 to 56.9 percent (see Table 3.11). While it is true that for both age cohorts significant differences existed in 1910, and some differences still existed in 1930, what is perhaps more striking is the identical upward tendency in all nativity groups and the flattening out of interethnic differences by 1930. Yet this trend occurred despite the existence before 1910 of highly variable matrices of child labor and school attendance among immigrant groups, and despite evidence that in 1907 differences in educational achievement were not related to differences in parental occupation, length of parental residence in the United States, standardized test scores, use of English in the home, and age of school entrance, but to group or ethnic values.[54] Moreover, children from all ethnic groups stayed on at school beyond the point required by compulsory education laws. The question then is Why? Why did more and more children, irrespective of ethnic (and presumably, class) background, stay at school for longer and longer periods of time even though they were not required to by law?

Of the possible reasons that could explain these changes in educational behavior, four in particular stand out. First, the persistent decline in the demand for the labor of children and youth, considered in the previous chapter, limited the opportunities of working-class youth to enter the work force. Second, the growth of credentialism and the putative association between length of school attendance and economic success engendered a reevaluation of the economic significance of education and a growing appreciation of the value of investment in human capital. The findings of a 1922 study by L. F. Merrill of the educational aspirations of 596 eighth-grade students in the Seventh District in Chicago, for example, provide a hint of this transformation. The Seventh District was a highly congested, poor immigrant area, one in which "many nationalities are represented," although "the standard of living in the various neighborhoods is fairly comparable." Overall, for all groups, 426, or 71.6 percent, of the eighth graders planned to go on to high school. (See Table 3.12.) The percentages varied from a high of 81 percent for Jews (discounting the one Greek case as statistically insignificant) to a low of 58 percent for Bohemian and Polish children. Of primary interest, however, is the high

Table 3.12 Educational Aspirations of District 7 Grade School Children, Chicago, 1922

Nationality or Race	Total in Group	Going to High School	Percent	Not Going to High School	Percent
Jewish	126	102	81	24	19
American white	96	71	74	25	26
Italian	92	54	59	38	41
Bohemian	84	49	58	35	42
Colored	63	59	90	4	10
Lithuanian	37	25	68	12	32
German	32	21	65	11	35
Polish	31	18	58	13	42
Swedish	9	4	89	1	11
Russian	9	8	90	1	10
Irish	8	7	89	1	11
English and Canadian	7	6	86	1	14
Greek	1	1	100	0	0

NOTE: The information about nationality was taken from the given birthplace of the father and does not necessarily imply foreign birth of the child.

Source: L. F. Merrill, "A Report Concerning the Plans of 596 Children on Leaving Eighth Grade," *The Chicago Schools Journal* 5 (1922–23): 156.

proportion of children from all ethnic groups who desired to go on to high school.

Of the 426 children going on to high school, over half were the first in their respective families to have gone beyond the grammar grades; and only 31 parents had ever attended a high school. *Many principals have mentioned the definite change that has come during the last few years in the attitude of both parents and children toward further education.* The social as well as the industrial value of high school is an important factor in increased high school attendance."

Third, it is likely that the improvement in the economic welfare of the immigrant family permitted parents to keep their children at school for longer periods of time. Michael Katz and Joel Perlman found that home ownership and school attendance were directly and positively related in Philadelphia and Providence in 1900. Their findings, together with the evidence for Chicago outlined above, suggest an intriguing hypothesis linking the immigrant family cycle, domestic economy, child labor, school attendance, and home ownership: As immigrant families acquired homes, immigrant parents felt increasingly able to keep their younger children at school for longer periods of time. Initially immigrant educational behavior reflected the struggle of the immigrant family to survive the vicissitudes of a wage labor system, for example, through generating sufficient money for a down payment on a home. But later, when a measure of economic security had been achieved, immigrant educational behavior reflected the efforts of parents to ensure the economic survival of their children in the same system.

Finally, partly out of a passionate desire to preserve their cultural-identity and ethnic solidarity, large numbers of Catholic immigrants actively and liberally supported the cause of Catholic parochial schooling, building by 1930 hundreds of elementary schools and more than two dozen high schools. In 1890 Chicago's Catholics enrolled 31,053 students in 62 elementary schools in the city and a further 1,571 students in schools in the suburbs; by 1930, 235 elementary schools in the city enrolled 145,116 students and 88 schools in the suburbs enrolled another 23,729 students. Catholic secondary schooling grew even more rapidly: from 1,348 students (city and suburbs) in 1890 to 17,913 students in 25 high schools in 1930. During the 1920s alone, the number of students in Catholic high schools almost doubled. (See Table 3.13.) Out of deference to interethnic aspirations and hostilities, however, Chicago's Catholics did not build a single uniform system of parochial schools. Rather, they built and supported parochial schools on an ethnically differentiated parish basis. Although absurdly uneconomical and inefficient, Chicago's Catho-

Table 3.13 Growth of Catholic School Enrollments, Chicago, 1880–1930

| Year | Elementary | | High School | |
	City	Suburbs	City	Suburbs
1880	16,710	1,019	950	65
1890	31,053	1,571	1,283	65
1900	49,638	2,313	3,640	69
1910	84,429	5,349	7,084	356
1920	112,735	12,169	8,685	427
1930	145,116	23,729	15,663	2,350

Source: Figures from *Official Catholic Directory of Chicago* (1880–1930) are cited in J. W. Sanders, *The Education of an Urban Minority* (New York, 1977), pp. 4, 5. Reproduced here with permission of Oxford University Press.

lics would have it no other way: They did not measure the benefits of their ethnically differentiated system in terms of economies of scale, but in terms of culture—the teaching of the native language, the protection of national identity, the binding of generations together. Along with the parish church and the voluntary associations connected with the church, the parochial school provided a major locus of social life and group relations, a principal instrument for what Thomas and Znaniecki called the "unification and organization" of the immigrant community. A 1900 diocesan publication, surveying the state of the Catholic church in Chicago at the beginning of the new century, organized the section on Catholic schools along ethnic lines, treating each group as a separate system.[66]

And well it should have. The two dominant Catholic groups prior to the 1890s—the Irish and the Germans—built separate parish churches and schools, even in neighborhoods in which both Germans and Irish resided. In Bridgeport in 1883, for example, the Irish supported three schools and the Germans two. By 1930, Irish children attended 29 Irish schools, while German children attended 33 German schools. Czech Catholics opened their first Czech Catholic parish in 1864; by 1937, they had opened ten more, each with its own school. Poles organized their first Catholic church, St. Stanislaus Kostka, in 1867. By 1900, the parish was the largest Catholic parish in the world with more than 50,000 members, a school enrollment of 4,000 pupils, and 50 different church organizations (including, it might be noted, a home savings and loan organization). By 1918, Poles supported 37 major Catholic parishes with 351,000 members and 37,976 children in parish schools. In 1930 Polish Catholics supported 42 schools in Chicago and 12 more in the industrial suburbs; even as late as 1940 some 50,000 pupils attended Polish elementary schools and six high schools. Slovaks opened their first parish, St. Michael's, in the stock-yards district in 1898; in 1914 they supported seven parishes, all but one with a parish school. Only Italians showed little interest in supporting parochial schools—or Catholic churches for that matter. In 1910, with some 45,000 native-born Italians and 28,000 second generation Italians in the city, all but one of the ten parishes had been established at the behest and with the financial support of the archdiocese; only one had a school. The difference of Italian Catholics should not obscure the fact, however, that in 1930, 56 percent of Chicago's Catholics attended ethnic churches, while 53 percent of Catholic school pupils attended separate ethnic schools.[57]

Each of these four developments—the decline in the demand for child labor, the changing perception of the economic value of schooling, the evolution of the domestic economy of the immigrant working class, and immigrants' efforts to protect their cultural identity and ethnic soli-darity—independently pushed school attendance upward. But immigrant families usually kept their children at school only after experiencing con-siderable conflict and tension between competing pressures. One involved a conflict between the decline in the demand for child labor and the immigrants' need for supplemental income; a second involved a tension between two conflicting forms of economic necessity—making a sufficient living to survive on a daily basis and sending children to school in order that they might make an adequate living after leaving school; a third involved a tension between the apparent economic necessity of investing in their children's education and the fears of many immigrant parents that prolonged schooling, public schooling especially, would undermine pa-rental authority, cultural identity, and ethnic solidarity.

Different immigrant groups handled these tensions in different ways, depending on their convictions about the role of children in the family economy, the economic value of schooling, and the relationship between schooling and cultural identity. Yet despite these initial differences, over time the differences eroded as immigrants gradually created common or parallel class practices—they kept their children at school for increasing lengths of time, although often in ethnically differentiated parochial schools. Increased levels of school attendance, on the one hand, reflected the economic remaking of the educational behavior of the Chicago work-ing class: the decline in the demand for child labor, altered perceptions of the economic importance of education in a society in which economic success in the market system seemingly depended on educational achieve-ment, and improvements in the family economy of the immigrant working class. The growth of parochial schooling, on the other hand, reflected the preferred solutions of many immigrant families to the conflict between investment in human capital and cultural identity. The transformation of the educational behavior of the immigrant working class did not result then from the activities of Progressive reformers, nor did it represent the creeping cultural "embourgeoisiement" or Americanization of the immigrant working class. Rather, it reflected two important aspects of the remaking of the Chicago working class: the structuration of educational behavior by the market system and the creation by immigrants and their children of viable ethnic communities.

Something of the character of this process can be illustrated by reference to the educational history of the various Slavic groups (Poles, Slovaks, Croatians, Czechs, Slovenians) in Chicago. High levels of child labor and home ownership, and relatively low levels of school attendance, attested to the Slavic belief that steady and reliable work and home ownership, not schooling, were the principal routes to economic security. In their homelands, education had been of no practical value, and it was inconceivable that it was of any value in the blast furnaces of South Chicago or the meatpacking plants of the stockyards district.[58]

The largest Slovak community in Chicago centered on St. Michael's parish, in the southwest part of the city, essentially a working-class parish whose location, as Stephen Palickar pointed out, "was due to its accessibility to manufacturing and packing plants offering employment to the Slovaks." Coming to Chicago "poor and industrially handicapped," they found employment "in many of the large industries near the site of [their] church. . . . The packing plants, steel and wire mills, rubber plants, and large corporation houses." Gradually, "through the practice of thrift, they . . . become the owners of homes." By 1920, St. Michael's had become "a district of home owners, of comfortable single or two-family houses, neat yards with well tilled gardens."[59] What characterized Slovaks also characterized, in varying degrees, other Slavic groups, reflected in the statistics for home ownership and child labor and the great vitality of Slav building and loan associations in Chicago.

Croatians established the first Croatian building and loan association in 1910, and despite the poverty of the Croats, deposits and loans steadily increased. By 1935, the organization had loaned over $4 million for mortgages.[60] Polish immigrants were similarly active in forming building and loan associations and banks in Chicago; by 1937, at least 30 Polish building and loan associations could be found in Chicago. In 1912, 106 of 227 building and loan associations in Chicago were Czech with assets of more than $10 million.[61] In 1904 J. M. McCullough, the Illinois auditor of building and loan associations, attested to the strength of the Polish and Bohemian building and loan associations. McCullough noted "their steady growth and general success," and counted 81 such associations "in the territory bounded by Twelfth Street on the north and Halstead Street on the east, embracing the great stockyards district," with $6.2 million in assets and a membership of twenty-eight thousand.[62]

The level of their home ownership reflected the vitality of the Slavic building and loan associations in Chicago. In 1910, 17.5 percent of foreign-born Poles owned homes; by 1930, the percentage had increased to 49 percent. In 1910, 17.7 percent of Bohemians and Moravians and 19.4 percent of Slovaks owned homes; by 1930, 43.9 percent of Czechoslovakians owned theirs, and 40.6 percent of Yugoslavians were homeowners.

High levels of home ownership accompanied high rates of child labor and low rates of school attendance. Like most immigrant groups, Slavs made extraordinary sacrifices in order to purchase a home as a form of economic insurance against unemployment, underemployment, and old age. One Polish family in Chicago in 1916 with nine children, the father a frequently unemployed teamster, was described by Breckinridge and Abbott as a "low grade family with an extremely dirty home and dirty, ragged children," yet significantly was "trying to buy the tenement in which they live, but it is mortgaged for $12,500."[63] Almost 21.0 percent of Polish families sent their children to work in 1907, providing 15.5 percent of the family's income. Among Czech-Moravian families, 37 percent sent their children to work, accounting for 33.8 percent of the family's income. The different proportions among the Slavic groups can be explained by the different propensities of each immigrant group to take in boarders and lodgers. Thus, while Czechs had a very high rate of child labor and acquired a high percentage of their family income from their children's earnings, only 17.1 percent of the Czechs derived income from boarders and lodgers, while among Polish families 21 percent sent their children to work but 43.5 percent took in boarders and lodgers (contributing 10.1 percent of the family budget).

Yet despite the heavy reliance in the Slavic community on child labor, from about 1910 influential voices in the community began to draw out the economic consequences of too little education. In May 1909 a Polish newspaper, *Dziennik Zwiazkowy*, observed that yesteryear education meant little in gaining employment, but that "today . . . whether we are laborers or office workers, it takes on a different meaning, and in many instances education is becoming a strict requirement."[64] The following month the same paper claimed that parents who did not send their children to school were "not looking after their children properly."[65] Another Polish newspaper, *Narod Polski,* a week later urged Polish parents to keep their children at school beyond the legal minimum age limit because, it said, "today we must seek the gold and treasures of this world not only by a spade or a shovel, but with the help of knowledge, and that with the help of it you can gain importance, influence, power and well-being."[66] In 1910 *Dziennik Zwiazkowy* argued that Polish children should be sent to school because "this would elevate our people from the ranks of ordinary manual laborers to that of civic and social leaders. Money should serve for the acquisition of education, and education will in turn bring monetary benefits to those who possess knowledge."[67] The following year the same paper told Polish workers, "Today you are a common workingman selling your energy and health for only a very small compensation, because you have no qualifications that would entitle you to a better position."[68] And it was not only a grammar school education that was required. By 1917, Polish newspapers were paying detailed attention to the value of high school education.[69] At the beginning of the school year in 1919, *Polonia* urged Polish parents to send their children on to "higher education" in order to protect the "future of their children."[70] In 1927 another Polish newspaper, *Przebudzenie,* put the immigrant argument in a nutshell when it commented that whereas in the past education had been an elite luxury, "Today it is a necessity. A man with no education is a cripple, and a burden to himself and his community."[71]

Similar sentiments appeared in the Czech press by 1915. At the beginning of the new school year in 1915, *Denni Hlastel* stressed the duty of Czech parents to send their children to school. Czech parents should give their children, "if possible . . . an opportunity to acquire the best and most complete education within their reach," since "if a man wants to get somewhat decent employment—and it may be far from being profitable—he is required to prove that he is educated, that he has schooling; lacking it, as well as some 'uncle' to give him the necessary pull, he has no chance whatsoever." The paper reminded its readers of the significance of the reserve army of the unemployed. "Labor is plentiful, and consequently, the employers are 'choosey.' Even for manual, unskilled labor they make their choice among the most likely men." Czech parents would be wise to send their children to school, not to work. Moreover, the paper went on, "Do not stop with primary school. Send your children to higher schools, send them to colleges, and you will never have to fear that life will be unkind to your children." The economic future of their children depended on education:

By keeping your children in school you will do them the most good. You may leave them money, but that will be spent. You may leave them a fine residence, it may burn; it may deteriorate sooner or later. You may leave them a farm, but a cyclone may turn valuable property into a desert. But give them an education, and there is nothing in the whole world that can take it away from them. . . . Education is a most valuable dowry. Without it their life struggle will be hard; with it, comparatively easy.[72]

Although Slavic parents sent growing numbers of their children to school for longer periods of time, they remained decidedly skeptical, however, about sending their children to public schools. If at all possible, Slavic parents enrolled their children in Slavic Catholic parochial schools where the children could be taught their particular native language and so become full members of their respective ethnic communities. The *Chicago Record Herald* reported in 1903 that although Polish parents appeared anxious to have their children learn English, Polish parents made sure that their children "never sacrifice their native language. In parochial schools . . . they are taught in English for four hours a day and the balance of the time in Polish, Polish history, literature and kindred subjects being studied in the native tongue." Eleven years later, a Polish newspaper, *Dziennik Zwiazkowy,* explained why:

One of the most important subjects awaiting the pupils of Polish schools and college is the Polish language, because knowledge of it will lead our young people to become acquainted with our history, our accomplishments, and the pearls of our literature. Even a slight knowledge of these things will be a shield against loss of our national identity and submergence in the boundless sea of Americanism.[73]

And as if unsure that Polish parochial schools were sufficient to protect the Polish language, Polish immigrants established by 1932 upward of sixteen "Polish Language Supplementary Schools" to teach Polish children the Polish language. Indeed, to know the Polish language was not only his obligation as a Pole, but his duty as a Catholic. "A Pole who says he is a Catholic but who is ashamed of or neglects the Polish language," one Polish writer wrote in 1904, "is not a Catholic."[74] Similar views pervaded the sentiments of other Slavic groups, and what Thomas and Znaniecki concluded of the Polish parochial schools was equally true of the others:

Good or bad, the parochial school is a social product of the immigrant group and satisfied important needs of the latter. The most essential point is neither the religious character of the parochial school, nor even the fact that it serves to preserve in the young the language and cultural traditions of the old country; it is the function of the parochial school as a factor of the social unity of the immigrant colony and of its continuity through successive generations.[75]

The educational remaking of Slavic immigrants in Chicago nicely illustrates how the interaction between immigrant traditions and social-structural conditions created a Slavic working class similar in its cultural practices to other ethnic groups but separated from them institutionally (churches, schools, voluntary associations, saloons, and so on). Arriving in America doubting the economic value of education and faced with the necessity of surviving low wages, frequent layoffs, injury, illness, and old age, Slavic parents devoted their early years to accumulating sufficient funds, in part through income derived from sending their children to work, to purchase a home; as they gradually came to recognize the economic importance of education, and as the condition of their family economy permitted, they kept their (younger) children on at school for longer periods of time. Out of a concern, however, to consolidate an emergent cultural identity and preserve group solidarity, they did not send their children to public schools, if they could help it, but to Catholic parochial schools. The interaction between immigrant traditions, social-structural conditions, and the desire for cultural identity and group solidarity in time produced an entirely new kind of cultural formation: a Slavic ethnic working class itself internally divided along ethnic lines.[76]

Other immigrant groups also undertook similar reevaluations of the economic significance of education. Southern Italians came to America deeply suspicious of the need for schooling, public or private. As one observer of Chicago's Italians commented:

"We are contadini." This phrase from the lips of the immigrant Sicilian is most revealing as to his social attitudes. The Chicago Sicilians have come largely from the villages and open country of Sicily, where they were poor, illiterate peasants, held down by the *gabelloti* or landlords in a state little better than serfdom. Generations of this condition have led them to look upon this status as fixed and as the horizon of their ambition. Why should *contadini* send their children to schools to bother their heads with letters? And besides, in Sicily, the boys go to work in the fields at fourteen. Why should they not go to work here?[77]

But not only did the South Italian immigrant believe schooling economically unnecessary, he also believed that it threatened the integrity of family life. Education was a family affair, not a matter of state, and the family, as Rudolph Vecoli suggests, was the focus of the South Italian's "most intense loyalties."[78] Leonard Covello remarked that given the primacy of the family in the affections of the South Italian, the South Italian considered "the home as the best institution for transmitting this knowledge in a manner calculated to maintain compliance to, and conformity with, the mores of his social group. The desire for security in his way of living was directly opposed to education from outside the home and its immediate environment." "Next to the difficulties of the parents themselves in making the necessary economic and social adjustments," Covello concluded, "the prospects of compulsory school education for their children threatened the very foundations of orderly family life."[79]

The desperate economic plight of the South Italian immigrant and his hostility to schooling resulted in extremely high levels of child labor and low levels of school attendance. A U.S. Commissioner of Labor study in 1897 of Chicago's Italians found that 5.88 percent of Italian children between the ages of five and fourteen were at work, while another 32.12 percent were kept at home and 4.3 percent both worked and went to school.[80] Ten years later, 12.7 percent of all South Italian children between six and sixteen worked, and a further 7.5 percent stayed at home; during the course of 1907–08, almost 25 percent of all South Italian families derived an income from their children. (See Table 3.4.) By the early 1920s, however, South Italian attitudes had begun to change. Merrill found that fully 59 percent of Italian eighth-grade children intended to go on to high school, a fact that surprised Merrill: "The 59 percent of the Italian children planning on high school calls for an interpretation, for this is not a nationality which ordinarily sends a large number on to high school." On further investigation, she discovered that the girls wanted sufficient education to enter the textile trades while one Italian boy told her, "I want an office job" so that he could be "clean and not digging in the dirt and building sewers."[81] Six years later, Giovanni Schiavo reported that "the Italians in Chicago, even the poorest and most ignorant, value education. . . . The poor Italian realizes that today education is more necessary than ever in the struggle for life and is anxious to give his children what he was unable to get for himself."[82]

In contrast to Slavic and Southern Italian immigrants, Jewish immigrants came to America strongly predisposed to value educational achievement.[83] For centuries, education had represented learning, the exigetical study of the sacred texts, and the survival of the Jews themselves. Louis Wirth, in his study of Chicago's Jews, noted that "the association between school and synagogue has always been close. Before and after the services, the Jews studied in the synagogue, read, and argued about the 'law' and the commentaries of the rabbis." Rabbis were the religious and intellectual leaders of the Jewish community, and "learning has always been a primary duty and a mark of distinction for every Jew."[84] In their European homelands, Jews had often enforced compulsory education upon their children as a matter of religious creed and racial survival. Polish Jews, for example, enforced compulsory education "centered around the Bible and the Tal-

mud, for all children between the sixth and thirteenth year."⁸⁵ Lest Jews
forget the role of education in the survival of Judaism, the *Daily Jewish
Courier* reminded its readers in 1914 that "Jerusalem was destroyed because it neglected the education of its children."⁸⁶

Chicago's Jews were no strangers then to a positive appreciation of
education. But where Jews had historically identified education with learning and learning with religious duty and cultural survival, the exigencies
of economic survival in America forced on Jewish immigrants a very different conception of the value of education. "The struggle to earn a living," reported the *Daily Jewish Courier* in 1916, had forced the retreat of
the traditional view of education:

At one time, Jews did not study with a view to earning a livelihood. Study was
wholly separated from material advantage! Individuals studied because it was their
sacred duty to do so. . . .
    In the last couple of generations, conditions in the . . . world have undergone
a complete change. The struggle to earn a livelihood has sharpened, and life has
begun to require more essentials.⁸⁷

Many Jewish parents found "modern conditions" difficult to accommodate to and inimical to the survival of Judaism. In 1914 the *Courier*
noted the painful dilemma faced by many Jewish parents: "Every Jewish
mother wishes earnestly that her child will grow up to be an educated man
or woman," the paper asserted. "Practically, without any exceptions, all
Jewish parents spare no efforts to give their children a good education.
But, unfortunately, all parents cannot attain their desire. Why? Simply
because of the high cost of living and the low wages people receive. To
keep a child in school doubles the cost of living."⁸⁸ Jewish parents and
community leaders also fretted about the survival of Judaism or the Jewish
"struggle for self-preservation," as the *Jewish Forward* put it in 1924.⁸⁹ To
allay their fears, Jews opened synagogue classes in the afternoons and
weekends to teach Jewish language and religion, established all-Jewish
elementary and secondary schools, and supported further literary, folk,
and musical societies.⁹⁰ Yet despite their economic situation and desire for
"self-preservation," more than 90 percent of eighth-grade Jewish children
(and 90 percent of "Russian" children) intended to go on to high school
in 1922, according to L. F. Merrill. She commented that "the Jewish
children, keen minded and ambitious, are usually anxious to take whatever
educational advantages come their way."⁹¹ Apparently Jewish parents felt
able in the long run to reconcile the sacred and the profane, as suggested
by the Yiddish lullaby: "My Yankale shall learn the law/The law shall baby
learn/Great books shall my Yankale write/Much money shall he earn."⁹²

America might not be the Promised Land, but it could surely be the land of promise.

In principle, several explanations of changes in the educational behavior of immigrants in Chicago (noted in Table 3.11) are possible. It is possible to argue that such changes reflect a successful strategy of social control—the imposition by Progressive reformers of "American" values and behaviors upon a recalcitrant and resentful immigrant working class. The evidence, however, does not support such an interpretation. It points instead to an explanation focused on the process of class formation: the remaking of the Chicago working class. The education history of immigrant groups in Chicago illustrates, first of all, the ability of the requirements of survival and success in a market system to mold the educational aspirations and educationally related behaviors (child labor, home ownership, school attendance, etc.) of immigrants, and second, the creation of an ethnically differentiated working-class culture. The first represents the structuration of working-class educational practices by the system of class relations, while the second illustrates something of the process through which immigrants created an identifiable working-class culture, characterized by distinctive working-class cultural practices, yet often internally differentiated along ethnic lines.[93]

Still, even if it is granted that processes of social control do not explain working-class educational behavior, it might yet be argued that neither does a theory of class formation, at least one that emphasizes the remaking of the Chicago working class. It could be argued, for example, that in sending their children to school beyond the age required by law, and doing so because they wished to enhance the value of their children's human capital, working-class parents adopted a form of behavior distinctively bourgeois in character. That is, the changing pattern of working-class educational behavior could well represent a form of embourgeoisie-ment, and not the remaking of the Chicago working class. The difficulty with this argument is that it arbitrarily assumes that school attendance is a purely bourgeois behavior when it makes far better sense to regard school attendance, whether by middle-class children or working-class children, as an accommodation to bourgeois social relations—above all, to markets in labor, including credentialing markets—by both middle- and working-class families as the condition of their respective family economies permitted. We might perhaps describe this accommodation as an instance of "structural" embourgeoisiement since it involved an accommodation of working-class educational behavior to bourgeois class relations, but there is certainly no evidence that the transformation of working-class educational behavior reflected a process of "cultural" embourgeoisiement, given the growth, vitality, and relative autonomy of a distinctive working-class culture throughout this period—the culture of parish churches and schools, saloons, union halls, work place associations and organizations, fraternal societies, and the texture of family and neighborhood life.[94] The remaking of the Chicago working class, not cultural embourgeoisiement, provides a more convincing explanation of changes in the educational behavior of the immigrant working class.

Progressive Reform and the Remaking of the Chicago Working Class

In the midst of widespread fears of a "growing separation of classes," bloody battles between labor and capital, severe economic depression, extensive poverty, rampant corruption, and a host of other social evils, Progressive reformers mounted during the 1890s a sustained attack on the abuses of the market revolution and the deterioration of class relations. They opened settlements in working-class neighborhoods, established mechanisms to arbitrate conflicts between employees and employers, secured or strengthened child labor and compulsory education laws, founded parks, playgrounds, kindergartens, a juvenile court, and a system of probation, provided temporary relief, and transformed charity into a professionalized social service function, organized civic reform groups, secured mother's pensions and mother's compensation legislation, and undertook moral purity and temperance crusades.

Despite the obvious success of Progressive reformers in creating a plethora of reform organizations, mounting one reform effort after another, and securing reform legislation or statutes, the extent and nature of the impact of all this activity on working-class people is not at all self-evident or obvious. Social settlements were not entirely trusted by working-class people, and there is no evidence that settlements ever became important working-class institutions or significantly influenced working-class life; there is no evidence that working-class people admired Jane Addams as much as her middle-class supporters in the suburbs. We have some idea of what the juvenile court did to delinquents, but we have little or no idea about the influence of probation on the working-class family or how working-class people might have put the juvenile court and the probation system to their own uses. Child labor declined and school attendance increased, but only in part because Progressive reformers secured child labor and compulsory education legislation. All-out assaults on capital by labor decreased after 1894 not because industrial arbitration settled labor-capital conflicts before they got out of hand but because the legal system severely restricted the ability of labor to confront capital and because organized labor increasingly focused its attention on bread-and-butter issues. Civic reformers assailed political corruption and machine politics, only to see their initial successes followed by levels of political corruption at least equal to that of the 1890s and a system of machine politics far more intractable than anything experienced before 1900. Jane Addams at least had the good sense to realize, after several unsuccessful efforts to unseat Johnny Powers in the Nineteenth Ward, that the working class needed Johnny Powers as much as he needed them.[95] Finally, while the threat of revolution receded, the separation of classes did not cease and the working class did not disappear.

Unwilling to reverse then the market revolution transforming American life, Progressive reformers could perhaps inhibit the growing separation of classes, but they could not halt the process of class formation— they could no more unmake the Chicago working class than they could prevent its remaking. Certainly reformers could and did alter the political and institutional contexts of working-class life and influence working-class behavior in one way or another. Child labor and compulsory education legislation, and the legislation creating the juvenile court and the probation system, limited parental autonomy in ways that had not been limited before and undoubtedly forced some parents to send or keep their children at school when they might not have done so before. Worker's compensation and mother's pensions facilitated the economic survival of the working-class family, but at the same time opened the door to the intrusion of professional case workers into the family. The introduction of manual training and vocational education courses made schooling more attractive to many working-class parents. Progressive reforms, however, were only one component of the overall social experience of the Chicago working class, and by no means the most important. Work experiences, neighborhood and community life, ethnic and racial antagonisms, the imperatives of survival imposed by wage labor, and the pursuit by working-class individuals and families of strategies of survival, resistance, accommodation and cultural identity also shaped working-class behavior. Child labor, school attendance, home ownership, and church membership were part of this process of class formation, representing the development of common class practices, albeit differentiated along ethnic and racial lines. The product of these social experiences and strategies was not a pale facsimile of middle-class culture but a "remade" working class organized around a bifurcated politics of the workplace on the one hand and machine politics, home ownership, saloons, churches, voluntary associations, and school attendance on the other.

Chapter 4

THE TRIUMPH OF VOCATIONALISM

Between 1880 and 1930 public education in Chicago underwent an industrial revolution. This revolution occurred at both institutional and ideological levels: new curricula, new pedagogies, new schools, and new purposes. Nothing like it had happened to public education before, and nothing comparable has happened to it since.

Rumblings of the impending revolution could be heard as early as the mid-1870s. In 1877, for example, Josiah Pickard warned the board of education that the "wants" of Chicago's schools "bear about the same relation to the wants of fifty years ago as the locomotive with its train bears to the lumbering coach." Circumstances change, he said; the "schools of half a century ago will not suffice for a model" to meet "the demands of the times." Agriculture had declined as the predominant form of productive activity, to be replaced by industry and commerce, "the minute subdivision of labor," and mechanization. The schools had to adapt themselves to these changes. Chicago required an education that provided students with practical skills, a virtuous character, a "wider intelligence and a more facile hand," "manual skill," and "habits of industry." By "giving our system of instruction more of an industrial bias," some headway would be made toward redirecting children's aspirations away from "office seeking, professional and mercantile life" and toward "manual pursuits" and reestablishing an equilibrium between the school and "the wants of the day."[1] Some years later, in 1884, and again in 1887, Superintendent George Howland, noting the growth of the city and the decline of the family, argued that the school had to begin "to aid the individual in gaining a living" by teaching children "the art of self-guidance and self-help" and the habits of "punctuality, order, system, subordination and industry."[2] In the half century that followed, a coalition of businessmen, Progressive reformers, and educational officials succeeded in transforming the curriculum and, in part, the pedagogy and the organization of public schooling in Chicago into "adjuncts" of the market economy.[3]

THE ORIGINS OF VOCATIONAL EDUCATION: THE TRANSFORMATION OF WORK

The origins of the demand for a practical vocational education lie in the transformation of work in the years following the Civil War. Four aspects of this transformation stand out: the growth in scale of the work site, the replacement of simple forms of control and supervision by technical and bureaucratic forms, the transformation of the labor process, and the development of differentiated labor markets.

Prior to the Civil War most manufacturing establishments in Chicago were small and catered to the local market, scattered around the city in small handicraft shops and manufactories (work settings with extensive division of labor but without external sources of power) making shoes, bread, jewelry, cigars, hats, metalware, soap, coffins, rope, and a thousand other items of daily existence. By 1870, iron and steel, transportation equipment, agricultural implements, slaughtering and meatpacking, clothing, cooperage, and furniture manufacture had been mechanized and often employed large numbers of workers in one plant. Before the war, factories were the exception; after the war, they rapidly became the norm.[4] Between 1870 and 1919, the average size of manufacturing establishments in Chicago increased from 25 employees to 48.[5] In those industries dominated by large corporations, the average size was far greater: In railroad car manufacturing the number of workers had reached 805 by 1919; in electrical machinery, 127; in iron and steel, 734; in slaughterhouses and meatpacking, 1,140. In 1850 the McCormick plant numbered 150; by 1900, it had grown to 4,000, and in 1916, to 15,000 workers. Pullman, in 1875, employed 600 men; ten years later, 2,700, and by 1893, 5,500.[6] By 1919, while the number of manufacturing establishments in Chicago employing less than five workers accounted for 46.1 percent of the total number of firms, such establishments employed only 24.9 percent of the total number of employees. On the other hand, the number of establishments employing over 1,000 workers accounted for only 0.4 percent of the total number of establishments, but they employed 29.3 percent of the total number of employees. Alternatively, while 92.1 percent of all establishments had fewer than 100 wage earners, they employed 28.7 percent of the labor force; those firms employing more than 100 wage earners accounted for 7.5 percent of the total number of manufacturing establishments, but employed 71.4 percent of the total number of wage earners. Clearly, by 1920, the large factory had replaced the manufactory and craft shop as the dominant mode of employment.[7]

The growth of large factories ruptured the simple personal forms of supervision and control of labor characteristic of smaller firms.[8] When firms were small, capitalists exercised power personally. When firms grew in size, bureaucratic modes of control appeared, although even in some of the larger factories founders and owners maintained active supervision on a day-to-day basis until the 1880s. At the McCormick works through the 1870s, for example, Cyrus and Leander McCormick personally ran the factory, knew most workers by their first names, and demanded hard work and loyalty from their men in exchange for good wages, fair treatment, and reasonable working conditions. One employee described the personal relations between Cyrus McCormick and his employees this way:

He knew how to get the spirit into his men. At Blue Island [the location of the McCormick factory after the fire of 1871], we worked seven a.m. to five thirty, with half an hour for lunch; and when there was a rush of orders, it would be often midnight for us. I don't mean we had to stay unless we wanted, but most of us did—not only because we got overtime pay, but because he would make us feel like that—because he was one of us, understand? No white-collar boss but right on the job, workin' hard with sleeves rolled up on some new gadget that had gone wrong. He knew machines like his own mother. While he was livin' we had one boss—and if anything went wrong, you could go right to him and get it fixed up. In these days of big companies, you have a dozen bosses—and where are you? With Old Cy, we knew. When he died, there were mourners in our crowd, for now we had lost him, and we knew we'd never have a boss like him again.[9]

By the late seventies this system of "simple" control had disappeared. A small army of foremen, supervisors, and superintendents exercised direct control of the labor force. They in turn reported to higher-level managers located miles away in downtown Chicago. Within the plant, bureaucratic procedures and rules institutionalized the impersonal exercise of power. Well might the Reverend H. Newton, in his testimony before the Senate committee investigating the relations between labor and capital, explain that modern industry had destroyed the close social relationships between employee and employer, thereby destroying the bond that kept labor and capital in harmony. The old community of interest between worker and employer had been superseded, he said, by a "new feudalism" in which "a master rarely deals directly with his hands. Superintendents, managers, 'bosses' stand between him and them. He does not know them; they do not know him."[10]

Simultaneously, as firms grew in size and complexity, they acquired the accoutrements of corporate expansion: growing numbers of accountants, management experts, industrial relations experts, production engineers, and marketing experts, who made plans and gave orders, and a small army of clerks with numerous titles and grades, who filled out orders, processed sales and inventories, and filed receipts and expenditures.[11] Between 1880 and 1920 the percentage of clerical, sales, and kindred workers in Chicago almost doubled, from 14.77 percent of the labor force to 27.86 percent of the labor force. Yet this percentage figure hides the dimensions of the absolute increase. Between 1890 and 1930, the number of clerical workers increased fivefold, from 55,352 to 255,495. Office hierarchies appeared. The basis of the hierarchy, as C. Wright Mills observed, was "the power and authority held by the managerial cadre, rather than . . . the level of skill."[12] The office hierarchy consisted of a ladder from stenographer-typist to secretary, and very infrequently to office manager. Firms recruited executives from alternative channels. A clear job ceiling existed for office workers, particularly women. Few ever became secretaries; even fewer had the chance of becoming the office manager.[13]

The organizational structure of the supervisory staff at the Hawthorne plant in Chicago in the late 1920s illustrates the nature of the social division of labor and bureaucratic control of employees. In general terms, the company combined both line and function organizational arrangements. The company divided the plant into functional units in which each unit performed a group of logically related and interdependent activities. But within each functional unit "line control" provided the general method of control. In their study of the Hawthorne plant, Roethlisberger and Dickson observed that the supervisory system was not so much "technical" as "social." The distinctions between workers, they argued, are

not distinctions of the fact but distinctions of sentiment, and they do not coincide with the technical discriminations of the organization. From a technical standpoint, that is, from the standpoint of manufacturing telephones efficiently, these distinctions are not implied. The supervisory organization as a method of control involves no such discriminations about social distance between ranks. . . . There is, from a strictly technical standpoint, no difference in importance between the work done by men and the work done by women, or between the work done by clerks and the work done at the bench.[14]

The dimensions of the growth of the bureaucratic white-collar work force in Chicago can also be illustrated by the growing importance of

administrative, relative to production, personnel in fifty major manufacturing industries in Chicago for the period 1890 to 1930. The number of
administrative personnel relative to the number of production workers
increased in 78 percent of the fifty industries, while it decreased in only
22 percent of the industries. The average ratio for all industries in 1890
was eleven to one; by 1930, five to one.[15] In 1910, approximately one in
twenty workers in manufacturing and construction held foreman status;
by 1940, one in ten.[16]

To some observers, these changes in the structure of authority within
the workplace suggested the appearance of an "industrial army." Charles
Bushnell described a packing plant in Chicago in terms of "a thoroughly
organized and highly trained industrial army." The superintendent, corresponding to the colonel of the regiment, commanded the unit. Immediately below him served an assistant superintendent (lieutenant-colonel),
and several division superintendents or staff aids (orderlies). The company
divided the plant itself into departments (battalions), each with its own
department superintendent (major) and its own staff of clerks and assistants. The company then divided each department into subdepartments
"at the head of which are sub-department superintendents, corresponding
to the captains of companies, and under these sub-department superintendents were assistants and subordinates, corresponding to the lieutenants,
sergeants, and corporals." At the bottom, the "rank and file" of the industrial army worked away.[17] The metaphor gained remarkable currency in
the years to come among Chicago's educational reformers.

Along with the expansion in the scale of the productive enterprise
and the creation of a new social division of labor to control the labor
force, the last quarter of the nineteenth century also witnessed a major
transformation of the labor process, and, as a consequence, a shift in the
character of the demand for skilled labor. Prior to the 1880s, workers in
most American industries exercised considerable control over the labor
process. Even after the industrialization of the labor process (the use of
external power and extensive mechanization) and the rise of the factory,
skilled workers in some industries, David Montgomery reminds us, still
exercised authority over decisions about input mix, rate of output, type of
technology, number of workmen, hours of work, wages, shop floor discipline and management, and often the hiring of their own co-workers. The
functional autonomy of craftsmen, Montgomery suggests, "rested on both
their superior knowledge, which made them self-directing at their tasks,
and the supervision they gave to one or more helpers."[18]

Toward the end of the late nineteenth century such situations grew
increasingly rare as skilled craftsmen lost control of the labor process.

Marx described this trend as the shift from "formal" to "real" subordination in order to differentiate between the development of capitalist property relations (the wage labor system) and the creation of a specifically capitalist labor process in which the organization and control of the labor process was under the aegis of capital rather than labor. The essence of the history of the labor process under capitalism is not to be found, as Harry Braverman and Kathy Stone suggest, in deskilling or the separation of conception and execution as a consequence of Taylorism and scientific management, but in the shift from formal to real subordination and reconstruction of the labor process upon a new social and technical basis. Deskilling characterized the labor process in some industries (shoemaking and textiles, for example) for much of the nineteenth century, decades prior to the advent of Taylorism. The shift from formal to real subordination provides a more comprehensive basis for approaching the history of the labor process under capitalism, and takes the burden of explanation away from any single development (the factory system, Taylorism) and locates it instead in the complex, varied, uneven process of the reconstitution of the labor process upon a new social and technical basis.[19]

The sources of this shift, and its scope, depth, and timing, varied from industry to industry, and from one time period to another: the effort to control and market the artisans' total product in order to prevent embezzlement; the attempt to increase output and productivity through specialization, lengthening the working day, speeding up the labor process, and mechanization; the desire to control the level and pace of technical innovation for the sake of accumulation rather than leisure. In the shift from formal to real subordination three mechanisms played particularly significant roles: specialization, mechanization, and Taylorism. Manufactories introduced specialization; mechanization arrived with the application of external sources of power and the invention of factories; and Taylorism appeared during the first two decades of the twentieth century. Of the three, mechanization proved the most important, a product of competition between capitalists seeking ways to lower unit costs through improving productivity, and of class conflict between labor and capital, from informal struggles over absenteeism and output restriction, to more "formal" struggles over control of the labor process and job conditions.[20] In real dollars, using capital per employee in 1880 and capital per wage worker in 1920 for close to fifty industries in Chicago, average capital per employee/worker increased nearly fifteen times from a mean of $1,112 in 1880 to $15,871 in 1920.[21] But whatever the motive, mechanization enabled capitalists to assume greater control of the labor process by destroying the irregular work patterns of handicraftsmen, displacing the intelligence of the artisan with the rhythms of the machine, and reconstituting the division of labor and wage hierarchies on an entirely new technical and social basis. Taylorism did little more than advance this process and legitimate it.[22]

The logic of the specialization of the labor process characteristic of corporate capitalism in Chicago did not escape Chicago's manufacturers. One newspaper reporter described how a Chicago manufacturer of railroad cars in 1890 would

> . . . make the manufacturing of cars as economical as possible. He compared it with the system used in Pullman for the construction of passenger and sleeping cars. At Pullman, the tracks are run into the building so as to stand across the width of it, and there the cars are built and remain on the same spot until finished, when they go to the paint shop. Mr. Harvey's plan is to run the tracks lengthwise through the building and have a certain part of the work done at one hand; then move the car along a little to a spot where the next stage of the construction is done; and so on until it is finished. This will keep the workmen, tools, and machinery for certain works at certain spots, and not only save time and expense, but also develop greater efficiency in the men, as they will be confined to a certain branch of work and always remain at the same spot.[23]

The meat slaughtering and packing industry employed the same strategy. Prior to the 1890s, highly skilled craftsmen slaughtered beef. Before the advent of large slaughtering and packing houses, and the extension of oligopolistic control over the industry and the reorganization of the labor process, cattle butchers were all-round skilled craftsmen. They knew the butchering business in all its details and could kill and dress a bullock with the aid of one or two helpers.[24] During the 1890s, however, the large packers introduced a new labor process based on an extensive division of labor. By 1894, when skilled workers went out on a sympathy strike with Pullman railroad workers, the division of labor had reached a point where skilled butchers found themselves replaceable with unskilled black strikebreakers.[25] According to Homer Call, the owners "divided the business up into groups consisting of enough to dress the bullock, one man doing only one thing . . . which makes it possible for the proprietor to take a man in off the street . . . and today the expert workers are, in many cases, crowded out and cheap Polackers and Hungarians put in their places."[26]

Ten years later the highly skilled workers—"the butcher aristocracy"—accounted for only a very small fraction of the workforce, according to John R. Commons. He suggested that "notwithstanding the high skill required, the proportion of skilled workers in the butchers' gang is very small, owing to a minute division of labor." In fact, Commons went on to argue,

It would be difficult to find another industry where division of labor has been so ingeniously and microscopically worked out. The animal has been surveyed and laid off like a map; and the men have been classified in over thirty specialties and twenty rates of pay, from 16 cents to 50 cents an hour. The 50 cent man is restricted to using the knife on the most delicate parts of the hide (floorman) or to using the axe in splitting the backbone (splitter); and, wherever a less skilled man can be slipped in at 18 cents, 18-½ cents, 20 cents, 21 cents, 22-½ cents, 24 cents, 25 cents, and so on, a place is made for him, and an occupation mapped out. In working on the hide alone there are nine positions, at eight different rates pay. A 20 cent man pulls off the tail, a 22-½ cent man pounds off another part where the hide separates readily, and the knife of the 40 cent man cuts a different texture and has a different "feel" from that of the 50 cent man. Skill has become specialized to fit the anatomy.[27]

Specialization in the clothing industry wrought similar consequences. Prior to the 1870s, a tailor made an entire garment. Following the introduction of "team work" in the 1870s, a division of labor crept into the production process, making it unnecessary for most of the workers to be skilled tailors. Unskilled immigrant labor, employed in teams by the contractors, replaced skilled journeymen. The clothing manufacturer, instead of keeping journeymen tailors in his own shop, or sending the clothing to the homes of individual workers, turned over the cut cloth to a contractor, who then employed one or more teams of workmen. Within a coatmaking team, for example, one man did the machine stitching, another sewed on the sleeves, another did basting, another made buttonholes, another did pressing. A girl did the "finishing" and sewed on the buttons. A minute division of labor characterized the whole process, reported the Illinois Bureau of Labor Statistics in 1892:

The minute subdivision of the work in the sweators shops reduces the skill required to the lowest point. The whole number of employees, therefore, in all the outside shops, includes, besides a few of the skilled, who would under the old system, be employed in the inside shops, a majority of unskilled hands of both sexes, earning low wages, easily replaced, and wholly at the mercy of the sweator. Subdivision thus reaches its highest development; operators stitch, pressers press, basters baste, button girls sew on buttons, others draw basting threads, and finishers finish. Sometimes one girl, with a buttonhole machine, makes a specialty of the inside bands of knee pants, making buttonholes by the thousand gross. On the other hand, coats requiring buttonholes made in cloth, and with more skill, are sent by the contractor to a buttonhole shop, where two or three young men work machines, and where small boys or girls shear the holes in preparation for them.[28]

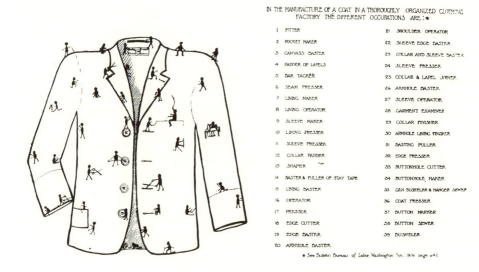

IN THE MANUFACTURE OF A COAT IN A THOROUGHLY ORGANIZED CLOTHING
FACTORY THE DIFFERENT OCCUPATIONS ARE : *

1	FITTER	21	SHOULDER OPERATOR
2	POCKET MAKER	22	SLEEVE EDGE BASTER
3	CANVASS BASTER	23	COLLAR AND SLEEVE BASTER
4	PADDER OF LAPELS	24	SLEEVE PRESSER
5	BAR TACKER	25	COLLAR & LAPEL JOINER
6	SEAM PRESSER	26	ARMHOLE BASTER
7	LINING MAKER	27	SLEEVE OPERATOR
8	LINING OPERATOR	28	GARMENT EXAMINER
9	SLEEVE MAKER	29	COLLAR FINISHER
10	LINING PRESSER	30	ARMHOLE LINING FINISHER
11	SLEEVE PRESSER	31	BASTING PULLER
12	COLLAR PADDER	32	EDGE PRESSER
13	SHAPER	33	BUTTONHOLE CUTTER
14	BASTER & PULLER OF STAY TAPE	34	BUTTONHOLE MAKER
15	LINING BASTER	35	GEN BUSHELER & HANGER SEWER
16	OPERATOR	36	COAT PRESSER
17	PRESSER	37	BUTTON MARKER
18	EDGE CUTTER	38	BUTTON SEWER
19	EDGE BASTER	39	BUSHELER
20	ARMHOLE BASTER		

* See Bulletin Bureau of Labor Washington Nov. 1906 page 642

Diagram 1.[29] The Division of Labor in Coat Production

By 1906, little had changed. Weyl and Sakoliski noted a complex and minute division of labor based on extensive mechanization and specialization, each garment passing through the hands of between 50 and 100 people.[30] In the manufacture of coats, they listed 39 separate occupational titles alone. R. J. Myers concluded in 1920 that textile mechanization and specialization brought about "appreciably reduce[d] skill requirements."[31] And, as in the meatpacking industry, the existence of a reserve army insured labor discipline and easy substitution of recalcitrant or militant workers.[32]

Much the same story can be told of the building industry after 1880. Over time, specialization in the various building trades increased. Factories began to prefabricate sheet metal products. "Greenhorns"—unskilled boys and immigrants—trained to do one specialized job, flooded the market.[33] Apprenticeship in the building trades atrophied, as a representative of the Chicago Trades Assembly, P. H. McLogan, testified before a congressional committee:

We find that in the various wood-working departments of trade there are thousands of children employed. Take cabinetmaking, for instance. Formerly a boy went into a cabinetmakers shop and learned the trade, but since the introduction of labor saving machinery, the cabinetmakers will put them into the cabinet shop to do a certain part of the work that they can easily learn to do in a short time. Take a bureau, for example; these boys will learn to make, say, one twenty-third part of a bureau; that is, they learn to do a certain little piece of work by means of labor saving machinery, and there they remain from year to year making that same little piece, and then all the pieces are put together, and the bureau is made. The same rule applies in other trades, in fact, in almost all the other branches of mechanical industry, so that it is very difficult for a boy to learn a trade at all.[34]

Specialization and mechanization also transformed the metal trades industries. Prior to the Civil War, the farm implements industry, for example, local mechanics, wheelwrights, and blacksmiths manufactured farm implements. Cyrus H. McCormick made the first Virginia reaper in a blacksmith shop in Virginia, and John Deere produced his steel plow in a blacksmith shop in Grand Detour, Illinois.[35]

For many years manufacturers were content with a shed and the most primitive implements. The essential in the production of casting was thought to be a group of skilled artisans. The moulder was supreme. He was supposed to be coremoulder, and cupola tender all in one. He cut over his own sand, shook out and cleansed his own castings, and had very little to work with except iron, fuel, sand and a few simple tools. Though rough and dirty; moulding was yet a highly skilled trade requiring technical proficiency, in which the processes, many of them apparently simple, demanded long training and experience.[36]

But gradually, over the years, mechanized methods replaced these hand methods as the McCormicks attempted to break the control of the skilled molders and machinists crafts over the production process.[37] Other skilled workers at McCormick—the machinists, blacksmiths, and pattern-makers—experienced a similar fate. During the late eighties and the nineties, all the "skilled crafts were broken down into a series of simple, repetitive operations to be performed by unskilled or semi-skilled workers with the aid of improved machinery."[38] And what was true at McCormick was true in other metal trades industries. By 1901, commentators estimated the existence of at least twenty-five different styles of molding machines in use in the country, and that machinery had replaced skilled labor with semiskilled or unskilled labor. Weyl and Sakolski noted that "a moulding machine put on the market in 1904 is almost completely automatic in its operation, merely requiring an attendant, who lifts the flask off and sets it to one side, blows the sand from the table by means of an air hose, and all is ready for renewing the process."[39]

These changes dramatically affected skill levels. Stecker concluded that while the introduction of machines lowered production labor costs, "probably more important than any other consideration to the employer, the installation of molding machines lessened his dependence on journeymen mechanics. Machines having been invested in, the working force in a foundry could be changed with but little inconvenience, for the skill required for molding was still present in the wood and metal of the machines, while new operators were easily broken in." Prior to mechanization, "brains" had been embodied in the molder; after mechanization, brains were embodied in the machine. By 1918, it took from only three to six weeks to "transform a common laborer into a first class machine moulder."[40] Not surprisingly, the demand for skilled labor decreased and the demand for semiskilled labor increased. In the farm implements industry, for example, the percentage of unskilled machine operators in the molding labor force increased from 9.4 percent to 22.9 percent, while the percentage of skilled workers dropped from 75.7 percent to 51.8 percent between 1900 and 1913.[41] Twenty years later the Federal Trade Commission observed "everywhere the development of the industry has meant increasing differentiation between the mental and the manual work, more intense simplification of processes, more minute specialization of tasks." Consequently,

Among the employees of farm equipment factories, a small proportion consists of highly skilled mechanics for tool making, experimental work, and pattern making; another small proportion is made up of skilled workers in certain operations such as tempering, welding, heat treating, moulding and coremaking; a large proportion consists of semi-skilled labor, conducting routine operations in which machines are adjusted to produce required accuracy of results and in assembling the various parts; and finally, there is a considerable number of purely unskilled laborers.[42]

In the steel industry, a similar transformation in the skill composition of its labor force occurred. Following the reorganization of the steelmaking process in the 1890s, the proportion of skilled workers steadily declined. By 1908, only about 17 percent of steel workers were skilled; 21 percent were semiskilled, and 62 percent unskilled.[43] Five years later the U.S. Labor Bureau reported that since 1890, the introduction of mechanical processes in the steel industry had replaced skilled workers "with unskilled laborers or with semi-skilled workers who can be recruited by the thousands whenever it is necessary."[44] The immediate effect of the new production process dramatically altered the composition of the labor force in the steel industry, decreasing the relative importance of skilled workers, and increasing the relative importance of semiskilled and unskilled workers.[45]

In a 1921 review of the effects of specialization and mechanization, Paul Douglas of the University of Chicago concluded that specialization lowered the amount of skill required in three major industrial categories: machine building industries, machine using industries, and machine repairing industries. In most machine using industries, specialization had reduced the need for skilled labor to a mere fraction of earlier levels.[46] In machine building industries, while there were a "large number of highly trained and competent engineers" in the drafting room, the remainder of the labor force required "muscle and endurance rather than skill and dexterity." Only in the small number of machine repairing trades did Douglas indicate a corps of highly trained and skilled workers, "the aristocracy of the labor force," who carried out repairs to the machines used in the production of goods or other machines.[47]

The transformation of the skill composition of the Chicago labor force can be measured quantitatively through an analysis of Chicago's occupational structure. Changes in the labor process were reflected in census statistics on changes in the occupational structure. The decline in skilled work as a result of the transformation of the labor process was reflected for manufacturing in general by a significant decline in the relative proportion of skilled workers in the Chicago labor force as a whole over the fifty-year period 1880–1930, dropping from 26.7 percent to 17.12 percent. Simultaneously, the various categories of semiskilled increased considerably: The percentage of "operatives" (semiskilled workers in factories) increased from 13.6 percent to 17.6 percent; the proportion of clerical, sales and kindred workers (semiskilled workers in offices and retail stores) increased from 14.77 percent to 27.86 percent; and the percentage of those workers in personal service (barkeepers) increased from 3.51 percent to 7.57 percent. Altogether, the percentage of skilled workers declined by 9.6 percent between 1880 and 1930 while the percentage of semiskilled in industry and commerce increased from 31.88 percent to 52.6 percent. In addition, 10.63 percent of the labor force in 1930 were unskilled laborers.[48]

The reconstitution of the labor process upon a new social and technical basis also generated a demand for new skills different in kind from those of the handicraft production process. The new skills were not so much cognitive as social and affective in nature, relying less on cognitive ability and judgment than attitudes and behavior appropriate to the new organization of the labor process. A superintendent of a meatpacking plant in 1920 took Frank Tannenbaum to the production line and pointed out a particular woman. Tannenbaum described what he saw and heard:

> She stood bending slightly forward, her dull eyes staring down, her elbow jerking back and forth, her hands jumping in nervous haste to keep up with the gang. These hands made one simple precise motion each second, 36,000 an hour, and all exactly at the same time.
> 'She is one of the best workers we have,' the superintendent was saying. We moved closer and glanced at her face. Then we saw the strange contrast. The hands were swift, precise, intelligent. The face was solid, vague, vacant. 'It took a long time to pound the idea into her head,' the superintendent continued, 'but when this grade of woman once absorbs an idea she holds it. She is too stupid to vary. She seems to have no other thought to distract her. She is a sure machine. For much of our work this woman is the kind we want. Her mind is on the table.' "[49]

The skills that this woman needed could be learned in a matter of hours or days. According to J. C. Kennedy, writing in 1914, the monotony, triviality, and repetitiveness of work in the meatpacking industry made "mental culture" entirely unnecessary. "Sixty percent of the workers in the packing industry don't need much previous instruction to do their work," he wrote. The industry has been so organized and developed that in one department after another, they depend upon machinery to do a great deal of the work, and by the subdivision of labor into small pieces, very, very small processes, they are able to get most of the work done by those who have had no particular training.[50] Kennedy added that because the "principle of the division of labor had been applied to all phases of the slaughtering and packing industry," the result was "that most workers perform very simple processes requiring strength and quickness rather than skill."[51] Whereas prior to the 1890s it required from three to five years for an apprentice to become proficient as a cattle or a sheep butcher, after the introduction of a minute division of labor, Weyl and Sakolski calculated in 1906, any ordinary unskilled laborer could be trained in most of the numerous packing occupations within a week.[52]

In other industries the story was much the same. In the steel industry, in 1910, many more workers were semiskilled than had been the case twenty years previously, but only because the skilled work of craftsmen and much of the heavy manual unskilled work had been eliminated by mechanization and replaced with semiskilled machine operating jobs.[53] And so on in industry after industry. Thorstein Veblen believed that "the machine process is a severe and insistent disciplinarian in point of intelligence. It requires close and unremitting thought, but it is which runs in standard terms of quantitative precision. Broadly, other intelligence on the part of the workman is useless or it is even more than useless."[54] Observers of the new labor process agreed that the "skill" required by modern industry involved the ability to withstand repetitive, monotonous work, hour in, hour out, day in, day out. Arthur Dean concluded in 1910 that the effect of specialization and mechanization had been to increase the demand for "speed and accuracy"—"quantitative" skills rather than "qualitative" skills.[55] Horace Eaton, general secretary-treasurer of the Boot and Shoe Workers Union, stated in 1899 that the worker himself had to become a "mere machine" in order to keep his job.[56] John Shedd, president of Marshall Field, described the intelligence required of modern industry as "mechanical intelligence," devoid of any real skill.[57] Paul Douglas believed that modern industry had rendered apprenticeship unnecessary.[58] During World War I, it took only nineteen days on average to train workers in seventy-one shipping yards.[59] In their comprehensive review of job requirements in American industry, Weyl and Sakolski concluded that, in general, the skill required of workers seemed to be "quantitative" rather than "qualitative":

The problem is complicated by the difficulty of defining skill. Under modern conditions, skill implies not only manual dexterity, but speed and accuracy. It is measured not only by the quality of the product. While there is a certain degree of skill and intelligence required in the commonest kind of labor . . . nevertheless, in the sense in which the terms skilled and unskilled are used, unskilled labor is generally understood as that labor which does not require experience in order to perform it with a degree of efficiency and rapidity of movement that will enable it to give the satisfaction desired by the employer. Skilled laborers, on the other hand, are those who have sufficient experience and training in the character of the work which they perform to do it both efficiently and speedily. The effect of new processes and machinery in modern industry has been to enhance quantitative skill, while decreasing the relative importance of qualitative skill. Quantitative skill implies close appreciation and the possibility of the worker enduring intense nervous strain. Qualitative skill, which we more generally recognize in the skilled worker, implies both manual dexterity and a thorough knowledge of the process of a trade.[60]

Whatever the motives of employers in reorganizing the labor process—control over the labor process, technical innovation, increased output, destruction of unions—the effects of the reorganization on skill requirements are quite unmistakable. "Mechanical intelligence," "quantitative skills," the capacity for "close application," the ability to endure "intense nervous strain" and to keep the "mind . . . on the table" necessitated a new kind of work force. Productivity, even economic survival, and not just control of the labor force or protection of capital's prerogatives, demanded a properly socialized and disciplined labor force. The shift from formal to real subordination made the proper socialization of the labor process into new work disciplines and rhythms a technical and not just a social or political necessity. When coupled with the desire to improve the "social efficiency" with which the school allocated students into an increasingly stratified labor market, that imperative profoundly affected the relationship between schooling and capitalism in Chicago.

THE POLITICS OF PRACTICAL EDUCATION

Following Superintendent Pickard's call for a more practical education in 1877, the board of education introduced drawing as an optional subject into the course of study. Pickard carefully emphasized that drawing was not part of "job training" or "shop work" but rather a component of a general common school education. If any child should be exposed to drawing or any other innovation, all children should be, for otherwise the ability of the school to provide common curricula experiences appropriate to a democratic society would be fatally compromised.[61] Drawing did not, however, go far enough to satisfy the demands of a number of leading businessmen and the *Chicago Tribune* for a practical education. In 1881 a business organization, the Citizens Association of Chicago, issued a report on education that criticized the public school system for its failure to provide "practical training, that training of the hand and eye which would enable those leaving our schools to become useful and productive members of society almost immediately after leaving school." But not only were the schools failing to provide the children with practical training, "the whole spirit of the education there given is against forming any taste whatever for manual labor of any kind."[62] Simultaneously, the *Chicago Tribune* began a year-long campaign to press home the need for "practical education," "manual training," or "industrial education" in view of the "new economic conditions."[63]

The combined pressure of the businessmen and the *Tribune* did not go unnoticed. The president of the school board noted in 1882 the pressure from "businessmen" and "commercial gentlemen, who have made stupendous fortunes" and who wanted "to see something practical in our schools."[64] The board agreed to transfer drawing to the regular list of subjects but would go no further. It refused to differentiate public education by giving "instruction of a different kind" so that "some useful trades might be acquired by the pupils." Practical subjects were acceptable provided they became a part of the common curriculum and of benefit to all.[65] Stymied by the recalcitrance of the board, several businessmen— Marshall Field, Richard Crane, George Pullman, and John Crerar—decided to apply their entrepreneurial skills to education: They would build a private manual training high school. At the regular monthly meeting of the Commercial Club in March 1882, "the establishment of a school was resolved upon, and $100,000 pledged for its support" in one night. The businessmen incorporated the Chicago Manual Training School (CMTS) Association on April 11, began construction September 24, 1883, and commenced classes February 4, 1884.[66]

The purpose of the school, according to Charles Ham, "was industrial, not educational reform." H. H. Bellfield, the principal of the school, insisted that the "primary idea of the secondary technical school" was not to fit boys for college but to fit boys "directly for business and for engineering schools," that is, "directly for life." Chicago's businessmen were well pleased with the result. "These schools in the future, we believe," reported a group of builders, "will break down the society lines, which all, or most all, building trade societies have fenced themselves in with, and will assist to send out able and skilled artisans in the building trades, regardless of their laws and edicts, and will also tend to so elevate the industrial arts to a degree that many a young man may be proud to be known as a *mechanic*."[67]

Faced with competition from the private sector, board sentiment shifted. In 1886 it established a manual training class at one of the rooms of the board's repair shop on West Monroe Street. Boys from surrounding schools who opted for the manual training classes spent from 9 to 12 A.M. in their normal "literary" classes, and between 1:30 and 4 P.M. in the manual training classes. The time spent on the traditional curriculum had been almost halved. Some members of the board opposed the innovation, although to no avail. In his report of 1886, board president Adolf Kraus lamented that the introduction of manual training into the Chicago school system represented the defeat of the common school ideal, the measurement of learning in terms of "its value in dollars and cents" and the transformation of Chicago's public schools into "trade schools" or "work shops."[68]

In 1888 the board extended the manual training course to the first two years of high school. In the same year Howland requested that the board establish a separate manual training school. Two years later the board opened English High and Manual Training School.[69] An entirely different type of high school, one with "different functions" and features that were "radical departures" from the traditional high school course

where a trade could be learned" and "the army of skilled workers thus . . . be recruited at home rather than imported labor."[74] In the years that followed, he continued to invest large sums of money in financing manual training in public schools. Between 1894 and 1900 he spent more than one hundred thousand dollars; in 1902 he outfitted four schools, and in 1909, five more. At the same time, he continued liberal support of the CMTS.[75]

The combination of private financial support and a set of educational, economic, and political arguments justifying a practical education proved sufficient to induce the board in 1895 to extend manual training into the upper grades of all grammar schools "so that every pupil may have an opportunity to bring himself into touch with the world of industry that surrounds him." The board reasoned that since most students would need to secure a livelihood through work, "to educate the mental faculties alone is discrimination of the worst kind in favor of the few against the many."[76] The same year, the board assumed complete financial responsibility for manual training, and Superintendent Lane embarked on a policy of rapid expansion. Within two years, some 19 manual training shops, teaching 5,500 seventh- and eighth-grade pupils from ninety schools, existed. Four years later, the number of manual training centers had increased to 122.[77] The board opened the Richard T. Crane Manual Training High School in 1903, and the same year introduced a two-year course in manual training and household arts into all of the high schools of the city. Within eleven years of the establishment of the first manual training class in the Tilden School by R. T. Crane, and eight years after the assumption of financial responsibility for manual training by the board, manual training had become a regular course in the elementary and the secondary schools.[78]

Never before had the schools been so quickly, so thoroughly, and so completely transformed within such a short period of time. For Otto Schneider, president of the board of education in 1909, practical education had revolutionized public education. "The entire apparatus of our school system is subordinate to the one subject: to give to the children the most practical education." The history of American education was replete with significant changes, he went on, but

at no time have greater changes been wrought in educational methods than during the past twenty years. Where formerly everything was concentrated upon the culture of the mind only, the tendency of modern times is to educate the hand as well. Manual training and everything pertaining to handicraft for industrial purposes now receives attention such as it never received before. With the growth of industries and the elevation of labor, it became a natural sequence of conditions, which demanded recognition.[79]

A revolution similar and parallel to the triumph of manual training occurred in the education of girls in Chicago's schools. Initially introduced into second, third, fourth, and fifth grades in January 1892 as a "form of manual training for girls" with a view of securing both pedagogical and practical benefits, sewing including "training in form and color" and the development of "the general discipline and training" necessary for "adaptation to many of the world's occupations." It proved to be a short-lived innovation, however, for the following year the board discontinued the sewing classes, a victim of the war on "fads and frills." But to at least two of Chicago's leading business families the household arts belonged in the school curriculum, so with the financial support of Mr. and Mrs. Cyrus McCormick and Mrs. Elizabeth Stickney, the board established classes in cooking and sewing in 1897 on an experimental basis in a room in the basement of the Hammond School. The success of the first year's efforts prompted Ella Flagg Young, then a district superintendent, to induce the Kindergarten Association of Chicago to open a room in the Kozminski School. At the close of the year, the Kindergarten Association requested the board of education to assume responsibility for "domestic economy," much as it had done in 1895 with manual training. A special committee of the board investigated the subject and reported favorably. Subsequently, during 1898–99 the board opened ten centers; girls in the seventh and eighth grades learned cooking, and girls in the sixth, seventh, and eighth grades, sewing and mending.[80] In 1911 the board established the Lucy Flower School to meet the need for a girls' technical high school. Between 1911 and 1915 the board opened three industrial schools in which girls devoted one-third of their time to "industrial work."[81]

The justification of household arts for girls closely paralleled the justification of manual training for boys. In 1910 Ella Flagg Young argued that every elementary school in Chicago "should be equipped with a manual training shop, a kitchen, and a sewing room," not so much for the pedagogical value of household arts, as its practical applications in the home. "The aim of the work in the elementary schools," she wrote, "is to give every boy some skill in using tools in manipulating wood and every girl the ability to be of some service to herself and to her family in arts that are almost invariably delegated to the women in the home." She also thought it would strengthen the home. "If every girl knew how to prepare a palatable meal, the tendency of the American people to drift away from a family life would be overcome to a large extent."[82]

In addition to manual training and household arts, the board also introduced commercial education into Chicago's schools during the 1890s.[83] A few businessmen had sought the introduction of commercial education in the 1880s, but most businessmen preferred to channel students into Chicago's rapidly growing industrial sector rather than into commercial occupations.[84] The board introduced stenography and type-writing into the English High and Manual Training School during the 1892–93 school year; the following year, Superintendent Lane recommended the extension of the work of the school "to include broader work in bookkeeping, stenography and typewriting, and the study of commercial law," and the establishment of such schools in other sections of the city. In 1896 President Cameron castigated the high schools for their "exclusively literary" character as a violation of the principle that as a public institution, the high school should serve the needs of all the people. Unless the high school acknowledged the legitimate claims of the "commercial interest," it failed to fulfill its "true mission." Cameron's successor, E. G. Halle, argued that the development of America's foreign commerce necessitated a thorough and extensive commercial training, that the development of Chicago as the preeminent commercial city of the country required men trained in commerce, and that Chicago ought to provide for that "great class of young men and women who are looking forward to occupation in commercial and mercantile pursuits" a secondary commercial education.[85]

The enthusiasm of the next president, Graham Harris, for the project was such that he posted five hundred letters to "practical and successful businessmen" seeking their opinions. To his delight, most supported the project. So, too, did the superintendent, E. Benjamin Andrews, the George Howland Club (composed of one hundred male principals of Chicago schools), the High School Council, and the Harper Educational Commission, together with leading Chicago businessmen. In an 1897 survey of leading Chicago businessmen, Charles H. Thurber of the University of Chicago found a fairly unanimous opinion that "college" and "literary" education was detrimental to a successful business career and that practical business courses ought to be introduced into the high school.[86] Within several years, Chicago's public schools offered commercial geography, commercial law, commercial arithmetic, bookkeeping, shorthand, and typing in the general high school curriculum. The board also announced plans for erecting a centrally located commercial high school "to train boys for a practical business career." (A year later, the board decided that the money would be better spent in broadening and expanding the commercial courses in the regular high schools and began to do so.[87])

By 1910, then, businessmen and their supporters on the board of education had self-consciously wrought a veritable revolution in public education in Chicago. Well might the superintendent of schools in 1910, Ella Flagg Young, celebrate the "permanent incorporation" of practical studies into the curriculum of the elementary and secondary schools.[88] By 1900, businessmen and sympathetic educational officials had reconceptualized the intellectual foundations of public education in Chicago and by 1910 had institutionalized this new public philosophy of education. They succeeded because they had convinced themselves and school board members that manual training, the domestic sciences, and commercial education were necessary to satisfy the labor requirements of industry and commerce and because they believed that common schooling violated the principles of a democratic education—it did not provide the children of the working class with the kind of education they needed or were capable of. By 1900 the school board and educational officials had caught up with Allan Story; a strictly liberal conception of educational arrangements, based on an acceptance of a differentiated society and the priority of labor market requirements, superseded earlier republican liberal conceptions of common schooling.[89]

Between 1900 and 1930 the school board and educational officials refined and extended this new public philosophy of education, but they did not alter it in any fundamental way. First, around 1910, reformers relabeled and extended but did not reconceptualize the economic and political justifications they provided for a practical education, and second, they replaced manual training with specific industrial job-related skills. Together, the conceptual revolution of the 1880s and 1890s and the institutional refinements of the period after 1910 constituted a wholly new public philosophy of education—vocationalism. Before 1900, reformers spoke of the practical needs of working class children; after 1910, they relabeled the issue the "fourteen to sixteen problem," referring to the large number of children, especially boys, who left school after turning fourteen to seek work without having completed grammar school. Of course, boys and girls had been leaving school at age fourteen long before 1910, and this had been a matter of great concern to educators and a principal motive behind the introduction of manual training, household arts, and commercial education.[90] But by 1910, with the level of "dropping-out" and truancy seemingly unaffected by manual training, educators and business groups began to look for new solutions.[91]

Once again, businessmen took the initiative. In 1909 the Chicago Association of Commerce published a major report, *Industrial and Commercial Education in Relation to Conditions in the City of Chicago*, in which it asserted that industrial and commercial education was necessary for those 70 to 90 percent of the total school enrollment "who of necessity have left school and gone to work, or will do so early, and will not take a high school course," and for those "who voluntarily turn away from the high school because it does not attract them but who have a taste for industrial and business activity." The report insisted that industrial and commercial education was of a different genre than manual training. The kind of commercial and industrial education that the association envisaged in Chicago involved an education that, if not quite "trade training" (an education that excludes everything not directly related to the trade), was nevertheless an education for "social efficiency" and was directly related to the future occupations of the children. The nature of public school education should be fundamentally reconceived: "The movement for Industrial and Commercial Education should be conceived and directed as an attempt so to reorganize public education as, while preserving the individual and social needs of education, to introduce, for pupils requiring them, subjects and processes that shall, beginning at the earliest practicable point of the pupil's life, directly prepare him for efficiency in the two great fields of modern activity—commerce and industry."[92]

The same year, 1909, that the Association of Commerce published its report, the Chicago City Club, founded in 1903 by members of the Municipal Voters League, embarked on a two-year investigation of vocational education. In late 1911 the Committee on Public Education, chaired by George Herbert Mead of the University of Chicago and funded by Mrs. Emmons Blaine of the McCormick family, concluded its research and in February 1912 published *A Report on Vocational Training in Chicago and in Other Cities.*

The very first sentence of the report indicated the primary concern of the committee. "In Chicago, as in other cities in America," the committee noted, "only a little over one-half the children complete the elementary course. Forty-three percent of those who enter the first grade do not reach the eighth grade at all, and forty-nine percent do not complete the eighth grade." Moreover, the report stated, there were "approximately 70,000 retarded children in Chicago elementary schools—or one-third of all the school children."[93]

Given such figures the committee concluded that the curriculum, "even with its manual training and household arts," did not meet the interests or needs of children, especially those over fourteen years of age. Unlike the 1909 report of the Association of Commerce, the City Club Education Committee believed "that the prevailing reason for leaving school is not to be found in the financial need of the family of the fourteen-year-old child." Rather, "the child's own lack of interest in the school as well as that of his parents is the unquestioned reason for the largest part of the elimination in our elementary schools." Since "a school which does not appeal to the vocational motive is bound to lose the interest of a great number of these children" the committee recommended that "industrial, i.e., vocational work, should be introduced into the seventh and eighth grades of the elementary school." For similar reasons, it recommended the introduction of commercial courses into these grades.[94]

The "fourteen to sixteen problem" redefined a democratic education; "social efficiency" relabeled the economic arguments of the 1880s and 1890s for a practical education. In the years following 1910, reformers insisted that practical education, in that it supplied the economy with a corps of workers well versed in the basic principles of modern work, improved the "social efficiency" of the schools and enhanced the competitive position of American industry in world markets. None doubted, moreover, that a practical education would create, in a manner comparable to Adam Smith's invisible hand, a happy congruence between the practical needs of individual students and the practical needs of the economy. In providing a practical education to the future workers of America, and channeling them into the appropriate slot in the labor market, the "social efficiency" of the school could be greatly enhanced, and the requirements of equal opportunity and a democratic education could be satisfied.

Two major developments prompted efforts to improve the "social efficiency" of schools around 1910. The first involved the continuing threat of European economic expansion—particularly German—to America's trade position. For members of the Chicago Association of Commerce, many of whose members invested heavily in international trade, this fear was particularly acute. The first signs of apprehension appeared among Chicago's businessmen during the 1890s; after 1905, the level of anxiety increased appreciably. In 1906 *The Bulletin* (forerunner of the *Chicago Commerce*) noted the rapidly growing column of German foreign trade, Germany's growing imperial power, and the fact that these two developments were seemingly associated with Germany's system of commercial and industrial education. Two years later the *Chicago Commerce* reprinted an article from the *London Times* that linked Germany's foreign trade power to the close connection between the German Chambers of Commerce and commercial education, and to the fact that "commercial education . . . permeates the whole country and is cultivated wholeheartedly on systematic lines."[95]

It did not take the *Times,* however, to tell Chicago's businessmen what they already knew. A January 24, 1908, article in *Chicago Commerce,* "Industrial Education—Industrial Supremacy," reported on a meeting of the ways and means committee in which speaker after speaker located the source of "industrial supremacy" in "industrial" or "vocational" education. Subsequent articles in *Chicago Commerce* hammered home the same point time and again: The source of German economic power was her system of industrial and commercial education and America must do likewise if she was to retain her competitive position.[96] The next year, the Commercial Club of Chicago commissioned former superintendent Edwin Cooley to travel to Europe, particularly Germany, to study industrial and commercial education, with a view to develop some "recommendations that would enable America to incorporate some practical scheme of vocational training with our public schools." Cooley's report to the Commercial Club of Chicago, and an address to the Association of Commerce, alluded repeatedly to Germany's industrial and training power, to the system of industrial and commercial education that made it possible, and for the need of America—and Chicago—to emulate the German example.[97]

The dramatic change in the nature, scale, and organization of work also prompted acceptance of social efficiency doctrines. Industrial capitalism had all but eliminated apprenticeship and the small artisan workshop; specialization, mechanization, and changes in the scale and organization of production placed a premium on the formation of new work habits, "quantitative" skills, and "industrial intelligence." For Theodore Robinson, vice-president of Illinois Steel and a member of the education committee of the Commercial Club, "unprecedented" industrial changes in America had destroyed the equilibrium between the school and society, such that "an educational system which fairly met the needs of our forefathers is insufficient for our modern conditions." The technical schools established to train America's industrial leaders were not sufficient: "Today our industrial necessities are demanding an elementary training for industrial workers." Manual training was also unable to provide an acceptable "practical foundation for the working class." Only a comprehensive system of industrial education such as that espoused by the Commercial Club of Chicago could meet the needs of the working class and the requirements of industry.[98]

Robinson's plea was far from a lonely cry in the wilderness. As part of the research for its *Report on Vocational Training*, the educational committee of the City Club of Chicago canvassed the attitudes of a large number of Chicago industrialists and businessmen toward industrial or commercial education. Among industrial employers, employing some 111,606 workers, mainly "skilled," the committee found that 74.7 percent of the firms had difficulty in obtaining or training foremen, and 88.0 percent of the firms believed that "industrial schools" would be of value to them. Moreover, 90 percent were in favor of trade schools for youths over the age of sixteen. Overall, the report concluded that in the industries surveyed, "nearly ninety percent believe that industrial schools of different types for the years between fourteen and eighteen would be of value to their concerns."[99]

A similar story emerged from the committee's analysis of the responses of three hundred "leading merchants, tradesmen, employment agents of the large department stores, railroad offices and mail-order houses" to a series of questions about commercial education. On the one hand, some 86.2 percent experienced "difficulty in obtaining efficient employees," and 60 percent reported that high school pupils were not efficient. On the other hand, 98 percent believed that a "broader commercial training" than currently offered in the public high schools or private commercial colleges "would be of material benefit to the business," and 73.2 percent thought it advisable to include in the first two years of high school a commercial education course that would give "specialized and intensive training in commercial branches (bookkeeping, stenography, English, penmanship, etc.)" as a means of supplying "efficient employees" for "clerical and office positions." Finally, 83.3 percent believed that a central high school of commerce "would be a good thing."[100]

Diagram 2.[101] *Diagram Showing Articulation of Proposed Schools and Courses With Existing Schools and With Occupations*

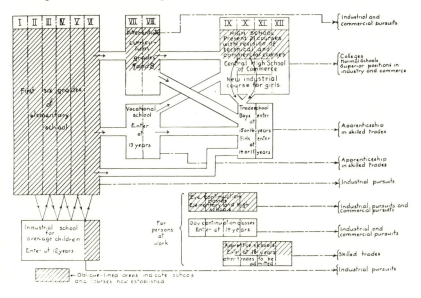

Reproduced with permission of the City Club of Chicago.

There can be little doubt about the breadth of support among large industrial and commercial employers in Chicago for vocational education. In the hope of satisfying this business demand for vocational education and the practical needs of the fourteen-to-sixteen age group, the City Club education committee recommended an extensive system of vocational education in Chicago's schools that "articulated" the educational system with the occupational structure. The City Club believed that a differentiated system of vocational education would institutionalize the connections between the school system and the occupational structure by linking various types and levels of schooling to the labor market. The high school would train noncommissioned officers of industry, while the elementary and trade schools would train the rank and file of the industrial army. "The high school," the report concluded, "is preeminently the place to train the leaders, at least the non-commissioned officers in the industrial army, whereas the rank and file are and probably will be obtained mainly from the lower academic levels."[102]

In addition to the clear institutional articulation of schooling and the social division of labor, the City Club and the Association of Commerce argued that pedagogical processes within the schools should be transformed to reflect more directly real work processes and situations. Vocational training, whether industrial or commercial, should be clearly distinguished from manual training:

The work done in these schools is not of a manual training character. It consists in actual trade processes and produces articles which have commercial value. The courses do not attempt in the nature of the case to make mechanics or artisans of the child. The training is of a preparatory trade character. It will unquestionably assist the child in his later trade training. It will also help him to select the trade for which he is to be adapted. It is our belief that it will hold the child in school who at present finds nothing there that interests him, and will quicken the interest of his parents in his further training.[103]

The committee insisted that vocational work be done "as far as possible under the conditions of the occupation outside the school." Students were to produce actual products through actual "commercial or trade processes." Thus, for example, in industrial courses, the shopwork required actual trade work, approximating as closely as possible the best conditions prevailing in the industries themselves: "the making of equipment, apparatus, and other articles of a distinctly commercial standard actually needed and put to use in the schools or elsewhere."[104] Similarly, in commercial education, according to William Bishop Owen, principal of the Chicago Normal School, school pedagogy should reflect the real world of commercial exchange:

The high school commercial course takes account of an *actual social world*, . . . it is a part of the world that can be brought into the schoolroom with the least departure from reality. The methods and processes of the world of commerce become the methods and processes of the schoolroom. . . . The standards of promptness, accuracy, definiteness, and responsibility of the business world are not interpreted as exactions of the artificial world of the schoolroom, but as a challenge of one's fitness to enter into the real order of things. It can always be said to him that this is the way the world does its business.[105]

In short, as Frank Leavitt, professor of industrial training at the University of Chicago and for a time chairman of the City Club's committee on schools, concluded, industrial education represented much more than a simple addition to the curriculum; it represented a new philosophy of education. "Industrial education means the complete and appropriate education of industrial workers of whatever grade," he wrote. "It means much more than the introduction of shop work into the present curriculum—the addition of another subject, however important that subject might be." Rather, it involved "a thorough revision of our school system with the purpose of furnishing for the working classes an education which bears somewhat the same relation to their prospective life work as does the college education of the future work of the professional and managerial classes."[106] Winfred McKinney, principal of Englewood High School, explained that "a great economic revolution in modes of production and distribution have wrought wonderful social and industrial changes, which in turn have made necessary a new kind of education and training in our public schools."[107]

Not even the traditional commitment of the public schools to citizenship could hold back the forces of vocationalism. Advocates of vocationalism simply redefined citizenship to include vocational training. Vocational training was as much a part of citizenship education as civics. One focused on the citizen as worker, the other on the citizen as voter. As one board of education committee suggested, "The duty of the school is to make good citizens, and no man can be a good citizen unless he has the skill and power to earn a living and accumulate property."[108] Similarly, for Superintendent Cooley. The problem of the school, he argued, was "to provide an education for citizenship, remembering that a good citizen must necessarily be able and willing to earn a decent living." He went on:

The good school, even of the old fashioned kind, had done much to develop good moral habits in the children, habits of a very practical kind. Such schools have always cultivated those habits of industry, punctuality, and obedience that must form the basis of good moral character, and which are essential for the preparation of life in society. . . . The child who has worked for eight years in a good school, where industry is made habitual, has done much to prepare him for citizenship and has done much toward the development of good moral character.[109]

To buttress the identification of vocational education with citizenship, supporters of vocational education advanced two kinds of arguments. Both focused on the capacity of vocational education to halt the growing separation of classes and to protect the structure of social relations. First, they placed human capital arguments in the service of social order arguments: vocational education enhanced the earning power of the individual, thereby increasing his chances of economic mobility, which, in turn, inhibited the growth of social discontent and radicalism. Theodore Robinson of the Commercial Club, for example, claimed that "the menace of socialism can be minimized by a vocational education which will increase the intelligence and future earning power of our children." Both the Association of Commerce and the City Club gathered extensive statistical "proof" of the economic rewards of vocational education to support this proposition.[110] Second, apostles of vocationalism focused upon the capacity of vocational education to properly socialize students. Reformers were keen to adopt a differentiated and stratified educational system, but they were by no means prepared to abandon the opportunity to use schools as a device to contain "the growing separation of classes" and regulate class relationships. One supporter intimated that vocational education would lessen the conflict between labor and capital. The "inculcation of industrial training and the teaching of the useful arts," Clifford Connelley assured an audience at the 1912 NEA convention in Chicago, would "bring about a better understanding between employer and employed."[111] Frank Leavitt thought that industrial education would teach more attention to "duties" than to "rights" and ensure the "contentment of the masses . . . essential to the stability of society."[112] Others emphasized the creation of "common motives," "social habits," and a "social point of view." By far the most important advocate of this view was Jane Addams.

For Jane Addams, a social democracy required a "socialized education" and a socialized education required vocational studies. A traditional literary education, she insisted, could not but be irrelevant to the future lives of the children of the immigrant poor, for it failed to prepare the great majority of children who left school at fourteen or fifteen for the world of work, and it failed to provide the immigrant child with an opportunity for "participation in the social and industrial life with which he comes in contact, nor any insight and inspiration regarding it."[113] A socialized education, including vocational training, would, however, do so. A socialized and practical education would "place the children into proper relation toward the industry which they will later enter." Since many children were "doomed to the unskilled work which the permanent specialization of labor demands," it was plainly preposterous to "graduate machine builders, but not educate machine tenders." Working-class children needed a practical education from the "social point of view":

Education must be planned so seriously and definitely for those two years between fourteen and sixteen that it will be actual trade training so far as it goes, with attention given to the conditions under which money will be actually paid for industrial skill; but at the same time, that the implications, the connections, the relations to the industrial world, will be made clear.[114]

Addams hoped that such an education would overcome modern work alienation and provide the social consciousness necessary to bridge the gap between the classes—to transform social relationships into those required by a social democracy. Moreover, a socialized education, she argued, would counteract the debilitating and fragmenting effects of the division of labor on the worker by providing him with an understanding of the historical, moral, social, and industrial value of his work. "If a working-man is to have a conception of his value at all," she explained, "he must see industry in its unity and entirety." Elsewhere she suggested that "a man who makes, year after year, but one small wheel in a modern watch factory, may, if his education has properly prepared him, have a fuller life than did the old watchmaker who made a watch from beginning to end." All he need be able to do is to see himself "in connection and cooperation with the whole."[115]

The influence of Jane Addams on the movement for vocational education in Chicago is difficult to gauge. Yet, given her stature in Chicago, it would be remarkable if her support of vocational education did not have a significant effect, providing as she did a rationale for vocational education rooted in a deep compassion for the welfare of adolescents and her quest to create "democratic" social relationships. Undoubtedly, many saw in her support of vocational education further proof of the righteousness of their cause.

THE INSTITUTIONALIZATION OF VOCATIONALISM

Along with the reconceptualization of manual training or practical education into vocational education, the Chicago Board of Education established "industrial" courses in the elementary schools and "vocational" courses in the high schools. The board introduced its first "industrial" classes February 1, 1910, at the Farragut Elementary School for children of grades six, seven, and eight who were one year or more behind a grade. One year later the board of education adopted an elementary industrial course for all schools for grades six, seven, and eight. Superintendent Young explained that the new course reflected "the necessity for a division into two lines in the upper grades so that provision may be made for those children whose power lies in practical rather than academic lines." President McFatrick of the board, on the other hand, emphasized "the readjustment of a traditional educational scheme . . . to the demands of a changing social order," particularly "the business world," the "great industrial institution" of American society.[116]

The industrial course introduced in February 1912 allowed pupils entering the sixth grade to choose between the industrial course and the academic course, the former leading to a two-year vocational course in the high school introduced in 1910. In the industrial course, 560 minutes (9 hours, 20 minutes) per week were to be allocated to the academic course (English, history, etc.) and 615 minutes (10¼ hours) per week to art and industrial arts. Students in the general course studied 795, 735, and 735 minutes per week for grades six, seven, and eight, respectively, in academic courses, and 270, 270, and 210 in art and industrial arts. Thus, in grade six a pupil in the industrial course received approximately four hours per week less academic instruction than did a pupil in the general course and nearly six hours a week more of art and industrial art. Furthermore, the work in the industrial arts, as outlined in the industrial course, included the following subjects not included in the general course: Venetian ironwork, plumbing, concrete construction, elementary electrical construction, photography, embroidery, millinery, and waitress work.[117]

In 1914 the committee of the survey of Chicago schools announced that in industrial schools, the academic subjects were also "to a certain extent correlated with shop work." For instance, it reported that in English composition, "industrial topics furnish a part of the subject matter, and the shop and the academic teacher cooperate." The committee unanimously recommended that the industrial course of study "be extended as rapidly as possible to all elementary schools." It further recommended differentiation of the pupils in up to 20 percent of their work in grades seven and eight, and that "the basis for differentiation be the individual ability of the pupil as determined by teacher and parent."[118]

The following year, the board extended the "industrial course" to twenty-three elementary schools. The board allocated approximately 50 percent of the students' time to industrial work and the other half to academic work. In the remainder of Chicago's elementary schools, "industrial work" (the old manual training course) occupied between one-fourth and one-third of the time. This organization apparently met the needs of the "motor children" in Chicago until the establishment of the junior high school when the board implemented a new organization of industrial work.[119]

The history of industrial education in Chicago's high schools is a more involved affair, largely because of the complexity of the organization of secondary education in Chicago. By 1913, Chicago had four types of high school: academic, composite, technical high schools for boys, and technical high schools for girls.[120] Each type of high school employed different combinations of industrial or vocational education—prevocational, technical, manual training, and commercial—for varying lengths of time (two years, four years).[121] The technical school, as conceived by Chicago's educators, prepared students to become skilled workers, foremen, superintendents, or engineers. At Lane Tech, for example, the four-year technical courses prepared students "for direct entrance into industry and for entrance into technical colleges." The purpose of the two-year vocational courses introduced in 1911—machine, electrical, mechanical drawing, carpentry, patternmaking, and printing—was to prepare those students who would otherwise drop out of schools for entrance into the ranks of "skilled labor." Pedagogically, the school existed, reported the City Club in 1911, in a "stage of transition from purely manual training to truly technical work," in which a considerable amount of time was allocated to shop work, and academic instruction was related to "shopwork and to industrial needs." Frank Leavitt wrote that "the distinguishing characteristic" of Lane Tech was that it trained "not school-boys" but "young workmen" in both specific job skills and proper habits of work by replicating in the workshop the machinery and work conditions of a typical patternmaking manufacturing plant. By the late twenties little had changed. As the *Annual Report of the Bureau of Technical Studies* in 1928 noted, the technical high schools aim "to offer a sequence of shop work that would parallel the production department of an industrial manufacturing plant." The purpose of the school shop, it continued, was "to give the boy training in the various shop processes."[122]

The board introduced the first overtly vocational courses in the general high schools in September 1910 as part of an overhaul of the high school curriculum.[123] The new program of study consisted of five alternative courses: a two-year vocational course in accounting, stenography, mechanical drawing, design, advanced carpentry, patternmaking, machine-shop work, electricity, household arts, and printing; a four-year vocational course in business, manual training, building, household arts, art, architecture; a four-year academic course in English, foreign languages, sciences; a teacher's college preparatory and a general course.[124] But in addition, as the City Club *Report on Vocational Training* pointed out in 1912, the board also "industrialized" academic subjects in the vocational courses: not history but "industrial history," not English but "business English," not math but "commercial math." In the two-year vocational program, two courses were commercial and the remaining eight industrial, a "large portion of time [from one-half to two-thirds] is alloted to shop work and drawing" and "specialization in a particular trade [is] required from the beginning."[125]

In August 1911 a special committee of the board of education recommended that technical and commercial courses for all boys and girls be offered in all the general high schools in the first and second years, and not simply in the three technical schools. On completion of the two-year course, if a student wished to continue a technical education, he or she would be transferred to a technical high school to undertake another two years of technical work. If a student wished to undertake a commercial or academic program, he or she would remain in the general high school.[126]

The adoption of the plan represented full and complete acceptance of vocational education in the general high school curriculum. By June 1913, sixteen of Chicago's twenty-one high schools had become "composite high schools," teaching in addition to the regular academic subjects, one or more years of manual training to both sexes (woodwork, forge, foundry, and machine shop for boys; cooking, sewing, and craft work for girls) as well as two-year vocational courses (including accounting, stenography, electricity, mechanical drawing, carpentry, patternmaking, machine shop, and household sciences). The schools offered eleven four-year courses and nine two-year courses, the number varying between high schools. Among the four-year courses, only eleven high schools offered the English program, sixteen general and the manual training programs, fifteen household arts and architecture, twelve business, and four carpentry. Among the two-year courses, sixteen high schools offered programs in accounting and stenography, twelve mechanical drawing, ten electricity, seven carpentry and household arts, five patternmaking, four designing, three machine shop. Of the 16,186 students in the sixteen composite high schools, 53 percent were enrolled in the general course and approximately 35 percent in vocational courses. An additional 10 percent of the pupils in the general course also took manual training in some form as an elective.[127] The pedagogy of the vocational high school courses did not consist of manual training but, as R. M. Smith, supervisior of technical training in the high schools observed in 1913, "technical training, directly applicable to trade and industry."[128] A 1914 survey of "vocational work" in Chicago schools found that in the wood shops, for example,

an effort to acquaint the boys with commercial shop methods is made in some of the schools. In one shop the group system of foremen and workers is being tried out. . . . Products are turned out in large numbers and commercial standards of technique are maintained. Care of material and tools, and a neat condition of the shops is required and this is an important item in the education of the boys as future industrial workers.[129]

The board first introduced commercial education courses in 1892–93. Despite several additions to the program, the City Club remained unsatisfied with these commercial courses. Late in 1911 the club requested the Chicago Association of Commerce to use its influence in the development of new courses. The association referred the matter to its vocational education committee, which submitted a report to the board of education's committee on school management, suggesting that the schools would be "provided with facilities whereby the pupils may learn the modern methods of transacting business, which, of course, will include the present-day methods of bookkeeping and accounting, as well as general office management, and the proper handling of office detail." If the schools adopted a program of specific training for commercial work, business would thereby be relieved of an "unprofitable" task.[130]

The proposals proved more than acceptable to the committee on school management. At a June 20, 1912, meeting of that committee and members of the association (and a Mr. S. Cody, a member of the City Club), the participants decided, reported the *Chicago Record Herald*, to develop jointly a commercial course for high schools. The two bodies appointed special subcommittees to confer with Superintendent Young and to work out a joint proposal, and the association announced the formation of a committee to "aid the city authorities to establish for high school pupils a system of commercial training conducted by practical men for youths to be doers rather than learners at the outset of their wage-earning career." On September 12 the association's committee on commercial courses in high schools met with the subcommittee of the committee on school management to iron out details of the proposed course. Mr. Pfalezer, on behalf of the board, outlined plans for a high school commercial course and for a downtown commercial high school to provide, in part, more vigorous instruction in "business discipline, thus preparing them for more efficient work in commercial life." The two bodies, and the ubiquitous Mr. Cody, met on several more occasions, one of which Superintendent Young attended.[131]

On October 25 the committee of the association submitted its report. It recommended a thorough drilling in the three R's; differentiation of pupils in the seventh and eighth grades so that "the future vocation of the pupil may be taken into consideration and provided for"; that the commercial subjects be taught by only those actually experienced in modern business enterprises; that modern text books reflecting modern business methods be used; that commercial education commence in the first year of the high school; that a commercial continuation school be established; that businessmen be invited into the schools to give lectures on commercial subjects; and that an "advisory" relationship exist between the businessmen of the association and the educators of the school system.[132]

Within twenty-four hours, Mrs. Young responded to this report, admitted "much justification for the Association of Commerce's criticisms," but indicated that the schools were trying to "mend these faults." By the end of 1912, sixteen of Chicago's high schools offered a regular commercial course and commercial subjects as electives. The subjects taught included bookkeeping, stenography and typewriting, commercial law and commercial geography, economics, "Business English," "Business Arithmetic," "Business Forms and Penmanship," and "Business Methods and Office Practice." In that year alone, fully 31.5 percent of all students in the high schools of Chicago enrolled in commercial courses.[133]

The board continued to "mend these faults" in subsequent years. The number of students continued to grow, and according to various annual reports, the quality of instruction as measured against modern commercial practices continued to improve. In 1913 the chairman of the committee of principals of the commercial department reported steady progress and urged the acquisition of adding machines, stenotypes, rotary duplicators, "and such other machines as are used in the largest offices," including filing cases, since the principals thought it important "to make the pupils familiar with office conditions." Likewise, teachers of commercial subjects should be familiar with office practice, since "there should be a close relationship between the school and the business classes, the teacher should be required to visit some large office at least once a month." Apparently, businessmen were impressed with the quality of student instruction, since "from fifty percent to one-hundred percent are placed within the first month and all the remainder during the second month." In 1914 the school survey reported that many of the teachers had experience in business offices, all of them were specially trained, and "actual business experience in accounting" was the basis of instruction.[134]

In the years that followed, the commercial curriculum expanded along new lines. In 1917 the board commenced classes in selling and advertising in some Chicago high schools. By 1922, ten high schools offered the course. The large department stores strongly supported the course, and in the spirit of cooperation advocated in 1912, eight of the Loop stores and two large stores outside the Loop organized the Chicago High School Salesmanship Club. Prominent businessmen spoke to student audiences. Teachers and businessmen cooperated to assist pupils to find jobs through a centralized file containing records of students' commercial work in the schools; when employers requested new employees, the supervisor of commercial work sent students the address of the employer. This procedure also kept "the schools in direct touch with the business world, thereby increasing the respect of the businessmen for the work the schools are doing and assisting the schools in adjusting their work to the practical needs of business." In November 1917 four commercial continuation schools opened: the Morris and Company School, the Armour and Company School, the Swift and Company School, and the Chicago Commercial Continuation School in the Loop district. In the last-named school, boys and girls from fourteen years up, employed by the Loop banks, department stores, and other business concerns, received an hour or so a day of instruction in "an almost complete list of commercial and allied subjects."[135]

By 1932, when the survey of Chicago schools released its findings, commercial education constituted "an important activity" in the junior high schools and a "major" activity in the senior high schools. The twenty-seven junior high schools provided elective courses in junior business training, filing and typewriting during the eighth and ninth school years. Twenty senior high schools maintained commercial departments offering two- and four-year courses of study. Some of the courses included a foreign language and formal high school math; others specialized in bookkeeping or stenography. Fourteen high schools offered courses in salesmanship. The commercial subjects offered in 1932 included junior business training A and B, commercial geography, elementary and advanced bookkeeping, typewriting, shorthand, clerical practice A and B, business organization A and B, commercial law, calculating machines A and B, salesmanship, filing A and B, office practice A and B, and advertising. As the City Club and the Association of Commerce had wished, the board had well and truly mended its ways.[136]

Finally, in addition to the introduction of vocational education courses in the elementary and high schools, the board of education established special prevocational classes for overage children in sixth, seventh, and eighth grades from fifteen schools. Inaugurated in September 1912 as special divisions of the four technical schools, these schools provided a highly practical industrial education to children who would otherwise leave elementary school without any vocational training. Between September 1912 and June 1914, 1,167 boys and girls were admitted to prevocational classes. By September 1918, the number of schools supplying pupils for the prevocational classes grew from fifteen to nearly seventy, and an additional 500 pupils of elementary age entered the schools.[137]

The curriculum of the prevocational schools devoted one-half of the school day to academic work (industrialized to fit in with the shop work) and the second half to industrial shop work. In the Jackson School, for instance, the industrial course for the boys included classes in woodworking, mechanical drawing, printing, and elementary science. In woodworking "the aim has not been far different from that of other manual training shops, but we try to emphasize those points which will be of value in future occupations," wrote principal William Hodges. The industrial character of the print shop was so pronounced that one visitor asked if the school taught the printing trade. Hodges responded that it did. He pointed out that "we follow the same lessons planned for apprentices in the trade, but we are doing much more than that." The school tried not only to give the boys specific skills but to train them in the proper work habits: "Here, as in the other shops, the shop rules must be observed, and each boy is required to give as good service as he would be expected to give if he were working for wages."[138]

The institutionalization of vocational education in Chicago's public secondary and elementary schools went hand-in-hand then with ideological victory of vocationalism. The triumph represented not so much a victory of businessmen over educators as a partnership between two groups equally committed to a common philosophy of education. On most issues businessmen took the initiative, but educators soon followed, eagerly pursuing the same goals. Both businessmen and educators had concluded by 1910 that the old practical education—the mix of manual training, commercial education, and domestic science—was not sufficiently practical and relied upon the informal alteration of student aspirations through exposure to practical activities in the classroom. They decided, therefore, to industrialize pedagogy, both in shop classes and in the academic components of the vocational curriculum, and to institutionalize a system of differentiated education that formally allocated and channeled students into different sectors of the labor market. In this manner, they expected education could be more "efficiently" calibrated with the labor process and the labor market requirements of the economy.

THE COOLEY BILL

Shortly after his retirement from the superintendency in 1909, the educational committee of the Commercial Club of Chicago sent Edwin Cooley on a twelve-month study tour of industrial education in Europe. Cooley first stopped in Munich. There he renewed his acquaintanceship with George Kerschensteiner, a leading advocate of continuation schools. Deeply impressed with Kerschensteiner's work and the Munich school system, Cooley persuaded Kerschensteiner to lecture in the United States and prevailed upon the Commercial Club to print an English version of one of his books.[139]

Upon his return to Chicago, he presented a summary of his findings to a special meeting of the Commercial Club on November 21, 1911. Subsequently, the club published in 1912 a partial report of his findings, *Some Continuation Schools of Europe,* and later a complete account, *Vocational Education in Europe.* Cooley traveled to Boston, New York, St. Louis, and other large cities to provide assistance in the development of vocational educational programs. During March–April 1912 he visited Wisconsin almost weekly. In February Theodore Robinson, the club's education committee chairman, reported that the Association of Commerce, the Hamilton Club, the Bankers' Club, and "other civic bodies" had decided to join with the Commercial Club in developing a vocational education plan that, according to Robinson, would "give to every boy and girl of fourteen to sixteen a better opportunity than exists at present for them to earn an honest livelihood, and to thus decrease the criminal and the pensioner classes." (He added, parenthetically, that "if the rising socialist tendencies are to be overcome, it must be largely through the result of industrial education.")[140]

In April Clayton Mark of the education committee announced that the club would seek legislation for a system of vocational education in Illinois similar to that in Wisconsin. During the spring and summer of 1912, the education committee of the Commercial Club met with representatives of the Association of Commerce, the Hamilton Club, and the Civic Federation. By August, a "tentative draft of a Proposed Bill" had been drawn up, outlining the administration, course of study, and financing of the vocational education scheme. This draft, along with Cooley's defense of the plan, "Statement of the Need of Vocational Schools in the United States," were widely distributed throughout Illinois.[141]

Cooley's plan proposed a state system of vocational education fully divorced from the existing school system. Full-time vocational schools and part-time continuation schools—"whose equipment, corps of teachers, and board of administration must be in the closest possible relation to the occupations"—would be established to render more efficient the practical work of the factory, shop, store, office, garden, or home. The dual system of schools, a general education system and a vocational educational system beginning at seventh grade, would have separate boards of control. The vocational school would be governed by independent boards of men with practical experience in industry and commerce, and funded by a special tax, one-half provided by the state in the shape of a grant, and the other half raised locally.[142]

In January 1913 sympathetic legislators introduced the "Cooley Bill" into the Illinois Legislative Assembly. The supporters of the Cooley Bill were not able to drum up sufficient support, however, and the bill failed to be enacted. Undeterred, the bill's supporters submitted it again in 1915. The Commercial Club urged its members to go down to Springfield in large numbers and circulate among the lawmakers to demonstrate "the extent of interest in the measure." Despite intensive lobbying, and the continued support of the Chicago *Daily News* and the *Record Herald,* opponents again defeated it. And again in 1917. At this point, the club ceased to agitate actively for the bill.[143]

A loose coalition composed of the Chicago City Club, the Illinois State Federation of Labor, the Chicago Federation of Labor, Superintendent Young, school teachers, and several educators of national significance led the opposition to the Cooley Bill in 1913, 1915, and 1917. The City Club opposed the Cooley Bill not because it opposed the principle of vocational education but because it opposed a dual system of public education. The City Club believed that in order to get children into vocational education classes, it would be much more effective to have a "democratic system of unitary control in which all work is under one roof or one management, and where the pupils form one student body." Comprehensive schooling and unitary control provided the most effective way to remove the "stigma" of vocational education, given the democratic ideological traditions of America. Citizenship training best took place in a common school although this obviously no longer entailed a common curriculum. "A democratic education," George Herbert Mead, principal architect of the City Club *Report* in 1912 suggested, "must hold together the boys and girls of the whole community; it must give them the common education that all should receive, so diversifying its work that the needs of each group may be met within the institution whose care and generous ideals shall penetrate the specialized courses."[144]

Superintendent Young also opposed the Cooley plan. She joined a committee composed of Julius Rosenwald, Frank Leavitt, E. A.

Wreidt of the City Club education committee, and Edmund James, president of the University of Illinois, to draw up an alternative to the Cooley Bill, the so-called Conference Bill of 1913. The Conference Bill supported vocational education but opposed a dual system. Mrs. Young also publicly attacked the dual system proposal, maintaining that "it is best to have the children of the rich and the poor in the same school and rubbing elbows with each other." It was not that she opposed vocational education—her sponsorship of the Conference Bill and the introduction of a whole range of industrial and commercial courses in the elementary and secondary schools during the years of her superintendency (especially between 1911 and 1913) amply testify to that—but that she believed a dual system was undemocratic.[145]

Teachers' organizations shared Superintendent Young's antagonism to the dual system. During December 1912 and the early months of 1913, the School-Masters Club, the Elementary Manual Training Club, the High School Teachers Club, the Principals Club, principals of the composite high schools, the Illinois State Teachers Association, and the Chicago Teachers Federation came out in opposition to the Cooley Bill, particularly to its provision for lay administrative control of the school boards and its provision for a dual system of control.[146] In November 1912 the Chicago Teachers Federation claimed that more than two thousand new teachers had joined it in protest against the Cooley Bill. A resolution adopted by the federation in early November challenged "the segregation of vocational training from the academic or liberal education on the ground that it is anti-democratic, anti-educational, anti-humanitarian, and anti-American."[147] Margaret Haley of the federation became one of the leading organizers of the successful fight against the Cooley Bill. In April 1913 she publicly debated Cooley in Oak Park on the subject of school governance and vocational training; in June she engineered the Chicago Federation of Labor's resolution condemning the Cooley Bill.[148]

Organized labor also condemned the Cooley plan in no uncertain terms. The Chicago Federation of Labor (CFL) viewed the plan as an attempt on the part of large employers to turn the public schools into a supply depot for docile, well-trained workers. The federation argued that the plan would establish a class system of education wherein the children of the workingman would be shunted into vocational schools and from there into the factories. One of the CFL's leading activists opposing the Cooley Bill, John C. Harding, an officer of the Chicago Typographical Union and the CFL, and a member of the board of education, claimed that the demand for a change in governance emanated from employers attempting to turn the schools into "scab factories."[149]

Although organized labor in Chicago opposed the Cooley Bill, it did not oppose the principle of vocational education. A 1901 questionnaire circulated by the federation to its 214 affiliated unions, representing 225,000 skilled workers, revealed overwhelming support (80 percent, 74 percent, and 83 percent, respectively) to each of three questions:

1. Do you favor a *public* industrial or *preparatory* trade school which would endeavor to reach boys and girls between fourteen and sixteen, that now leave the common school in very large numbers before graduation? *Such a school would not teach a trade,* but would give a wide acquaintance with materials and fundamental industrial processes, together with drawing and shop mathematics, with the object of giving a better preparation for entering the industries at sixteen and better opportunities for subsequent advancement.

2. Do you favor *public trade* schools for boys and girls between sixteen and eighteen, that would give two years of practical training, together with drawing and mathematics, *provided* that graduates of such schools should serve two years more as apprentices or improvers?

3. Do you favor public *evening* industrial schools giving instruction as indicated in questions 1 and 2, and furnishing also *supplemental* trade education for those already at work in trades during the day?[150]

The unions responded thus:

Number Answering

	Number Replying	Yes	Percent Yes	No	Percent No
Question 1	111	92	82.8	19	17.2
Question 2	112	88	78.5	24	21.5
Question 3	112	87	86.6	15	13.4
Total			82.6		17.4

The support of skilled workers, however, depended upon several important conditions. Some unionists claimed that they supported industrial education only on the condition that such an education made "all round mechanics of them, not specialists." Others supported it if and only if "cultural studies be not eliminated from the course of study, and that these schools be conducted in the same buildings and in connection with the common school." Still others insisted that such programs be "conducted for the benefit of boys and girls only, and not to be used as a profit system for somebody else." Even among those unions that voted no, the primary reason was not opposition to the principle of vocational education per se, but a fear that the proper safeguards or conditions could not be enforced.[51]

But while organized labor in Chicago approved of the principle of vocational education, it stridently opposed vocationalism and the Cooley Bill. At the 1914 convention of the Illinois State Federation of Labor (ISFL) in Peoria, a committee of the ISFL reported in favor of the principle of vocational education but opposed establishment of a separate school system and the creation of a separate state or district board of administration to take responsibility for vocational education in the state. The committee, headed by Victor Olander, noted a "vigorous demand for vocational education among unionists" throughout Illinois but pointed out that this demand was invariably coupled with a further demand "for greater skill and less automatic and monotonous labor." No discussion of industrial education could get very far without taking cognizance of changes in the labor process in the previous two or three decades. It was "vital to a fair discussion of the subject," argued the committee, "to note that in our industrial life many vocations, which formerly offered to the workers opportunities more than mere sustenance of physical existence, have been divided and subdivided until the vocation itself, in many instances, is rapidly becoming almost a lost art." The committee concluded:

Through this subdivision and extreme specialization of labor the workers are prevented from acquiring the skill and training necessary to the continued development, or even the proper maintenance of various trades and callings, without which the continuance of the industries is jeopardized. As specialization increases still further, these evil results will logically increase in proportion unless some stringent measures are adopted to avoid the evils of monotonous and automatic employment, which only results in a less mentally and physically equipped worker.[52]

To remedy the situation, the committee made two recommendations. First, the committee suggested that the children of Illinois have practical training in the schools, but that, as the early proponents of manual training had insisted, such industrial training not be a substitute for general education. Indeed, all children must be given a "broad and general education" so that "class distinctions in our public schools such as practiced in the German system of education could be avoided." Any attempt on the part of employers "to limit the opportunities of the workers for obtaining a general education and thus render them more submissive and less independent" should be resisted. To guard against such an eventuality, the committee suggested that the schools be continuously monitored to determine "whether the education fostered and encouraged . . . tend[s] to a full development of the spirit of American freedom and of American manhood and womanhood."[153]

Second, the committee recommended a reorganization of the labor process in such a manner as to allow the worker to develop and utilize a wide range of technical skills. The simple inclusion of vocational education in the public school system would not suffice. The organization of production itself, particularly the "extreme specialization, semi-automatic and monotonous labor" must be abolished if the vocational education received by children was to have any value. "What good will come from giving vocational training in the public schools," the ISFL asked, "if we continue to permit our children to be chained to machines which require but the repetition of a few muscular motions?"[154]

The following year, 1915, when reformers submitted the second version of the Cooley Bill to the Illinois legislature, the ISFL led the successful opposition to the bill. When the bill went down to defeat, the ISFL's *Weekly Newsletter* noted that "it is hoped that [this] will put a stop to the vicious attempt which has been made to destroy the democracy of the public schools, and that commercial interests and others who are trying to split the schools, create class distinctions and prevent proper education of children of working people will realize schools are held too sacred by working people to permit misuse."[155]

Finally, a number of prominent national educators opposed the bill. John Dewey, for example, attacked the Cooley Bill on three grounds. First, the proposed plan could not but be administratively inefficient, since the plan divided and duplicated educational administration. Second, the segregation of academic from vocational education would "inhibit the transformation of traditional pedagogy along progressive lines." And third, the segregation of students into general and vocational schools would injure "the true interests of the pupils who attended the so-called vocational schools" since they would be denied an education in which industrial training was integrated into an education for citizenship. Dewey was not in any way opposed to industrial training—indeed, he agreed that its "right development will do more to make public education truly democratic than any other single agency now under consideration." But the only "economical and effective" way to do this was "to expand and supplement the present school system," not to establish separate vocational schools but to integrate industrial training into the composite high school. In this fashion, Dewey believed, training for employment could be happily married to training for citizenship.[156]

The combined attack of the City Club, organized labor, Ella Flagg Young, the various teacher organizations, and prominent educators prevented passage of the Cooley Bill. Within a few years, the passage of the Smith Hughes Act in 1919, the opening of a continuation school system, and the progressive improvement in the quality of vocational education in Chicago's schools convinced the Commercial Club that a separate system of vocational schools was indeed unnecessary. Satisfied, the club disbanded its education committee.[57]

VOCATIONAL GUIDANCE

The early history of vocational guidance in Chicago is largely the history of two developments: first, the initial introduction of vocational guidance procedures by reformers and the very gradual adoption of vocational guidance by the school board; and second, the development and justification of vocational guidance as a "democratic" means of linking the labor market and vocational education.

Vocational guidance began in Chicago when two inveterate child-savers, Edith Abbott and Sophonisba Breckinridge, in the course of a study of truancy and nonattendance, opened an "employment bureau."[58] In effect, however, the bureau was a vocational guidance office and not simply a job placement bureau. Abbott and Breckinridge described their work as an attempt to ascertain the job opportunities available to the children and the characteristics of the children themselves. The first involved "a thorough-going investigation into opportunities of employment open to children under sixteen" and the second "a careful study of the particular child."

On the one hand, it means interviews with employers and foremen, and on the other, interviews with the child before he leaves school, with his teachers, with the parent in the home. . . . This is, of course, only half the battle. There is also the selection from among all the available jobs that can be found, the one to which the boy seems best adapted, and then frequently the task of persuading the boy to give up being a messenger boy or some other wasteful occupation.[59]

Their effort to study and reconcile the individual to the available job structure became the principal feature of the vocational guidance movement. From its beginning, vocational guidance in Chicago developed on the basis of the assumption that the practical needs of industry and the distinctive capacities and needs of children could be reconciled through a close integration of the output of the schools and the requirements of industry. Vocational guidance, in effect, would fine tune the calibration of schooling with the labor market.

For the next three or four years, vocational guidance remained privately funded and limited to a small number of schools. In June 1911 Abbott and Breckinridge opened another office at the Washburne School; meanwhile, an office sponsored by a consortium of women's clubs opened at the Lucy Flower Technical High School.[160] At this point, the president of the board of education suggested that the board seriously consider the establishment of a vocational guidance department for Chicago's schools. He thought it appropriate for the board to devise a system of vocational guidance that would simultaneously help children find employment "adapted to their natures and abilities" and help the business world find the "young people suitable to enter their services for permanent employment."[161] When the board failed to act on his suggestion, the Association of Commerce decided to make its influence felt. At a summer meeting of the association in 1912, Dr. Nathaniel Butler, dean of education at the University of Chicago and chairman of the committee on vocational education of the Association of Commerce, reported to the executive committee that because large numbers of boys were leaving school before completing seventh or eighth grade without "proper training or vocational guidance" many of them were entering jobs "for which they were not . . . naturally qualified." Butler recommended the establishment of a Bureau of Vocational Guidance to provide advice "to juveniles as to the opportunities for which they are by ability, taste, character and education suited." On October 15 the association established the Vocational Guidance Bureau and appointed Raymond Booth as its field representative. Booth immediately started holding office hours in the head office of the association and in four elementary schools under the general direction of District Superintendent Roberts.[162]

By December, the organizing principles of the association's approach to vocational guidance had crystallized. The association wanted to keep children between fourteen and sixteen in school, particularly those that had no employment—a number estimated to be about twenty thousand in 1912. In May 1913 the association brought a lawsuit against a "delinquent" fifteen-year-old boy to see whether it could solve the fourteen-to-sixteen problem through legal compulsion. The court decided in favor of the association. The bureau also hoped to place a child in a job suited to his abilities. "Social efficiency" improved, the *Chicago Commerce* claimed, when the distinctive characteristics of a child—his needs, abilities, and background—were matched by a job suitable to those characteristics. The matching of children and jobs, the *Chicago Commerce* wrote, would eliminate "misfits" and allow each child to utilize "his talents to serve society."

Vocational guidance, Dr. Butler argued, was "the connecting link in bringing into closer relationship the educational and industrial interests of Chicago."[163]

Meanwhile, other agencies continued to fund research into job opportunities in various districts.[164] The praise lavished on these private investigations and counseling services eventually shamed the board into taking some action. In 1914 two committees of high school principals, district superintendents, and teachers recommended that Chicago's public schools officially adopt vocational guidance procedures and establish a Bureau of Vocational Guidance. The officials insisted, however, that vocational guidance ought not be an authoritarian command to a child to take up a particular job, but a "democratic" process of "self-guidance." "Self-guidance" represented a principle of the utmost importance to the leaders of the vocational guidance movement, for at all costs they wished to avoid the impression that vocational guidance counselors themselves made decisions about the child's future. Their function was to "know the child" through intensive examination of "the child's abilities and desires" and to "understand the requirements, chances, and remuneration of many occupations." Rather than telling the child what to do, the counselor would "lead him to know himself, and let this information speak for itself." The committee then added, "The responsibility will then rest upon those who make the decision."[165]

Self-guidance proved a brilliant formula: It simultaneously reconciled the democratic tradition of individual choice with the desire to match the needs of industry with the abilities and capacities of the child. Not only would it eliminate misfits, it would also eliminate discontent, for the individual would have no one to blame but himself. The individual student made the decision, not the vocational guidance counselor, not the board of education, not "society," not the child's parents. The individual would alone be responsible for his fate. With a single stroke, failure and discontent would be eliminated, industry would get its supply of "efficient and contented employees," the "individuality" of the individual would be "respected and fostered," democracy preserved, and industrial efficiency secured.

Still, the board temporized. Impatient with the board, the Association of Commerce in late 1915 and again in January 1916 recommended that the board take over the existing quasi-private forms of vocational guidance and "establish, maintain and manage a Vocational Guidance Bureau." To the chairman of the association's educational committee, it seemed perfectly "logical" that "the school system, in addition to turning out its product, that is, training the children and fitting them to take a place in the world, should also assist in some degree in bridging the span between school and commercial and industrial life." No longer able—or willing—to resist, the board committed itself to the creation of such a bureau. On March 1, 1916, the board officially took over the semiprivate Bureau of Vocational Supervision. Evidently pleased with the result, the Association of Commerce commented that it had completed the task it had set out to accomplish, namely, "of undertaking this work in the initial stages with a view to developing it to a point where the public educational authority might see the way clear to proceed with it."[166]

The objectives of the new bureau replicated those of the private agencies, as the first report of the Bureau of Vocational Guidance made clear. In its statement of purposes, the bureau articulated four goals:

First. To study industrial opportunities open to boys and girls with respect to wages and the requirements necessary to enter an occupation, . . . in short, to gather the greatest possible amount. . . . Second. To advise the children about to leave school and retain them in school when possible. . . . Third. When every effort to retain them in school has failed, to place them in positions. . . . Fourth. To follow up and supervise every child who has been placed.[167]

The board enlarged the responsibilities of the new bureau in January 1918 when the board of education assigned it the duty of issuing employment certificates for fourteen- to sixteen-year-olds, a task that up to that time had been carried out by the compulsory attendance department. For the year ending June 30, 1919, the bureau issued 36,605 certificates alone. The bureau also acquired responsibility for the physical examination of children applying for work certificates. And in September 1919 the work of the bureau further expanded with the appointment of a staff of visiting teachers assigned to individual schools but working under the supervision of the director of the bureau. By 1924, the Vocational Guidance Bureau had a permanent staff of forty-seven employees, committed to carrying out the principles of vocational guidance established in the early teens: ascertain individual abilities, determine available job opportunities, and match the two in the name of social efficiency.[168]

Vocational guidance thus consummated the marriage reformers had arranged between public education and the economy in Chicago. Through vocational guidance, businessmen could reasonably expect that students would be channeled into the appropriate level of the labor market and even into particular jobs, and it would be done so without in the least violating democratic traditions of individual choice and responsibility. It was a powerful and extraordinary omnibus, this vocationalism.

MENTAL TESTING AND JUNIOR HIGH SCHOOLS

During the 1920s, two innovations rounded out the structure of differentiated education: the introduction of mental testing and homogeneous grouping, and the establishment of a system of junior high schools.

Teachers in Chicago were first officially exposed to the idea of intelligence tests in an article published by Mildred Hall in the *Educational Bi-Monthly* in late 1914, in which she discussed the work of Binet, Simon, and Terman.[169] By the early twenties, the pages of the *Chicago Schools Journal* reflected a serious interest in the use of "mental tests" to provide a basis for classroom grouping, as a means of protecting individual differences, and as a device to improve educational efficiency.[170] Two assumptions pervaded these articles. First, the authors assumed that individual differences were explained by differences in intellectual ability and could thus be measured by intelligence tests. Second, they believed that individual differences required homogeneous grouping in order to satisfy the demands of democratic equality of opportunity, "social efficiency," and the efficient organization of the learning environment. A 1924 article by Frank Freeman of the University of Chicago captured the essence of meritocratic defense of the new procedures. "The fundamental basis for the practice of homogeneous grouping," he wrote, "is the psychological fact of extreme differences in the capacity of children to do school work. Every test that has been given in recent years, whether it is an educational test or a special capacity test or a general intelligence test, shows that these differences exist." Only with honest and democratic recognition of individual differences would America accept the unequal outcomes of schooling as fair and legitimate. "The business of the school," Freeman concluded, is "to help the child to acquire such an attitude toward the inequalities of life, whether in accomplishment or in reward, that he may adjust himself to its conditions with the least possible friction."[171]

The board supplied some schools with mental tests as early as 1921; by 1924, all high schools had been supplied with them. However, the actual extent to which teachers used intelligence testing as the basis for homogeneous grouping in Chicago is difficult to determine. The U.S. Bureau of Education reported in 1926 that in Chicago the practice of classification "varied from school to school at the elementary level" with many schools simply relying on extensive use of nonpromotion or acceleration of pupils to group students by ability. The bureau did find, however, that at the junior and senior high school levels, a more consistent use of IQ tests became the basis of classification: After determining a pupil's mental age on the basis of his performance on an IQ test, junior and senior high school personnel then placed the student in one of the three or more ability groups. The 1932 survey of schools likewise found a "more or less haphazard and sporadic program of testing in some of the Chicago elementary schools and the almost complete lack of testing in others." In the junior and senior high schools, however, the survey found sufficient homogeneous grouping and differentiation of curricula catering to "individual differences to a fair degree" and urged the school system to press on with the good work.[172]

As in so many educational controversies in the second and third decades of the century, Victor Olander led the opposition to intelligence tests. In an article on the issue he wrote for the June 26, 1924, edition of the *Weekly Newsletter*, he argued that intelligence tests relied on two assumptions. The use of intelligence tests assumed, first, that children choose their curriculum specialization on the basis of ability and ability alone. But to Olander, the fact that some children selected difficult academic courses, others the technical and commercial course, and yet others the two-year vocational course, did not reflect innate differences of ability but the "economic and social status" of the pupil's family. "The boy whose family requires his services as a wage earner at the age of sixteen, will, probably select a two-year commercial or industrial course," he wrote. "The girl whose family can afford to keep her in school until she is approximately eighteen years of age will most likely select a four-year commercial course, while the pupil whose economic status permits will prepare to enter a college or university." The exigencies of family economy, not "mental ability," decided curricula and, therefore, occupational choice.[173]

Olander also rejected outright the assumption that the American social structure should reflect a meritocratic hierarchy of intelligence and ability. Such an assumption, he argued, in effect introduced into America "the ancient doctrine of caste," according to which "by alleged divine or natural law, the people are organized in groups according to the occupations for which they are supposed to be fitted, the merchant in the merchant caste, the teamster in the caste of the teamster, the carpenter in the carpenter's caste, and so on through the long list of vocations." Such a philosophy, Olander thought, would "demoralize" industry by implicitly teaching American youth to despise manual work or productive labor and would "Europeanize" American society into "more or less permanent class divisions."[174]

The solution, Olander continued, was not to degrade productive labor or citizens who did manual work. Nor was it sufficient to raise wages or shorten working hours: "Man does not live by bread alone." The solution rather was to give "the children of all classes . . . a full education no matter what occupation they may follow." Only in this way would the "master passion of humanity," the "desire for equality," be satisfied, and the basic principle of the American political birthright, the equality of all citizens, be realized.

> The basic principle upon which our nation is founded recognizes this truth in candid language, written so plainly that none can misunderstand its meaning and purpose. For this reason, and this alone, America has become the great nation of the earth, until within recent years the public school system has responded more and more to the great truth and as a result the education of all citizens has been growing apace. Now comes the effort to stem the tide of human progress in this country by overthrowing the great principle of American life within the public school system and thus, through the children of the nation, to degrade it by destroying the one vital principle which marks our nation as different from all others—the great principle of human equality as proclaimed in the American Declaration of Independence.[75]

Olander's lament fell upon deaf ears. Social efficiency, and the Progressive interpretation of equal opportunity, not the equal rights philosophy of Painite republicanism, guided the actions of the guardians of American education. When labor opposed the introduction of junior high schools on similar grounds, education officials again refused to listen.

The history of junior high schools in Chicago dates from 1917, when the board opened three junior highs, only to close two of them the following year. In 1923, however, the board decided to embark on a major expansion of the junior high school network. It appointed a committee to investigate the possibility of establishing a system of junior high schools in the city. In March 1924, when Superintendent McAndrew met with the Elementary General Council (composed of representatives of elementary teachers), he refused to answer questions the teachers put to him about the junior high school. On the last day of April, the committee tendered its report to the board, including a recommendation that junior high schools be established in seventh, eighth, and ninth grades. On May 14 the board voted to establish the junior high school in accordance with the recommendations of the report. The board held no public hearings, nor did it consult with any interested organization. McAndrew, without further ado, immediately took steps to open five junior high schools in the fall.[76]

The high-handed manner of the board and McAndrew alarmed labor, which suspected that the board and McAndrew intended to introduce another "class" system of vocational training different in name and form but similar in intent to the Cooley Plan. Labor accordingly requested a hearing with the board. The board granted the request. On June 3 representatives of the CFL, the ISFL, the High School Teachers Council, and the Elementary School Council met with the school administration committee of the board. Alderman Nelson, vice-president of the CFL, accused the board of attempting to establish the junior high schools in a cavalier fashion "without the slightest conference, without any element of citizenry, parents or teachers, being given an opportunity to discuss it with you." Victor Olander argued that the junior high school was an "attack against the democracy" (of the elementary school) by cutting from it "two years" so that the common education of children, so central to the development of proper citizenship, would in effect be reduced by two years. This reminded Olander of the Cooley Plan, and like the Cooley Plan, the junior high school "seemed to be nothing more than the German idea of compelling, through the public pressure of public authorities upon the parents, a class division being made clear and distinct when the child reaches the age of twelve years." But, insisted Olander, this plan "ran counter to all that is best and truest in American life." Calling on the political heritage of democratic republicanism, Olander rejected the idea of meritocratic testing and selection and called the junior high school plan a violation of "the meaning of the Declaration of Independence" with respect to "what it means to the equality of men," and to "the meaning of the Constitution."[177]

The committee waited until labor's spokesmen had finished, and then presented them with a typewritten statement of the policy of the board which had been prepared in advance of the meeting. The board, in its collective wisdom, had already made up its mind and would not change it. Labor's representatives felt that the meeting had been a charade. This was made all the more galling by the fact that labor was prepared to try out the junior high school as an "experiment" to see how it in fact worked, what its curriculum would be like, and whether it tracked students away from high school. At a discussion of the junior high school at the Chicago City Club on June 16, Olander pointed out that he saw no danger in an "experimental policy," particularly if labor had an opportunity "to watch, to suggest improvements, and to consult with the Superintendent of Schools and the Board of Education." He believed that the "average man among our people, no matter what class he moves in, is opposed to anything endangering Americanism," which he defined in terms of "the fact that our political structure is founded, as stated in the Declaration of Independence, on the equality of man." But it appeared, given the board's high-handed, undemocratic procedure, that the board intended to develop another form of "class education."[178] Insofar as the junior high school "switched" children away from the high school, the American school system would lose its democratic bearings, assume an elitist character, and create class divisions along European lines.[179] Junior high schools would, in effect, institutionalize "class" in American society:

Exactly the division proposed in the Cooley Bill which put the commercial interests in Illinois attempted to put through the Illinois legislature about ten years ago, the purpose of which was to classify the children at the age of twelve years into two separate groups, one of which was to be destined for higher education and the other for industrial life. The plan was defeated by the trade-unionists of the state then, but in a different form it is now being imposed upon the people of Chicago by the Chicago Board of Education.[180]

Labor had little doubt who was behind the junior high school plan. The CFL declared that "the new changes proposed in the public schools are degrading and the schemes proposed to be in force were conceived by representatives of the Chamber of Commerce and large industrial concerns as a hindrance to the children's obtaining a good education and to restrain their mental faculties to the extent that they might be able to induce them to work in their cheap industrial plants at low wages and under inhuman conditions."[181] Olander held similar views. The Chicago Association of Commerce, not the board of education, ran the schools. The association's interest in the junior high school could be traced, he believed, to the transformation of the production process and the effect of that transformation upon the demand for labor:

No kind of labor out of which there does not come pleasure to him who does it is safe to work or safe labor. And right there we are going to have the struggle, right upon that point, because through the establishment of new and efficient methods, so called of one kind or another, they have succeeded in dividing and subdividing until there is nothing left but a few mechanical motions, and they now want to bring in a new class of workers, who are to be turned out by the public schools for the purpose of doing this monotonous, mechanical, degrading, mean labor.[182]

Others besides organized labor opposed the junior high school. They held mass meetings in various parts of the city, particularly in areas designated to have junior high schools. Counts described the protest movement thus:

Groups of irate parents held indignation meetings, petitioned the board for hearings, and appeared at the board rooms for conference. . . . The bitterness of the struggle increased. In one junior high school the parents are reported to have destroyed $5,000 worth of equipment in protest against the change. At least one school strike was organized.[183]

Following rebuttal by the school administration committee, the CFL filed a protest with the board of education and began to drum up support: through the columns of the *New Majority*, organizing mass meetings, placing pressure on the board through the City Council, and carrying the issue to all the local unions of the state through the help of the ISFL. At the June 16 meeting of the executive board of the ISFL, the ISFL committed itself to the fray. The executive committee concluded that the junior high school

is cunningly devised and furnished a means whereby pupils at age of twelve years can be led into side-tracking courses which frequently do not qualify them for entry into regular high school although in its inception the system may be so administered as to disarm suspicion by providing a curriculum which actually does connect with the high school in the case of all pupils.[184]

Business and other supporters of junior high schools came to the defense of the board. In September the City Club and thirty-six participating organizations sponsored a conference in Chicago in support of the junior high school. The *City Club Bulletin* reported, in fact, that the conference "was one of the largest, if not the largest, ever held at the City Club." The *Bulletin* did not list the names of the organizations, but it did report that Superintendent McAndrew was the keynote speaker.[185]

The support of the City Club and other organizations swamped labor's opposition. By 1926, the number of junior high schools had increased to sixteen, and by 1932 to twenty-seven. Within eight years, a completely new division of schooling had been added at considerable cost to the school system. The growth of enrollments tells a similar story: From a total enrollment of 4,496 in 1924–25, junior high enrollments had climbed to 39,911 in 1931–32, nearly an eight-fold increase. In effect, fully one-third of all students at the end of sixth grade proceeded to a junior high school.[186]

The course of studies outlined by the board on September 3, 1924, for the junior high schools, and intended to reflect "immediate life experiences of the pupil," contained five courses: general academic, technical, commercial, practical arts, and household arts. In the seventh grade all pupils took the same academic subjects; in the eighth and ninth grades, differentiation commenced, with each pupil required to take a core group of subjects and specialize in one of the five curricula.[187]

In each of these courses, there is a core of subjects which are identical, and one featured subject which identifies the course. The Academic course, with its foreign language, prepares for any senior high school course and for general professional training. The Commerical course is good preparation for general office work and the commercial courses in senior high schools. The Technical course gives good training and leads into the Technical or Shop courses in senior high. The Household Arts course leads into the same or short Household Arts courses in senior high. The Practical Arts course is designed to give good shop training.[188]

Shop courses included practical experiences in electrical, print, metal, and woodworking processes. Students in nonacademic curricula spent five times as many periods in shop classes as did students in the academic curriculum. Over 68 percent of boys enrolled in the vocational courses (55.3 in the technical above), and 60.1 percent of the girls (including 55.1 percent in the commercial curriculum).[189]

The junior high school system, according to the board, existed "to provide youth with equality of opportunity without undue insistence upon equality of achievement." For Walter Hatfield, principal of Parker Junior High, the shop courses represented the core of the new program. "The shop courses develop deftness of hand with tools and machines, experience in working in different kinds of materials," he said, and promoted "shop habits of orderliness, care, thrift, industry, shop attitudes toward work and fellow workers, and appreciation of the value and dignity of manual labor." The inclusion of the various industrial courses reflected an attempt, he said, to give children of twelve to thirteen the "democratic opportunity" to try out the various industrial "experiences" to see which was most suitable to their individual "bent" and least likely to allow "failure," and to acquire the requisite "industrial intelligence" that would minimize the risk of failure in the workplace.[190]

Something of the character of these shop courses can be gleaned from a series of reports of visits made in 1927 and 1928 by members of the South End Public School Association to several junior high schools in the South Side. On a May 2, 1927, visit to the Sabin Junior High School, Mrs. Fred Rutz and Mrs. Clyde McAtee inspected the print shop: "Room 105, 7-A, the print shop. Found 49 boys in this room. Three boys, Solly, aged 12, 2014 West Division Street, Morris Cohen, aged 12, 1531 North Artesian Avenue, and Isidor Iken, 1224 North Oakley Avenue, were operating three power-driven printing presses."[191] In the tin shop, Mrs. Rutz and Mrs. McAtee found forty-five children at work, using the "usual knives and other tools of such work." The sewing room "was equipped with electric sewing machines which were being operated by eleven, twelve, and thirteen-year-old girls." In another seventh-grade class ostensibly studying "social studies," they found nothing but vocational guidance:

Found 41 children in portable social study class. It was raining. The children were obliged to pass into the main building without wraps. One boy was advised by the instructor to write to the Chicago and Milwaukee Railroad to find out "just how he could take up the 'work' he had in mind." Another boy, aged 12, was given a book edited by R. R. Donnelly & Sons Co., Chicago, to "guide" him and show him how he could best "fit himself" into a position with the firm. A business card came with the book, which was given to the child to take home for his parents to look over also. The card read, "E. E. Sheldon, Supervisor of Training Department, Lakeside. R. R. Donnelly & Co., 731 Plymouth Court, Wabash 2980." The instructor then gave us a number of folders from the vocational guidance department of the Board of Education. They were given to these seventh grade children so that they may "begin to train now."[192]

Subsequent visits to other schools revealed conditions in industrial education shops similar to those found at Sabin. On a May 6 visit to the Harper Junior High School, the visitors inspected the printing shop and found it to be "equipped with power machines—electric printing presses, etc."[193] Three days later, visitors to Stockton Junior High School found that the wood shop, the electric shop, and the print shop were all outfitted with standard industrial equipment.[194]

The following year, similar conditions prevailed. At Herzl Junior High, members of the South End Association "visited the class where children [boys] were sent from repairing the school furniture, screws, etc., to learning how to repair bells, lamp shades, bookcases, plumbing, etc." Some thirty years after the board of education had sought the passage of child labor laws, the visitors reported they were told that these seventh-grade children were "working for the Board of Education." (And without even paying child wages, and without fear of inspection by factory inspectors and compulsory education officers trying vigorously to get the children into the schools.) All of the industrial shops in the school the visitors found to be "equipped with power (Hersey Universal) drills, lathes, band saws, printing presses, etc." The children in the woodshop assured the visitors "they they used this power-driven machinery. One boy named Bennett Lion, pointed to a saw labelled #29763 (Oliver Machine) and told us that all the kids used the machines."[195] Victor Olander would hardly have been surprised.

VOCATIONAL EDUCATION AND THE MARKET REVOLUTION

The origins, politics, and significance of the triumph of vocationalism in Chicago are inextricably linked to the Great Transformation of the nineteenth century. The origins of vocationalism lie in the market revolution, particularly in the expansion of trade and markets in labor and the transformation of the labor process—the shift from formal to real subordination—accomplished through the increased division of labor and mechanization. A conceptual revolution in the 1880s and 1890s transformed the purposes of public education, long before social efficiency doctrines had become fashionable, and made possible the transformation of public education into an "adjunct" of the labor process and the labor market. In addition, the differentiation of the public school curriculum stratified educational credentials in a wholly new way and strengthened the connection between schooling and the system of stratification: students were no longer stratified in terms of the number of years of schooling completed, but also by the kind of knowledge they had been exposed to.

Ideologically, the triumph of vocationalism marked the victory of the market revolution in education and the defeat of Whig and radical republican conceptions of society and education premised on visions of a "classless" society and common schooling. The victory of vocationalism did not, of course, go uncontested. Superintendent Howland clung to Whig social and educational ideals. Tommy Morgan, Margaret Haley, John Fitzpatrick, and, above all, Victor Olander repudiated vocationalism and its accoutrements in the name of radical republicanism: differentiated education, IQ testing, and junior high schools violated the principle of equal rights and represented the establishment of a system of "class education." None of them rejected the inclusion of practical studies in the curriculum, but they insisted that such studies be part of the general course of studies. With the sole exception of the Cooley Bill, the opponents of vocationalism did not prevail, and even in the case of the Cooley Bill they prevailed only with the support of reformers who thought the Cooley Bill took matters too far. Few reforms of the Progressive Era better symbolize the efforts of reformers to reconcile the antinomies of commerce and virtue than the comprehensive high school.

Chapter 5

CENTRALIZATION AND THE TRANSFORMATION OF PUBLIC EDUCATION

In 1892 John D. Rockefeller founded the University of Chicago and made William Rainey Harper its president. Two years later, in 1894, the Chicago Civic Federation selected Harper the first chairman of its educational committee; the same year, the federation nominated Harper for appointment to the board of education. Two years later, Mayor Swift appointed him. Then, in January 1898, following representations from businessmen, Progressive reformers, and the Civic Federation, Harrison created a blue-ribbon Educational Commission to investigate and report on the state of public education in Chicago. Members of the commission then chose Harper as chairman.[1]

Exactly one year later, the commission reported to the mayor, recommending "radical" reform of the "largely defective" administrative structure of public education in Chicago. In particular, the commission found that the administrative structure, with its "large" board of 21 members and 17 committees inefficient, subject to graft and corruption, and prone to unwarranted political influence or "pull." The commission recommended that the board be reduced from 21 to 11 members; that board members continue to be appointed by the mayor rather than popularly elected; that administrative and legislative functions be clearly differentiated, with the administrative functions exercised by a highly paid superintendent acting as an educational "expert" with greatly enhanced powers and a six-year contract, and a business manager who would have "a free-

*Coauthored with Marjorie Murphy.

dom similar to that of the executive head in any well-conducted business enterprise." The superintendent alone would determine the course of study, hire all teachers, determine "efficiency," and recommend promotions. The commission concluded that "the established laws of business cannot be violated with impunity in the management of the professional details of our schools."[2]

Prominent national educational figures praised the commission's report, but to the fledgling Chicago Teacher's Federation (CTF), formed two years prior to protect teachers' pensions, raise salaries, and to "study parliamentary law," the Harper Report boded ill tidings.[3] The commission had included no teachers, women, or labor figures; it had not consulted teachers; it had made no provision for tenure; it had recommended that the process of teacher training and certification be revised to include a college education; and although it had recommended creating a system of teacher councils, they were to be advisory only and to have no say in the design of school policy or in the administration of the school system. When Harper engineered the appointment of Benjamin Andrews, a mentor of Harper's at Denison University, to the superintendency, and supported through the good offices of the leading expression of political progressivism in Chicago, the Civic Federation, a bill in the state legislature to institute the recommendations of the commission, the CTF feared that the material welfare and professional autonomy of Chicago's teachers stood in jeopardy. The union quickly mobilized to contest Harper and the Civic Federation in Springfield. The battle lines between business and the "administrative progressives," as David Tyack calls them, and the CTF were drawn, and remained so throughout the next three decades.[4]

At an immediate political level, three issues pitted the business community, the board of education, and the administrative progressives against the CTF: (1) business domination of the board, (2) imposition of a centralized and hierarchical administration modeled upon corporate industry and nourished by the same ideological developments that nourished political progressivism generally, and (3) the teachers' conditions of employment. The conflicts generated by these differences were often characterized by sharp expressions of class consciousness and antagonism, but the origins, character, and significance of these conflicts cannot be adequately captured in terms of a simple categorical notion of "class politics." Rather, the origins and significance of the centralization movement derived from the common vision of class relations and institutional alignments shared by progressives in education and civic reform and the complicated relationship between centralization politics and complex processes of class formation during the Progressive Era.

THE POLITICS OF CENTRALIZATION

When teachers founded the CTF in 1897, they were concerned with bread and butter issues—above all, salaries and pensions. Indeed, protection of their pensions against a proposed change in the state law regulating pensions for public servants precipitated the establishment of the CTF in 1897.[5] When the Civic Federation proposed a bill based on the recommendations of the Harper Commission (the Harper Bill) in Springfield in 1899, the concerns of the CTF expanded from pensions and salaries to include teacher training, job security (entry, promotion, and tenure), and their professional rights and autonomy. Within a short time the leaders of the CTF articulated a philosophy of administrative structure and professional autonomy very different from that proposed by the administrative progressives.

To contest the Harper Bill, the CTF circulated a petition, gathered fifty thousand names, enlisted the support of the Chicago Federation of Labor, and lobbied extensively in Springfield. Margaret Haley, who with Catharine Goggin was at the time running for election to the top leadership positions in the CTF, compared the teachers' role under the Harper Bill with factory employees. "The teacher is the only person under the civil service law who has no right to trial before the Civil Service Commission," she argued. "Every other person from Superintendent to janitor has that right. We are given no more consideration than factory employees and our places will be dependent on the good will of the Principal and Assistant Superintendent." In terms resonant with the radical republican idiom of antimonopolism, equal rights, and fear of class privilege, the CTF warned that if passed, the Harper Bill would give the superintendent "autocratic powers unknown to the Czar of Russia." The direct relationship between the despotic power of Rockefeller—the greatest example of "one man power in American business"—and the feudal implications of the Harper Bill should escape no one.[6] Moreover, the Harper Commission's recommendation that a college degree be made a prerequisite for entrance into teaching, thereby replacing the old apprenticeship system, outraged the teachers. Harper had impuned their cultural background (mainly working class) and their professional competence:

Uncouth and uncultured are terms which they freely apply to the unspecified element they desire to see eliminated from the schools. What constitutes culture they do not define, nor what incompetence. A college degree, however, they would probably accept as a certificate of culture. With all due respect for a college degree—there are many emergencies in the life of the public school teacher where it would be of considerable less value than the experience she has acquired during the four years usually spent in college. . . . To make it a condition of entrance to teaching or to lower the requirements in favor of those who hold a degree would be to put a premium on the conventional and the conventional is the last thing to rely on the problem of dealing with children.[7]

Teachers were not the only individuals upset. Members of the Chicago Central Labor Council argued that "making a college education a requisite for the position as a teacher" would severely limit the ability of working-class women to enter teaching, still, around 1900, the principal avenue of social mobility and respectability for working-class daughters. The new procedures represented "an unjust discrimination against the children of the common people who, with few exceptions, find it impossible to secure a college education, and who, for this reason, although qualified in all practical essentials, must give way to the college graduate."[8] Two months later, after Andrews claimed that since schools had to teach morality, it was necessary that teachers had to be "properly" educated, another delegate to the Central Labor Council denounced Andrews as a "moral leper." "He is the creature of Rockefeller and his purpose is to promote Rockefeller's ideas. He talks about outsiders in the schools. The outsider he refers to is the child of the proletariat."[9]

The combined opposition of the CTF and the CFL blocked passage of the Harper Bill, much to the chagrin of Superintendent Andrews, Harper, and the Civic Federation. Andrews blamed the failure of the bill directly on the teachers "who protect mediocrity and incompetency." The CTF, on the other hand, witnessed its membership soar to thirty-three hundred and confirmation of its political power in Chicago.[10]

Defeated but not intimidated, Andrews decided to pursue the goals of the Harper Report indirectly, through administrative fiat. In June 1899 he fired a woman music teacher and replaced her with a man as part of a "reorganization plan" without notifying the school management committee, nominally responsible for such decisions. A week later, Andrews again irritated the committee when he issued a memorandum requiring a college degree for admittance to principal examinations, another Harper innovation. Immediately, school management committee members argued that they were not consulted and countermanded the memorandum. Nevertheless, Andrews was not without friends in higher places, for at the National Education Association (NEA) meeting that summer, Nicholas Murray Butler came to the aid of Andrews, angrily denouncing the teachers in Chicago as "revolutionist" and successfully sponsoring a resolution lauding Andrews.[11]

Buoyed by his support at the NEA, in the fall of 1899 Andrews continued to implement the recommendations of the Harper Bill through administrative fiat. He announced that all principals were to make reports on teachers, noting "their fidelity and consecration," ability to govern, books they had read, and personal inquisitiveness. The teachers called it a police system "like in Russia."[12] In November Andrews proposed a plan of reorganization that included his own four-year tenure and a salary raise. The board refused. Andrews then rejected four principals recommended by the school management committee, and the committee ruled him out of order.[13] The following day, board president Graham Harris announced he would accept Andrews's resignation.[14] Andrews refused to oblige, and continued to fight throughout the winter months of 1900 for the reorganization of the administrative structure. The board frustrated each effort. In February newspapers announced that "President Harper, the Civic Federation and the members of the Superintendents' Department of the NEA are about to fire a 13-inch gun in defense of 'one-man power' in the Chicago Public Schools."[15] But Andrews had lost his will to fight; in March he took a vacation and upon his return resigned.

During the search for a new superintendent, the Civic Federation announced the formation of a Commission of One Hundred to study the "reorganization" of the school system and set up committees around each of the major recommendations of the Harper Report. Among others, Nicholas Murray Butler and Andrew Draper, president of the University of Illinois, addressed the Commission of One Hundred. Draper, like Butler, encouraged the federation to pursue administrative reform and to secure the reduction of the size of the school board and the appointment to it of men "representative of the business and property interests, as well as of the intelligence and genuine unselfishness of the city."[16] Meanwhile, the board appointed Edwin Cooley to succeed Andrews.[17] Cooley entirely sympathized with Andrews's objectives but proved to be far more adroit politically than his predecessor, actively seeking out the support of leading board members and the business community while introducing administrative reforms with considerable bureaucratic finesse.

Cooley first concentrated on gaining control over entry into the teaching force. At the time of his appointment, high school graduates entered teaching either through an apprenticeship system or through graduation from a two-year program at the Chicago Normal School (until 1896, the Cook County Normal School). Upon completion of their apprenticeship or graduation from the Chicago Normal School, local school committees of the board of education hired the teacher for a local neighborhood school, very often the same neighborhood the teacher had grown up in, a situation highly suited to patronage politics and local control of neighborhood schools.[18] Shortly after his appointment, Cooley acted to overturn the existing system and locate control of the hiring process in the superintendent's office. At the beginning of the new school year, Cooley convinced a member of the board to introduce an "anti-pull' regulation to prevent political influence in the hiring of teachers. In November the board approved the regulation. Under the provisions of the new rule, Cooley drew up a list of all personnel appointments and submitted it as a whole to the school management committee in June. Should any board member, alderman, or political person discuss with Cooley any individual teacher, Cooley would expose both the lobbyist and the teacher, placing that person on the ineligible list.[19]

Next, Cooley turned to the system of promotions. At the time, principals and local school committees controlled the promotions process; primarily they evaluated teachers for their ability to govern and to teach. When a financial crisis hit the school system in late 1901, Cooley took the opportunity to announce the introduction of a "new promotional scheme" and "merit pay system" in which salaries were tied to secret "efficiency grades" or "ratings." "Efficiency grades," in turn, were to be measured in terms of professional attainments, systematic work and results in scholarship, and "school interest"—cooperation with other teachers and with the principal—as determined by the principal. Efficiency grades determined whether a teacher could then take a promotional examination to gain a salary increase. From these evaluations a teacher was graded from 95 to 100 as "superior," 90 to 94 as "excellent," 80 to 89 as "good," 70 to 79 as "fair," and below 70 as incompetent. The grades were kept secret "to avoid comparisons" and to avoid political "pull." The teachers were never notified of their exact grade and if they had attained above 80, they were simply told they were eligible to take a promotional examination. "The merit system," Cooley claimed in unconscious irony, "will make teachers progressive, not time servers."[20]

With the antipull campaign in full swing and the new promotions scheme in place, Cooley turned to the transfer system. Normally, teachers transferred on the basis of seniority with the approval of the local school committee and the district superintendent. Cooley decided to "base transfers according to 'merit' " and the "needs of the entire system." Teachers had no court of appeal; those who appealed to their district superintendent, to board members, or their alderman Cooley accused of using pull.[21]

The CTF reacted with immediate hostility to Cooley's proposals. The "efficiency ratings" failed "to take into account the qualities of soul and heart and mind, the really vital part, the character and personality of the teacher" and threatened to undermine collective solidarity. The new transfer system, on the other hand, would destroy the ability of teachers to teach in the school of their choice, often in neighborhoods where they had grown up. The CTF leadership decided to boycott Cooley's proposals, but the membership split: While many teachers would boycott the system, others felt they could not afford to, a situation that created considerable conflict and "bitterness" among the teachers, and ineffective opposition. Not until 1905, with the appointment of the first Dunne board and the selection of Jane Addams to head the school management committee, did the teachers get their first real chance to force Cooley to retract his promotions scheme.[22]

Cooley's antipull crusade and his new promotions and merit pay scheme won him immediate prestige and invitations to speak at the Merchants Club, the Commercial Club, the Union League Club, and the Civic Federation, a prestige he used in turn to further centralize power in the superintendent's office.[23] He engineered the reduction of the number of board committees, organized along district lines, from more than sixty to four on a city wide basis: school management, buildings and grounds, finance, and compulsory education. In a series of moves, he gained control of the appointment of Normal School faculty, the admission of students, and the general policy of the Normal School. To destroy the power of local superintendents and centralize power in his office, in 1902 Cooley reduced the number of district superintendents from fourteen to six, significantly reduced their powers (e.g., over transfers, curriculum, and textbooks), created three new assistant superintendents in the head office to oversee day-to-day administration, and formed the six remaining district superintendents into an at-large board of superintendents. The next year, he codified the rules of the board of education, carefully delineating the prerogatives of the board and inserting those prerogatives of the superintendency outlined in the Harper Bill although not approved by the state legislature. He began to refine cost per student categories in his annual reports, and in 1904 started publishing the Chicago Board of Education *Bulletin*. The contents of the *Bulletin* accurately reflected the more prosaic preoccupations of the administrative progressives: average school membership, total cost of educational supplies, and average cost per pupil of supplies including chalk, crayons, erasers, drawing paper, arithmetic paper, spelling paper, language paper, unruled paper, pencils, pens, and penholders. The *Bulletin* listed these calculations by school so principals could compare their cost-effectiveness in issuing supplies to that of other schools. It also included curriculum outlines, suggested reading lists, and recommended study lists for teachers preparing for exams, aiming to achieve uniformity throughout the system. Pleased with the success of Cooley's efforts to achieve efficiency and economy, the board put aside its financial worries momentarily to vote him a five-year contract and a $10,000 per annum salary.[24]

Yet for all his success in securing administrative centralization, Cooley remained discontented: He also wanted legislative endorsement of what he had accomplished covertly through bureaucratic fiat. In 1901 the Civic Federation, with the support of Cooley and board member Clayton Mark, a Chicago businessman and later head of the Commercial Club's educational committee, sponsored legislation in the Illinois legislature proposing further reforms along the lines advocated by the Harper Report. But opposition lead by the CTF defeated the bill. Undeterred, the Civic Federation in 1903 supported another bill to increase the power of the superintendent to enable him to control appointment, promotion, and firing of teachers, to determine the course of study, and to reduce the size of the board from twenty-one to nine members. At the same time, Cooley and Mark supported a bill similar to the Civic Federation's, except that the Cooley-Mark Bill did not stipulate any particular size for the school board. Both bills were designed to give legal sanction to what Cooley had already accomplished.[25]

The state legislature refused to pass either bill, again due to the energetic opposition of the CTF and the Chicago Federation of Labor. The Civic Federation's bill, Margaret Haley claimed, "is fundamentally wrong because it creates an administrative officer and confers on him all the duties and powers naturally and necessarily inherent in the whole teaching force, and the people, through their representatives, thereby setting aside the principles of democracy in the internal administration of schools, precisely as the same principles are set aside in the government of the schools, so far as the whole people of Chicago are concerned. . . ."[26] To Haley, the bill expressed a nationwide antidemocratic sentiment:

The situation in Chicago as far as the relation of the teacher to the system is concerned, is not peculiar to Chicago, but is general throughout the country. The tendency in the field of education today is the same as the tendency in the commercial, the financial and the political world—that of concentration of power in one man or one set of men. This centralization of power has the effect of bringing the top captains of the world with untold power for good or ill to those under them and to those dependent on them.[27]

But the bill threatened more than democratic principles and the professional autonomy of teachers. It also attacked their material security:

The whole bill is a denial of the rights of the rank and file, whether they be teacher or people. Teachers who have not only spent years in professional training, but have devoted their lives to the actual work of teaching, who are in fact the real educators of the children, have no security of tenure of office or salary except that which the will of one man assures, and no more voice in the educational system of which they are a part than the children they teach.[28]

Contesting the Civic Federation's bills in Springfield represented only part of the CTF's efforts to protect democracy and the material interests of teachers. In 1900 and 1902 the union committed teachers to two unusual and controversial steps that challenged the board even further: In 1900 the CTF filed a tax suit against corporate tax evaders, and two years later it affiliated with the Chicago Federation of Labor.

In the wake of a threatened salary cut in late 1899, Margaret Haley instigated an investigation of the Cook County tax system. She found that several hundred corporations had avoided paying city taxes. She persuaded the CTF to file suit against the tax delinquent firms in the hope of increasing the revenues of the board of education—and the salaries of its teachers. Five public utility corporations alone owed taxes of $2,358,295. The courts decided in favor of the CTF in May 1901; in October the Illinois Supreme Court upheld the decision. Plaintiffs appealed to the U.S. District Court; the court upheld the decision but reduced the sum to $600,000. In 1903–04, the delinquent corporations paid the sum to Cook County, which, in turn, passed the money on to the Chicago Board of Education. But in a quite remarkable display of arrogance and callousness, the board, rather than paying the increases in teachers' salaries it had promised years before, decided to pay the coal bill, reinstitute kindergartens, give the janitors a raise, and contribute money to the building fund. The board then added insult to injury by introducing the Cooley "merit pay" scheme. Their material needs denied and their professional competence impuned, the members of the CTF voted to affiliate with the Chicago Federation of Labor.[29]

Haley justified affiliation as necessary to protect the material welfare of the teachers as wage earners and the need to join forces with those organizations struggling for a better education and democracy in America. "Two ideals are struggling for supremacy in American life today," she argued, "one the industrial ideal, dominating through the supremacy of commercialism, which subordinates the worker to the product and the machine; the other, the ideal of democracy, the ideal of educators, which places humanity above all machines, and demands that all activity shall be the expression of life." Because of the growing dominance of the industrial ideal and "the increased tendency toward 'factoryizing education,' making the teacher an automaton, a mere factory hand, whose duty is to carry out mechanically and unquestionably the ideas and orders of those clothed with the authority of position, and who may or may not know the needs of the children or how to minister to them," teachers needed to affiliate with organized labor. Affiliation offered a means through which teachers could "rid themselves of the reactionary conditions in and out of the classroom which are crushing out their lives and that of the children." Through organization and cooperation the teachers could "save the schools for democracy and save democracy in the schools."[30]

Affiliation with the CFL proved to be a bitter pill for a number of teachers, who resigned from the CTF in protest. But the dissatisfaction did not hinder the growing involvement of the leadership of the CTF in a number of reform movements, particularly municipal ownership and women's suffrage, both of which Haley and Goggin identified with the expansion of democracy in America.[31] The same year (1902) the CTF affiliated with the Chicago Federation of Labor, it joined the Illinois Federation of Womens Clubs. Affiliation with the two organizations provided the necessary ingredients for a strategy of coordinated reform encompassing labor, teachers, and women, representing the factory, the school, and the home for the pursuit of social reform. While labor would "improve the standard of living of the poorest and weakest members of society" and democratize industry, and women would protect the integrity of the home and the nation through the ballot, teachers would fight to protect the material interests of teachers and to extend "democracy in the schools."[32] Haley's hopes for the alliance appeared well founded, at least in the short run. During the 1905–07 debates over a new charter for Chicago, the CTF, the CFL, and the women's organizations combined to help defeat the educational provisions of the charter prepared by the Merchants Club and Theodore Robinson of the Commercial Club that proposed the selective appointment of school boards and administrative centralization. The CFL, for example, attacked the educational articles of the charter as an effort to transform public schools into "a cog in the capitalistic machine, so that . . . children reach manhood's estate content in a condition of abject servitude." There could be no other reason for centralized and autocratic authority, declared the CFL, than to impart a "reactionary mold to the minds" of future workers. Control of the school board and administrative centralization went hand in hand with controlling the content, pedagogy, and function of public education.[33]

Meanwhile, in early 1904 the CTF brought a suit against the board for the board's failure to increase teacher salaries with funds derived from the successful tax evasion suit; in August 1904 Judge Edward F. Dunne decided against the board and for the teachers. The following year, the CTF energetically supported Dunne's successful bid to become mayor of

Chicago. Dunne responded by appointing seven new board members friendly to the CTF and, according to Jane Addams, "for the most part adherents to the new education": Jane Addams herself; Cornelia DeBey, a physician and child labor reformer; John Harding, business agent for the Chicago Typographical Union; Mrs. Emmons Blaine, the widowed daughter of Cyrus McCormick; Emil Ritter, a manual training teacher and president of the Referendum League; and two others to represent the Polish and Jewish ethnic groups in the city.[34]

In one of the board's first acts, it appointed Ella Flagg Young, an ardent advocate of democratic decentralized administration and teacher councils, to the principalship of the Chicago Normal School. Addams secured appointment to the chairmanship of the powerful school management committee, a role she believed would enable her to mediate between Cooley's "commercialistic" administration and Haley's CTF, since the "whole situation between the superintendent supported by the majority of the board, and the Teachers' Federation had become an epitome of the struggle between efficiency and democracy; on the one side a well-intentioned expression of the bureaucracy necessary in a large system but which under pressure had become unnecessarily self-assertive, and on the other side a fairly militant demand for self-government made in the name of freedom."[35]

It was not long, however, before Addams and Haley came to a painful parting of the ways. In May 1906 a dispute arose as to whether the teachers who had borne the cost of the tax fight should be the only ones to receive a salary increase. The CTF and Addams divided; Addams suggested that the CTF was "self-seeking." But what ultimately forced the issue was Addams's failure to allow the CTF to petition the board against implementation of the Cooley promotional system. Addams thought that Cooley's proposals would be of "undoubted benefit" and proceeded to find a compromise with Cooley: Cooley could keep his promotional scheme if he would allow teachers to substitute course work for the promotional examination. Cooley accepted. Haley was appalled and described the affair as "one of her keenest disappointments" and a sign that Addams had "compromised her principles." Haley decided to give up on Addams—who had become known as a "strong" supporter of Cooley—and to wait for seven more Dunne appointments before mounting a campaign to dismantle the Cooley administrative structure.[36]

Dunne made seven new appointments in July 1906. Uniformly sympathetic to the vision of democratic administration sponsored by the CTF, the new members, particularly Ritter, Post, and DeBey, systematically attacked the administrative philosophy of the centralizers. Ritter complained that former boards of education had been dominated by businessmen who had run "the schools on the factory plan."[37] Post criticized the "spoilsmen" and the "business" board, denounced the "commercialistic ideal of the system," the replacement by the "ethics of the counting room" of "democratic tendencies and educational ideals," "high salaries for administrators with low salaries for teaching," and the "conception of authoritative sequence" based on a docile board of directors, a dictatorial superintendent, department managers, bureau chiefs, and a body of teachers responsive as a vast mechanism, like factory workers, to orders transmitted from above. Post ticked off the despotic character of the administrative system under Cooley's aegis—"the absurdly aristocratic marking methods, . . . the arbitrary salary-promotional device, . . . the silencing of the teaching body"—and decried "the irresponsible control which the Superintendent has over examinations for entrance, salary promotion and functional promotion," the "atmosphere of secrecy in which the system is immersed," and "the demand that the Superintendent be allowed complete control, either without supervision or under a Board with little other power than to register his decrees." Finally, Post found fault with Addams's compromise promotions and salary scheme of the previous year: "The recent modifications of the promotional test appear to have been introduced by way of compromise at a time when the Chicago Teachers' Federation was urging the abolition of promotional examinations," he argued. "While not open to some of the objections urged against the examinations, this test is equally objectionable as to its purpose, which is to create arbitrary conditions for salary advancement." Instead, he recommended a new policy including strict probationary requirements for new teachers, a board of three examiners to conduct entrance examinations, that all teachers graded by their principals as "efficient" per se advance through the salary schedule on an annual basis, semiannual reports of principals on each teacher, and that teachers have time off to attend classes at the Normal School.[38]

Cornelia DeBey added her voice to the chorus of criticism. Calling attention to the writings of John Dewey, Ella Flagg Young, and Albert Hart, DeBey decried the "despotic manipulation" of teachers by the "masterhands" and the hierarchical "methods of management . . . from the top downward." She proposed instead a new system of management that worked "from the bottom upward": the teaching force should have "advisory authority and responsibility on educational subjects and the relation of the teaching body to the school system," while the superintendent should have "administrative authority and advisory direction." DeBey also recommended that teachers be organized at the local, district, and central levels.[39]

The broadsides against the philosophy of centralized administration provided the intellectual justification to dismantle the system of centralized administration desired by the reformers. The board repealed the Dawes antipull rule, altered the promotions scheme, dropped the previous board's appeal to the state supreme court in the tax case, raised teacher salaries, debated the Post and DeBey reports, increased the membership of the board of superintendents from six to ten, appointed women to the four new district superintendent positions, voted to make decisions in teacher transfers, changed textbooks to include teacher choices in spellers and union-printed textbooks, and, finally, reorganized administration into a decentralized structure that included district councils with teacher representatives.[40] For the moment, at least, "democracy" had triumphed over "efficiency."

Partisans of business control and centralized authority did not, however, take all this lying down. Throughout the life of the Dunne board, the *Daily News* and the *Chicago Tribune* kept up an unremitting barrage of invective that was at times as inventive as it was vicious: "Freaks, cranks, monomaniacs and boodlers," the *Tribune* called the reformers. Jane Addams commented that "the newspapers had so constantly reflected and intensified the ideals of a business Board" that "from the beginning, any attempt the new Board made to discuss educational matters only excited their derision and contempt."[41] At the same time, Chicago's leading businessmen continued their campaign to extend administrative centralization. Declaring that the schools should be run on a "rational and business-like basis," the Merchants Club, through the good offices of Cooley, brought Nicholas Murray Butler back to Chicago to define once again the goals of the efficiency movement and to rally the faithful. Butler ridiculed the idea of teacher councils for he would "as soon as think of talking about the democratization of the treatment of appendicitis" as to allow "the democratization of schools." For Butler, "democracy is a principle of government; and a democracy is as much entitled as a monarchy to have its business well done." He concluded—to great applause—that if he were a board member he would do his "best to have adopted a by-law which would remove from the school service any teacher who affiliates . . . with a labor organization."[42]

In the 1907 mayoral race, the Republican candidate, Fred Busse, defeated Dunne and installed a "business" board as he had promised.[43] The new board, dominated, wrote Jane Addams, by men "representing the leading Commercial Club of the city," immediately went about dismantling the work of the previous board and reactivating the centralization program. In a symbolic gesture of class consciousness, the board renamed the Henry George School the George Pullman School.[44] The board also supported legislation, drawn up by members Theodore Robinson (vice-president of Illinois Steel, chairman of the education committee of the Commercial Club, and a leading advocate of charter revision and vocational education), to vest executive authority in the hands of a tenured superintendent and to reduce the size of the school board to fifteen members. The bill, however, went down to defeat, again largely due to the intense lobbying of the CTF and the CFL. Frustrated, Cooley resigned his position in March 1909, exclaiming as he did that no school reorganization program would be successful so long as the CTF existed.[45]

Although a final showdown between the business-dominated board and the CTF appeared imminent, in a surprise move the board appointed Ella Flagg Young superintendent to succeed Cooley. Young's administrative philosophy, articulated as a student of John Dewey's at the University of Chicago and published in 1901, was almost an antipode of Cooley's. Where Cooley desired to centralize power in the superintendent's office, Young preferred a system of decentralized administration that gave teachers a significant role through a system of teacher councils. Mrs. Young acknowledged the increasing size and complexity of urban school systems but did not view centralization and bureaucratization as their inevitable concommitants. Indeed, Mrs. Young argued, centralization and bureaucratization were undemocratic and un-American: "No more un-American or dangerous solution of the difficulties in maintaining a high degree of efficiency in the teaching corps of a large school system can be attempted than that which is effected by what is termed 'close supervision.' " Power should be decentralized and decisions implemented through a federal system of teachers' councils ascending from the individuals' schools to districts to a central council. The councils would consider policy proposals and make recommendations; the superintendent would act according to her judgment but she would "be held responsible for the outcome."[46]

Discerning the motives of the board's members who appointed Mrs. Young can only be guesswork. Perhaps they wished to lower the level of political conflict between the CTF and the superintendent's office; perhaps they imagined that the appointment of Mrs. Young would facilitate the implementation of a differentiated vocational curriculum. Mrs. Young, after all, strongly supported vocational education, and Theodore Robinson, a leading member of the board, was a major figure in the vocational education movement. In any event, the appointment of Mrs. Young certainly reduced the level of conflict between the CTF and the office as Mrs. Young adopted policies near and dear to the hearts of the CTF membership. She reduced classroom size, eliminated the secret marking system, modified the Cooley promotional plan, supported increased salaries, introduced teachers' councils, and consulted teachers on the selection of textbooks and curriculum development. As might be expected, the CTF thought very highly of Mrs. Young.[47] The relationship between Mrs. Young and the board proved far less cordial, however, particularly after Mrs. Young publicly opposed the Cooley Bill in the state legislation in 1913.[48] When she also refused to go along with the requests of two board members, William Rothmann and Jacob Loeb, to demote teachers who were leaders of the CTF or who opposed the efforts of Rothmann to gain control of the teachers' pension fund, relations between Young and the board deteriorated even further.[49] In an intriguing move, wholly inconsistent with the philosophy of administrative centralization but accurately reflecting the concerns of the board with curriculum matters, the board voted to remove control over the course of study from the superintendent's office.[50] Twice in 1913 Mrs. Young resigned her position (the second time the board split evenly on her reappointment), only to be reinstated by the board following widespread protests and pressure from Mayor Harrison.[51]

Meanwhile, tensions between the CTF and the board also accelerated steadily. In 1912 and 1913 Harrison appointed several members—Rothmann, a lawyer, and Loeb, a real estate and insurance agent—intent on destroying the federation and gaining control of the teachers' pension fund. In 1913 the CTF secured the defeat in the state legislature of a board-sponsored bill designed to increase board control of its pension fund.[52] In 1913 and 1915 the CTF led the opposition against the board-supported Cooley Bill. Thwarted by the CTF, Loeb bided his time. He eventually succeeded following a fiscal crisis in early 1915, the creation by the board of a committee of "efficiency and economy" to devise ways to lower costs (the committee recommended in May that teacher salaries be cut 7½%), the election of William Hale Thompson to the mayor's office in April 1915, the creation of a state commission (the Baldwin Commission) to investigate the board and the CTF (an investigation probably intended to be a CTF witch hunt), and the effort by a CTF sympathizer in the Chicago council to investigate the financial records of the board of education.[53] On August 23, 1915, Loeb introduced a motion into the board committee meeting that denied the teachers the right to belong to any organization affiliated with trade unions or having paid business agents. On September 1 the full board adopted the motion by eleven to nine.[54]

The Loeb Rule provides a classic example—indeed one of the first in American history—of the application of the open shop philosophy to public employees. As in the battles between labor and capital, the issue centered on control of the workplace, but with one important difference: The rhetoric of "professionalism" and "service" replaced the "harmony of interests" doctrine of industrial life. "Teaching is not a trade, it is a profession, and one of the noblest professions," explained Loeb. "In principle and in practice, trade unionism is inconsistent with and unnecessary to a professional career. In the schools it makes for a divided allegiance, it breeds suspicion and discontent. It destroys harmony and creates strife. It interferes with discipline and halts efficiency."[55] The CTF was "a curse to the school system," its leaders "lady labor sluggers."[56] "We've got to stop this unionization of teachers once and for all. It has gone far enough. These unions are growing like fire. They are taking over the schools and turning labor on us. We will cut them off from labor. We'll cut their professional throats if we have to."[57]

Nine days after the adoption of the Loeb Rule, the Chicago Federation of Labor called a mass protest meeting at the Auditorium Theater. Samuel Gompers and Louis Post, now assistant secretary of labor, came from Washington to speak. For Post, the Loeb Rule represented yet another effort by business to turn schools into factories by reducing teachers into factorylike workers. Alderman John Kennedy declared that businessmen and their representative, Jacob Loeb, wished to transform the school system "from a system of education for the development of the child, to a system to prepare the raw material for their factories and their shops and their mines and their stores. . . ." John Walker of the Illinois State Federation of Labor (ISFL) compared "the difference between school teachers who are free and untrammeled and independent, who have the right to act towards the school system as their knowledge of it and judgement leads them to believe is right, and, on the other hand, school teachers who will be held in the hollow of the hands of the direct representatives of the business interests."[58] The ILSF and CFL sent letters of protest to the governor of Illinois, denouncing the Loeb Rule as an effort by "big business" to have the schools "create for them a body of trained, efficient, and somewhat servile workers" while providing "the cheapest possible sort of education."[59] Margaret Haley linked the "determination of 'Big Business' to reduce the teachers to a state of servility" to the ongoing struggle between democracy and monopoly:

The attack upon the teachers of Chicago . . . reveals the dearest ambition of the financial feudal lords of America who have agreed upon one economic and political principle that looks to the control of the Public School system in the country. The motive is simple. Profits are being reduced by a growing experimental control. Democracy demands that this control shall become more powerful in the future. The selfish interest of the wealth classes depends upon the breaking down of the popular power, therefore, your fight for life is as profound and as precious as the early struggles of the men who founded this nation.[60]

On September 23 the CTF obtained an injunction against the enforcement of the Loeb Rule on the grounds that it was too sweeping. In response, the board on September 29 amended the rule to read "membership in *some* teachers organizations which have officers, business agents or other representatives of the teaching force."[61] The courts held, however, that no action could be taken until June 1916 when the teachers would be up for reelection. In June Loeb, now president of the board, dismissed sixty-eight teachers for failure to comply with the Loeb Rule (twenty-eight were federation members, including all eight of its officers). A storm of protest broke upon the board.[62] On July 17, 1916, a public meeting, chaired by Mary McDowell, addressed by Janes Addams, Charles Merriam, and Helen Hefferan of the Women's City Club and president of the Illinois Congress of Parents and Teachers and provided with a statement prepared in part by Victor Olander and John Fitzpatrick, condemned the firings and called for the creation of a new citizens association.[63] Shortly afterward, representatives from twenty-eight civic organizations, along with Jane Addams, Grace Abbott, George Herbert Mead, Charles Merriam, John Fitzpatrick, and Victor Olander, founded the Public Education Association (PEA).[64] Not to be outdone, the Illinois Manufacturers' Association (IMA) wrote the school board and Mayor Thompson supporting the Loeb Rule and created a rival organization, the Public School League (PSL). Two of the league's directors were former presidents of the IMA; its president was president of the Rock Island Mining Company. Declaring that its goal was to "increase educational efficiency," the PSL sought the "entire elimination of the Teachers' Federation and its politico-labor activities."[65] Later that year, Loeb joined the PSL.

In the early months of 1917, the PEA, the PSL, and Robert Buck of the Chicago City Council each sponsored a bill in the Illinois legislature to settle the disputes over administrative structure and control once and for all.[66] The PEA-sponsored bill (the Otis Bill) provided for an eleven-member, unpaid, appointed board, three principal administrators (the superintendent, a business manager, and an attorney), and teacher tenure after three years' service. Angus Shannon, the attorney responsible for drawing up the major provisions of the bill, explained to a City Club audience that the "primary idea" behind the bill "was to place the administrative phase of school affairs in the hands of experts, removed from political influence, and subject only to the approval or disapproval of a board of education, in matters of policy. Thus, all details of the actual work would be in the hands of specialists."[67] The PEA declared that among other objectives, the Otis Bill would allow "the board of education to organize the schools so that they shall employ the most expert people" while allowing for sufficient "progressiveness" in policy without jeopardizing "efficiency."[68] Although the bill included no provisions for teacher councils, increased the powers of the central administration, and provided for an appointed rather than an elected board, the CTF did not oppose the bill since it did include a tenure clause for teachers.[69] On April 20 a version of the Otis Bill passed the state legislature. After nearly twenty years of intense battle, the major goals of the original Harper Bill had been enacted into law. Centralization by statute had at last come to Chicago.

The very same day that the Otis Law passed, the Illinois Supreme Court, in a decision that Ella Flagg Young called the "Dred Scott Decision of Education," decided that "the board has the absolute right to decline to employ or re-employ any applicant for any reasons or for no reason at all. . . ." Elated, Loeb exclaimed that it was "the happiest day in my life, . . . there will be no more labor unions in the public schools." Defeated, the CTF disaffiliated with the CFL, the ISFL, the AFT (founded the year before in Chicago with the CTF as Local No. 1) and the Women's Trade Union League. The CTF never fully recovered from the blow.[70]

The sequel to the passage of the Otis Law reveals little more than a series of comic opera sideshows, including doublecrosses between old allies, court battles between competing boards of education, hastily arranged marriages of convenience, the wholesale looting of educational funds on a scale unparalleled even for Chicago, three indifferent and colorless superintendents, a lawsuit by one superintendent against a board of education, a grand jury investigation, the jailing of several board members for corruption, and the defeat of Mayor Thompson in 1923.[71] Under the circumstances, very little further centralization took place despite the demoralization of the CTF. When in 1924 a new board appointed a new superintendent, a disciple of Nicholas Murray Butler, the efficiency-conscious, single-minded, strong-willed William McAndrew, the process of centralization resumed with a vengeance.

Very little irritated William McAndrew more than "inefficiency," "lax standards," and the usurpation of the superintendent's autonomy, whether by teachers or the board of education. As much as anything else, Mc-Andrew believed in social efficiency, the prerogatives of the superintendent, and "close supervision." He roundly condemned the board of education's meddling in the superintendent's affairs. Referring to the "tragi-comedy" prior to his appointment, McAndrew traced its source to "the outworn fallacy that a superintendent is the board's . . . executive to carry out their policies. He isn't. . . . They can't say what medicines shall be used or what operations shall be performed. Somebody had to tell 'em that."[72] Similarly, McAndrew had no use for the CTF or teacher councils. In 1927 he informed an audience that he had been brought to Chicago for the purpose of "loosening the hold of this 'invisible empire' within the schools, a weird system, a selfish system, doing everything to indicate a selfish purpose and demanding the right to govern the schools."[73] And although required by board regulations to call meetings of the teachers' councils on a regular basis, he either refused to do so or allowed them to meet only under conditions specified by himself: meetings were not to be held during school hours, and principals could not be excluded as has been the custom, since to do so was "repugnant to experience, discipline and efficiency." The system of teachers' councils, he argued, violated the principles of "the standard works on school management in which there is a direct line of control from Board through superintendent and principal down to teacher. . . ." Teachers required not autonomy but "close supervision."[74]

McAndrew's regime of "close supervision" introduced a series of reforms. He required every teacher to check a report sheet four times a day, established fixed criteria of performance that made no allowance for the size of classes or children's backgrounds, and introduced standardized tests and a system of "line and staff" supervision to ensure strict compliance. McAndrew's "Official Notice on Teacher Efficiency" for 1925–26 contained little that was different from Cooley's original scheme. Knowledge of subject accounted for 10 percent; teaching ability 20 percent; progress of pupils 30 percent; cooperation with pupils and community 10 percent; cooperation in school management 15 percent; professional standing and growth (including adaptability to suggestion for professional improvement) 15 percent. Finally, an open-ended category for "demerits" allowed a principal for any reason at all to take off as many points as he wished. McAndrew informed principals that they had "the iron hand" and should use it.[75]

Although McAndrew flatly opposed efforts by politicians, businessmen, or teachers to dictate educational policy to the superintendent's office, he was by no means hostile to businessmen or to their interests.

McAndrew insisted on a "100 percent mastery program" in the basics—reading, writing, and arithmetic—favored by businessmen and solicited their opinion on the "efficiency" of the schools by sending out letters to members of the Association of Commerce under the heading "Customers' Estimate of Service." McAndrew did not send similar letters to leaders of the labor movement or to the parents sending their children to school.[76] In May 1926 McAndrew organized the first of a series of "Citizens' Sampling Days" to demonstrate to the school system's "stockholders"—representatives from leading civic organizations—the quality of the schools' "human output" and the degree to which the "human output" satisfied the "requirements" of the stockholders. On the appointed day, representatives from business firms, the Chicago Association of Commerce, the Union League Club, the City Club, the Women's City Club, the Chicago Bar Association, the settlement movement, and other organizations plied the children with questions and tests of skill.[77] For one invited citizen stockholder who did not attend, John Fitzpatrick of the CFL, there could be no doubting the meaning of "Citizens Sampling Day."

I cannot understand what you and your assistants are thinking about when you talk about 'output customers, Stockholders and Sampling Day' unless you imagine that you are running some kind of a mill or factory while you are grinding out a certain kind of product or material and you are going to get the 'stockholders and customers' together and bring forth 'samples' as an exhibit of your 'output.'

. . . Thus 'sampling day,' as you present it, is nothing more or less than an exhibition of the effort and result of eight years' schooling to make the youngsters think and act alike. . . . And the customers will be shown that the products of our public schools jump when the string is pulled, and they will be splendid material to draw upon for employees in stores, offices, shops, factories, or elsewhere.

The parents are not consulted as to whether or not they are satisfied with the kind of schooling their children are getting. But why should they be consulted? The schools are not being run for them but for the 'stockholders and customers.'[78]

The following year, 1927, the voters of Chicago reelected William Hall Thompson as mayor of Chicago. During his campaign, Thompson, perhaps wishing to establish his presence in international affairs before running for the office of president of the United States, attacked McAndrew for allowing "pro-British" books into the schools and promised to "punch King George in the snoot." After his election, Thompson promptly engineered a "trial" of McAndrew by the board and McAndrew's dismissal.[79] In a symbolic parting of the ways, the CTF and the CFL supported Thompson, while the Joint Committee on Public School Affairs, an umbrella organization of twenty-nine civic organizations and aging Progressive reformers, supported McAndrew.[80] Yet, although Thompson dismissed McAndrew, the dismissal did nothing to undo the centralization of educational administration or to roll back the business-oriented ideology of social efficiency that dominated the administration and curriculum of Chicago's public schools. McAndrew's demise did not presage an assault on centralization or on the ideology of social efficiency. McAndrew went, but centralization stayed; Thompson won, but social efficiency prevailed.

CENTRALIZATION, BUSINESS, AND PROGRESSIVE POLITICS

Between 1899 and the mid-1920s, a coalition of school superintendents and businessmen, with the occasional support of other Progressives, managed to secure, through a combination of administrative fiat and legislative statute, the major recommendation of the Harper Report of 1899: "radical" reform of the "largely defective" administrative structure of public education in Chicago. The victory of this coalition raises three general questions: first, the character and significance of their victory; second, the nature of the coalition that achieved it—the relationship between the administrative progressives, the business community, and Progressive reform generally; and third, the character of the opposition that centralization generated.

The phenomenology of success is readily apparent. The coalition succeeded in securing the reduction in the size of the school board, the appointment rather than the election of school board members, and the nonremuneration of members. Board members had been appointed rather than elected prior to the Progressive Era, and they had not been remunerated for their services either, but in light of the demands of the CTF and the CFL for the election and payment of school board members, the continued appointment and nonpayment of school board members should count as victories for the reform coalition. The net effect of the reforms is also not difficult to discern. Although businessmen were highly overrepresented on the board prior to 1899, after 1900 they dominated it, with the sole exception of the Dunne board between 1905 and 1907. George Counts, in his study of school politics in Chicago, reveals that all 120 members of the board he studied between 1903 and 1926 "were drawn entirely from the middle and favored classes. . . . The Chicago Board of Education has been composed almost exclusively of persons engaged in proprietorial, managerial, professional, and commercial occupations—lawyers, physicians, corporation presidents, manufacturers, merchants, publishers, real estate agents, bankers, architects, contractors, insurance agents, and dentists." Moreover, after the formation of the Association of Commerce in 1904, the association had, on average, three or four members serving on the board at any one time; during the first three years of McAndrews's administration, five of the eleven members were members of the Association of Commerce.[81]

In addition, the coalition drastically altered the administrative structure of public education in the decades after 1899: It secured the clear differentiation of legislative and administrative functions, and it imposed a hierarchically organized structure of authority, modeled on corporate industry, that located centralized power over the teaching force, the educational process, and the day-to-day operation of the school system in the superintendent's office. Cooley's "anti-pull" rule and his "promotional scheme" secured centralized control over the hiring, promotions, and salaries of teachers; other reforms secured centralized control over their training as well, while Loeb's Rule severely hampered the ability of the CTF to wield political power over the board or resist the superintendent's will. Although McAndrews failed to wrest control of the day-to-day operation of the school system from the local school management committees, Cooley succeeded. Securing control over the educational process proved a more complicated task. The organizational structure of the educational process—the fact that teachers taught in self-contained classrooms free from direct supervision of principals, and with some immunity from the imposition of more technical forms of control characteristic of industrial work processes—limited the ability of the superintendent's office to gain control over the educational process.[82] Nevertheless, the administrative progressives succeeded in securing as much control over the educational process as its organizational structure would permit. Each superintendent, but above all McAndrew with his regime of "close supervision" and constant measurement, increased the control of the superintendent's office over grading standards, student promotional policies, textbook selection, and pedagogical methods—the bureaucratization of pedagogical practices described in chapter 2. Finally, the superintendent's office exercised monopoly powers over the course of study, although for a brief period during Ella Flagg Young's incumbency the board removed authority over the course of study from her office. In effect, centralized control over the day-to-day operation of the school system, over teachers, and—within the limits imposed by the classroom system—over the educational process represented the successful imposition of a hierarchical structure of social relations and the creation of what Willard Waller described as a "punishment-centered bureaucracy" in which superintendents exercised "dominative" authority over teachers, an educational version of the shift from formal to real subordination characteristic of corporate industry.[83]

Two groups could fairly claim responsibility for the success of the centralization movement: businessmen and their organizations, and an ambitious but clearsighted cadre of aspiring professional educational administrators who, with one exception, occupied the superintendent's office between 1899 and 1927—Harper, Andrew, Cooley, and McAndrew. Of the two groups, the administrative progressives were far more committed in principle to centralization. Indeed, there are ample grounds for believing that many of the businessmen who supported centralization did so not because they supported educational centralization as a matter of principle but because they wished to engage in various forms of petty accumulationist activity or pursue an open shop campaign. Membership on the board, support for centralization, and opposition to the CTF were far from one and the same thing.

Chicago's administrative progressives pursued centralization for a variety of reasons, although not because they were forced to, as Raymond Callahan suggests. Callahan argues that educational administrators advocated centralization for purely defensive reasons: by virtue of the "vulnerability" of their positions to business-dominated boards of education, administrators adopted the ideology of social efficiency and pursued centralization to protect their jobs.[84] This does not seem to have been the case in Chicago. True, businessmen dominated the board of education and superintendents served at the pleasure of the board. But the business-dominated board of education did not impose the ideology of social efficiency or the particular model of centralized and hierarchical administration on a recalcitrant Edwin Cooley or an unwilling William McAndrew. Both men viewed themselves as apostles of the new order. Both wholeheartedly, even passionately, believed in social efficiency and centralization, proselytized on its behalf, and attempted, against bitter opposition from the CTF and the CFL, to advance the cause of one and institutionalize the other. The explanation of the adoption of social efficiency doctrines and centralization by the administrative progressives lies elsewhere than in the "vulnerability" of their positions.

In part, the centralized and hierarchical bureaucratic structure that the administrative progressives and their business allies imposed reflected a response to a genuine crisis of financial solvency and administrative coordination associated with the rapid expansion of the school system in the years after 1890. But problems of coordination and financial solvency can explain only part of the popularity of the corporate model of administration. Administrative coordination can be achieved through a variety of administrative structures: the administrative progressives sought not just coordination but centralized, hierarchical, bureaucratic control.[85] The administrative problems facing the administrative progressives were real enough, but the administrative structure they imposed expressed a particular political construction of administration—the assumption, shared with other followers of administrative progressivism writ large, that administrative efficiency necessitated a centralized, hierarchical, and bureaucratic administration characteristic of corporate industry. The fact that the board frequently turned a blind eye toward corporate tax evasions and low property assessments, that it sold prime inner city land to resolve immediate fiscal problems, and that it leased valuable school land at a fraction of its real value to major corporations in Chicago only exacerbated the problem.[86] Moreover, administrative progressives, like their ideological compatriots in civic reform, were intensely leary of machine politics and imagined that a clear separation between legislative and administrative functions, and the centralization of educational decision-making in the superintendent's office, would limit the capacity of "politics" to corrupt the administrative process. Again, the fledgling science of educational administration developing at Stanford, Columbia, and Chicago lauded the corporate model for its efficiency, economy, and parsimony.[87] Finally, insofar as educational centralization promised to create a profession at once powerful, respected, and remunerative, it provided a means of advancing the claims of meritocratic expertise as a legitimate form—and source—of social authority and secured the "collective mobility" of an aspiring professional group of educational administrators. In a word, centralization was part and parcel of a process of class formation—the making of the professional middle class.[88]

The administrative progressives did not succeed alone and unaided. Indeed, businessmen, business organizations, and a business-dominated political reform organization (the Civic Federation) aided and abetted them in important ways. The Civic Federation sponsored Harper's entrance into public school politics when it nominated him for the board of education in 1894, supported the formation of the Harper Commission in 1898, sponsored the Harper Bill three times in the state legislature, in 1899, in 1901, and again in 1903, and created the Commission of One Hundred to advance the cause of centralization; the business-dominated board gave unwavering support to the efforts of Andrews, Cooley, and McAndrew to centralize educational administration; representatives from the Merchants' Club and the Commercial Club drew up the education provisions of the revised city charter in 1905–07; Clayton Mark of the

Commercial Club collaborated with Edwin Cooley in drawing up another bill submitted to the state legislature in 1903; Theodore Robinson, also of the Commercial Club, assumed responsibility for drafting another version of the Harper Bill in 1909; Jacob Loeb broke the affiliation of the CTF with the CFL; the Illinois Manufacturers' Association created the Public School League in 1916 to support Loeb's efforts to dismember, as it were, the CTF.

But although businessmen dominated the board during the period when it imposed centralized administration, and although they assumed major responsibility for securing legislation sanctioning centralization, for the most part, businessmen supported centralization, or what is not quite the same thing, opposed the CTF, for very different reasons than those motivating the efforts of the administrative progressives. In general, relatively few businessmen were seriously interested in centralization per se, and even fewer supported centralization because they were philosophically committed, as a matter of principle, to centralization. Indeed, while reform of the conditions of board membership helped consolidate business domination of the board of education, it is fairly clear that in part business domination of the board did not so much reflect business preoccupation with principles of social efficiency and centralized administration but a belief among many businessmen that board membership represented an opportunity to engage in one form or another of petty accumulation. Some, like William Rothmann, for example, were little more than greedy, avaricious opportunists interested in tapping the revenues of the board (or the teachers' pension fund) to line their own pockets, or they wished to punish, hobble, and, if possible, destoy the CTF for its efforts to expose public utilities, a major newspaper (the *Tribune*), and several dozen large corporations (including Pullman and Armour) for tax evasion, low property assessments, and the leasing of valuable school board property to businessmen for a fraction of its market value. For such businessmen, centralization, or opposition to the CTF, were matters of immediate economic gain, not political principle. On occasion some businessmen supported centralization or opposed the CTF as a matter of principle: The businessmen associated with the Merchants' Club who drew up the educational provisions of the proposed city charter in 1905–07 were "better government" businessmen interested in keeping school costs and, therefore, taxes to a minimum as a matter of economic principle, while Jacob Loeb and the members of the PSL who battled the CTF were apostolic, anti-union, open shop ideologists committed to the destruction of the CTF and the labor movement generally.

Yet, not all businessmen supported centralization or opposed the

CTF simply because board membership provided an opportunity to engage in petty accumulationist activity or indulge in open shop demagoguery or to keep taxes low. Some, at least, had a broader view. The very same Civic Federation that sponsored Harper and then the Harper Bills in 1899, 1901, and 1903, also supported municipal reform through the Municipal Voters League, whose approach to public administration and politics differed not a whit from the views of the administrative progressives. Both looked askance on the corruption of democratic politics, both wished to separate as far as possible legislative and administrative functions, both endeavored to ensure economy and efficiency in government and the election of responsible citizens to elective office, and both imposed a hierarchical and centralized model of governance on public administration. Moreover, individuals and organizations closely linked to the centralization movement were also closely linked to the movement to vocationalize and differentiate the curricula of public education in Chicago. Both Clayton Mark and Theodore Robinson took responsibility for drafting versions of the Harper Bill and participated in the vocational education movement. Edwin Cooley advanced the cause of centralization and vocational education as superintendent between 1901 and 1909, and after 1910 played a key role in attempting to secure a system of differentiated education. Both Mark and Robinson, it will be recalled, were chairmen of the educational committee of the Commercial Club—the very same organization that sponsored Cooley's campaign to differentiate the public school system. In effect, the same individuals, the same organizations, and the same philosophy—social efficiency—guided both centralization and vocational education to victory. Where one set of reforms ensured that businessmen formally governed the school system and that superintendents administered the school system in a businesslike manner according to businesslike principles, the second transformed schooling into a business institution, an adjunct to the market economy.

Two groups, businessmen and the administrative progressives, deserve the bulk of the credit for the success of the centralization movement. But, on occasion, mainline Progressive reformers also provided important support. This is particularly apparent in the support of the Harper Bill by the Civic Federation in 1899, 1901, and 1903, in Jane Addams's qualified support for Cooley's promotional scheme in 1906, the foundation of the PEA in 1916 by Addams, Merriam, McDowell, Mead, Abbott, and others, passage of the Otis Bill in 1917, and the support of McAndrew by the Joint Committee on Public School Affairs in the mid-1920s (when McAndrew fought to introduce junior high schools, the platoon system, intelligence testing, and "close supervision," and fought off political interference in the administration of the school system). The fact that Addams, Merriam, Mead, Abbott, and others protested the Loeb Rule in 1916, or that Addams supported the affiliation of the CTF with the CFL, did not represent an ambivalent or limited commitment to centralization; it merely indicated that they did not identify the cause of centralization with opposition to the affiliation of the CTF with organized labor.

If support among Progressive reformers for centralization did not necessarily involve opposition to the CTF, there can be no doubting the opposition of the CTF itself to centralization. At the time of its founding in 1897, the concerns of the CTF membership were limited to two issues: salaries and pensions. At the time, the question of tenure was not a live issue—Governor Altgeld in 1895 had managed to insert a limited tenure provision for teachers in the pension law of 1895. Yet within the space of three and a half years, between January 1899 and mid-1902, a series of events rapidly expanded the preoccupations of the CTF: the release of the Harper Report in early 1899, the sponsorship of the first of the Harper Bills in the state legislature later that year and again in 1901 and 1903 by the Civic Federation, the appointment of two self-confessed centralizers, Andrews and Cooley, as superintendents, the refusal of the board to increase teacher salaries in 1899 on the grounds of insufficient funds, Cooley's "anti-pull" crusade and his introduction of a "new promotional scheme" and merit pay system in 1901–02, and the refusal of the board to increase teachers' salaries in 1901 following the CTF's court victory in the tax case. In response to these events, the agenda of the CTF expanded to include issues involving conditions of entry and promotion, job control, and social reform. That agenda changed little for more than thirteen years until 1916 when the board's firing of sixty-eight teachers added tenure to the list. For almost two decades, the CTF actively pursued the cause of "democracy in the schools" and "democracy for the schools." The former focused on resisting the imposition of "close supervision" and hierarchical, centralized, and bureaucratic control within the workplace while attempting to secure a system of teacher councils, decentralized control, and professional autonomy, as well as job security. The latter, "democracy for the schools," centered on a variety of reform movements after 1900: tax reform, municipal ownership, antimonopoly, women's suffrage, and support for organized labor.

Teacher councils represented the core of the CTF's campaign for "democracy in the schools." Ironically, the Harper Commission first raised the possibility of a system of teacher councils in 1899, but the commission intended the councils to be without any formal authority—a mere tea-and-biscuits device, not an administrative agency or policy-making body.

But the influence and writings of Francis Parker, John Dewey, Ella Flagg Young, and Cornelia DeBey suggested a far more substantial and agreeable system of teacher councils and decentralized administration. Many teachers, certainly the leadership of the CTF, were thoroughly familiar with Ella Flagg Young's *Isolation in the Schools,* and many had been deeply influenced by Parker and Dewey, some as students, or through attending their public lectures and reading their published works. Margaret Haley, for instance, drew upon Parker and Dewey to explain and justify her conviction that teachers, by virtue of the great responsibility they assumed for the training and cultivation of the minds, personalities, and character of children, required sufficient professional autonomy to be able to respond meaningfully to individual student differences and needs and a level of material security and professional prestige befitting the importance of their responsibilities:[89]

To the teacher it means freedom from care and worry for the material needs of the present and future—in other words, adequate salary and old age pensions; freedom to teach the child as an individual and not to deal with children en masse. In other words, fewer children for each teacher. Last but not least, the teacher must have recognition in the educational system as an educator. The tendency is to relegate her to the position of a factory hand, or to the orders from above.[90]

Indeed, teachers found the demand for teacher professionalism voiced by administrative progressives hypocritical and contradictory. They dismissed "professionalism as service" as a ploy to keep teachers' salaries low. To insist on professionalism while denying teachers control over the conditions of entry and certification requirements common to other professions, failing to provide adequate tenure, job security, and salaries, and refusing to institute a system of councils was sheer hypocrisy. What else could the teachers conclude of the decision of the Board to refuse to give teachers time off to attend a public lecture by G. Stanley Hall on the grounds that the board believed the teachers were not ready for Hall's ideas.

Teachers pursued job security, teachers' councils, decentralized administration, and professional autonomy under the banner of "democracy in the schools." But the quest for democracy also involved a wider political commitment to the extension of democratic principles to all aspects of social life. Like John Dewey, the CTF leadership argued that democracy in the schools could not be separated from—indeed in the long run necessitated—democracy in the wider society. Certainly, the fights against tax evasion by the utility corporations and the leasing arrangements between the board and several Chicago companies were motivated in part by the decision of the board to renege on promised salary increases. But these struggles also expressed an antimonopoly and equal rights philosophy with ideological roots in Populism, Greenbackism, and the Knights of Labor (all of which were part of the political culture of Margaret Haley's family), and the single tax philosophy of Henry George's *Poverty and Progress,* a book that Margaret Haley had read and described as having "had a profound effect on me."[91] Again, the support of the CTF for the municipal ownership movement, like the fight against the "industrial ideal" and "one-man rule" in education, expressed an antimonopoly and equal rights sentiment against "money power," class privilege, and the "concentration of power in one man or one set of men."[92] The battle to elect Dunne mayor of Chicago, and the appointment of the Dunne school board, particularly Louis Post, a Georgite single taxer, reflected the CTF's efforts to secure a popularly based school board inspired not by the "industrial ideal" but by democratic principles. Affiliation with the Chicago Federation of Labor in 1902 represented more than a tactical move by the CTF to protect the material and professional interests of its membership. It also represented the commitment of the CTF to broader democratic political objectives. While the depth of support among the membership of the CTF for women's suffrage is unknown, Haley herself worked tirelessly on its behalf for more than a decade, lecturing, traveling, lobbying, organizing, and answering mail.[93]

Finally, in pursuit of "democracy for the schools," the CTF played a leading role in founding the American Federation of Teachers in 1916, and in effecting, between 1903 and 1910, a number of significant reforms within the National Education Association.[94] Through adroit political maneuvering, feminist fellowship and the garnishing of widespread grassroots support, the CTF fractured the power of the ruling oligarchy (led by William T. Harris and Nicholas Murray Butler) of the NEA, reformed selection procedures, elected Ella Flagg Young president in 1910, enlarged the size of the National Council on Education, refocused some of the NEA's energies and funds onto questions of teachers' salaries, pensions, and tenure, and secured the creation of the Department of Classroom Teachers.[95]

The involvement of the CTF leadership in this broad array of reform movements on behalf of democracy for the schools and the protracted struggle of the CTF to secure professional autonomy and decentralized administration in the workplace preclude the conclusion, advocated by some historians, that the goals of the CTF were little more than expressions of an economistic philosophy of pure and simple unionism.[96] Certainly the CTF leadership believed that the pursuit of these political objectives would enhance the material and professional well-being of teachers, but their commitment also reflected a larger political commitment to the extension of democratic social relations in America. Indeed, the politics of the CTF closely resemble the politics of "reform unionism" characteristic of the Knights of Labor during the 1880s rather than the narrow econ018omistic policies of "pure and simple" unionism of the 1900s. Like the unions that flocked to the Knights of Labor, the CTF pursued a program that combined improved material welfare, job autonomy, and the preservation—or restoration—of democratic social relations in America, and nourished its politics with the traditions of antimonopolism and equal rights radical republicanism. The CTF did not, admittedly, protest proletarianization as the Knights had, but it did protest the threat that the new training and appointment procedures represented to working-class women seeking respectability and a measure of economic independence.

Other parallels, besides those of politics and ideology, can also be found. Some historians of the Knights of Labor (Commons, Perlman, and Grob, for example) argue that the Knights articulated a "transitional" "pre-industrial labor consciousness" prior to the triumph of pure and simple unionism. Similarly, it could be argued (indeed, it is implicit in Robert Reid's history of the CTF) that the CTF represents, as it were, a transitional or pre-professional consciousness prior to the triumph of pure and simple professionalism (to coin a phrase) and the organizational revolution.[97] Neither interpretation, however, can withstand close scrutiny. To describe the consciousness of the Knights of Labor as a form of "pre-industrial labor consciousness" ignores the critique of industrial capitalism articulated by the Knights and the vision of democratic industrial organization that the Knights proposed. Moreover, the labor historians who described the Knights as a transitional phenomenon assumed a particular telos: the inevitable (and laudable) triumph of pure and simple unionism. But the Knights were not defeated by teleology. Rather, Haymarket, the shift from formal to real subordination, and the process of working-class formation—the replacement of the first generation of industrial workers by the second (largely immigrant) generation and the development of the labor aristocracy—destroyed the Knights. Likewise, a pre-professional consciousness did not characterize the CTF; instead, it developed an informed critique of centralization, while at the same time articulating an alternative model of administrative structure and professional autonomy. Moreover, the defeat of the CTF did not reflect the realization of an omniscient logic of professionalization or express an immutable bureaucratic imperative toward administrative rationalization. Rather, it reflected the combined effect of particular and highly contingent political events and processes. Two of these were particularly significant.

First, the social authority of the ideology of social efficiency and the political power of the administrative progressives and their business allies enabled the apostles of centralization to push through a series of reforms that radically circumscribed the power of the teachers and limited the ability of the CTF leadership to sustain a militant unionist and radical political posture. The board's adoption of the Loeb Rule in 1916, for instance, destroyed a major power base of the CTF—affiliation with organized labor—and broke the spirit of the CTF membership, or at least the spirit of its leadership. The success, moreover, of the administrative progressives in gaining control of teacher training and appointment enabled the superintendent to socialize teachers to the new pedagogical and administrative order and to tie the careers of teachers to the superintendent's office rather than to local district committees. In effect, Cooley succeeded in breaking the nexus between working-class neighborhood politics, represented by the local school committee, and control of the work place—training, appointment, and promotion. Finally, the expansion of the school system and the lengthening of job ladders (for women as well as men) created new job opportunities for ambitious middle-class college educated women and created a new faction, a labor aristocracy, within the teaching force—principals, vice-principals, specialists of various kinds—whose fortunes were closely tied to the new administrative order.

Second, the changing social composition of the teaching force undermined the capacity of the CTF leadership to foster the growth and maturation of a radical working-class organization. During the closing years of the nineteenth century, the social composition of the teaching force changed quite dramatically: between 1880 and 1900, for instance, the percentage of daughters of semi- and unskilled workers in the labor force dropped from 17.7 percent to 7.9 percent, and the proportion for all blue-collar daughters declined from 47.7 percent to 35.6 percent, while the percentage of daughters from high white-collar homes increased from 15.4 percent to 27.2 percent. A similar decline characterizes the ethnic pattern: among immigrant families, the percentage of daughters from households with one or more foreign-born or semiskilled or unskilled parents dropped significantly from a high of 22.7 percent in 1880 to 7 percent in 1900.[98] A noticeable shift in the demographic profile of the teaching profession thus occurred between 1880 and 1900, the very year the first cohort of teachers required to have three years of postsecondary education entered the teaching force, although we do not know whether, or to what extent, the latter contributed to the former. There is every reason to suspect, moreover, that the demographic trend apparent by 1900 continued after 1900. Edwin Cooley had only to pay low wages (relative to office and factory work) to push the daughters of low white-collar and blue-collar origins out of a profession in the process of redefinition to accommodate middle-class daughters seeking temporary employment before marriage. Expanding opportunities in clerical work attracted women out of teaching, but the disincentives to stay in education encouraged the most assertive and militant to give up any ambitions they may have had in the schools and leave. What had initially been an occupation of working-class women was still, in 1902, the year the CTF affiliated with the CFL, dominated by women from a working-class background, but the writing was on the wall. By the time the board adopted the Loeb Rule in 1916, the membership of the CTF had probably become predominantly middle class in character, and after 1916, middle class in outlook as pure and simple professionalism replaced reform unionism.

In opposing centralization, the CTF received support from several sources. It received support from mainline Progressive reformers in 1916 during the crisis over the Loeb Rule, not because Progressives opposed centralization, but because Progressive reformers were dismayed by Loeb's hard line, open shop tactics and confrontational politics. Indeed, in the aftermath of the Loeb crisis, the organization created by the Progressives, the PEA, worked energetically to secure passage of the Otis Bill, which gave legislative sanction to centralization. The CTF also received support from members of the Dunne board, particularly Ritter, Post, and DeBey. Jane Addams supported the CTF on some issues (e.g., affiliation with organized labor) but opposed it on others (e.g., with regard to Cooley's promotions and merit pay scheme). Ella Flagg Young supported the right of the CTF to affiliate with the CFL, but more importantly, supported decentralized administration and teacher councils.

The CTF's most important and persistent support, however, came from organized labor, particularly the CFL. The CFL strenuously supported the industrial policies of the CTF to improve conditions of employment and gain a measure of job control through decentralized administration and teacher councils, but the support of the CFL for the CTF went far beyond fraternal duty. The CFL's support also expressed a deep sympathy to the political orientation and commitments of the CTF—its efforts to create a democratic education for a democratic society. Like the leadership of the CTF, the CFL feared that centralization represented an effort to prevent the democratic control and administration of education in order to create a class-stratified system of education to serve the needs of business. Hence, the considerable resiliency and potency of the factory metaphor in the rhetoric of the CFL (and the CTF): their belief that businessmen and Superintendents Andrews, Cooley, and McAndrew wanted to create a factorylike education, governed autocratically by businessmen and the superintendent's office, in which factorylike workers (teachers) would train in a factorylike manner in specialized production processes (differentiated curricula) future factory workers.

For a little over a decade and a half, the coalition between the CTF and the CFL, with the support of the Dunne board and the occasional support of Progressive reformers, hampered the efforts of the administrative progressives to secure centralization through administrative fiat and blocked passage of legislation imposing centralization. In the long run, the coalition proved unable to prevent the triumph of centralization.

Its failure strikingly illustrates the character of progressive reform and the larger social processes associated with America's Great Transformation that shaped the reform movement. Essentially the failure of the CTF and its allies does not so much reflect the inevitable triumph of an organizational imperative as it does the greater political, ideological, and industrial resources of the administrative progressives, the impact of on-going processes of class formation and reformation, and the transformation of public education into a labor market institution. The Loeb Rule destroyed the CTF as an industrial force, while the slow accretion of centralized power under Andrews and Cooley and the Otis Bill doomed the vision of decentralized power and professional autonomy that the leadership of the CTF supported. In a sense the imposition of a hierarchical and centralized system of educational governance, the bureaucratic rationalization of pedagogical practices, and the day-by-day control of teachers through "close supervision" constituted an educational version of the shift from formal to real subordination characteristic of corporate industry. At the same time the clash between the CTF and the administrative progressives reflected the impact of processes of class formation and contributed to them in turn. On the one hand, administrative progressives aspired to advance the claims of meritocratic expertise as a legitimate source of social authority, to proselytize on behalf of social efficiency, institutionalize a hierarchical structure of social relations and administrative arrangements within public education, and create an occupation at once lucrative and prestigious. Their successes in this enterprise contributed to the making of a nascent professional middle class. On the other hand, the political conflicts associated with centralization at first advanced the making of a radical working-class organization practicing a politics of reform unionism. Later, the Loeb Rule, the changing social composition of the teaching force, and the successful redesign of administrative arrangements within public education stopped this process of working-class formation dead in its tracks. In effect, the CTF appears to have been both a product and a victim of processes of class formation.

Finally, the victory of centralization is closely related to the transformation of public education into a labor market institution. Because the CTF and organized labor opposed not only the Harper Bill but also the Cooley Bill, not merely the imposition of a corporate model of educational administration and the formal control of public education by businessmen but the stratification of the curriculum under the aegis of social efficiency, opposition to the CTF and support for centralization came to be closely connected, in terms of ideology and personnel, with the drive to vocationalize and differentiate public education. In short, centralization consolidated business control of the board of education, transformed the administration of the school system along corporate lines, and advanced the transformation of public education into an adjunct of the market economy. In the last analysis, the defeat of the CTF symbolized the triumph of one form of social organization over another: the imposition of hierarchical social relations and centralized, corporate, and bureaucratic structures of control on a public institution against the wishes of a radical reformationist movement protesting the subordination of public education to the imperious demands of the market and advocating nothing more revolutionary than democracy in education and an education for democracy.

Chapter 6

CONCLUSION
Progressive Reform and the Market Revolution

The origins of Progressive reform are revealed in the dominant images of the reform rhetoric of the 1890s: rapacious monopolists, heartless sweatshop owners, boodlers, working children and mothers, deracinated youth, fiery socialists, immigrant neighborhoods, destitute families, striking employees, and burning railroad cars. The appearance of this iconography in the 1890s reflected a pervasive sense of social crisis created by the growth of monopolies, civic corruption, immigration, depression, poverty, delinquency, irrelevant schooling, "the growing separation of classes," and the threat of working-class radicalism. What started out, however, as a response to a social crisis and a protest against the abuses and the excesses of the market revolution quickly evolved into a two-decade-long series of attempts to reform and rationalize the market revolution itself through the elimination of "social injustice" and "corruption," the moral regeneration of American society, restrictions on "commerce," the extension of equal opportunity, the recalibration of institutional arrangements, and the bureaucratic and normative regulation of social relationships. Progressive reform was both the creation and the agent of America's Great Transformation.

Progressive educational reform was very much an integral part of Progressive reform generally, a product of the same causal matrix, inspired by the same fears and aspirations, led by the same people or the same kinds of people, supported by the same broad middle-class constituency, and closely linked to Progressive social and political reform generally. Its origins were not idiosyncratic, its guiding principles not unique, its leadership and support not distinctive. Lawrence Cremin then was surely right: Progressive educational reform represents the educational equivalent of Progressive reform "writ large."[1] Yet it is clear that Cremin's account misleads in two respects. First, Cremin's argument that a single, unitary reform ideology—what he labels "Progressivism"—characterized Progressive reform, writ large or small, cannot be sustained. In Chicago, at least three languages of reform, or what Daniel Rodgers calls "languages of discontent . . . and social vision," can be identified: social justice, social democracy, and social efficiency.[2] On occasion, Progressives also used the language of antimonopoly, but when they did, it bore very little of the political meaning and passion that it did to equal rights republicans like Henry Demarest Lloyd, Victor Olander, and Margaret Haley, or socialists like Tommy Morgan and (after 1896) Eugene Debs. And second, Cremin misleads in his insistence that the origins, goals, and significance of Progressive reform can be reduced to a simple "humanitarian effort to apply the promise of American life—the ideal of government by, of and for the people."[3] A common objective did link the three languages of Progressive reform, but it was not "government by, of and for the people." Progressives pursued, rather, the reform and rationalization of the market revolution. Advocates of social justice protested humanitarian abuses of the market revolution and inequalities of opportunity. They did not abandon the market revolution—they merely wished to secure social justice within a market society. Supporters of social democracy did not urge abolition of markets in labor but the moral regeneration of American society, the reconciliation of the classes, and the regulation of social relationships. Apostles of social efficiency found machine politics disagreeable and reliance on the invisible hand in social policy ineffective but rather than advocate radical republican or populist solutions they proposed to replace politics and the invisible hand with scientific administration and to realign social institutions with the logic of the market economy.

But while Progressive reform ideology cannot be described in Cremin's terms, neither can it be reduced to the mirror image of Cremin's account—social control—either by scheming capitalists or anxious liberals, even though Progressive reformers came almost exclusively from the business and upper middle classes. Social justice and social democracy were not languages of social control. They were languages of protest against the abuses of the market revolution and of individual and social redemption. The growth of monopolies, commercialized vice, commercialized leisure, child labor, commercialized pedagogy, and the growing separation of classes appalled them. So too, "social efficiency" provided a grammar of institutional engineering with intellectual roots in Horace Mann's social mechanics, not a program of class domination. Even when Progressives employed the language of social control, as E. A. Ross did, social control did not generally denote class repression but moral and political consensus or some kind of institutional realignment to enhance "social efficiency." "Social control" simply fails to capture what is central to the intentions and beliefs of Progressive reformers.

Nonetheless, although it does not make sense to characterize Progressive reform as a "social control" movement, Progressive reform was very much a class movement. First of all, Progressive reformers were almost exclusively upper middle class and business class individuals, either by birth or achievement. Second, Progressive reforms often provoked class-conscious opposition from working-class groups or constituencies expressed in the equal rights rhetoric of "class privilege" and "class education," notably over the Cooley Bill, testing, junior high schools, the "fads and frills" controversy at the turn of the century, and educational centralization. And third, in their preoccupation with the reform and rationalization of the market revolution, Progressive reformers promoted the making, or precipitated the remaking, of a class society.

Of the three reasons, the third is the most important. The first and second rest on categorical conceptions of class—what social class reformers belonged to, whether or not class consciousness attended Progressive reform. Categorical conceptions of class are useful analytical tools, but they are not the only or even necessary criteria of class politics. In principle, there is no reason why the social composition of reformers or the presence of class consciousness should provide the basis for determining whether or not a reform movement is a class movement, or an ethnoreligious movement. Indeed, while it is true that Progressive reformers were overwhelmingly upper class and middle class, and that instances of class consciousness and class conflict can be found, working-class groups often supported particular Progressive reforms—manual training, mother's pensions, and worker's compensation, for example—or did not actively oppose others. Moreover, while some Progressive reforms provoked class-conscious opposition, not all of them did so. Class-conscious oppositional politics did not necessarily accompany Progressive reform; it developed rather when working-class groups or constituencies judged that a particular Progressive reform violated the maxims of equal rights republicanism, or for some, like Tommy Morgan, socialist visions of justice and democracy.

The third reason, however, does not assume a categorical conception of class but rests on a conception of class as a particular kind of historical process: the making of a class society. Individuals do not merely belong to a class; class also "happens" through time as a process of "structuration," that is, in the development and organization of cultural formations, social relations, social relationships, social practices, patterns of inequality, and institutional arrangements around the market economy. The concept of class does not merely delimit categories of individuals; it also denotes a structuring process—the continual organization and reorganization of social relations, institutional arrangements, and cultural practices around the market system. It is in this sense above all that Progressive reform constitutes a class movement.

First of all, processes of class formation were both the cause and consequence of Progressive reform. On the one hand, the growing separation of classes, conflicts between labor and capital and the making of a class-conscious immigrant working class provide a major part of the explanation of the origins of Progressive reform and the making of the Chicago business and middle classes. On the other hand, Progressive reform altered the institutional ecology of working-class life and contributed to the remaking of the Chicago working class. Compulsory education, child labor laws, the juvenile court, probation, mother's pensions, and professional casework all affected working-class life, although the extent is difficult to judge, since the structure of class relations, the texture of social relationships, the Catholic church, machine politics, housing patterns, racial antagonisms, ethnic differences, and the continual reorganization of the labor process also affected it. Again, educational centralization initially promoted class-conscious politics among Chicago's elementary school teachers; later it contributed to the unmaking of the Chicago Teachers Federation. Second, Progressive reformers succeeded in transforming childhood, the family, and schooling into "adjuncts" of the market economy: childhood through a preoccupation with the proper socialization and training of children for their entry into the labor market, the family through adjusting the domestic economy of the working class to wage labor, and schooling through the calibration of school curricula, pedagogies, and guidance procedures to the labor process and market and the stratification of the curriculum. In addition Progressives created an array of new institutional mechanisms—industrial arbitration, professional casework, compulsory schooling, parks, kindergartens, playgrounds, child-centered pedagogies, and probation—intended to prevent class conflict and to regulate the social relationships of a market society.

Primarily, then, Progressive reform can be characterized as a class movement because it was essentially a response to a crisis of class relations and because it advanced the making of a class society—above all because it expressed and advanced processes of class formation and the structuration of social relations and institutional arrangements around a market economy. But if Progressive reform represents a particularly important moment in the making of a class society, it was also a distinctively American version of the Great Transformation. The social vision that animated Progressive reform was not simply liberal or republican but republican liberal—a society organized around markets in labor, individual achievement (in education as in society generally), equal opportunity, and periodic exercises in moral regeneration. Unwilling to break free of the cognitive dissonances of the eighteenth century, Progressives simultaneously embraced the market revolution and reformed it. Progressive conceptions of equality ("social justice") and social order ("social democracy," "social efficiency") expressed an intramural critique, not a repudiation, of the market revolution transforming all aspects of American life. In much the same manner that Western expansion, the doctrine of separate spheres, evangelical revivalism, and ante-bellum social reform had expressed nineteenth-century anxieties over sustaining a proper balance between commerce and virtue, so too Progressive reform. On the one hand, child labor, the closing of the red-light district, the reform of classroom pedagogy, the regulation of monopolies, municipal reform, and prohibition, for example, imposed limits on "commerce" without abandoning the market revolution, while worker's compensation and mother's pensions legislation provided a measure of protection against the ravages of the marketplace. On the other hand, Progressives intended compulsory education, probation, kindergartens, playgrounds, parks, and child-centered pedagogies to promote "virtue," and the comprehensive high school to reconcile commerce and virtue in its internal organization and guiding philosophy.

Even the social theory bequeathed by the Progressives failed to transcend the intellectual legacy of republican liberalism. Robert Wiebe has stressed the bureaucratic and processual character of Progressive social theory, and Morton White its contribution to the revolt against formalism.[4] Both are correct, but what both accounts lack is a recognition that Progressive social theory, particularly its theory of democracy, eschewed the analysis of social relations in favor of a social-psychological and moralistic conception of society that centered analytical attention upon social relationships and moral consensus. Jane Addams, for example, conceived *Democracy and Social Ethics* as a study of the social relationships appropriate to a "democratic" society. Paternalist social relationships, she insisted, whether between employees and employers, charity workers and clients, fathers and daughters, household heads and servants, or teachers and students, contravened the egalitarian premises of a democratic society and prevented the development of "social morality" and "social democracy." *Democracy and Social Ethics* contains a very astute analysis of paternalistic social relationships, but it is also significant for what it reveals about the changing ontology of social thought of the late nineteenth and early twentieth centuries. *Democracy and Social Ethics* repudiates the individualistic assumptions of nineteenth-century social thought and reform ideology and substitutes for it an entirely different conceptual schema based on moralistic, anthropological, and socio-psychological contructions of social relationships and democracy—the moral language of "social ethics," "social morality," and "social democracy," and the cultural language of "community," "social intercourse," "social interdependence," "social expression," and "social communion." The language of class, like the language of individual moral responsibility, contradicted not only her aspirations for a classless society and a social democracy—one free of class consciousness and class conflict—but her basic theoretical assumptions about the nature of social life itself. For all her enormous compassion for the poor, for all her concern for social justice, for all her awareness of class conflict, Jane Addams could not imagine these as systematically linked to a structure of social relations because she had no notion of social relations—only of social relationships—and she could do no better than call for a politics of "social amelioration" and "social adjustment." Class analysis remained both politically unacceptable and conceptually inaccessible.[5]

Much the same can be said of G. H. Mead and John Dewey. Mead drew upon socio-psychological concepts to develop a social interactionist account of the development of personality and moral community. Mead frequently used the example of Hull House because "it illustrates concretely how the community ought to form moral judgments." The task of politics, or "method," he wrote, was to develop a kind of "community" that would evoke moral behavior and facilitate "the rational solution of conflicts."[6] John Dewey, meanwhile, rejected all "monistic" theories of society and all intellectual procedures based on dualistic categories and a "logic of general notions under which specific situations are to be brought" as "fatal to understanding and the intelligent action."[7] Social theorists needed to build social theories that employed pluralistic causal frameworks and that recognized the fundamental significance of the psychological and the interactional in social life. Society, Dewey insisted, was nothing more than a maze of social interactions and relationships, covering "all the ways in which by associating together men share their experiences, and build up common interests and aims."[8] And, like other Progressive intellectuals, Dewey articulated an essentially socio-psychological rather than structural conception of democracy as a form of community—"primarily a mode of associated living of conjoint communicated experience."[9] Democracy, Dewey insisted, would only be secured when Americans abandoned "the idea that the conflict of parties will, by means of public discussion, bring out necessary public truths" and embraced the assumption that politics should be modeled on the "procedure of organized co-operative inquiry which has won the triumphs of science in the field of physical nature."[10] With politics reconstituted as "scientific method" or "the method of intelligence," the creation of a new moral consensus, "The Great Community," "a life of free and enriching communion," would be possible.[11]

The intellectual revolution carried out by Progressive intellectuals in Chicago and elsewhere promoted, then, the development of an interactionist and pluralist conception of political society that provided, in turn, an intellectual foundation for a "pragmatic" politics of moral regeneration, class reconciliation, and social engineering. (The role of G. H. Mead, John Dewey, and Charles Merriam in both the intellectual and political wings of this revolt simply underlines the close connection between the two.) When Herbert Schneider examined the intellectual achievements of the Progressives, he concluded that they created what he described as a "conscious ideology of social experience" to intellectually underwrite "pragmatic habits of political thinking" and that "the headquarters of this philosophy were in Chicago":

> The social psychology developed there by Dewey, Tufts, Mead and Veblen . . . formulated a theory of democracy not merely as a form of government but also as a mode of associated living based on the ideas that individuality and freedom are themselves social products and that a democratic society is one which subordinates its institutions to the basic aim of permitting its members to grow intellectually and emotionally by widening their "areas of shared concern" by promoting means of communication and public expression, and by giving all a responsible participation in the process of social and physical control. This ideal was applied by Dewey to the reform of education, by Jane Addams to the reform of urban society and international relations, by Veblen and Ayres to the reform of industrial management and vested interests. The philosophy was given a more technical and systematic elaboration as a theory of government by Arthur F. Bentley and by the Chicago Trinity—Charles E. Merriam, H. D. Lasswell, and T. V. Smith. Bentley, Beard and Merriam have been leaders in formulating politics in terms of the interaction of pressure groups and in thus providing a practical, pluralistic substitute for the Marxian concepts of class conflict in a society where classes are vague, but conflict continual. In the form of "experimental economics," this philosophy was then carried by Tugwell and other New Dealers to Washington, where it passed through the ordeal by fire.[12]

In the final analysis, the intellectual habits of the Progressives—their failure to transcend the dialectic of commerce and virtue, their inability to generate a family of concepts suitable to the analysis of social relations, their socio-psychological conception of democracy as community, their

preoccupation with moral regeneration and social engineering, their cele-
bration of pragmatic habits of political thinking—explain a great deal
about the nature and the legacy of Progressive reform.[13] Progressive educational reform contributed to the making of a class society, not because
reformers advocated class domination or social control but because they
subscribed to a republican liberal ideology of the American experience,
because they believed that justice would be secured if they merely expanded educational opportunity, because they believed it necessary and
desirable to adjust schooling to the labor market and the labor process,
because they embraced a stratified curriculum and a stratified student body
in the name of social efficiency, because they believed that schools should
be run on a bureaucratic, hierarchical, and centralized basis, and because
they failed to attack, with the partial exception of Parker and Dewey, the
pedagogy of possessive individualism—the competitive individual appro-
priation of knowledge.

Visiting Chicago in 1893 to attend the Columbian Exposition,
Henry Adams came to the conclusion that Chicago "asked for the first
time whether the American people knew where they were driving." He
sensed that they did not, nor knew what drove them, nor indeed, who
was in the driver's seat. Later that year, following the great debate over
free silver and the gold standard, he realized that at least they had decided
which carriage to ride in. After a hundred years of oscillating ambivalence
toward the new order, in accepting the gold standard America had at last
"declared itself, once and for all, in favor of the capitalistic system with all
its necessary machinery." American politics, and America itself, would
never be the same again; Chicago, not Washington, symbolized the nascent "unity" of the new America. The new politics would be a politics
of "method," of "running machinery," and "economy," not a matter of
"disputed principle." The Pullman strike and the election of 1896 might
have caused him to doubt his conclusion that in 1893 his "education in
domestic politics stopped," but Progressive reform certainly did not
do so.[14] With Progressive reform, the market revolution, moralized and
rationalized, rolled on unencumbered into the 1920s until a second
"Années Terrible" in the 1930s provided yet another opportunity for a
new generation of reformers to again play out that idiosyncratic and ata-
vistic dialectic of commerce and virtue that has characterized America's
Great Transformation.

NOTES

PREFACE

1. J. Dewey, *The School and Society* (Chicago, 1899), 8–9.
2. G. S. Counts, *School and Society in Chicago* (New York, 1928), 340.
3. L. Cremin, *The Transformation of the School* (New York, 1961), viii.
4. M. Katz, *The Irony of Early School Reform* (Boston, 1968); idem, *Class Bureaucracy and School* (New York, 1971).
5. C. Karier, *Shaping the American Educational State* (New York, 1975); C. Karier, P. Violas, J. Spring, *Roots of Crisis* (Chicago, 1973); P. Violas, *The Training of the Urban Working Class* (Chicago, 1978); J. Spring, *Education and the Rise of the Corporate Liberal State* (Boston, 1972); M. Lazerson, *Origins of the Urban School* (Cambridge, Mass., 1971); E. A. Krug, *The Shaping of the American High School, 1880–1920* (Madison, 1969).
6. D. Tyack, *The One Best System* (Cambridge, Mass., 1974).
7. S. Bowles and H. Gintis, *Schooling in Capitalist America* (New York, 1976).
8. E. P. Thompson, *The Making of the English Working Class* (Harmondsworth, Middlesex, 1973); idem, *The Poverty of Theory* (London, 1978); G. S. Jones, *Outcast London* (Harmondsworth, Middlesex, 1976); R. Gray, *The Labor Aristocracy of Victorian Edinburgh* (Oxford, 1976); A. Dawley, *Class and Community: The Industrial Revolution in Lynn, Massachusetts* (Cambridge, Mass., 1976); G. Nash, *The Urban Crucible: Social Change, Political Consciousness, and the Origins of the American Revolution* (Cambridge, Mass., 1979); B. Laurie, *The Working People of Philadelphia, 1800–1850* (Philadelphia, 1980); H. Gutman, *Work, Culture and Society in Industrializing America* (New York, 1975); J. Foster, *Class Conflict and the Industrial Revolution* (London, 1975); R. Connell and T. Irving, *Class Structure in Australian History* (Melbourne, 1980); P. Anderson, *Arguments Within English Marxism* (London, 1980); R. Johnson, "Edward Thompson, Eugene Genovese, and Socialist-Humanist History," *History Workshop,* no. 6 (Autumn 1978), 79–100; idem, "Three Problematics: Elements of a Theory of Working Class Culture," in J. Clarke, C. Critcher, and R. Johnson, *Working Class Culture* (New York, 1979); N. Poulantzas, *Classes in Contemporary Capitalism* (London, 1978); R. Connell, *Which Way Is Up* (Sydney, 1983).
9. Recently structuralist theorists have expanded the criteria from the wage-labor relations to the structure of social relations in general—political, ideological,

as well as economic—within the definition of class and define a class in terms of its "place" in the overall structure of social relations. Thus, Nicos Poulantzas: "What are social classes in Marxist theory? They are groups of social agents, of men defined principally but not exclusively by their place in the production process, i.e., by their place in the economic sphere. The economic place of the social agents has a principal role in determining social classes. But from that we cannot conclude that this economic place is sufficient to determine social classes. . . . The economic does indeed have the determinant role in a mode of production of a social formation; but the political and the ideological (the super structure) also have an important role. . . . We can thus say that a social class is defined by its place in the ensemble of the division of labor which includes political and ideological relations" ("On Social Classes," *New Left Review* 78 [1973]: 26). See also his *Classes in Contemporary Capitalism*, 14–18.

10. Thompson, *Making*, 9.

11. Ibid., 939; idem, "The Peculiarities of the English," *Socialist Register*, 1965, 357.

12. Thompson, *Making*, 10–11; idem, "Eighteenth Century Society: Class Struggle Without Class?" *Social History* 3, 2 (May 1978); idem, *The Poverty of Theory*, 298.

13. For discussions of a class as a "situation," see Connell and Irving, *Class Structure in Australian History*, ch. 1; R. Gray, *The Labor Aristocracy of Victorian Edinburgh* (Oxford, 1976), introduction.

14. See, in particular, Anderson, *Arguments within English Marxism*, ch. 1; Johnson, "Edward Thompson," 83–89; idem, "Three Problematics," 214–17, 227–30; Connell and Irving, *Class Structure in Australian History*, ch. 1.

15. Thompson, *Making*, 10. See also his *Poverty of Theory*, 298–99.

16. Anderson, *Arguments within English Marxism*, 40–41.

17. R. W. Connell, *Which Way Is Up?* (Sydney, 1983), chs. 5, 6, 7; R. W. Connell, D. J. Ashenden, S. Kessler, G. W. Dowsett, *Making the Difference: Schools, Families and Social Division* (Sydney, 1982), 33.

18. G. A. Cohen, *Karl Marx's Theory of History* (New York, 1979), 73.

19. Connell, Ashenden, Kessler and Dowsett, *Making the Difference*, 33.

20. For analyses of the notion of cultural production, see Connell, *Which Way Is Up?* ch. 12; P. Willis, *Learning to Labor* (Westmead, England, 1977); idem, "Cultural Production and Theories of Reproduction," in L. Barton and S. Walker, eds., *Race, Class and Education* (London, 1983), 107–38.

21. Thompson, *Making*, 212–13. For a further discussion, see Anderson, *Arguments within English Marxism*, 32. Anderson insists, and he is absolutely right to do so, that it is impossible to judge the truth, or relative truth, of the claims without a detailed and explicit account (whether descriptive or quantitative) of the manner, and the extent to which, experiences were structured by class relations. Or, in Anderson's terms, "if the claim for co-determination of agency and necessity was to be substantiated, we would need to have at a minimum a conjoint exploration of the objective assemblage and transformation of a labour-force by the Industrial Revolution, and of the subjective germination of a class culture in response to it."

22. K. Polanyi, *The Great Transformation* (Boston, 1957), 57; A. Giddens, *The Class Structure of the Advanced Societies* (New York, 1973), 110; Connell and Irving, *Class Structure in Australian History*, 15. See also A. Giddins, *Central*

Problems in Social Theory (Berkeley, 1979), ch. 2; idem, *New Rules of Sociological Method* (New York, 1976), ch. 3; P. Abrams, *Historical Sociology* (Ithaca, N.Y., 1982), ch. 1.

23. R. Hofstadter, *The Age of Reform: From Bryan to F.D.R.* (New York, 1955); G. Mowry, *The California Progressives* (Berkeley, 1951); P. Kleppner, *The Cross of Culture* (New York, 1970); R. Jensen, *The Winning of the Midwest* (Chicago, 1971); J. Allswang, *A House for All Peoples* (Lexington, 1971); J. Wrigley, *Class Politics and Public Schools* (New Brunswick, 1972).

24. J.G.A. Pocock, *The Machiavellian Moment* (Princeton, 1975); idem, "Virtue and Commerce in the Eighteenth Century," *Journal of Interdisciplinary History* 3 (1972): 119–34.

25. On the structural aspects of America's Great Transformation during the late seventeenth century and the eighteenth century, see R. Bushman, *From Puritan to Yankee: Character and Social Order in Connecticut* (Cambridge, Mass., 1967); Nash, *The Urban Crucible;* J. Henretta, *The Evolution of American Society, 1700–1815* (Lexington, Mass., 1973); J. Appleby, "The Social Origins of American Revolutionary Ideology," *Journal of American History* 64, 4 (March, 1978): 935–58; idem, "Liberalism and the American Revolution," *New England Quarterly* 49 (March, 1976): 3–26; J. Greene, "Search for Identity: An Interpretation of the Meaning of Selected Patterns of Social Response in Eighteenth-Century America," *Journal of Social History* 3 (1970): 189–220; idem, "The Social Origins of the American Revolution: An Evaluation and an Interpretation," *Political Science Quarterly* 88, 19 (1973): 1–22; K. Lockridge, "Social Change and the Meaning of the American Revolution," *Journal of Social History* 6, 4 (1973): 403–39.

26. Neo-Whig historians deny that Lockean liberalism had any significant influence on revolutionary thought. To J.G.A. Pocock, for example, the Revolution was a "Machiavellian moment," not a Lockean moment. "Locke et praetera nihil." The dominant ideology of the Revolution was the "country" ideology of the eighteenth-century commonwealthmen. The politics of the 1770s and 1780s, moreover, should be described not in Lockean terms but in terms of a conflict between "court" and "country" traditions. While neo-Whig historians have considerably expanded our understanding of revolutionary politics, I am not convinced that Lockean liberalism was insignificant. Nor am I convinced by Gary Wills's attempt to replace Locke with the sentimentalist moral philosophy of Francis Hutcheson. For the neo-Whig position, see G. Wood, *The Creation of the American Republic* (New York, 1972), pt 2, 5; B. Bailyn, *The Ideological Origins of the American Revolution* (Cambridge, Mass., 1976); S. N. Katz, "The Origins of American Constitutional Thought," *Perspectives in American History* 3 (1969): 474; J. Dunn, "The Politics of Locke in England and America in the Eighteenth Century," in *John Locke: Problems and Perspectives,* ed. J. W. Yolton (Cambridge, 1969); Pocock, "Commerce and Virtue," 124, 127, 129, 130–31; idem, *The Machiavellian Moment,* ch. 14; J. Murrin, "The Great Inversion of Court versus Country: A Comparison of the Revolution Settlements in England (1688–1721) and America (1776–1816)," in *Three British Revolutions,* ed. J.G.A. Pocock (Princeton, 1980), 368–455; L. Banning, *The Jeffersonian Persuasion: Evolution of a Party Ideology* (Ithaca, 1978); G. Stourzh, *Alexander Hamilton and the Idea of Republican Government* (Stanford, 1970). For Wills, see his *Inventing America: Jefferson's Declaration of Independence* (Garden City, 1978). For a more convincing view, see M. White, *The Philosophy of the American Revolution* (Oxford, 1978); and

R. Hamony, "Jefferson and the Scottish Enlightenment: A Critique of Gary Wills's *Inventing America: Jefferson's Declaration of Independence*," *William and Mary Quarterly* 36 (1979): 502–23.

27. For details see Pocock, "Virtue and Commerce," 120–24, 129–30; idem, *The Machiavellian Moment*, pt. 2, 3; Bailyn, *The Ideological Origins of the American Revolution;* Wood, *The Creation of the American Republic*, pt. 1; C. Robbins, *The Eighteenth-Century Commonwealthman* (Cambridge, Mass., 1959); I. Kramnick, *Bolingbroke and His Circle: The Politics of Nostalgia in the Age of Walpole* (Cambridge, Mass., 1968); D. McCoy, *The Elusive Republic: Political Economy in Jeffersonian America* (Chapel Hill, 1980), ch. 1; D. W. Howe, "European Sources of Political Ideas in Jeffersonian America," in *The Promise of American History*, ed. S. J. Kutler and S. N. Katz (Baltimore, 1982), 28–44; J. Appleby, "The New Republican Synthesis and the Changing Political Ideas of John Adams," *American Quarterly* 25, 5 (1973): 568–95; R. Shalhope, "Toward a Republican Synthesis: The Emergence of an Understanding of Republicanism in American Historiography," *William and Mary Quarterly* 29 (1972): 49–80.

28. See, in particular, Appleby, "Liberalism and the American Revolution"; idem, "The Social Origins of American Revolutionary Ideology"; idem, "What is Still American in the Political Philosophy of Thomas Jefferson?" *William and Mary Quarterly* 39, 12 (April 1982): 287–309; I. Kramnick, "Republican Revisionism Revisited," *American Historical Review* 87, 3 (June 1982): 629–64; E. Foner, *Tom Paine and Revolutionary America* (New York, 1976), ch. 5; M. Curti, "The Great Mr. Locke: America's Philosopher, 1783–1861," *Huntington Library Bulletin*, no. 11 (1937): 107–51; A. Hirschman, *The Passions and the Interests: Political Arguments for Capitalism Before Its Triumph* (Princeton, 1977); J. Appleby, *Economic Thought and Ideology in Seventeenth-Century England* (Princeton, 1978); M. Myers, *The Soul of Modern Economic Man* (Chicago, 1983); J. Fliegelman, *Prodigals and Pilgrims: The American Revolution Against Patriarchal Authority, 1750–1800* (Cambridge, Mass., 1982); L. Hartz, *The Liberal Tradition in America* (New York, 1955); E. Morgan, "The Puritan Ethic and the American Revolution," *William and Mary Quarterly*, 3d ser., 24 (January 1967); J. E. Crowley, *This Sheba Self: The Conceptualization of Economic Life in Eighteenth Century America* (Baltimore, 1974).

29. For details, see Stourzh, *Alexander Hamilton;* Wood, *The Creation of the American Republic;* Banning, *The Jeffersonian Persuasion;* Murrin, "The Great Inversion"; Foner, *Tom Paine;* Appleby, "Thomas Jefferson"; idem, "Liberalism and the American Revolution"; R. Berthoff, "Independence and Attachment, Virtue and Interest: From Republican Citizen to Free Enterpriser, 1787–1837," in *Uprooted Americans: Essays in Honor of Oscar Handlin*, ed. R. Bushman (Boston, 1979); McCoy, *The Elusive Republic;* R. L. Kelley, *The Cultural Patterns in American Politics: The First Century* (New York, 1978); L. Kerber, *Federalists in Dissent: Ideology and Imagery in Jeffersonian America* (Ithaca, 1979); R. Buel, *Securing the Revolution* (Ithaca, 1973); D. Sisson, *The American Revolution of 1800* (New York, 1974).

30. For details, see Berthoff, "Independence and Attachment," 98–124; D. W. Howe, *The Political Culture of the American Whigs* (Chicago, 1979); E. Foner, *Free Soil, Free Labor and Free Men* (New York, 1970); idem, *Politics and Ideology in the Age of the Civil War* (New York, 1980); K. K. Sklar, *Catherine Beecher* (New Haven, 1973); M. Ryan, *Cradle of the Middle Class: The Family in Oneida County,*

New York (New York, 1981); A. M. Schlesinger, Jr., *The Age of Jackson* (Boston, 1945); S. Wilentz, "On Class and Politics in Jacksonian America," in *The Promise of American History*, ed. Kutler and Katz, 45–63; A. Dawley, *Class and Community;* B. Laurie, *Working People of Philadelphia;* D. Montgomery, *Beyond Equality: Labor and the Radical Republicans, 1862–1872* (New York, 1967); Y. Arieli, *Individualism and Nationalism in American Ideology* (Cambridge, Mass., 1964); M. Meyers, *The Jacksonian Persuasion: Politics and Belief* (Stanford, 1957).

31. On the importance of evangelical Protestantism and/or the Scottish Enlightenment in the eighteenth century, see Perry Miller, *Errand into the Wilderness* (New York, 1956), ch. 6; C. B. Cowing, *The Great Awakening and the American Revolution: Colonial Thought in the Eighteenth Century* (Chicago, 1971), chs. 2, 5, 6; S. Ahlstrom, *A Religious History of the American People* (New York, 1975), vols. 1, 3; H. May, *The Enlightenment in America* (New York, 1976), pt. 1; A. Heimert, *Religion and the American Mind* (Cambridge, 1966), pt. 2; E. Flower and M. Murphy, *A History of American Philosophy* (New York, 1977), vol. 1, chs. 4, 5; White, *The Philosophy of the American Revolution*, esp. chs. 3–6; Wills, *Inventing America;* N. Hatch, *The Sacred Cause of Liberty* (New Haven, 1977); S. Lynd, *Radicalism* (New York, 1968); Howe, "European Sources," 37–39. On their influence in the nineteenth century, see Howe, *The Political Culture of the American Whigs*, esp. chs. 1, 2, 4, 218–21; D. Meyer, *The Instructed Conscience: The Shaping of the American National Ethic* (Philadelphia, 1972); W. Smith, *Professors and Public Ethics: Studies of the Northern Moral Philosophers* (Ithaca, 1956); T. Martin, *The Instructed Vision: Scottish Common Sense Philosophy and the Origins of American Fiction* (Bloomington, 1961); Sklar, *Catherine Beecher.*

32. Wilentz, "On Class and Politics," 54–55. See also, Howe, *The Political Culture of the American Whigs*, chs. 1, 2, 4, 7; D. Ross, "The Liberal Tradition Revisited and the Republican Tradition Addressed," in *New Directions in American Intellectual History*, ed. J. Higham and P. Conkin (Baltimore, 1979), 116–31; Foner, *Politics and Ideology*, 10.

33. My view of the conceptual significance of the antinomies of commerce and virtue draws upon Pocock's writings on conceptual orders and language. See, in particular, his *Politics, Language and Time* (New York, 1971). See also Arthur Lovejoy, who argued that each age is dominated by a set of "implicit or incompletely explicit assumptions, or more or less unconscious mental habits" which predisposes it "to think in terms of certain categories or of particular types of imagery." Lovejoy called these "endemic assumptions" or "unit ideas" that controlled "the course of man's reflections on almost any subject." A. O. Lovejoy, *The Great Chain of Being* (New York, 1960), 7, 10, 15.

34. Pocock, "Commerce and Virtue," 134; Ross, "The Liberal Tradition," 118–24; Berthoff, "Independence and Attachment," 105; D. Rodgers, *The Work Ethic in Industrializing America* (Chicago, 1974), chs. 1, 2.

35. Foner, *Tom Paine*, xix, 89, 92–96, 105, 143, 145–46, 154, 155–56, 157, 158–59, 234.

36. Stourzh, *Alexander Hamilton*, esp. chs. 2, 3; Pocock, "Commerce and Virtue," 131; McCoy, *The Elusive Republic*, chs. 4, 5, 6, 7.

37. For details, see McCoy, *The Elusive Republic*, chs. 8, 9; Banning, *The Jeffersonian Persuasion;* Foner, *Tom Paine*, 101–5.

38. Foner, *Tom Paine*, 88–89; McCoy, *The Elusive Republic*, chs. 5, 6, 7; Wood, *The Creation of the American Republic*, pts. 4, 5.

39. See, in particular, Meyers, *The Jacksonian Persuasion*, chs. 2, 5, 6; Schlesinger, *The Age of Jackson*, chs. 7, 8, 15, 24, 26–28; M. P. Rogin, *Fathers and Children* (New York, 1976), ch. 9. R. Hofstadter characterizes Jackson as a simple opportunist and possessive individualist in *The American Political Tradition* (London, 1967), ch. 3.

40. Howe, *The Political Culture of the American Whigs*, passim; Schlesinger, *The Age of Jackson*, ch. 22; Wilentz, "On Class and Politics," passim.

41. Laurie, *Working People of Philadelphia*; Dawley, *Class and Community*; L. Goodwyn, *The Populist Moment* (New York, 1978); Montgomery, *Beyond Equality*.

42. On the doctrine of separate spheres, see Sklar, *Catherine Beecher*, pts. 2 and 3; Ryan, *Cradle of the Middle Class*, chs. 2, 3; N. Cott, *The Bonds of Womanhood: "Women's Sphere" in New England, 1780–1835* (New Haven, 1977); B. Welter, "The Cult of True Womanhood, 1820–1860," *American Quarterly* 18 (1966): 151–74; C. Degler, *At Odds: Women and the Family in America from the Revolution to the Present* (New York, 1980).

43. A. de Tocqueville, *Democracy in America* (Garden City, 1969), vol. 2, 601. Randy McGowen, at the University of Oregon, pointed out this passage to me and suggested the relationship between liberal social theory and middle-class marriage in his "Two Spheres: Family, Ideology, and the Making of the Middle Class," (paper presented at the meeting of the Organization of American Historians, Detroit, April 1981). Perhaps the quintessential expression of the antinomies of liberal social theory and the bifurcation of bourgeois gender roles is to be found in Talcott Parsons's "binary opposites" of "instrumental" and "expressive," "differentiation" and "socialization," "male" and "female," "husband" and "wife." See T. Parsons, *Social Structure and Personality* (London, 1964).

44. On the common school reform movement, see R. Church, *Education in the United States: An Interpretative History* (New York, 1976), pt. 2; C. Kaestle and M. Vinovskis, *Education and Social Change in Nineteenth Century Massachusetts* (New York, 1980); C. Kaestle, *Pillars of the Republic: Common Schools and American Society, 1780–1860* (New York, 1983).

45. J. Brown, *An Estimate of the Manners and Principles of the Times* (London, 1757), 217, cited McCoy, *The Elusive Republic*, 75. See also James Madison's "10th Federalist" in *The Federalist*, ed. E. M. Earle (New York, 1938).

CHAPTER ONE: *Social Order and Progressive Reform in Chicago*

1. In part Marx had the United States in mind when he wrote of the achievements of nineteenth-century capitalism: "The bourgeoisie, in its reign of barely a hundred years, has created more massive and more colossal productive power than have all previous generations put together. Subjection of nature's forces to man, machinery, application of chemistry to agriculture and industry, steam navigation, railways, electric telegraphs, clearing of whole continents for cultivation, canalization of rivers, whole populations conjured out of the ground—what earlier century had even an intimation that such productive power slept in the womb of social labor?" (K. Marx, "The Communist Manifesto" in *The Marx-Engels Reader*, ed. R. C. Tucker [New York, 1978], 473–75).

On various aspects of the market revolution of the nineteenth century, see A.

Dawley, *Class and Community: The Industrial Revolution in Lynn, Massachusetts* (Cambridge, Mass., 1976); G. R. Taylor, *The Transportation Revolution, 1815–1860* (New York, 1951); P. Johnson, *A Shopkeeper's Millennium: Society and Revivals in Rochester, New York* (New York, 1978); E. C. Kirkland, *Industry Comes to Age: Business, Labor and Public Policy, 1860–1897* (Chicago, 1961); T. C. Cochran and W. Miller, *The Age of Enterprise* (New York, 1961); A. D. Chandler, *The Visible Hand: The Managerial Revolution in American Business* (Cambridge, 1977); W. A. Williams, *The Contours of American History* (Chicago, 1966), pts. 3 and 4; D. Rodgers, *The Work Ethic in Industrial America, 1850–1920* (Chicago, 1974); K. Kolko, *The Triumph of Conservatism* (Chicago, 1963); P. Gates, *The Farmers Age: Agriculture, 1815–1860* (New York, 1958); D. C. North, *The Economic Growth of the United States, 1790–1860* (Englewood Cliffs, N.J., 1961); M. Horowitz, *The Transformation of American Law, 1780–1860* (Cambridge, 1977); R. D. Brown, *Modernization: The Transformation of American Life, 1600–1865* (New York, 1976); B. Laurie, *Working People of Philadelphia, 1800–1850* (Philadelphia, 1980); N. Cott, *Bonds of Womanhood: "Women's Sphere" in New England, 1780–1835* (New Haven, 1977); H. Gutman, *Work, Culture and Society in Industrializing America* (New York, 1975); M. Katz, M. Doucet, and M. Stern, *The Social Organization of Early Industrial Capitalism* (Cambridge, 1982); E. F. Genovese and E. Genovese, *Fruits of Merchant Capital* (New York, 1983), pt. 1.

2. F. Norris, *The Pit* (New York, 1901), 50.

3. On Chicago's industrial development, see B. Pierce, *A History of Chicago, 1871–1893* (New York, 1957), chs. 3, 4, 5, 6; H. Hoyt, *One Hundred Years of Land Values in Chicago* (Chicago, 1933); J. Carlin, *Chicago* (Chicago, 1940), 71–73; U.S. Department of Commerce, Bureau of the Census, *Thirteenth Census, 1910, Abstract* with supplement for Illinois, ch. 4; idem, *Fourteenth Census, State Compendium: Illinois*, 155–81; W. W. Belcher, *The Economic Rivalry Between Chicago and St. Louis, 1850–1880* (New York, 1947).

4. See P. F. Greesey, "Population Succession in Chicago: 1898–1930," *American Journal of Sociology* 44, 1 (1938): 59–70; Hoyt, *Land Values*, 284; J. Allswang, *A House for All Peoples* (Lexington, 1971), 18–19; R. Roberts, "Ethnic Groups" in *Chicago Lutheran Planning Study*, ed. W. Kloetzle, vol. 1, pt. 2 (Chicago, 1963), 1–37.

5. *Chicago Tribune*, June 29, 1877.

6. Illinois Bureau of Labor Statistics (IBLS), *Report, 1902*, 496–502. See also idem, *Report, 1886*, 412–17; idem, *Report, 1888*, 223–26. For general accounts of the conflict between labor and capital in Chicago, see E. Staley, *History of the Illinois State Federation of Labor* (Chicago, 1930); E. C. Bogart and C. M. Thompson, *The Industrial State, 1870–1893, Centennial History of Illinois*, vol. 4 (Springfield, 1920), chs. 19, 20; E. C. Bogart and J. M. Mathews, *The Modern Commonwealth, 1893–1918, Centennial History of Illinois*, vol. 5, ch. 8; J. H. Keisner, "John Fitzpatrick and Progressive Unionism, 1915–1925" (Ph.D. dissertation, Northwestern University, 1965); N. Fine, *Labor and Farmer Parties in the United States, 1828–1928* (New York, 1928); H. B. Sell, "The American Federation of Labor and the Labor Party Movement of 1918–1920" (M.A. thesis, University of Chicago, 1922); B. Newell, *Chicago and the Labor Movement* (Urbana, 1961); E. R. Beckner, *A History of Labor Legislation in Illinois* (Chgicago, 1929); J. Keisner, "John H. Walker: Labor Leader from Illinois" in *Essays in Illinois History*, ed. D. F. Tingley (Carbondale, 1968), 75–100; R. Hunter, *Labor in*

Politics (Chicago, 1915); R. W. Scharnau, *Thomas J. Morgan and the Chicago Socialist Movement, 1896–1901* (DeKalb, Ill., 1966); A. J. Townsend, *The Germans of Chicago* (Chicago, 1927), ch. 3; E. B. Mittelman, "Chicago Labor in Politics, 1877–1896," *Journal of Political Economy* 28 (1920): 407–27; M. J. Schaack, *Anarchy and Anarchists* (Chicago, 1889); H. David, *The History of the Haymarket Affair* (New York, 1936); G. Schilling, "History of the Labor Movement in Chicago" in *Life of Albert R. Parsons,* ed. L. Parsons (Chicago, 1889); and K. Kann, "Working Class Culture and the Labor Movement in Nineteenth-Century Chicago" (Ph.D. dissertation, University of California, Berkeley, 1977).

7. IBLS, *Report, 1902,* 496–502; idem, *Report, 1886,* 412–17; idem, *Report, 1888,* 226.

8. *Workingmans Advocate,* April 12, May 26, June 2, June 16, August 18, August 25, September 8, 1866; November 23, 1867; May 30, 1868; February 19, July 19, 1870; December 20, 1873; September 12, 1886; Bogart and Thompson, *The Industrial State,* 451–52; D. Montgomery, *Beyond Equality: Labor and the Radical Republicans, 1862–1872* (New York, 1967), 256–57, 306–11. The producer ideology divided society into two classes: the producers and nonproducers, a dualism often expressed in the language of "wealth-producers vs. wealth-owners," "the people vs. the plutocrats," "democracy vs plutocracy," "the many vs. the few." Unlike the labor theory of value at the core of Marxist theories of class, the producer ideology rested upon a labor theory of wealth. For discussions of the producer ideology, see M. Neufeld, "Realms of Thought and Organized Labor in the Age of Jackson," *Labor History* (Winter 1969): 5–43; Montgomery, *Beyond Equality,* 90–134, 230–60; H. Gutman, "The Workers' Search for Power," 31–54, "Class Status and Community," 263–87, and "Protestantism and the American Labor Movement," 137–74 in *Dissent: Explorations in the History of American Radicalism,* ed. A. F. Young (DeKalb, Ill., 1968); N. Pollack, *The Populist Mind* (New York, 1967), 404–6; Dawley, *Class and Community,* chs. 2, 3; L. Goodwyn, *The Populist Moment* (New York, 1978); D. Rodgers, *The Work Ethic in Industrial America, 1850–1920* (Chicago, 1978), 212–19.

9. For general discussions of the strike, see Kann, "Working Class Culture," 273–77; W. J. Adelman, *Pilsen and the West Side* (Chicago, n.d.); J. Brecher, *Strike!* (Greenwich, Conn., 1972), ch. 1; J. R. Commons et al., *History of Labor in the United States* (New York, 1921), II: 185–91; R. V. Bruce, *1877: Year of Violence* (Indianapolis, 1959), ch. 12; S. Lens, *The Labor Wars* (New York, 1974), ch. 3; W. Andrews, *Battle for Chicago* (New York, 1946), 105–6; Pierce, *A History of Chicago,* 3: 242–56; S. Yellen, *American Labor Struggles, 1877–1934* (New York, 1974), 27–31. Traditional interpretations of the Great Upheaval as a series of local strikes or a great strike born of frustration with years of depression are put forward by M. Hillquit, *History of Socialism in the United States* (New York, 1965), 199; Commons et al., *History of Labor 11,* 185–91; P. Foner, *History of the Labor Movement in the United States* (New York, 1955), 1: 464–74. Kenneth Kann, however, convincingly argues that from the very beginning, the Great Upheaval represented something more than a general railroad strike or a series of local strikes over specific job or wage and hour grievances. Rather, the crowd-enforced work stoppages, the transcendence of differences in nationality, neighborhood, age, sex, and occupation, the disciplined and discriminating running battles with police, state militia, federal troops, and businessmen constitute the "first assertion of a national working class, of a common anger against the transformation of life being

imposed upon them with the development of industrial capitalism, and a collective power to impose their own will upon future social development." The strike of 1877 represented a class-conscious, anticapitalist insurrection by an emergent working class with decidedly radical views (Kann, "Working Class Culture," 273–75).

10. Andrews, *Battle for Chicago*, 108; Pierce, *A History of Chicago*, 3: 252; Kann, "Working Class Culture," 146, 277–78.

11. Cited in S. Buder, *Pullman: An Experiment in Industrial Order and Community Planning, 1880–1930* (New York, 1967), vii–viii, 34, 40, 41–42, 43, 77, 92, 96.

12. David, *Haymarket*, 57–60; IBLS, *Report, 1886*, 198–99; testimony of P. H. McLogan, *U.S. Senate Committee on the Relations Between Labor and Capital* (Washington, 1885), 1: 578. In 1886 the United States Supreme Court declared armed associations unconstitutional.

13. Schilling, "History," xix; Kann, "Working Class Culture," 329–31, 346–47; Commons et al., *History of Labor*, II: 279–82; Bogart and Thompson, *The Industrial State*, 433.

14. David, *Haymarket*, 69–75; J. J. Rayback, *A History of American Labor* (New York, 1966), 153–54.

15. Rayback, *History*, 150; Yellen, *American Labor Struggles*, 48–49; Commons et al., *History of Labor*, 2: 297–98; Pierce, *A History of Chicago*, 266–67; Kann, "Working Class Culture," 400–402.

16. Bogart and Thompson, *The Industrial State*, 455, 457. For further accounts of the growth of the Knights, see IBLS, *Report, 1886*, 186–94, 203–13; J. Garlock, "A Structural Analysis of the Knights of Labor: A Prolegomenon to the History of the Producing Classes" (Ph.D. dissertation, University of Rochester, 1964), 188.

17. IBLS, *Report, 1886*, 192, 213.

18. Ibid., 21, 233, 161. While the Knights armed for a broad inclusion within its ranks of all those who were wage earners, its strategy as enunciated by its leadership was a peaceful, arbitrated conciliation between labor and capital, with the eventual aim of establishing a cooperative commonwealth. So while it aimed, in effect, for the abolition of the wage labor system, its leadership did not believe that strikes or violence were necessary in order to achieve it.

19. IBLS, *Report, 1886*, 479–80.

20. For detailed discussions of the ideology of the Eight-Hour Movement, see David, *Haymarket*, ch. 7; Kann, "Working Class Culture," 396–430.

21. Commons et al., *History of Labor* II: 373–74.

22. For details of the events of late April and early May, see David, *Haymarket*, ch. 38.

23. For details, see David, *Haymarket*, chs. 8–11; Kann, "Working Class Culture," 430–58.

24. For the law and order campaign of 1886 and the Haymarket trial, see David, *Haymarket*, chs. 10–21. The quote is from Adelman, *Haymarket Revisited*, 21.

25. David, *Haymarket*, 370–71, 537. Labor fought the bill bitterly. The Chicago Knights of Labor argued that it was framed "to hold for murder every member of a labor organization, if in an attempt to secure remunerative wages a man is killed by somebody" (ibid., 537). In 1891 labor managed to have the law

repealed. Nevertheless, Haymarket had significant effects upon the labor movement and the process of class formation. The combined effect of the law and order
campaign, the counter-offensive staged by capital, and the recriminations and
feuds within the ranks of organized labor opened up by the Haymarket explosion
incapacitated the Eight-Hour Movement for two decades or more, dealt a mortal
blow to the Knights of Labor, so badly wounded the socialist movement that it
never again attained the relative strength it had gained in 1886, and left the way
open for the growth and consolidation of the pragmatic and defensive politics of
the aristocracy of labor and pure and simple unionism.

Opinion was and still is divided on the significance of the Haymarket Affair
for the subsequent history of the Eight-Hour Movement and the Knights of
Labor. Powderly, Gompers, the *Arbeiter-Zeitung*, and the local journal of the
Knights of Labor believed that the Haymarket did irreparable damage. George
Schilling believed that it was a "serious mistake" to assume "that had the bombs
not exploded on the Haymarket, the eight-hour movement would have been a
success" (Schilling, "History," xxiv). But if the law and order campaign and the
counter-offensive by capital are made part of the Haymarket Affair, the conclusion
arrived at by Powderly and others seems undeniable, a judgment that Henry
David, in his cautious way, seems to concur with (*Haymarket*, 536–37).

The issue of labor aristocracy and the victory of pure, simple unionism is
more complex. With respect to the labor aristocracy, its appearance in the late
nineteenth century was fundamentally the outcome of the reorganization of the
technical basis of the labor process (creating new kinds of skilled workers) and the
development of a defensive political structure within the labor place (unions) by
the skilled workers to protect themselves from any further encroachments by
capital and to strengthen their hand in the bargaining process with capital over
job conditions and wages. But essentially the horse had already bolted, since capital
had already penetrated sufficiently far into the labor process to give it basic control;
the appearance of the labor aristocracy was, in fact, transitional, and signaled a
major success in capital's campaign to restructure the labor process on a new basis
and paved the way, through scientific management and Taylorization, for the
further rationalization of the entire labor process, the eventual displacement (with
a few exceptions, notably in mining and printing) of the labor aristocrat by the
modern skilled worker, and the stabilization of capitalist control of the labor
process. Finally, with regard to the ascendency of pure and simple unionism, I am
not at all sympathetic to the arguments of Commons, Grob, Perlman, and others
who have argued that the Knights represent a "transitional" phenomenon, express-
ing a "preindustrial labor consciousness" or a "politics of reform unionism" prior
to the inevitable triumph of the only "realistic" form of labor politics in the context
of American capitalism, pure and simple unionism.

26. My view of antebellum and Gilded Age moral reform ideology has
been influenced by C. S. Rosenberg, *Religion and the American City* (Ithaca,
1971); L. Banner, "Religious Benevolence as Social Control: A Critique of an
Interpretation," *Journal of American History* 60, 1 (June 1973): 23–41; Laurie,
The Working People of Philadelphia; and Johnson, *A Shopkeeper's Millennium*. While
Boyer's survey of the moral reform during the Gilded Age is comprehensive and
well researched, I remain unconvinced by his equation of moral reform with social
control. See P. Boyer, *Urban Masses and Moral Order in America, 1820–1920*
(Cambridge, Mass., 1978), pt. 3.

27. The most useful, although conceptually flawed, general account of the temperance movement in America is Joseph Gusfield's *Symbolic Crusade* (Urbana, 1963). In my account of the temperance movement in Chicago, I have leaned heavily upon Kann, "Working Class Culture," 157–60.

28. C. Bonney, *The Present Conflict Between Labor and Capital* (Chicago, 1966), cited in Kann, "Working Class Culture," 158.

29. Senate testimony of J. Medill, *Relations Between Labor and Capital*, 960.

30. Minutes of the Methodist Episcopal Church annual conference, 34th sess., 1874, 25, quoted by Kann, "Working Class Culture," 158; Citizens League of Chicago for the Suppression of the Sale of Liquors to Minors, *Third Annual Report, 1881*, 6. Among the business members of the league were Marshall Field, Potter Palmer, George Pullman, C. H. McCormick, M. Ryersen, O.S.A. Sprague, and Franklin MacVeigh. See Pierce, *A History of Chicago*, 3: 459

31. Kann notes that temperance workers established missions, schools, day care centers, and homes for the inebriates. Temperance workers regularly visited hospitals and jails and charity homes, and staged regular meetings at churches, meeting halls, and street corners. They invaded saloons, questioning patrons whether they were ready to meet their Maker, and they invaded the homes of the poor. They especially sought contact with lower-class children through the Sunday schools and industrial schools, where they succeeded in recruiting thousands to sign the temperance pledge (Kann, "Working Class Culture," 159). See also the Chicago Women's Christian Temperance Union, *Annual Reports, 1878–1887* (Pierce, *A History of Chicago*, 3: 457–59).

32. Chicago Baptist Association, *Proceedings, 1882*, 11; P. J. Stachause, *Chicago and the Baptists* (Chicago, 1913), 112.

33. Chicago Missionary Society, *First Annual Report, 1884*, 12, 14.

34. Cited in W. G. McLoughlin, *Modern Revivalism* (New York, 1959), 311.

35. For the reaction of the Protestant churches generally to the events of 1877, 1886, and 1892–94, all of which, except for Homestead in 1892, were centered on Chicago, see H. May, *Protestant Churches and Industrial America* (New York, 1967), 91–111.

36. *Chicago Tribune*, July 30, 1877.

37. Cited by J. Findlay, *Dwight L. Moody, American Evangelist, 1837–1899* (Chicago, 1969), 327.

38. Chicago City Missionary Society, *Annual Reports, 1884–1895;* Chicago Baptist Association, *Proceedings, 1882–1886; Baptist City Mission Society of Chicago* (Chicago, n.d.); C. F. Gates, "The Work of the Chicago Missionary Society," "The Needs of Chicago: An Address Delivered before the Congregational Club at the Palmer House," May 21, 1883; Pierce, *A History of Chicago*, 3: 425; Kann, "Working Class Culture," 156; McLoughlin, *Modern Revivalism*, 267.

39. Dwight L. Moody's first evangelical act was part of this movement. In early 1859 he opened a Sabbath school for the urchins of "The Sands," a slum area with a predominantly immigrant population. Not hesitant about doing God's work in one of Satan's abandoned institutions, he opened the Sunday school in an old, unused saloon; with the aid of some "missionary sugar" to entice the children into the school, the school soon became so large that he persuaded the mayor to help in God's work by providing the city's North Market rent free. He boasted that with one thousand pupils in the Sunday School it was "the best school there

is this side of New York." Chicago's leading businessmen listened and were impressed. Cyrus McCormick, George Armour, Isaac Burch, and particularly John Fairwell, a dry-goods merchant, not only listened, but made generous donations to Moody's work. That Moody was less interested in the pedagogical guidelines laid down by the American Sunday School Union than in inspiring children with God's word in whatever way he knew how apparently did not bother businessmen in the least. See Findlay, *Moody*, 72–81; McLoughlin, *Modern Revivalism*, 174–75; Boyer, *Urban Masses and Moral Order*, 182.

40. Findlay, *Moody*, 73–74; R. Perry, "The Mission Sunday School as a Social and Ethical Lever," *Biblioteca Sacra* 56 (1899): 481; Pierce, *A History of Chicago*, 3: 426; J. M. Gillette, "The Culture Agencies of a Typical Manufacturing Group: South Chicago," *American Journal of Sociology* 7, 1 (July, 1901): 91–121.

41. Findlay, *Moody*, 232, 326, 328, 329. Several days later Moody wrote that the institute represented his desire "to work out the greatest problem of this century." "The greatest subject before the people today," he stated, is "what should be done with and for the workingman?" His answer was simple and straightforward: "Save their souls." McLoughlin, *Modern Revivalism*, 272–73.

42. Cyrus McCormick, Jr., T. W. Harvey, N. S. McCormick, Jr., N. S. Benton, E. G. Keith, and John Farwell were charter members. Nettie Fowler McCormick, the widow of Cyrus McCormick, Sr., was also actively involved; she contributed $50,000 to the institute. Farwell donated $100,000; Cyrus McCormick, Jr., $25,000; Harvey, $10,000; Keith, $10,000; Marshall Field, $10,000; Levi Zeiter (Marshall Field's original partner), $10,000.

43. Findlay, *Moody*, 327–35; McLoughlin, *Modern Revivalism*, 272–74.

44. Cited in B. Weisberger, *They Gathered at the River: The Story of the Great Revivalists and Their Impact on Religion in America* (Boston, 1958), 211–12. Moody's theology is discussed by Findlay, *Moody*, ch. 7; McLoughlin, *Modern Revivalism*, 167–70, 247–57; and Weisberger, 171–77, 196–97, 211–12. Moody was a premillennialist who believed that the millennium would come only after the present world had been destroyed by God's agents with his second coming. For discussions of Moody's social views, see McLoughlin, 252–59, 278, 311–12; Weisberger, 189–90; and Findlay, 274–84.

45. McLoughlin, *Modern Revivalism*, 168, 262–70; Weisberger, *They Gathered at the River*, 205, 229–30; Findlay, *Moody*, 174. In any case, the numbers estimated to have been converted are not impressive. For Moody's early revivals in Chicago, totaling sixteen weeks, estimates varied from 2,500 to 10,000. The *Chicago Tribune*, for example, reported in 1877 after one revival that "about 2,500 have been converted, between 6,000 and 8,000 have been seriously impressed." There is no evidence that Moody's revivals added appreciably to the number in Chicago's churches. It was true that in the Third Ward, some fourteen churches and two synagogues served the ward's 20,212 inhabitants in 1886, but the ward was the residence of Chicago's well-to-do. In the First Ward, on the other hand, in which 16,241 persons resided, only six churches served the population. See McLoughlin, 262–65; *Chicago Tribune*, January 17, 1877; Pierce, *A History of Chicago*, 3: 424.

46. H. Nelli, *Italians in Chicago, 1880–1930* (New York, 1970), 283–84; Weisberger, *They Gathered at the River*, 204; Findlay, *Moody*, 272–73.

47. Cited in McLoughlin, *Modern Revivalism*, 308.

48. Ibid.

49. Pierce, *A History of Chicago,* 3: 437–38; May, *Protestant Churches,* 118–21. The quote is from Pierce, 3: 438.

50. Pierce, *A History of Chicago,* 3: 423–24.

51. Chicago Relief and Aid Society, *Report of the Chicago Relief and Aid Society of Disbursement and Contributions for the Sufferers by the Chicago Fire* (1874), 126–27. For details of the early history of the CR&AS, see J. Brown, *The History of Public Assistance in Chicago, 1833–1893* (Chicago, 1941); O. M. Nelson, "The Chicago Relief and Aid Society, 1850–1874," *Journal of the Illinois State Historical Society* 49, 1 (Spring 1966): 48–66; J. A. Mayer, "Private Charities in Chicago from 1871 to 1915" (Ph.D. dissertation, University of Minnesota, 1978), 26–72; T. J. Nayler, "Responding to the Fire: The Work of the Chicago Relief and Aid Society," *Science and Society* 39, 4 (Winter 1975–76): 450–64; A. Johnson, *Adventures in Social Welfare* (Fort Wayne, 1923), 61–62.

52. CR&AS, *First Annual Report, 1867–1868,* 8 (the numbering of annual reports by the society varied after 1867; therefore the report for 1867 was known both as its first and its fifteenth); idem, *Report of the Chicago Relief and Aid Society of Disbursement . . . , 1878,* 126–27; E. B. McCagg, "The Charities of Chicago," Sixth Annual Conference of Charities and Corrections, *Proceedings, 1879,* 146–47; Brown, *History of Public Assistance,* 38–44, 101, 112.

53. McCagg, "The Charities of Chicago," 149; CR&AS, *Twenty-Seventh Annual Report, 1884,* 2, 6; idem, *Twenty-Third Annual Report, 1880,* 5.

54. For histories of the COS, see H. S. Tishler, *Self-Reliance and Social Security, 1870–1917* (Port Washington, N.Y., 1971), chs. 1, 2; W. I. Trattner, *From Poor Law to Welfare State: A History of Social Welfare in America* (New York, 1974), ch. 5; R. Lubove, *The Professional Altruist* (New York, 1977), ch. 1; Boyer, *Urban Masses and Moral Order in America, 1820–1920,* ch. 10. The best study of the charity reform movement is G. S. Jones, *Outcast London* (Harmondsworth, Middlesex, 1976), pt. 3. For drawing my attention to the importance of the Charity Organization Society, I am indebted to Michael Katz.

55. Johnson, *Adventures in Social Work,* 59, 61.

56. Johnson, *Adventures in Social Work,* 61; idem, *Methods and Machinery of the Organization of Charity* (Chicago, 1887), 1, 3; *Annual Report of the Charity Organization Society of Chicago, 1886,* 4.

57. Henderson was also a founder of the Terra Haute, Ind., COS, a leading official of the "new" charity in Chicago from the mid-1890s until his death in 1915, and in 1889, president of the National Conference on Charities and Corrections.

58. C. Henderson, "Public Outdoor Relief," National Conference of Charities and Corrections, *Proceedings, 1891,* 40. See also idem, "The Relations of Philanthropy to Social Order and Progress," National Conference of Charities and Corrections, *Proceedings, 1899,* 15; idem, "Definition of a Social Policy Relating to the Dependent Group," *American Journal of Sociology* 10, 3 (November 1904): 323–27, 331; idem, "How to Care for the Poor Without Creating Pauperism," *Charities Review* 5, 4 (February 1896): 185.

59. Jones, *Outcast London,* 252.

60. Ibid., 252.

61. F. H. Wines, *Lend A Hand,* 8 (1892): 37. See also S. H. Gurteen, *A Handbook of Charity Organization* (Buffalo, N.Y., 1882), 39, 182, 224–25, 117; idem, *Hints and Suggestions to the Visitors of the Poor* (Buffalo, N.Y., 1896), 6.

62. Johnson, *Adventures in Social Work,* 76–83; CR&AS, *Thirty-First Annual Report, 1888,* 4; Brown, *The History of Public Assistance in Chicago,* 125; Pierce, *A History of Chicago,* 3: 461; Mayer, "Private Charities in Chicago," 69–123; K. Kusmer, "The Functions of Organized Charity in the Progressive Era: Chicago as a Case Study," *Journal of American History* 60 (December 1973): 659.

63. On the Social Gospel movement, see May, *Protestant Churches,* pts. 3 and 4.

64. Allen Nevins described the twelve months that began in the middle of the year 1894 "the Année terrible of American history between Reconstruction and the World War," a point of view endorsed by C. Vann Woodward in a chapter ("Année Terrible") of his *Tom Watson:* "As the national depression reached its nadir, a new record was attained in unemployment, in the intensity of organized labor's struggle for existence, in the brutality of capitalist oppression of labor, and in the distress of the agricultural masses. When the paralysis of the farming sections had suffered so long and finally gripped the vitals of the industrial East, it called forth an expression of new radicalism which, joined to the older agrarian radicalism, formed a flood of discontent, protest, exposure, and some astute analysis of a corrupt capitalist economy" ([New York, 1963], 259). I think their use of the singular "Année," however, too limiting: distress and radical politics were widespread before mid-1894, certainly in Chicago.

65. On the elections of 1890, see H. Faulkner, *Politics, Reform and Expansion, 1890–1900* (New York, 1959), ch. 5; and J. D. Hicks, *The Populist Revolt* (Omaha, 1959), ch. 6.

66. The Omaha platform is cited in full in Hicks, *The Populist Revolt,* 439–44. On the formation of the Peoples party, see Hicks, ch. 8; and Goodwyn, *The Populist Moment,* ch. 4.

67. On the political culture, ideology, and language of the Peoples party, see Goodwyn, *The Populist Moment,* chs. 5 and 6; and N. Pollack, *The Populist Response to Industrial America* (New York, 1962), chs. 1, 2, 3.

68. On the elections of 1892, see Hicks, *The Populist Revolt,* ch. 9; Faulkner, *Politics, Reform and Expansion,* ch. 6; Goodwyn, *The Populist Moment,* ch. 6; R. Jensen, *The Winning of the Midwest* (Chicago, 1971), 219–21; H. Barnard, *Eagle Forgotten: The Life of John Peter Altgeld* (Indianapolis, 1938), ch. 17; J. P. Altgeld, *Live Questions* (Chicago, 1899); W. R. Browne, *Altgeld of Illinois* (New York, 1924), ch. 5.

69. H. D. Lloyd to Samuel Gompers, July 10, 1892, American Federation of Labor archives, cited in C. McA. Destler, *American Radicalism, 1865–1901* (New London, 1946), 168. See also Pollock, *The Populist Response,* ch. 3.

70. *Official Annual Labor Gazette, 1893,* 42, 135–37; Destler, *American Radicalism,* 165.

71. H. D. Lloyd, *Wealth Against Commonwealth* (New York, 1894), 510–11; C. McA. Destler, *Henry Demarest Lloyd and the Empire of Reform* (Philadelphia, 1963), 292, 300. For an assessment of Lloyd's analysis of monopoly and monopoly power, see Destler, *American Radicalism,* ch. 7.

72. *Chicago Tribune,* December 15, 1893; Destler, *Henry Demarest Lloyd,* 263–65.

73. Faulkner, *Politics, Reform and Expansion,* 141–42; S. Reznick, "Unemployment, Unrest and Relief in the United States During the Depression of 1893–1897," *Journal of Political Economy* 61 (August 1953): 324–28; C. Hoff-

man, "The Depression of the Nineties," *Journal of Economic History* 16 (June 1956): 138–41; J. A. Schumpeter, *Business Cycles* (New York, 1939), 341–42, 388–89; Bogart and Thompson, *The Modern Commonwealth*, 399–400.

74. L. H. Feder, *Unemployment Relief in Periods of Depression* (New York, 1936), 76–83; *Chicago Times*, September 30, 1893; *Chicago Daily News Almanac for 1894* (Chicago, 1894), 360–374.

75. *Chicago Searchlight*, August 2, 1894, cited in Destler, *American Radicalism*, 177.

76. R. S. Baker, *American Chronicle* (New York, 1945), 2.

77. *Chicago Tribune*, August 21, 22, 1893; *Chicago Times*, August 27, 29, 31, 1893.

78. J. Addams, *Twenty Years at Hull House* (New York, 1960), 159–60.

79. G. Taylor, *Pioneering on Social Frontiers* (Chicago, 1930), 110.

80. The Civic Federation of Chicago, *First Annual Report of the Central Council, 1895*, 10–11.

81. For details of the wage cuts and the hardship they caused, see A. Lindsey, *The Pullman Strike* (Chicago, 1942), 90–103; and the United States Strike Commission, *Report of the Chicago Strike of June–July, 1894*, executive document of the U.S. Senate, 53d Cong., 3d sess., no. 7 (Washington, D.C., 1895).

82. Eugene Debs founded the ARU in 1892 as an industrial, rather than craft, union, encompassing all workers in the railroad industry, regardless of craft or skill level. Soon after its formation, in 1893, it won a major victory over the Great Northern Railway, comparable to the victory of the Knights of Labor over Jay Gould in 1885. As in the Knights' victory, workers swarmed into the victorious organization. Within a year of its establishment, the ARU had 150,000 members, more than the combined membership of the conservative railroad brotherhoods and only 25,000 less than the entire membership of the AFL. For further details, see Brecher, *Strike!* 113–14; R. Ginger, *The Bending Cross* (New Brunswick, 1949), 97–98; Lindsay, *The Pullman Strike*, ch. 6.

83. For descriptions of the strike, see Lindsay, *The Pullman Strike*, chs. 7–11; Brecher, *Strike!* 112–32.

84. *Public Opinion*, July 5, 1894, cited in Brecher, *Strike!* 119.

85. For Debs's antimonopolism, see N. Salvatore, *Eugene V. Debs: Citizen and Socialist* (Urbana, 1982).

86. Cited in Lens, *The Labor Wars*, 89–90. Perlman did not exaggerate: The Pullman strike reflected a half century of class formation, beginning with the artisanal politics of the 1850s and 1860s, the spontaneous neighborhood-based riots of 1877 accompanied by extensive violence, and the Eight-Hour conflicts over condition of employment within wage labor.

87. U.S. Strike Commission, *Report*, 609.

88. *New York Times*, June 29, 1894; *Chicago Tribune*, July 3, 1894.

89. Cited in R. Ginger, *Altgeld's America* (Chicago, 1965), 158.

90. U.S. Strike Commission, *Report*, 179–80; *Report of the Attorney-General, 1894*, xxxi–xxxiv.

91. G. Cleveland, *Presidential Problems* (New York, 1904), 79–117; U.S. Strike Commission, *Report*, xiv–xvi; Browne, *Altgeld of Illinois*, 153–56; Barnard, *Eagle Forgotten*, ch. 31. Henry Demarest Lloyd, remarking on Cleveland's action, wrote that "the Democratic Party for a hundred years has been the pull back against centralization in American politics. . . . But in one hour here last July, it

sacrificed the honorable devotion of a century to its great principles and surren-
dered both the rights of states and the rights of man to the centralized corporate
despotism to which the presidency of the United States was then abdicated" (C.
Lloyd, *Life of Henry Demarest Lloyd* [New York, 1912], 1: 146–47).

92. *Chicago Tribune*, May 20, 1893; Destler, *American Radicalism*, 168.

93. *Chicago Tribune*, May 29, 1893; Destler, *American Radicalism*, 169–70.

94. Lloyd, *Henry Demarest Lloyd*, 1: 243; *Chicago Tribune*, July 6, 1893;
Destler, *American Radicalism*, 171–76; idem, *Henry Demarest Lloyd*, 268–70.

95. Destler comments: "The consummation of the Labor-Populist alliance
at Springfield, Illinois, was especially significant. The Springfield conference had
grafted on to the Omaha platform, with its limited program of state ownership,
nine of the planks of the political program of British labor, a vogue single tax
plank, and a modified version of Plank 10, which endorsed the extension of
collective ownership of the means of production and distribution as far as the
voting public should approve through the initiative and referendum. Even apart
from this last plank . . . the Springfield platform extended its application of the
collectivist principle far beyond the Populist position" (*American Radicalism*, 176).
While the arrest of Debs and the collapse of the Pullman strike in July 1894
generated widespread support in Chicago for the alliance in the 1894 elections,
the alliance did not do particularly well, despite the hard work of Lloyd to tempt
labor away from the Democratic party to the Peoples party. Instead, the Republican party, rather than the Populists, benefited from disaffection with the Democratic party. See Destler, ch. 9.

96. Barnard, *Eagle Forgotten*, 321–22, 350.

97. Ibid., 352–53; H. Wish, "John P. Altgeld and the Background of the
Campaign of 1896," *Mississippi Valley Historical Review* 24 (March 1938): 504–10;
Ginger, *Altgeld's America*, 174–79.

98. Wish, "Campaign of 1896," 511–12.

99. Ibid., 512–14; K. K. Porter, comp., *National Party Platforms* (New
York, 1924), 181–87; Barnard, *Eagle Forgotten*, ch. 34.

100. W. G. Bryan, *The First Battle* (Chicago, 1896), 199–206.

101. Clarence Darrow reported that Altgeld remarked to him the morning
after Bryan's speech, "It takes more than speeches to win real victories. Applause
lasts but a little while. The road to justice is not a path of glory; it is stony and
long and lonely, filled with pain and martyrdom. . . . I have been thinking over
Bryan's speech. What did he say, anyhow?" (C. Darrow, *The Story of My Life* [New
York, 1932], 92). See also Wish, "Altgeld and the Election of 1896," *Journal of
the Illinois State Historical Society* 30 (October 1937): 357, 363–64.

102. H. F. Pringle, *Theodore Roosevelt* (New York, 1931), 164, cited in
Faulkner, *Politics, Reform and Expansion*, 200.

103. Upon Bryan's nomination by the Peoples party, a deeply chagrined
Henry D. Lloyd declared in a memorable metaphor: "The Free Silver movement
is a fake. Free Silver is the cow-bird of the reform movement. It waited till the
nest had been built by the sacrifices and labor of others, and then it laid its eggs in
it, pushing out the others which it smashed on the ground. . . . The People's Party
has been betrayed. No party that does not lead its leaders will ever succeed"
(Lloyd, *Henry Demarest Lloyd*, 1: 259).

104. On the election of 1896, see Faulkner, *Politics, Reform and Expansion*,
ch. 9; Hicks, *The Populist Revolt*, ch. 13; Jensen, *The Winning of the Midwest*, ch.

10; Goodwyn, *The Populist Moment*, ch. 8; P. Glad, *McKinley, Bryan and the People* (New York, 1964); S. Jones, *The Presidential Election of 1896* (Madison, 1964); Wish, "John Peter Altgeld and the Election of 1896," 353–84.

105. *Chicago Tribune*, March 8, 1889.

106. R. Woods and A. J. Kennedy, eds., *Handbook of Settlements* (New York, 1911), 37–72.

107. Addams, *Twenty Years*, 91–94, 95, 97. See also idem, *Democracy and Social Ethics* (New York, 1920), 73–77, 79, 81–82, 94, 101; idem, "A New Impulse to an Old Gospel," *Forum* 14 (November 1892): 348, 356–57; A Davis, *Spearheads for Reform* (New York, 1967), 27–29, 14–17, 33–39; idem, *American Heroine* (New York, 1973), 73–74; L. Wade, "The Social Gospel Impulse and Chicago Settlement House Founders," *Chicago Theological Seminary Register* 55 (April 1965): 1–12.

108. Addams, *Twenty Years*, 45.

109. Idem, *Democracy and Social Ethics*, 2–3; idem, *Twenty Years*, 100.

110. Idem, *Twenty Years*, 89, 98; idem, "Hull House, Chicago: An Effort Toward Social Democracy," *Forum* 14 (October 1892): 226; "The Objective Value of a Social Settlement," in *Philanthropy and Social Progress*, ed. J. Addams, R. Woods et al. (New York, 1893), 27–56; Davis, *Spearheads*, 19. See also Davis, *American Heroine*, ch. 4. Graham Taylor, founder of Chicago Commons, was of a similar mind. He intended Chicago Commons to be "a common center where representatives of the masses and classes could meet and mingle as fellow men." John Dewey, a close observer of the settlements in Chicago, summarized the settlement house as primarily a "social clearing house," a place "for bringing people together," "doing away with barriers of caste, or class, or race, or type of experience that keep people from real communion with each other." The Taylor quote is cited in Davis, *Spearheads*, 19; Dewey's quote is from "The School as a Social Center," National Education Association, *Addresses and Proceedings* (1902): 381. See also Taylor, *Pioneering on Social Frontiers*, ch. 1; L. Wade, *Graham Taylor: Pioneer for Social Justice, 1851–1938* (Chicago, 1964), chs. 1, 2, 3; Davis, *Spearheads*, 13, 26–27.

111. Cited in L. Wade, "The Heritage from Chicago's Early Settlement Houses," *Illinois State Historical Journal* 4 (Winter 1967): 415. See also G. Taylor, *Chicago Commons through Forty Years* (Chicago, 1936), 21; and T. Philpott, *The Ghetto and the Slum* (New York, 1979), ch. 3.

112. Addams, *Twenty Years*, chs. 2, 7, 8, 10, 13, 14, 18; Davis, *Spearheads*, chs. 3–9; Residents of Hull House, *Hull House Maps and Papers;* Ginger, *Altgeld's America*, ch. 5; S. Rothman, *Woman's Proper Place* (New York, 1970), chs. 3, 4.

113. Addams, "Hull House," 226; idem, *Twenty Years*, 83, 92 (see also 113, 242, 243, 257, 258, 259, 261).

114. Addams, *Twenty Years*, 83–84, 85–86, 179–83, 202, 205, 247, 248, 251, 301–4.

115. Or, as several historians have explained, settlement house work represented an expression of "social feminism." See W. O'Neill, *Everyone Was Brave* (Chicago, 1969), esp. chs. 1, 3, 4, 5; C. Degler, *At Odds: Women and the Family in America from the Revolution to the Present* (New York, 1980), ch. 13; Rothman, *Woman's Proper Place*, ch. 3.

116. J. Addams, *The Second Twenty Years at Hull House* (New York, 1930), 89, 91, 92; idem, "Women's Conscience and Social Amelioration," in *Social Appli-*

cations of Religion, ed. C. Stelze (Cincinnati, 1908), 41; idem, *Twenty Years,* 204; idem, "Why Women Should Vote," *Ladies Home Journal* 27 (January 1910), reprinted in *New Ideals of Peace* (New York, 1970), 202. See also idem, *Democracy and Social Ethics,* 73–77, 80–87, 94–101, 106, 110. In a 1906 address to the convention of the National American Woman Suffrage Association, Addams claimed that "city housekeeping has failed partly because women, the traditional housekeepers, have not been consulted as to its multiform activities" to which women could bring "a sense of obligation for the health and welfare of young children and a responsibility for the cleanliness and comfort of other people" (I. H. Harper, *History of Woman Suffrage* [New York, 1922], 178).

117. Addams, *Twenty Years,* 98, 133–34; *Second Twenty Years,* 381.

118. For details, see Addams, *Twenty Years,* passim; Davis, *Spearheads,* passim.

119. Addams, *Second Twenty Years,* 23, 29, 31, 30.

120. Ibid., 39, 40–41; Davis, *Spearheads,* 202–7. At the December 12, 1912, meeting of the National Progressive Committee, Jane Addams convinced the committee to approve the creation of national ominibus reform organization: the National Progressive Service (NPS). Divided into two bureaus—the Legislative Reference Bureau and the Speakers Bureau—and four departments (conservation, popular government, cost of living and corporation control, and social and industrial justice, co-directed by Jane Addams), the NPS carried on a two-decade-old effort to end social injustice and create a social democracy.

121. T. Veblen, *Theory of the Leisure Class* (New York, 1959), 224.

122. W. T. Stead, *If Christ Came to Chicago* (Chicago, 1895), 397–99.

123. In 1870, relatively modest residential segregation characterized Chicago. After 1870, however, with the introduction of cable cars, elevated steam railroads, and electric surface lines, the spatial separation of classes accelerated rapidly. For details of the process of residential segregation in Chicago, see S. B. Warner, *The Urban Wilderness* (New York, 1972), ch. 4; H. M. Mayer and R. C. Wade, *Chicago: Growth of a Metropolis* (Chicago, 1969), chs. 3, 4; Hoyt, *Land Values,* chs. 3, 4, 5, 6; H. Hoyt, *The Structure and Growth of Residential Neighborhoods in American Cities* (Washinton, D.C., 1939), 106; H. Zorbaugh, *The Gold Coast and the Slum* (Chicago, 1929), 242.

124. Stead, *If Christ Came to Chicago,* 315, 399, 410; *Chicago Tribune,* November 12, 1893; Ginger, *Altgeld's America,* 249.

125. A. Small, "The Civic Federation of Chicago: A Study in Social Dynamics," *American Journal of Sociology* 1 (July 1, 1885): 85, 88–90; Addams, *Twenty Years,* 158; B. Grant, *The Fight for a City—The Chicago Unions Leagues Club* (Chicago, 1955), ch. 11; D. Sutherland, *Fifty Years on the Civic Front* (Chicago, 1943), ch. 1; D. Levine, "The Civic Federation of Chicago" in *Varieties of Liberal Reform* (Madison, 1964), ch. 3. On the National Civic Federation, see Kolko, *The Triumph of Conservatism,* and J. Weinstein, *The Corporate Ideal in the Liberal State* (Boston, 1968).

126. Civic Federation of Chicago, *First Annual Report of the Central Council, 1894–1895,* 7, 10.

127. Mayer, "Private Charities in Chicago," 143–58; "Relief by Extra Public Service," *The Charities Review* III (1894): 133; *Report to the Central Relief Association to the Civic Federation,* 4, 14, 28; Civic Federation of Chicago, *First Annual Report, 1895,* 28, 33–36; M. H. Coonley, "Private Relief Agencies in Chicago

(M.A. thesis, University of Chicago, 1921), 44–45; E. Bicknell, "Problems of Philanthropy in Chicago," *Annals of the American Academy of Social and Political Science* 21 (May 1903): 44. Settlement house workers were closely associated with the CRA in the mid-1890s. See R. Hunter, "The Relation Between Social Settlements and Charity Organizations," *Journal of Political Economy* 11 (December 1902); 77, 79. The leaders of the CRA included Jane Addams, Graham Taylor, Albion Small, Lucy Flower, Sarah Hackett Stevenson (president of the Chicago Womens Club), W. R. Stirling (a former COS official), Julian Mack (late a judge of the juvenile court), John Dewey, and Lyman Gage. Franklin MacVeagh, like Gage a banker, was president of the Bureau of Associated Charities until 1909 and a very active participant in the municipal reform movement in the late 1890s and early 1900s. William T. Baker, vice-president of the bureau for almost a decade, was one of Chicago's "grain kings," president of the Board of Trade in the 1890s, and a supporter of a variety of Progressive issues. Kusmer reports that between 1886 and 1908, a director of the COS, CRA, or BAC in Chicago was, typically, a large-scale merchant, banker, or lawyer, "between forty-five and fifty-five years of age; he was likely to be a Protestant in religion and a Republican in politics." The majority held college degrees, mainly from eastern schools. The typical director, finally, belonged to two prestigious clubs (Kusmer, "The Functions of Organized Charity," 672–73). Business also ensured that it controlled the funding of private charity in Chicago. When Sophinisba Breckinridge attempted in 1911 to establish a centralized voluntary system of investigation and certification of private charitable agencies soliciting public funds, and to base it at the School of Civics and Philanthropy at the University of Chicago, the Association of Commerce stepped in to thwart the move. The association appointed a committee "to investigate the solicitors and beneficiaries by or for whom donations are solicited" and asked the committee to make its findings public. This it did the next year, and every year thereafter, as an annual *Classified List of Local Philanthropic and Charitable Organizations*. For further details, see S. Diner, *A City and Its Universities* (Chapel Hill, 1980), 122–23; Kusmer, "The Functions of Organized Charity," 672–76; Ginger, *Altgeld's America*, 58, 60, 280; E. C. Kirkland, *Dream and Thought in the Business Community, 1860–1900* (Chicago, 1956), 141–42; C. Baker, *Life and Character of William Taylor Baker* (New York: 1908), 65–69, 116–39, 171–73.

128. In London, argues Stedman Jones, the COS assumed that friendly visiting would end the growing separation of classes and establish social harmony by creating a "deference community" in which "the relations between rich and poor would be braced by personal ties by obligation and dependence (Jones, *Outcast London*, 228).

129. C. Henderson, "Three Months in a Workshop," *Charities Review* 4, 5 (March 1895): 258.

130. J. Addams, "The Subtle Problems of Charity," *The Atlantic Monthly* 83 (February 1899): 163–76; idem, *Democracy and Social Ethics*, 14–69. Robert Hunter developed a similar analysis of friendly visiting (Hunter, "The Relation Between Social Settlements and Charity Organizations," 81). Paul Boyer also describes the mocking, satiric send-up of the dilemma of the friendly visitor by Mary McDowell of the University of Chicago settlement at the National Conference of Charities and Corrections in 1896 (*Moral Order*, 155). In later years, G. H. Mead, then teaching at the University of Chicago and for a while president of the City Club, developed a philosophical and socio-psychological critique of char-

ity and a defense for social insurance. See G. H. Mead, "The Psychology of Punitive Justice," *American Journal of Sociology* 23 (March 1918): esp. 596–602; idem, "Philanthropy from the Point of View of Ethics" in *Intelligent Philanthropy*, ed. E. Faris (Chicago, 1930), 133–48; and T. V. Smith, "George Herbert Mead and the Philosophy of Philanthropy," *Social Service Review* (March 1932): esp. 47–53.

131. For general accounts of the Progressive social insurance movement, see R. Lubove, *The Struggle for Social Security, 1900–1935* (Cambridge, 1968); Tishler, *Self-Reliance and Social Security;* Trattner, *From Poor Law to Welfare State;* R. Bremmer, *From the Depths* (New York, 1956). I have been particularly influenced by both Lubove's and Tishler's treatments of the ideological conflicts associated with the social insurance movement, and by an essay by M. Katz, "American Historians and Dependency" (unpublished paper, University of Pennsylvania, August, 1980).

132. For the history of worker's compensation legislation in Illinois, see Beckner, *A History of Labor Legislation in Illinois,* 429–62; J. L. Castrovinci, "Prelude to Welfare Capitalism: The Role of Business in the Enactment of Workers Compensation Legislation in Illinois, 1905–1912," *Social Science Review* 50 (1976): 82–86; C. R. Henderson, "Workingmens Insurance in Illinois," American Association for Labor Legislation, *Proceedings of the First Annual Meeting* (1907): 69–84; idem, "Industrial Insurance," *American Journal of Sociology* 12 (January 1907): 472; idem, *Industrial Insurance in the United States* (Chicago, 1909); Illinois Employers Liability Commission, *Report* (Springfield, Ill., 1910), 18–19; Tishler, *Self Reliance and Social Security,* 115–21; Weinstein, *The Corporte Ideal in the Liberal State,* ch. 2; Lubove, *The Professional Altruist,* 115–116, 119, 126–27, 128, 134–37; *Chicago Tribune,* November 15, 1909. For the history of the mother's pension movement, see the White House Conference on Child Health and Protection, *Dependent and Neglected Children* 4, C-1 (New York, 1933), 9, 59; M. W. Pickney, "Public Pensions to Widows: Experiences and Observations Which Led Me to Favor Such a Law," NCCC, *Proceedings* 39 (1912): 473; G. Abbott, *The Child and the State* (Chicago, 1938), II: 229–331; J. P. Zetland, "Private Agencies and the Development of Public Assistance in Chicago, 1911–1935" (M.A. thesis, University of Chicago, 1947). On the opposition of the COS to mother's pensions, see, for example, the *Proceedings* of the NCCC between 1894 and 1904; and Boyer, *Urban Masses and Moral Order,* 157–58.

133. Cf. R. Lubove: "The Social Insurance Movement, launched in the early twentieth century, marked a decisive episode in the history of social welfare. In contrast to the middle class reform tradition of the past, with its emphasis upon economic independence and mobility, the sponsors of compulsory social insurance addressed themselves to the requisites of security in a wage-centered, industrial economy. They maintained that neither the public welfare system, nor private social work, nor voluntary insurance institutions sufficed to provide 'indemnity against financial losses from . . . ordinary contingencies in the workingman's life' " (Lubove, "Economic Security and Social Conflict in America," *Journal of Social History* 1 [Fall 1967]: 61; Lubove quotes Louis Brandeis).

134. Henderson, "Industrial Insurance," 472; "Workingman's Insurance," 69–84.

135. The creation of this binary structure of social security and public assistance can be linked, as James O'Conner suggests, to the existence of dual labor

markets and the different functions of "social capital" (social security) and "social expenses" (public assistance). Similarly, Piven and Cloward have persuasively argued that public assistance is an instrument of general labor discipline and social order. See F. F. Piven and R. A. Colward, *Regulating the Poor* (New York, 1971); J. O'Conner, *The Fiscal Crisis of the State* (New York, 1973); and M. Katz, "American Historians and Dependency."

136. Eli Zaretsky, in a recent essay, cites I. M. Rubinow to the effect that social security was made necessary by the decline of the extended family and the "increasing dependence of the majority of mankind . . . upon a wage contract for their means of existence." Zaretsky comments that "workmen's compensation tied insurance to the wage contract, as well as protecting the insurance companies that served as private carriers." He goes on to conclude that "the shift the Progressives helped accomplish from a laissez-faire outlook to one appropriate to a highly integrated corporate capitalist welfare state masked the continuity of market relations both in society and as incorporated into government reforms. . . . As with government intervention into business, government intervention into social life presupposed wage labor and private property" (E. Zaretsky, "The Place of the Family in the Origins of the Welfare State" in *Rethinking the Family,* ed. B. Thorne and M. Yalom [New York, 1982], 211).

137. By the late 1920s, disbursements from mother's pensions accounted for approximately 40 percent of all relief distributed by all relief agencies, public and private, in Chicago. "The widows pension, mothers assistance funds, for example," wrote Edith Abbott, "have almost revolutionized social work within recent memory. In the city of Chicago, the expenditures in this field, on an excellent case-work basis and with good social workers as probation officers, many of them graduates of our University School of Social Service, were $1,200,000 last year, exclusive of overhead. . . . " Mother's pensions, along with the opening of professional schools of social work (for example, the Chicago School of Civics and Philanthropy), the appropriation of psychoanalytic theory as the theoretical base of social work, the development of scientific case work, and the growth in size and bureaucratization of private and public welfare organizations (particularly the United Charities of Chicago after 1909 and, after 1913, the Chicago Department of Public Welfare) might thus be credited with responsibility for the growth of professional social work in Chicago. For further details, see H. K. Jeter and A. W. McNillen, "Some Statistics of Family Welfare and Relief in Chicago, 1928," *Social Service Bureau* 3 (September 3, 1929): 450; E. Abbott, *Social Welfare and Professional Education* (Chicago, 1931), 84, 105, 150.

138. Chicago Council of Social Agencies, *Social Service Directory, Chicago, 1930* (Chicago, 1930), i; M. F. Krughoff, *Salaries and Profesisonal Qualifications of Social Workers in Chicago, 1935* (Chicago, 1937), 4–5; H. R. Jeter, "Salaries, Education, Training and Experience of Social Workers in Family Welfare and Relief Agencies in Chicago, October 1, 1932," *Committee on Research of the Chicago Council of Social Agencies and the Advisory Committee on Relief and Service of the Cook County Bureau of Public Welfare,* February 6, 1933 (from a copy in the University of Chicago Library).

139. It is not insignificant that the two major texts of social work education in the 1920s, *Social Diagnosis* (1917) and *What is Social Casework* (1922), were both written by Mary Richmond, a leading figure in the COS.

140. It is in these developments that the underlying significance of the

growth of case work and the shift from "cause" to "function" noted by Lubove can be found. Lubove, *The Professional Altruist*, 14–16, 22–23, 52, 121, 157–58.

141. Civic Federation of Chicago, *Congress on Industrial Conciliation and Arbitration, November 13–14, 1894* (Chicago, 1894), 94; idem, *First Annual Report of the Central Council, 1895*, 78.

142. U.S. Senate, *Report of the Chicago Strike*, 250.

143. J. P. Altgeld, "Labor Day Address, 1892," cited in Browne, *Altgeld of Illinois*, 195; H. Wish, "Altgeld and the Progressive Tradition," *American Historical Review* 46 (July 1941): 819–20; *First Annual Report of the State Board of Arbitration, March 1, 1896* (Springfield, 1896); Addams, *Twenty Years*, 214; Beckner, *A History of Labor Legislation in Illinois*, 76–78.

144. Addams, "A Function of the Social Settlement," *Annals of the American Academy of Political and Social Science* 13 (May 1899): 335; idem, *Democracy and Social Ethics*, 210; idem, "The Objective Value of a Social Settlement," *Philanthropy and Social Progress* (New York, 1893), 52–54; idem, *Twenty Years*, 214, 218; idem, "The Present Crisis of Trade Union Morals," *North American Review* 179 (1904): 187–88; Residents of Hull House, *Hull House Maps and Papers*, 183–84, 194–203; Davis, *American Heroine*, 110–16.

145. G. Taylor, "The Social Settlement and the Labor Movement," *23rd Annual Conference of Charities, 1896*, 143–49; idem, "A Word to Labor Unions," *Commons* 1 (September 1896): 7; idem, *Pioneering on Social Frontiers*, 138–73; idem, "Between the Unions in Chicago's Industrial Civil War," *Commons* 14 (April 1904): 141–46; Wade, *Graham Taylor*, 144–45.

146. Mary McDowell, Alzina Stevens, Raymond Robbins, and Florence Kelley usually supported labor in strikes. See A. Stevens, "As for Trade Unions," *Commons* 4 (June 1897): 12; H. Wilson, *Mary McDowell: Neighbor* (Chicago, 1928), 25–28; Davis, *Spearheads*, 103, 104, 105, 106, 109, 112–19.

147. Addams, *Twenty Years*, 158–61; idem, *Democracy and Social Ethics*, 139, ch. 5; idem, "A Modern Lear," in *American Social Thought*, ed. R. Ginger (New York, 1961), 189–203. Jane Addams apparently believed, however, that not all benevolence was misguided. In 1903 she was involved in the introduction of "welfare capitalism" at the McCormick works in Chicago. On the recommendation of Addams, the McCormick Company appointed a "social secretary," Gertrude Beeks, later the wife of Ralph Easley, secretary of the CCF and later the NCF, in order to gain labor's "good will" and "cooperation." Miss Beeks was to engage in "betterment work," the meaning of which was indicated in a *Chicago Tribune* report twelve months later: "Girl an Angel of Peace. McCormick Company Hires Anti-Strike 'Social Agent.' Firm Employs Miss Gertrude Beeks to Aid in Solving the Problems of Capital and Labor." Miss Beeks's first gesture was modest—"She Wins Women by Placing Plenty of Mirrors in Their Dressing Room," the *Tribune* reported—but in 1903 the company took a further step by granting a stock gift to some of its workers as a means of preventing a strike at the works. *Chicago Tribune*, September 24, 1902; May 1, 1903. See also, R. Ozanne, *A Century of Labor Management Relations at McCormick and International Harvester* (Madison, 1967), 71–95, 118–20, 142–43, 182.

148. Cited in Davis, *Spearheads*, 209.

149. Ibid, 209–13; idem, "The Campaign for the Industrial Relations Commission, 1911–1913," *Mid America* 45, 4 (October 1963): 211–28; Weinstein, *The Corporate Ideal in the Liberal State*, ch. 7.

150. On Jane Addam's abortive attempt to unseat alderman Johnny Powers in the Nineteenth Ward, see Addams, "Objective Value of Social Settlement," 29; idem, "Ethical Survivals in Municipal Corruption," *International Journal of Ethics* 8 (April 1898): 372–91; idem, *Democracy and Social Ethics*, ch. 7; Davis, *American Heroine*, 120–25; idem, "Jane Addams vs. the Ward Boss," *Illinois State Historical Society Journal* 53 (1960): 250–56; H. S. Taylor, "John Powers and the Italians: Politics in a Chicago Ward, 1896–1921," *Journal of American History* 57 (June 1970), 67–84.

151. Civic Federation of Chicago, *First Annual Report of the Central Council, 1894–1895*, 10.

152. In 1895 Taylor organized a Seventeenth Ward Civic Federation (later renamed the Seventeenth Ward Community Club) affiliated with the Civic Federation of Chicago and the Municipal Voters League and set out to defeat corrupt local politicians at the voting booth. His candidate lost the 1896 elections but won in 1897 and again in 1898 and 1901. Wade, *Graham Taylor*, 129–33, 188–89, 227.

153. As a consequence of its rapid development and its failure to acquire a city charter granting it home rule from the Illinois legislature, Chicago's political structure by the mid-1890s was a Byzantine labyrinth of overlapping and competing jurisdictions. With power radically decentralized among eight principle and up to twenty-five or thirty minor municipal governing bodies, Chicago lacked the centralized organization of power characteristic of New York or Philadelphia. Instead, a series of four or five major factions and numerous minor ones were distributed throughout the three thousand precincts of Chicago and Cook County. The result was, as Charles Merriam, a University of Chicago political scientist and inveterate Progressive reformer, observed, a "feudal system," although during the 1890s among the Republicans, Bill Lorimer began building a political machine on the West Side that was eventually inherited by Fred Lundlin and William Hall Thompson, and among the Democrats, John Hopkins and Roger Sullivan built the beginnings of a political machine that eventually grew, in the 1930s, into the most successful urban government in the nation's history. During the 1880s and 1890s an interlocking directorate or "unholy alliance" developed between a number of ward level bosses (the most infamous of whom were R. E. Burke, Johnny Powers, "Hinky Dink" Kenna, and "Bathhouse John" Coughlin), the Lorimer Republicans, and the Sullivan-Hopkins Democrats, on the one hand, and on the other, a group of utility magnates (principally Charles Tyson Yerkes) and bankers (particularly John R. Walsh) interested in utility franchises and the deposit of public funds. The combination of decentralized political power, opportunism, greed, graft, and "boodlerism" produced, by the mid 1890s, one of the most notoriously corrupt city governments in the country. For further details, see C. Merriam, *Chicago: A More Intimate View of Urban Politics* (New York, 1929), 20–22, ch. 2, 94–98; H. Gosnell, *Machine Politics, Chicago Model*, 2d ed. (Chicago, 1968), ch. 1, postscript; E. Kantowicz, *Polish American Politics in Chicago, 1888–1940* (Chicago, 1975), chs. 2, 4; C. Harrison, *Growing Up with Chicago* (Chicago, 1944); A. Gottfried, *Boss Cermak of Chicago* (Seattle, 1962); L. Wendt and H. Kogan, *Bosses in Lusty Chicago* (Bloomington, 1971); E. M. Levine, *The Irish and Irish Politicians* (Notre Dame, 1966), ch. 6; "The Kelly-Nash Machine," *Fortune* (August 1936); C. Merriam, S. D. Parratt, A. Lepawsky, *The Government of the Metropolitan Region of Chicago* (Chicago, 1933); H. Zink, *City*

Bosses in the United States (Durham, 1930), 275–90; J. Bught, *Hizzoner "Big Bill" Thompson, an Idyll of Chicago* (New York, 1930); L. Lewis and H. Smith, *Chicago: The History of its Reputation* (New York, 1929); J. Tarr, *A Study in Boss Politics: William Lorrimer of Chicago* (Urbana, 1971), 75–80; idem, "The Urban Politician as Entrepreneur," *Mid America* 49 (January 1967): 55–67; idem, "J. R. Walsh of Chicago: A Case Study in Banking and Politics, 1881–1905," *Business History Review* 40, 4 (Winter 1966): 451–61; S. I. Roberts, "Portrait of a Robber Baron: Charles T. Yerkes," *Business History Review* (Autumn 1961); idem, "The Municipal Voters League and Chicago's Boodlers," *Journal of Illinois State Historical Society* 53 (1960): 122; L. Steffens, *The Shame of the Cities* (New York, 1904, 1957), 162–66, 175–76.

154. At the national level, Walter Lippmann, Herbert Croly, Louis Brandeis, among others, voiced a similar ideology. See S. Haber, *Efficiency and Uplift* (Chicago, 1964); C. Forcey, *The Crossroads of Liberalism* (New York, 1961); R. Wiebe, *The Search for Order* (New York, 1967), ch. 6; D. Noble, *The Paradox of Progressive Thought* (New York, 1958).

155. Small, "Civic Federation of Chicago," 97.

156. F. MacVeagh, "A Programme of Municipal Reform," *American Journal of Sociology* 1 (March 1896): 552–54; idem, "The Business Man in Municipal Politics," *Proceedings of the Louisville Conference For Good City Government and of the Third Annual Meeting of the National Municipal League, May 1897* (Philadelphia, 1897), 136.

157. Roberts, "Municipal Voters League," 122–27; Taylor, *Pioneering,* 55–56; Wendt and Kogan, *Bosses in Lusty Chicago,* 118–20; E. F. Dunne, "The Story of the Street Car Companies in Chicago," in *Dunne: Judge, Mayor, Governor. The Papers of Edward F. Dunne,* ed. W. L. Sullivan (Chicago, 1916). The speakers at the March 3 meeting included Lyman Gage, Henry Demarest Lloyd, Marshall Field, and William Rainey Harper (president of the University of Chicago).

158. Browne, *Altgeld of Illinois,* 231–42; Wish, "Altgeld and the Progressive Tradition," 824–25; Altgeld, "Veto of the Monopoly Bills," in *Live Questions,* 940–43 (cited by Wish, loc. cit.); Wendt and Kogan, *Bosses in Lusty Chicago,* 125–30, 149; *Chicago Tribune,* May 15, 1895; Wish, "Altgeld and the Progressive Tradition," 825–26.

159. Roberts, "The Municipal Voters League," 127–37; Wendt and Kogan, *Bosses in Lusty Chicago,* 125–30, 136–49; C. Harrison, *Stormy Years* (Indianapolis, 1938), 112–13; Municipal Voters League, "Objects of the Municipal Voters League," *Minute Book* (April 13, 1896). See H. King, "The Reform Movement in Chicago," in *The Annals of the American Academy of Political and Social Science* (1905): 235–45; E. B. Smith, "The Municipal Voters League of Chicago," *Atlantic Monthly* 125 (June 1900): 834–39; L. Steffens, *The Shame of the Cities,* 162–94; E. B. Smith, "Council Reform in Chicago," *Municipal Affairs* (June 1900), 347–50; J. Frank Aldrich, "Eighteen Hundred and Ninety Six," *Union League Club Bulletin* (October 1926): 13–14.

160. *Chicago Tribune,* February 19, March 9, 11, 12, 13, 17, 18, 21, 24, 28, April 13, 14, 15, 16, 18, 20, 29, 30, May 13, 19, 20, 21, 23, 24, 25, 26, 27, June 6, 1897; ibid., December 6, 7, 8, 9, 10, 11, 12, 13, 1898; Roberts, "Charles T. Yerkes," 354–55; S. W. Norton, *Chicago Tradition: A History, Legislative and Political* (Chicago, 1907), 81; W. T. Hutchinson, *Lowden of Illinois* (Chicago, 1957), 87; The Chicago Committee of One Hundred, *The Street Railway Bills*

(Chicago, 1897); Norton, 87–90; Harrison, *Stormy Years*, chs. 10, 12, esp. 156–59, 170–73; Chicago, *Council Proceedings, 1898–1899*, 1,059–61; Wendt and Kogan, *Bosses in Lusty Chicago*, 184–99; C. H. Lawson, *Victor Lawson: His Time and Work* (Chicago, 1935), 285.

161. Roberts, "The Municipal Voters League," 139–48; M. P. McCarthy, "Businessmen and Professionals in Municipal Reform: The Chicago Experience, 1887–1920" (Ph.D. dissertation, Northwestern University, 1971), 23–24.

162. Steffens, *The Shame of the Cities*, 162.

163. Ibid., 171, 177; idem, *The Autobiography of Lincoln Steffens* (New York, 1931), 426. See also, F. C. Home, "The Municipal Character of Achievements of Chicago," *Worlds Work* 5 (March 1903): 32–43; Municipal Voters League, "Objects of the Municipal Voters League," *Minute Book* (April 13, 1896); King, "The Reform Movement in Chicago," 235–45; Smith, "The Municipal Voters League of Chicago," 834–39; Steffens, *The Shame of the Cities*, 162–94; Smith, "Council Reform in Chicago," 347–50; Aldrich, "Eighteen Hundred and Ninety-Six," 13–14.

164. *Chicago Tribune*, March 21, April 12, 1895; Altgeld, "The Civil Service Law," in *Live Questions*, 725–26; *Laws of the State of Illinois, 1895* (Springfield, 1895), 585–94; Small, "Civic Federation," 82, 85; J. B. Kingsbury, "The Merit System in Chicago from 1895 to 1915: The Adoption of the Civil Service Law," *Public Personnel Studies* (November 1925): 308–9. See also, Bogart and Mathews, *The Modern Commonwealth, 1893–1918*, ch. 13. Other business organizations were also active in the passage of the act: The Commercial Club, Oakland Club, Republican Central Committee, Ashland Club, Civil Service Reform League, Chicago Club, Jefferson Club, Iroquois Club, Real Estate Board, Board of Trade, Union League Club, Hamilton Club, Chicago Athletic Club, Bankers Club, Citizens Association, Illinois Club, Marquette Club, and the Columbus Club. The Democratic party strongly opposed the bill.

165. J. B. Kingsbury, "The Merit System in Chicago From 1895 to 1915: The Administration of the Civil Service Law under Various Mayors," *Public Personnel Studies* 4 (May 1928): 154–56; Bogart and Mathews, *The Modern Commonwealth 1893–1918*, 272, 274–76; W. Kent to L. Steffens, June 9, 1904, cited in M. J. Schiesl, *The Politics of Efficiency: Municipal Administration and Reform in America* (Berkeley, 1977), 72.

166. J. H. Gray, "New Charter for Chicago," *The Northwestern* 15 (February 28, 1895): 3; Civic Federation of Chicago, "Report on Reform Legislation," *Civic Federation Papers*, no. 16, 6; J. Gray, "Home Rule for Chicago," *The Voter: A Monthly Magazine of Politics* (1905): 32–33, 39; Diner, *A City and Its Universities*, 156–58.

167. *Chicago Tribune*, October 29, 1902; November 8, 1904; C. Merriam, "The Chicago Charter Convention," *American Political Science Review* 11 (November 1907): 1–14; McCarthy, "Businessmen and Professionals," 51–54.

168. Chicago Charter Convention, *Proceedings*, November 30, 1906–February 18, 1907; Merriam, "The Chicago Charter Convention"; idem, *Report on an Investigation of the Municipal Revenues of Chicago* (Chicago, 1906), esp. v–vi, 71–76, 141–42; idem, "Home Rule in Chicago's New Charter," *The Voter: A Monthly Magazine of Politics* (1907): 30–31; idem, "Home Rule Features of the New City Charter," *City Club Bulletin* (June 1907): 148–52; "Chicago's New Charter," *Outlook* 86 (June 8, 1907): 269–70; H. Ickes, "Political Features of the

Proposed City Charter," *City Club Bulletin* (July 10, 1907): 167–72; McCarthy, "Businessmen and Professionals," 56–67. The City Club, to which Merriam belonged (along with G. H. Mead), had been formed in 1903 as an offshoot of the MVL to promote public welfare. See H. E. Fleming, "Twenty Years of Service: High Points in the History of the City Club of Chicago," *City Club Bulletin* 16 (December 17, 1923): 415–25; idem, "City Club of Chicago and its Committee Plan," *Charities and the Commons* 17 (November 3, 1906): 217; McCarthy, 41–43. On the Merchants Club's educational proposals, see the *Chicago Tribune*, December 21, 22, 1906, and ch. 5, below.

169. The details of the defeat of the charter referendum are described in McCarthy, "Businessmen and Professionals," 67–81.

170. C. E. Merriam, "The Charter Situation: What Next," *City Club Bulletin* 1 (October 23, 1907): 212–15; idem, "Investigations As a Means of Securing Administrative Efficiency," *Annals of the American Academy of Political Science* 41 (May 1912): 281–313; R. Robbins, "The Charter Situation: What Next," *City Club Bulletin* 1 (October 23, 1907): 217–20.

171. Chicago Harbor Commission, *Report to the Mayor and Aldermen of the City of Chicago by the Chicago Harbor Commission* (Chicago, 1909), 3; Merriam to J. P. Goode, March 2 and 16, 1908, Merriam Papers, box 12, folder 18, University of Chicago Library (cited in Diner, *A City and Its Universities*, 164).

172. C. E. Merriam, "The 1910 Budget," *City Club Bulletin* 3 (December 15, 1909): 80–81, 83–84; idem, "The Work and Accomplishments of the Chicago Commission on City Expenditures," *City Club Bulletin* 4 (August 16, 1911): 198–204; idem, "Investigations As a Means of Securing Administrative Efficiency," 282, 284–88, 289–95, 298; idem, "The Work of the Chicago Bureau of Public Efficiency," *Philadelphia City Club Bulletin* 3 (November 2, 1910): 64. See also, Merriam, *Chicago*, ch. 5; *Final Report of Municipal Efficiency Commission, City of Chicago, March 8, 1911*, 14–19; B. Karl, *Charles Merriam and the Study of Politics* (Chicago, 1974), 1–68; Schiesl, *The Politics of Efficiency*, 106–7; Diner, *A City and Its Universities*, 168–70.

173. Merriam, "The Work of the Chicago Bureau of Public Efficiency," 66–68; idem, "The Chicago Bureau of Public Efficiency," *City Club Bulletin* 3 (June 8, 1910): 325; G. A. Weber, *Organized Efforts for the Improvement of Methods of Administration in the United States* (1919), 227; Merriam, *Chicago*; Schiesl, *The Politics of Efficiency*, 123–24.

174. H. Ickes, *Autobiography of a Curmudgeon* (New York, 1943), 115–44; McCarthy, "Businessmen and Professionals," 151–67; Diner, *A City and Its Universities*, 170; Karl, *Merriam*, 68–72; *Chicago Daily News*, April 3, 1911.

175. *Chicago Tribune*, April 26, 1896; McCarthy, "Businessmen and Professionals," 36–37.

176. Steffens, *Autobiography*, 426.

177. Andrews, *Battle for Chicago*, 176.

178. W. K. Ackerman, *Report of Investigation into the Affairs of the Street Railways of Chicago, Made to the Civic Federation* (Chicago, 1898); Civic Federation of Chicago, *The Street Railways of Chicago* (Chicago, 1901). In the late 1890s, Morgan, Altgeld, and Lloyd led an unsuccessful municipal ownership campaign in Chicago; in 1902–03, Lloyd, Edward Dunne, Jane Addams, Margaret Haley of the Chicago Teachers Federation, the Referendum League, and several other civic organizations, mounted yet another campaign, but it too failed, as did a third

attempt between 1905 and 1907. For details, see Destler, *Henry Demarest Lloyd*, 515–24; C. Lloyd, *Henry Demarest Lloyd*, vol. 2, ch. 26; Sullivan, ed., *Dunne: Judge, Mayor, Governor*, 133–38, 257–59.

179. Civic Federation of Chicago, *Chicago Conference on Trusts* (Chicago, 1900). Ralph Easley organized the convention. The success of the convention prompted Easley to go national; the next year he organized the National Civic Federation. See Weinstein, *The Corporate Ideal in the Liberal State*, 7–38; Ginger, *Altgeld's America*, 252–53.

180. Sutherland, *Fifty Years on the Civic Front*, 18–19; Civic Federation of Chicago, *Tax Inequities in Illinois* (Chicago, 1910). The federation did not propose increasing the city's taxing and bonding abilities until after the threat of municipal ownership had receded.

181. "Ways and Means Session: Association's Largest Committee Hears Discussion Enlightening on Functions and Merits of Charter," *Chicago Association of Commerce Bulletin* 3 (August 23, 1907): 1.

182. Commenting on the prominence of bankers in political progressivism (J. P. Morgan in the National Civic Federation, Lyman Gage in the Chicago Civic Federation), Ray Ginger notes, "Bankers such as Morgan and Gage sometimes sought class conciliation because of their values as individuals, or because bankers more often than industrialists had been born into the cultured upper class and had been taught a type of aristocratic responsibility. But bankers had good business reasons for moderation. Income came to them, not as a maximum rate of profit in the short run, but as a fixed rate of interest over long periods of time. The major consideration for them was stability, routine, an ordered and predictable society in which the safety of investments was unthreatened" (*Altgeld's America*, 280).

183. Steffens, *Shame of the Cities*, 188–89; idem, *Autobiography*, 429.

184. W. R. Werner, *Julius Rosenwald: The Life and Times of a Practical Humanitarian* (New York, 1939), 42. Michael McCarthy argues that, at least in part, Merriam's defeat in 1911 was the result of changes in the social demography of Chicago. The annexation law of 1889 added a great many new voters—most of them middle class—to the Chicago electoral region. The annexed areas, which throughout the 1890s attracted middle-class voters, were the heart of the MVL's hardcore supporters. After 1900, and particularly 1910, the annexed areas attracted mainly ethnic working-class and lower-middle-class families who were less likely to vote for reform candidates. In addition, the rapid growth of the black population provided another electoral base for William Thompson's Republican machine during the 1920s. But demographic changes alone are insufficient to account for the failure of the reform movement to destroy machine politics in Chicago. Three other causes were also significant. First, machine politicians repeatedly outmaneuvered the reformers in electioneering and coalition formation, a factor of some significance in Harrison's defeat of Merriam in 1911. Second, municipal reformers paid the price of the Progressive's inability to enact a system of social insurance and public works. The failure of such reforms left intact the economic base of machine politics—jobs, welfare, coal in winter, turkeys at Christmas—upon which the immigrant and native-born working class depended for economic survival. And finally, businessmen deserted political progressivism, at least as early as 1903, if Steffens is correct. See McCarthy, "Businessmen and Professionals in Municipal Reform," 139–44, 162–67.

185. Merriam, *Chicago*, 21–22.

186. Gosnell, *Machine Politics*, 11.

187. Ibid., 5, 8. See also, D. Richberg, "Gold Plated Anarchy: An Interpretation of the Fall of the Giants," *Nation* (April 5, 1933): 361–69; Andrews, *Battle for Chicago*, ch. 7; F. McDonald, *Insull* (Chicago, 1962).

188. Gosnell, *Machine Politics*, 13, 16, 24–25; *Fortune* 14 (August 1936): 114.

189. Merriam, *Chicago*, 108–9.

190. Kolko, *The Triumph of Conservatism*, 3.

191. Gosnell, *Machine Politics*, 183.

192. Marx was not alone in looking upon the bourgeoisie as a revolutionary class intent upon the "constant revolutionizing of production, uninterrupted disturbance of all social relations, everlasting uncertainty and agitation," and because of which "all that is solid melts into air, all that is holy is profaned" (see note 1). Henry Demarest Lloyd also thought so—as did Debs, Morgan, and to some extent, Altgeld. In an address at the Central Music Hall in October 1894 (almost a year after the meeting that created the Civic Federation), Lloyd declared, "The Revolution has come. . . . It is a revolution which has given the best parts of the streets that belong to all the people to street-railway syndicates, and gas companies, and telephone companies, and power companies. It is a revolution which has created national-bank millionaires, and bond millionaires, and tariff millionaires, and land-grant millionaires. . . . It is a revolution by which great combinations, using competition to destroy competition, have monopolized entire markets, and as the sole sellers of goods make the people buy dear, and as the sole purchasers of labor make the people sell themselves cheap. . . ." Lloyd went on to announce, mistakenly as it turned out, "a counter-revolution of the people" (H. D. Lloyd, "The Revolution is Here," in Destler, *American Radicalism*, 216–17).

193. Small, "The Civic Federation of Chicago," 92.

194. Davis, *Spearheads*, 33–36.

195. J. Miller, "The Politics of Municipal Reform in Chicago During the Progressive Era: The Municipal Voters League as a Test Case, 1896–1920" (M.A. thesis, Roosevelt University, 1966), 23–25; Tarr, *Boss Politics*, 68–69.

196. E. Anderson, "Prostitution and Social Justice: Chicago, 1910–1915," *Social Science Review* 48 (1974): 209–10.

197. Ibid., 216–18.

198. R. J. Buroker, "From Voluntary Association to Welfare State: The Illinois Immigrant Protective League, 1908–1926," *Journal of American History* 58, 3 (December 1971): 648–49.

199. S. D. London, "Business and the Chicago Public School System, 1890–1966" (Ph.D. dissertation, University of Chicago, 1968), 52.

200. Kusmer, "The Functions of Organized Charity," 673.

201. Diner, *A City and Its Universities*, 195.

202. Ibid., 196.

203. Ibid., 70.

204. R. Hofstadter, *The Age of Reform: From Bryan to F.D.R.*, (New York, 1955), ch. 4.

205. Wiebe, *The Search for Order*, ch. 5.

206. S. Hays, "The Politics of Reform in Municipal Government in the Progressive Era" in *Progressivism: The Critical Issues*, ed. D. Kennedy (Boston, 1971), 91–95.

207. Wiebe, *The Search for Order,* 166, 129.
208. Small, "The Civic Federation of Chicago," 93.
209. Late nineteenth-century versions of "corruption" and "conspiracy" thus differed in important respects from those of the eighteenth century. In the eighteenth century, commonwealthmen feared corruption of the people by luxury and commerce and of the legislature by the court or the executive; late nineteenth-century republican liberals feared corruption of the legislature and the executive by commerce ("boodlerism"), corruption of the people not by luxury but by economic deprivation and demoralization and corruption of social order by class conflict.

CHAPTER TWO: *The Ironies of Progressive Child-Saving*

1. On the common school reform movement, see R. Church, *Education in the United States* (New York, 1976), chs. 3, 4; D. Tyack, *The One Best System* (Cambridge, 1974), pt. 2; S. Schultz, *The Culture Factory* (New York, 1973); K. Kaestle, *The Evolution of an Urban School System* (Cambridge, 1973); idem, *The Evolution of an Urban School System* (Cambridge, 1973), chs. 4, 5, 6; K. Kaestle and M. Vinovskis, *Education and Social Change in Nineteenth Century Massachusetts* (New York, 1980); M. Katz, *The Irony of Early School Reform* (Boston, 1968).
2. H. Mann, "The Twelfth Annual Report of the Board of Education," in *The Republic and the School,* ed. L. Cremin (New York, 1957), 87.
3. On the history of child-saving in the nineteenth century, see J. M. Hawes, *Children in Urban Society* (New York, 1971); R. Mennel, *Thorns and Thistles* (Hanover, 1973); Katz, *Irony of Early School Reform;* S. Schlossman, *Love and the American Delinquent* (Chicago, 1977); A. M. Platt, *The Child Savers: The Invention of Delinquency,* 2d ed. (Chicago, 1977); P. Coveney, *The Image of Children* (Harmondsworth, Middlesex, 1967); B. Wishey, *The Child and the Republic* (Philadelphia, 1972); D. Rothman, *The Discovery of the Asylum* (New York, 1971).
4. "If humanitarian progressivism had a central theme," wrote Robert Wiebe in *The Search for Order,* "it was the child. He united the campaigns for health, education, and a richer city environment, and he dominated much of the interest in labor legislation. . . . The child was the carrier of tomorrow's hope whose innocence and freedom made him singularly receptive to education in rational, humane behavior. Protect him, nurture him, and in his manhood he would create that bright new world of the progressives' vision" ([New York, 1967], 169).
5. J. Addams, *Twenty Years at Hull House* (New York, 1960), 100.
6. Ibid., 148.
7. Ibid., 148–50.
8. D. R. Blumberg, *Florence Kelley: The Making of a Social Pioneer* (New York, 1966), 121–26; J. Goldmark, *Impatient Crusader* (Urbana, 1953), 22–23; F. Kelley, "Our Toiling Children," *Our Day* 6 (1980): 33–192.
9. Residents of Hull House, *Hull House Maps and Papers* (New York, 1895), 43, 45; Blumberg, *Florence Kelley,* 127–28; Goldmark, *Impatient Crusader,* 33–34. The quote is from a letter of Kelley to Friedrich Engels, cited in Blumberg, 128.
10. F. Kelley, "I Go to Work," *The Survey,* June 1, 1927, 273.

11. Ibid.; Addams, *Twenty Years,* 150.

12. E. Abbott and S. Breckinridge, *Truancy and Non-attendance in the Chicago Schools* (New York, 1970), 50, 440–41; E. R. Beckner, *A History of Labor Legislation in Illinois* (Chicago, 1929), 150–53; F. Kelley and A. Stevens, "Wage Earning Children," in *Hull House Maps and Papers.*

13. Blumberg, *Florence Kelley,* 134–35; Goldmark, *Impatient Crusader,* 34–35; Addams, *Twenty Years,* 150–51. In 1895 the Illinois Supreme Court ruled the eight-hour employment of women provision unconstitutional.

14. Factory Inspectors of Illinois, *First Annual Report, 1893,* 90, 122; *Second Annual Report, 1894,* 13, 14, 17, 19, 20; *Third Annual Report, 1895,* 40, 41, 46.

15. Factory Inspectors of Illinois, *Fourth Annual Report, 1896,* 21; Beckner, *A History of Labor Legislation in Illinois,* 159; Abbott and Breckinridge, *Truancy and Non-attendance,* 81–84; F. Kelley, "The Illinois Child Labor Law," *American Journal of Sociology* 3, 4 (1898): 494.

16. Factory Inspectors of Illinois, *Fifteenth Annual Report, 1907,* 15, 16; Beckner, *A History of Labor Legislation in Illinois,* 161; Addams, *Twenty Years,* 153.

17. F. Kelley, "Has Illinois the Best Laws in the Country for the Protection of Children?" *American Journal of Sociology* 10, 3 (1904): 299–314. In subsequent years, a number of unsuccessful attempts were made both to weaken and to strengthen the law. Finally, in 1917 the state passed a new act that altered the certification system along lines required by the federal Child Labor Act of 1916, and in 1921 the employment of children under sixteen was prohibited in any employment found by the Department of Labor to be dangerous to life, limb, health, or morals, and completion of six years of schooling was required instead of only five as previously. Beckner, *A History of Labor Legislation in Illinois,* 169–77. Jane Addams also thought that child labor legislation would eventually add to "industrial efficiency" by ensuring a better educated workforce. Jane Addams, "Child Labor Legislation—A Requisite for Industrial Efficiency," *Annals of the American Academy of Political and Social Sciences* 25 (May 1905): 123–25.

18. Indeed, between 1897, when the new Republican governor replaced Kelley, and 1901, the child labor laws were not enforced at all. Kelley's successor, Louis Arrington, had been associated for twenty-seven years with the Illinois Bottle Company of Alton, Illinois, one of the companies subjected to scathing criticism by Kelley in a special report on the glass industry in 1895.

19. Chicago Board of Education, *Proceedings,* August 21, 1889, to July 9, 1890, 105.

20. Chief State Factory Inspector, *22nd Annual Report, 1915,* 30–36.

21. Illinois Factory Inspector, *Annual Report, 1896,* 30.

22. See the annual reports of the Illinois Factory Inspector for 1893–1900 and 1902–06.

23. Illinois Factory Inspector, *Annual Report, 1908,* 830–31.

24. Ibid.; J. Kett, *Rites of Passage: Adolescence in America, 1790 to the Present* (New York, 1977), ch. 6.

25. Kelley and Stevens, "Wage Earning Children," 75; Factory Inspectors of Illinois, *Second Annual Report, 1894,* 14. See also, the *Third Annual Report, 1895,* 15.

26. Chicago Board of Education, *37th Annual Report, 1891,* 152–53; *38th Annual Report, 1892,* 61; *41st Annual Report, 1895,* 48; *43rd Annual Report, 1897,* 53.

27. Chicago Board of Education, *34th Annual Report, 1888,* 38–39; idem, *Proceedings, 1889–1890,* 106.

28. Abbott and Breckinridge, *Truancy and Non-attendance,* 57–58; H. B. Chamberlain, "The Chicago School System," *Chicago Record Herald,* February 7, 1906.

29. On the basis of an analysis of voting patterns in Illinois, Richard Jensen argues that the defeat of Edwards in 1890, the Democratic victories in 1892, and the repeal of the Edwards Law in 1893 demonstrate the salience of "ethnocultural" politics over "class" politics in "the winning of the midwest." Five criticisms might be leveled at his argument. First, Jensen employs a straightforward categorical conception of class (and ethnicity) derived from stratification theory, rather than an approach that uses either a Marxist categorical definition of class, or preferably, an approach based on processes of class formation. Second, Jensen's own data does not establish any clear-cut political division between the liturgicals and the pietists with respect to voting behavior: His analysis of four midwestern counties ignores the very high percentage of the population (as high as 50 percent in Geneseo County) listed as "no-denomination" (see Tables 2, 3, 25). Third, since he infers individual behavior from aggregate group behavior, he runs the risk of committing the ecological fallacy. Moreover, the high correlation of religious identification with voting at a group level does not establish a causal relationship between the two at an individual level. That kind of argument requires multivariate analyses rather than zero-order correlational analyses. Fourth, Jensen fails to adequately control for the relationship between religion and ethnicity, and both with occupation, as James Wright argues. Finally, Jensen's analysis of the substantive issues involved in the conflict over the Edwards Law greatly exaggerates the differences between pietists and liturgicals on the three relevant issues involved: the English language requirement, regulation of the private schools by local public school boards, and the principle of compulsory education. Neither pietists nor liturgicals disagreed with the principle of compulsory education, and both pietists and liturgicals believed that an amicable compromise could be found on the English language requirement and the private school controversy. For further discussion, see G. Wright, "The Ethnocultural Model of Voting," *American Behavioral Scientist* 16, 5 (1973): esp. 662–63; W. D. Burnham, "Quantitative History: Beyond the Correlation Coefficient," *Historical Methods Newsletter,* March 1971, 65; P. Kleppner, "Beyond the New Political History: A Review Essay," *Historical Methods Newsletter* 6, 1 (1972): 17–26; D. Hogan, "Historians and the Edwards Law in Illinois," unpublished essay. Jensen develops his analysis in chs. 3 and 5 of *The Winning of the Midwest* (Chicago, 1971).

30. *Chicago Tribune,* June 14, 1895; May 5, 1899.

31. Chicago Board of Education, *44th Annual Report, 1898,* 170.

32. Chicago Board of Education, *54th Annual Report, 1908,* 17; *60th Annual Report, 1914,* 405.

33. Chicago Board of Education, *36th Annual Report, 1890,* 126.

34. Abbott and Breckinridge, *Truancy and Non-attendance,* 94, 147, 145. The annual reports of the board of education regularly contained an analysis of the causes of truancy and nonattendance in terms of "poor homes" or "bad family life." The 1911 report of William Bodine, superintendent of compulsory education, claimed, for example, that while "a good boy may come from a bad home and a bad boy may come from a good home, the fact remains that the environment of the insanitary and improvident home is now, and always has been, the dominant

breeder of the backward, truant, delinquent or subnormal child." Yet in the very same paragraph, Bodine reported that of the 4,230 cases of truancy, nearly a quarter came from "good homes," almost a half from "fair homes," and only a third from "poor homes" (Chicago Board of Education, *57th Annual Report, 1911*, 136). It should be noted, moreover, that during the 1890s, school officials and reformers supported the creation of special "parental" schools for incorrigible truants and delinquent children. In 1890 Superintendent Howland outlined the need for such schools. "One of the greatest needs of the city," he wrote, "made almost imperative by the compulsory law, is a *family school* in each of the several sections of the city, with facilities for some simple work, as well as study, under the charge of well-prepared teachers, in which the little waifs of the community, now growing up in want and wickedness, may be tenderly cared for, and trained to habits of industry, intelligence and honorable citizenship." Construction of a family school eventually commenced in June 1900 through the "generosity" of an unknown donor who gave a substantial amount of money, followed by other "public spirited anonymous citizens." In January 1901 the board of education approved funds, and on January 31, 1902, the school finally opened. Chicago Board of Education, *36th Annual Report, 1890*, 39–40; *Chicago Record*, October 22, 1898, 5; T. H. MacQuery, "Schools for Dependent, Delinquent and Truant Children in Illinois," *The American Journal of Sociology* 9, 1 (1903): 16; "The Parental School Law," in the *Report on Parental Schools*, Chicago, January 10, 1900, 11; *Chicago Record*, December 22, 1899, 4; *Chicago Tribune*, December 17, 1899; ibid., June 11, 1900; *Chicago Record Herald*, April 4, 1906, 8; Chicago Board of Education, *38th Annual Report, 1892*, 61, 64; *39th Annual Report, 1893*, 66–67; *40th Annual Report, 1894*, 39; *41st Annual Report, 1895*, 48–49; *43rd Annual Report, 1897*, 53, 57; *44th Annual Report, 1898*, 169–70; *Report of the Educational Commission of the City of Chicago*, W. Harper, chairman (Chicago, 1899), 160–63, app. G.

35. Citizens Association of Chicago, *Report of the Committee on Education*, (Chicago, 1881), 8, 14, 15; *Chicago Tribune*, March 7, 1882; February 8, 1883; August 1, 1885; May 19, 1886; May 23, 1886; November 23, 1886; November 25, 1888; July 4, 1887; July 11, 1887; March 31, 1889; January 7, 1890; Chicago Board of Education, *42nd Annual Report, 1896*, 18; *Chicago Commerce*, March 20, 1920, 36, 12.

36. Chicago Board of Education, *23rd Annual Report, 1877*, 46–47; *38th Annual Report, 1892*, 62; *40th Annual Report, 1894*, 60; *42nd Annual Report, 1896*, 16; *43rd Annual Report, 1897*, 20, 21.

37. Cited in Hawes, *Children in Urban Society*, 162–63.

38. C. Kelsey, "The Juvenile Court of Chicago and Its Work," *Annals of the American Academy* 17 (1901): 119, 299.

39. Board of State Commissioners of Public Charities for the State of Illinois (BRPC), *Eleventh Biennial Report*, 194. A reform school established in 1855 had been destroyed by the Great Fire in 1871. A reform school at Pontiac for boys between eight and eighteen (created in 1867 for "the discipline education, employment and reformation of juvenile offenders and vagrants") began after 1872 to admit boys under eighteen convicted of robbery, burglary, or arson. Boys convicted of lesser offenses were committed to the already overcrowded county jail for adult offenders. A court case in 1870 (the O'Connell decision) placed fundamental limits on the power of the courts to commit minors to reformatories

without due process. In 1879 the state had authorized the establishment of privately organized industrial schools for dependent and delinquent children; eight years later, four such schools existed in Chicago. A Supreme Court decision in 1888, however, prohibited charitable organizations who placed children in these schools from doing so unless they directly conducted an industrial school themselves. Care for dependent and neglected children was almost nonexistent.

The history of the care of delinquent, dependent, and neglected children in Illinois from the early nineteenth century through to the act of 1899 are surveyed in Platt, *The Child Savers*, 101–32; Hawes, *Children in Urban Society*, 161–64; Mennel, *Thorns and Thistles*, 124–30; H. R. Jeter, "The Chicago Juvenile Court," U.S. Children's Bureau, *Publication No. 104* (Washington, D.C., 1922), 1–5; T. D. Hurley, *Origin of the Illinois Juvenile Court Law* (New York, 1977), 9–26; J. C. Lathrop, "The Background of the Juvenile Court in Illinois," in *The Child, the Clinic, and the Court*, ed. J. Addams (New York, 1925), 290–97; Schlossman, *Love and the American Delinquent*, ch. 4.

40. Hurley, *Origin of the Illinois Juvenile Court Law*, 139–40.

41. Platt, *The Child Savers*, 126–29; Mennel, *Thorns and Thistles*, 129. The school was established under board of education auspices. A high percentage of the inmates in the city jail were truants; in one estimate, in 1898 the John Worthy School processed an average of thirteen hundred boys a year, of which over a quarter were truants. Platt, 129.

42. Cited in Platt, *The Child Savers*, 129.

43. Illinois Board of State Commissioners of Public Charities, *Fifteenth Biennial Report* (1898), 63, 366. See also Lathrop, "The Background of the Juvenile Court in Illinois," 290.

44. The act is reprinted in G. Abbott, *The Child and the State* (Chicago, 1938), II: 392–401. See also, Platt, *The Child Savers*, 130–34. Platt comments that the act was a consequence of the "efforts of a group of feminist reformers," "career women and society philanthropists, women's clubs and settlement houses, and political and apolitical groups," and particularly of the untiring efforts of Louise De Koven Bowen, Jane Addams, Julia Lathrop, Lucy Flower, and Mrs. Perry Smith (75, 77, 79, 83–89). While true, this ignores the very substantial role played by male judges, the men of the all male Chicago Association and the Chicago Visitation and Aid Society. Platt also (77–78, xxiii, xxiv) links the class membership of the juvenile reform movement to a policy of "social control."

45. For Grace Abbott, the act represented a profound break with the past because the child was no longer to be regarded "as a criminal, but as a delinquent." Homer Folks, then secretary of the state Charities Aid Association of New York, suggested that "although some of its beginnings were had in some of the eastern states, its great progress and development, its distinctive character, its propaganda, all took their origin in the city of Chicago. And I think it is from this city that we have drawn some of the best ideas of what the Juvenile Court should be and what it should do. . . . The central idea . . . is that the Juvenile Court is the community pondering upon the problem of the exceptional child." Both Abbott and Folks are cited in Mennel, *Thorns and Thistles*, 133, 134. Within five years of passage of the act, ten states had implemented similar procedures, and by 1920 every state except three provided for a juvenile court. See D. Rothman, *Conscience and Convenience* (New York, 1980), 215.

46. The act construed dependency and neglect in very general terms to

mean "any child who for any reason is destitute or homeless or abandoned; or dependent on the public for support; or has not proper parental care or guardianship; or who habitually begs or receives alms; or who is found living in any house of ill fame or with any vicious or disreputable person; or whose home, by reason of neglect, cruelty or depravity on the part of its parents, guardian or other person in whose care it may be, is an unfit place for such a child; and any child under the age of eight years who is found peddling or selling any article or singing or playing any musical instrument upon the street or giving any public entertainment." Cited in Abbott, *The Child and the State*, 393.

The point of making no provision in the act for the expenditure of public monies on the salaries of probation officers was, of course, to make the court rely upon volunteers. The first volunteer to be appointed by Judge Tuthill was Alzina Stevens, a resident of Hull House. Lucy Flower of the Chicago Women's Club convinced some of her friends to pay Mrs. Stevens's salary. One probation officer, however, was not enough. Within a year of the opening of the court, the juvenile court committee of the Chicago Women's Club was paying the salaries of six probation officers. In 1904 the various private organizations interested in the support of probation officers incorporated as the Juvenile Court Committee, by which time the number of probation officers had increased to fifteen. In addition, some twenty police officers were assigned to probation work, and representatives of various social agencies (most importantly, the Illinois Children's Home and Aid Society, the Visitation and Aid Society, and the Bureau of Personal Service) were commissioned as probation officers. In 1905 an amendment to the 1899 act permitted the Board of County Commissioners to pay the salaries of probation officers. By 1911, the number of officers paid by the county had reached thirty-seven. For further discussion, see Howes, *Children in Urban Society*, 173, 178–79; Mennel, *Thorns and Thistles*, 140–41; Jeter, "The Chicago Juvenile Court," 6–8.

47. Cited in Rothman, *Conscience and Convenience*, 212. See also Hawes, *Children in Urban Society*, 171–72.

48. V. Arnold, "What Constitutes Sufficient Grounds for the Removal of a Child from His Home," *Proceedings of the Child Conference for Research and Welfare* (New York, 1910), 345; cited by Rothman, *Conscience and Convenience*, 221.

49. An Illinois superior court put the matter this way: "It is the unquestioned right and imperative duty of every enlightened government in its character of parens patriae to protect and provide for the well-being of such of its citizens as by reason of infancy, defective understanding. . . . The performance of this duty is justly regarded as one of the most important of governmental functions and all constitutional limitations must be so understood and construed as not to interfere with its proper and legitimate exercise" (H. Hurd, "Juvenile Court Law," *Charities* 13 [1905]: 327). The doctrine of parens patriae, however, was not without its critics. See, for example, E. Lindsay, "The Juvenile Court Movement from a Lawyer's Standpoint," *Annals of the American Academy of Social and Political Science* 52 (1914): 140–48; Hawes, *Children in Urban Society*, 125; Platt, *The Child Savers*, 103ff.; Mennel, *Thorns and Thistles*, 156ff.; Schlossman, "End of Innocence," 213.

50. Abbott, *The Child and the State*, 134.

51. *Juvenile Court Record*, December 1900, 4.

52. Ibid., 5.

53. Kelsey, "The Juvenile Court of Chicago and Its Work," 118–19; Platt, *The Child Savers*, chs. 2, 3; and Mennel, *Thorns and Thistles*, ch. 3, survey environmentalist theories of delinquency in the late nineteenth century.

54. J. Addams, *The Spirit of Youth and the City Streets* (Urbana, 1972), 31.

55. E. Abbott and S. Breckinridge, *The Delinquent Child and the Home* (New York, 1970), ch. 11.

56. Kelsey, "The Juvenile Court of Chicago and Its Work," 118–19; *Juvenile Court Record*, June 1902, 5. See also, J. Mack, "The Chancery Procedure in the Juvenile Court," in *The Child, the Clinic, and the Court*, ed. Addams, 315.

57. H. Thurston, "Ten Years of the Juvenile Court of Chicago," *The Survey*, February 5, 1910, 656–57. See also Kelsey, "The Juvenile Court of Chicago and Its Work," 122–23; Jeter, "The Chicago Juvenile Court," 35–42; Hawes, *Children in Urban Society*, 158–59; Platt, *The Child Savers*, 141–44; and Mennel, *Thorns and Thistles*, 135.

58. R. Tuthill, "Address," National Prison Association, Annual Congress, *Proceedings* (1902): 121.

59. J. Mack, "Legal Problems Involved in the Establishment of the Juvenile Court," in *The Delinquent Child and the Home*, ed. Abbott and Breckinridge, 198. After 1909, for eight or so years the juvenile court utilized the psychiatric services of Dr. William Healy at the Psychopathic Institute founded by women associated with the Juvenile Protective League. For details, see Hawes, *Children in an Urban Society*, 246–59; Mennel, *Thorns and Thistles*, 160–71, 195–97; S. Schlossman, "End of Innocence: Science and the Transformation of Progressive Juvenile Justice, 1899–1917," *History of Education* 7, 3 (October 1978), 216.

60. Abbott and Breckinridge, *The Delinquent Child and the Home*, 40. Of the remainder, the court dismissed or "continued indefinitely" 16.9 percent of the cases for boys and handed .8 percent over to the grand jury. (For girls, the respective figures are 10 percent and .1 percent.)

61. Illinois Association for Criminal Justice, *The Illinois Crime Survey* (Chicago, 1929), 685. For boys, a further 23.3 percent were held over, 8.6 percent dismissed, and 5.2 percent placed in the care of guardians. (For girls, the respective figures are 3.3 percent, 12.7 percent and 9.8 percent.)

62. Ibid., 685–86.

63. Platt, *The Child Savers*, 139, 135, 77–78. See also C. Lasch, *Haven in a Heartless World* (New York, 1977).

64. See Schlossman, *Love and the American Delinquent*, chs. 1, 2, 3, 4; Rothman, *Conscience and Convenience*, chs. 6, 7, 8; Rothman, *The Discovery of the Asylum*; Mennel, *Thorns and Thistles*, chs. 1, 2.

65. Paul Boyer's neglect of the creation of juvenile courts and child-saving generally is all the more notable given the focus of the act of 1899, the procedures of the court, and the pedagogy of probation upon individual moral uplift; P. Boyer, *Urban Masses and Moral Order in America* (Cambridge, Mass., 1978). It should also be mentioned that it is highly likely that working-class parents used the courts, probation, and institutions as a means of shoring up their often fragile authority over their children or to ensure that they were properly disciplined, as Steven Schlossman found in his study of Milwaukee.

66. A. S. Holbrook, "Map Notes and Comments," *Hull House Maps and Papers*, 5. The 1894 publication of the Labor Department was published as the Seventh Special Report of the Commissioner of Labor, *The Slums of Baltimore*,

Chicago, New York and Philadelphia (Washington, D.C., 1894). The 1892 survey of slums in Chicago was not the first time that attention had been given to the housing conditions of the poor. In 1878, for example, the Chicago Department of Health reported that almost 4,900 tenements existed in the city; four years later, the department reported "dangerous over-crowding in all of the poor districts" (most of which were immigrant districts) and appealed to the conscience of the city to build model tenements. In response, the Chicago Citizen's Association (a watch-dog committee composed of leading capitalists of the state of law and order in Chicago) appointed a committee to investigate "Tenements for the Working Classes." The committee concurred with the judgment of the Health Department; the association subsequently appointed a committee to draw up plans for model tenements in Chicago. A year later, the *Report of the Committee on Tenement Houses of the Citizens Association of Chicago* recommended that in order to preserve harmony between labor and capital, the wealthy men of Chicago should construct model tenements for the poor. Of course, the report recommended, the tenements should return not less than 6 percent on capital invested to make the investment attractive. But because of labor unrest in 1884–86 in Chicago (culminating in the Haymarket riot) and press criticism of the Pullman project as "un-American," the association shelved its plans and lobbied instead for a new armory in Chicago to house the Illinois First Infantry to protect "law and order." Two years after the publication of *Hull House Maps and Papers* in 1895, Northwestern University Settlement sponsored a citywide conference on tenements, out of which grew the City Homes Association (CHA). In the years that followed, the CHA scored a number of minor victories: It pressured the city council into opening a municipal lodging house for homeless men (the first superintendent was Raymond Robbins, a Chicago Commons resident) and enacting a "New Tenement" ordinance in 1902. The association installed Charles Ball, formerly the chief inspector of New York City's Tenement Department, as the chief of the Sanitary Bureau in Chicago, where for the next twenty-five years he conducted, against considerable opposition from machine politicians, a protracted, and under the circumstances, successful war against tenement owners who violated the city's sanitation code. Finally, in 1901, the CHA sponsored an intensive survey of three "representative" tenement housing districts. Conducted by Robert Hunter, an itinerant political radical then living at Hull House, the survey was later published as *Tenement Conditions in Chicago*. See the Chicago Department of Health, *Report, 1878,* 10–11; *1882,* 47–50; *Report of the Committee on Tenement Houses of the Citizens Association of Chicago* (Chicago, 1884); Philpott, *The Ghetto and the Slum,* 53–60, 92–94, 98–109; "Bad Tenements: Chicago's Need of Radical Reform," *Chicago Commons* 1 (February, 1897): 1–3; R. Hunter, *Tenement Conditions in Chicago* (Chicago, 1901).

67. W. T. Stead, *If Christ Came to Chicago* (Chicago, 1894), pt. 1, chs. 2, 3, 6; pt 2, chs. 1, 4, 5; pt 4, chs. 1, 2, 3, pp. 410, 413, 416, 421–22, 423, 429, 430.

68. Addams, *The Spirit of Youth,* 14; C. R. Henderson, "The Theory and Practice of Juvenile Courts," *Proceedings of the National Conference of Charities and Corrections* (Chicago, 1904), 364.

69. Addams, *The Spirit of Youth,* chs. 1, 3; M. Haller, "Urban Vice and Civic Reform," in *Cities in American History,* ed. K. J. Jackson and S. Schultz (New York, 1972), 291–92; P. G. Cressey, "Report on Summers Work with the

Juvenile Protection Agency in Chicago," in the Ernest Burgess Papers, University of Chicago Library, 2-A, box 39; F. Thrasher, *The Young: A Study of 1,313 Gangs in Chicago* (Chicago, 1927); C. Shaw, *The Jack-Roller: A Delinquent Boy's Own Story* (Chicago, 1930); C. Shaw, *The Natural History of a Delinquent Career* (Chicago, 1931).

70. "Work of the Juvenile Protection Association" (1911), JPA Papers, Library of the University of Illinois, Chicago Circle, folders 84, 85, 86, 156; Addams, *The Spirit of Youth*, ch. 4; Haller, "Urban Vice and Civic Reform," 296–97; P. G. Cressey, *The Taxi-Dance Hall: A Sociological Study in Commercialized Recreation and City Life, 1933* (New York, 1971); L. Bowen, *Our Most Popular Recreation Controlled by the Liquor Interests: A Study of Public Dance Halls* (Chicago, 1912); idem, *Five- and Ten-Cent Theatres* (Chicago, 1911); idem, *The Public Dance Halls of Chicago* (Chicago, 1917); Chicago Motion Picture Commission, *Report* (Chicago, 1920), 50–51, 75; "Work of the Juvenile Protective Association," folder 15.

71. J. Addams, "Public Recreation and Social Morality," *Charities and the Commons* 18 (August 3, 1907): 492, 494; idem, *The Spirit of Youth*, 7, 18–19, 27, 53, 56, 6, 8, 5.

72. Addams, *The Spirit of Youth*, 27, 29, 30, 25, 44, 47, 45.

73. Ibid., 6, 14, 47, 96–97, 98–99, 101–3.

74. Ibid., 154, 109, 126; idem, *Twenty Years*, ch. 18; idem, *Democracy and Social Ethics*, 180–81.

75. Addams, *Twenty Years*, 205–6; A. Davis, *Spearheads for Reform: The Social Settlements and the Progressive Movement, 1890–1914* (New York, 1967), 61–62; *Report of the Chicago Vocation School Committee of Women's Clubs* (Chicago, 1899), 30; G. S. Counts, *School and Society in Chicago* (New York, 1928), 210–11; S. Curtis, *The Play Movement and Its Significance* (New York, 1917), 12; P. Boyer, *Urban Masses and Moral Order in America, 1820–1920* (Cambridge, Mass., 1978), 242, 243; R. Woods and A. J. Kennedy, eds., *Handbook of Settlements* (New York, 1911), 37–80.

76. For details, see F. L. Olmstead, "Public Parks and the Enlargement of Towns," in *Civilizing America's Cities: A Selection of Frederick Law Olmstead's Writings on City Landscapes*, ed. S. B. Sutton (Cambridge, 1971), 75–76. See also Boyer, *Urban Masses and Moral Order*, 237–39; A. Fein, *Frederick Law Olmstead and the American Environmental Tradition* (New York, 1972); G. Blodgett, "Frederick Law Olmstead: Landscape Architecture as Conservative Reform," *Journal of American History* 62 (March 1976): 869–89.

77. C. Zueblin, "Municipal Playgrounds in Chicago," *American Journal of Sociology* 4, 2 (September 1898): 145–58; H. Foreman, "Chicago's New Park Service," *Century Magazine*, February 1903, 610–20; M. P. McCarthy, "Businessmen and Professionals in Municipal Reform: The Chicago Experience" (Ph.D. dissertation, Northwestern University, 1970), ch. 4; E. Halsey, *The Development of Public Recreation in Metropolitan Chicago* (Chicago, 1940); F. F. Stephan, *Public Recreation in Chicago* (Chicago, 1918); C. Rainwater, *The Play Movement in the United States* (Chicago, 1922), 70–190; Curtis, *The Play Movement and Its Significance*, ch. 5; B. McArthur, "The Chicago Playground Movement: A Neglected Feature of Social Justice," *Social Science Review* 49 (1975): 376–93.

78. Halsey, *Development of Public Recreation*, 27; Commercial Club of Chicago, *The Merchants Club of Chicago, 1890–1907* (Chicago, 1922), 5–7; *Chicago*

Tribune, November 12, 1899; McCarthy, "Businessmen and Professionals," 88–89; McArthur, "The Chicago Playground Movement," 380; *The Daily News,* November 13, 1899.

79. A. W. O'Neil, "Chicago Playgrounds and Park Extension," *Charities* 12 (August 1904): 198–99; McCarthy, "Businessmen and Professionals," 90.

80. Cited in Rainwater, *The Play Movement in the United States,* 95. G. Taylor, "Recreation Developments in Chicago Parks," *Annals* 15 (March 1910): 304–21. Rainwater describes at length an innovation undertaken by the South Park Board that he describes as a "turning point in the play movement." This was the building of a large "fieldhouse" or "recreation center" with cafeteria, auditorium, meeting rooms, gymnasiums, and bathing facilities, open all year round, costing close to a half million dollars. The impact of the innovation upon public opinion was immediate. President Roosevelt characterized it as a great civic achievement. The newly organized Playground and Recreation Association of America selected Chicago for its first national convention, which in turn prompted the creation, in 1907, at Hull House of the Chicago Playground Association (CPA) to host the convention. Of the eighteen directors of the CPA, six were businessmen (including Harold McCormick), five professionals (including Judge Julian Mack of the juvenile court), and six welfare and settlement workers (including Jane Addams, Mary McDowell, and Amalie Hofer). See McArthur, "The Chicago Playground Movement," 385.

81. McArthur, "The Chicago Playground Movement," 383.

82. A. H. Jerome, "The Playground as Social Center," *American City* 5 (August 1911): 33; E. B. Mero, ed., *American Playgrounds: Their Construction, Equipment, Maintenance and Utility* (Boston, 1908), 256; Rainwater, *The Play Movement,* 326; J. Addams, "Public Recreation and Social Morality," *Charities and Commons* 18 (August 3, 1907): 494; G. Taylor, "How They Played at Chicago," *Charities and Commons* 18 (August 3, 1907): 473–74; Commercial Club of Chicago, *The Merchants Clubs of Chicago, 1890–1907,* 7; *Chicago Tribune,* November 12, 1899; *Daily News,* November 13, 1899.

83. Curtis, *The Play Movement and Its Significance,* 92, 316, 322–23.

84. Rainwater, *The Play Movement in the United States,* 267.

85. Stead, *If Christ Came to Chicago,* 410; C. Zueblin, "The White City and After," *Chautauquan* 38 (December 1903): 374–75; idem, "The Making of the City," *Chautauquan* 38 (November 1903): 275; C. W. Robinson, *Modern Civic Art or the City Made Beautiful* (New York, 1903), 371; W. S. Rainsford, *The Story of a Varied Life* (Garden City, 1922), 329; J. Lee, *Play in Education* (New York, 1915), 388–89. See also, J. J. Ingals, "Lessons of the Fair," *Cosmopolitan* 16 (December 1893): 141–49; P. Bourget, "A Farewell to the White City," *Cosmopolitan* 16 (December 1893): 134–40; A. F. Palmer, "Some Lasting Results of the Worlds' Fair," *Forum* 16 (December 1893): 517–23; J. C. Adams, "What a Great City Might Be—A Lesson from the White City," *New England Magazine* 14 (March 1896): 3–13. Robinson and Rainsford are quoted by Boyer, *Urban Masses and Moral Order,* 182, 183.

86. T. J. Hines, *Burnham of Chicago, Architect and Planner* (New York, 1974), ch. 14; D. H. Burnham and E. H. Bennett, *Plan of Chicago* (Chicago, 1909), 8, 48, 108, 53, 121, 116, 118, 4; C. Condit, *Chicago, 1910–1929* (Chicago, 1973), ch. 3; P. Duis, *Chicago: Creating New Traditions* (Chicago, 1976), 48–55, esp. 53; Boyer, *Urban Masses and Moral Order,* 270–76. My analysis of Burnham follows closely that developed by Boyer.

87. J. Addams, *A New Conscience and an Ancient Evil* (New York, 1912), 212, 210, 206, 207. Charles Rosenberg argues that an important component of Victorian sexual thought supported an identical attack upon the innateness of male lust and the inevitability of the double standard and proposed instead an alternative model of male sexual ideology, "the Christian Gentlemen." See, C. Rosenberg, "Sexuality, Class and Race in Nineteenth-Century America," *American Quarterly* 25 (May 1973): 131–53.

88. G. K. Turner, "The City of Chicago: A Study of the Great Immoralities," *McClure's Magazine* 18 (April 1907): 575–92; C. Barnes, "The Story of the Committee of Fifteen of Chicago," *Social Hygiene* 14 (1918): 146. W. T. Stead had written about prostitution in the mid-1890s in *If Christ Came to Chicago*, but his discussion did not generate a campaign as Turner's article did in 1907. See Stead, *If Christ Came to Chicago*, pt. 3, ch. 5.

89. Turner, "The City of Chicago," 576, 577, 578–79, 582–85, 580, 582.

90. Barnes, "The Story of the Committee of Fifteen," 145–46; *Chicago Tribune*, September 26, October 17, 1909.

91. Barnes, "The Story of the Committee of Fifteen," 146; C. Roe, *The Prodigal Daughter: The White Slave Evil and the Remedy* (Chicago, 1911), 169, 182. Cited in R. Lubove, "The Progressives and the Prostitute," *The Historian* 24 (1962): 308. S. P. Wilson, author of *Chicago and Its Cess Pools of Infamy* (Chicago, n.d.), held a similar view: the economics of commercialized prostitution spelled inexorable doom for twenty-two thousand daughters every five years:

Listen, father, mother, there are twenty-two thousand, dearly-beloved young girls growing up in our midst today who within five years must undergo the present system of white slavery, put aside father, mother, home, friends and honor and march into Chicago's ghastly flesh market to take the place of the twenty-two thousand helpless, hopeless, decaying chattels who now daily behind bolts and bars and steel screens satisfy the abominable lust of approximately two hundred and ten thousand brutal, drunken adulters. (55)

92. Barnes, "The Story of the Committee of Fifteen," 146–47; G. Taylor, *Pioneering on Social Frontiers* (Chicago, 1930), 87; idem, "The Story of the Chicago Vice Commission," *Survey* (May 6, 1911): 239; L. Wade, *Graham Taylor: Pioneer for Social Justice, 1851–1938* (Chicago, 1964), 199–200; L. Wendt and H. Kogan, *Bosses in Lusty Chicago* (Bloomington, 1971), 282–93; E. Anderson, "Prostitution and Social Justice: Chicago, 1910–1915," *Social Science Review* 48 (1974): 208–9; Haller, "Urban Vice and Civic Reform," 294.

93. Membership of the commission included six physicians, the president of Northwestern University, two University of Chicago professors, eight clerics (including Graham Taylor), lawyers, judges, and businessmen, and the former national president of the General Federation of Women's Clubs. Some of Chicago's most famous anti-vice crusaders were not members: Clifford Rae, temperance organization leaders, the head of Chicago Law and Order League, and evangelical red-light "rescue missionaries." For further details, see Anderson, "Prostitution and Social Justice," 208–9; Taylor, "Vice Commission," 239; Wendt and Kogan, *Bosses in Lusty Chicago*, 282–93.

94. Chicago Vice Commission, *The Social Evil in Chicago. A Study of Existing Conditions with Recommendations by the Vice Commission of Chicago* (Chicago,

1911), 32 (emphasis in original). The commission also included that while white slavers might work together informally, "it has been demonstrated" that they were "not organized" (41). Clifford Roe, on the other hand, argued that an "invisible government" made up of "low and degenerate, grasping and avaricious" vice tycoons organized and ran on a national scale the "great hideous business" of the white slave trade. C. Roe, *The Girl Who Disappeared* (Chicago, 1914), 200; idem, *The Prodigal Daughter: The White Slave Evil and the Remedy*, 185, 189. The United States Immigration Commission reported in 1911, however, that it found no evidence "of a great monopolistic [vice] corporation" and did not believe, therefore, that any such monopoly organization existed. U.S. Senate, *Reports of the Immigration Commission: Importation and Harboring of Women for Immoral Purposes*, doc. 753, 61st Cong. 3d sess. (Washington, D.C., 1910), 76.

95. Ibid., 32, 27. Graham Taylor later wrote in *Survey* that "the greed which has commercialized this vice to wring from it such enormous profits, artificially and even coercively stimulates, increases, perpetuates, and spreads its growth far beyond what might be considered its natural supply and demand" ("Vice Commission," 242). Abraham Flexner was of a similar mind. The basic assumption of the anti-vice crusade, he wrote in 1914, is the belief that "certain forms of vice represent not the human weakness of the participants but the commercial interest of the exploiter," and that repression could only suppress that part of the demand created by "sheer artificial stimulation" (A. Flexner, "Next Steps in Dealing With Prostitution," *Social Hygiene* 1 [1914–15]: 522, 535. Cited in Lubove, "The Progressives and the Prostitute," 320).

96. Chicago Vice Commission, *Social Evil in Chicago*, 263, 45, 43, 46, 25, 57. In 1916 the Illinois Vice Commission also concluded that "poverty" was "the principal cause, direct and indirect, of prostitution." Thousands of young girls, it argued, were forced into prostitution out of a "sheer inability to keep body and soul together on the low wages received by them" (Illinois Senate Vice Committee, *Report of the Senate Vice Committee* [Chicago, 1916], 23, 28).

97. Chicago Vice Commission, *Social Evil in Chicago*, 45–55, 245, 40. In a review of the commission's report two years later, Walter Lippmann argued that what the commission wanted to accomplish was the annihilation of lust. "The members assumed without criticism," he wrote, "the traditional dogma of Christianity that sex in any manifestation outside marriage is sinful" and failed to realize that "a forcible attempt to moralize society from the top" would not work. W. Lippmann, *A Preface to Politics* (New York, 1914), 129–31. Cited in Anderson, "Prostitution and Social Justice," 220–21. But as Anderson points out, Lippmann missed the point of the report: The primary focus of the commission's work was commercialized sex, not private lust.

98. Barnes, "The Story of the Committee of Fifteen," 146–50. By April 1913, the committee had expanded to fifty members.

99. Committee of Fifteen, *Annual Report of the Committee of Fifteen for the Year Ending April 30, 1918*, 6; Anderson, "Prostitution and Social Justice," 215–16, 212–13, 207; Chicago Immigrants Protective League, *First Annual Report, 1909–1910* (Chicago, 1910), 4, 13–15; idem, *Fourth Annual Report, 1913* (Chicago, 1913), 13; G. Abbott, "The Chicago Employment Agency and the Immigrant Worker," *American Journal of Sociology* 14 (November 1908): 289, 291–92; J. C. Burnham, "The Progressive Era Revolution in American Attitudes Toward Sex," *Journal of American History* 59 (March 1973): 885–908; E. Feld-

man, "Prostitution, the Alien Woman and the Progressive Imagination, 1910–1915," *American Quarterly* 19, 2 (1967): 192–206; H. B. Leonard, "The Immigrants Protective League of Chicago," *Illinois State Historical Society Journal* 66, 3 (Autumn 1973): 271–84. The members of the Immigrants Protective League included Jane Addams, Margaret Drier Robbins, Mary McDowell, Graham Taylor, Julius Rosenwald, Sophonisba Breckinridge, and Judge Julian Mack.

100. S. Breckinridge and E. Abbott, "Housing Conditions in Chicago," *American Journal of Sociology* 16 (January 1911): 442. Philpott argues that "according to the business creed, housing was a commodity for private enterprise to provide at profit. . . . Restrictive legislation, zoning and city planning were within the scope of government. Building, selling and managing houses fell within the private domain, and it was all business, not philanthropy." The color line referred to the informal policy of containing blacks within clearly segregated areas of the city. The Chicago Real Estate Board policed the business creed and the color line. Reformers, whether those on the Chicago Commission of Race Relations, or the Chicago Housing Commission (largely the product of Mary McDowell's efforts), whatever their private convictions, did not cross either line. Housing reform for blacks in Chicago's ghettos and for white ethnics in Chicago's slums was both limited and frustrated by the business creed. Only one, however, had to carry an additional burden, and settlement reformers did little to lighten the load. Philpott, *The Ghetto and the Slum*, 204–6, and pts. 2, 3, and 4, generally.

101. E. C. Moore, "The Social Value of the Saloon," *American Journal of Sociology* 3, 1 (July 1897): 1–12; R. Calkins, *Substitutes for the Saloon* (Boston, 1901); R. Melendy, "The Saloon in Chicago, I," *American Journal of Sociology* 6, 3 (November 1900): 289–464; idem, "The Saloon in Chicago, II," *American Journal of Sociology* 6, 5 (January 1901): 433ff.; J. F. George, "The Saloon Question in Chicago," *Economic Studies* 2 (1897): 77; Chicago Commission on the Liquor Problem, *Preliminary Report* (December 1916): 3–17; Haller, "Urban Vice and Civic Reform," 295.

102. J. D. Buenker, "The Illinois Legislature and Prohibition, 1907–1919," *Illinois State Historical Society Journal* 62, 4 (Winter 1969): 371, 372; J. H. Timberlake, *Prohibition and the Progressive Movement* (New York, 1970), 141–42, 150; F. P. Stockbridge, "The Church Militant against the Saloon," *The World's Work* 26 (October 1914): 709–10.

103. Buenker, "Illinois Legislature," 373–75, 379; J. Allswang, *A House for All Peoples* (Lexington, 1971), 119, 120; C. E. Merriam, *Chicago: A More Intimate View of Urban Politics* (New York, 1929), 60. While more research is required on the social basis of support for and opposition to the amendment, it seems likely, as Buenker reports, that the major division was between the state's old stock, traditionally Protestant groups located primarily in the southern and rural parts of the state, and the new stock, Catholic groups who for the most part lived in Chicago. Harold Gosnell's study of the Prohibition movement in Chicago led him to a slightly different but by no means incompatible interpretation. On the whole, he concluded, "the Catholics, the foreign born, the unemployed, the persons who pay the lower rents, and the non-home owners tend to be wet. Inversely, the Protestants, the native whites of native parentage, the employed, the persons paying the highest rents, the home owners, the persons with superior educational attainments tend to be dries" (Buenker, "Illinois Legislature," 371–72, 375–84; H. Gosnell, *Machine Politics: Chicago Model* (Chicago, 1968), 149.

John Allswang, using the pietist-liturgical framework of recent ethno-cultural history, came to a different conclusion. For Allswang, "prohibition was the greatest ethnic issue, both for its precise aims and for the more general ethnic-native-American conflict which it epitomized." It was not a "class" issue, he argued, but ethnic: "There are sufficient reasons to conclude that ethnicity provided the strongest frame of reference for the ethnic voters of Chicago in the first third of the twentieth century" (Allswang, 118). Allswang's argument rests upon the misconception that a categorical definition of "class" and "ethnicity" establishes the credibility of class analysis in political history. To establish significant ethnic differences in voting behavior does not validate an ethno-cultural interpretation of voting behavior at the expense of class theory. From the standpoint of class analysis, such ethno-cultural interpretations simply beg the question. In addition, it takes a large leap of faith to assume that voting behavior is a useful index of ethnic or class consciousness, or that ethnic and class position directly reflect or represent class position or social status. From the perspective of class analysis, voting behavior is more usefully related to long-term processes of class formation within which ethnicity plays a significant role.

104. Buenker, "Illinois Legislature," 372–84.

105. Boyer, *Urban Masses and Moral Order*, 227–78, 175, 179, 190, 198–200, 278–79, 281, 213–14.

106. Ibid., 281–82. Roy Lubove, like Boyer, stresses the "social control" objectives of the urban reform movement. Lubove, "The Progressives and the Prostitute," 330.

107. Both Mark Haller and Michael Katz have argued the centrality of child-saving to urban reform. Haller concluded that "the central thrust of urban reform was . . . to supervise and uplift the lives of the city's children" ("Urban Vice," 301). Michael Katz notes, apropos Boyer, "Although Boyer briefly notes the attention to children so prominent in the late-nineteenth and early-twentieth centuries, he does not use the term *child-saving*, which became ubiquitous in both public and private reform literature. Reformers and public officials who otherwise differed on various issues united in the belief that the ineffectual results of attempts to change adult behavior pointed unmistakably to the need to concentrate energy on children who should be rescued from faulty homes, inadequate legal protection, and unhealthful surroundings. Child-saving does not fit easily into either of Boyer's positive or negative environmental categories since it had elements of both" (Katz, *Poverty and Policy in American History* [New York, 1983], 192–93).

108. Taylor, "Vice Commission," 239; idem, *Pioneering*, 87; *Chicago Tribune*, October 16, 17, 1909.

109. Anderson, "Prostitution and Social Justice," 217–18. See also, Haller, "Urban Vice," 301.

110. E. A. Ross, *Social Control: A Survey of the Foundations of Order* (New York, 1901), 432, 435. Cited by Boyer, *Urban Masses and Moral Order*, 278.

111. C. P. Dozier, "History of the Kindergarten Movement in the United States," *Educational Bi-Monthly* 2 (1907–08): 354, 357–58; Chicago Board of Education, *38th Annual Report, 1892*, 56–57.

112. Counts, *School and Society in Chicago*, 209; N. C. Vandewalker, *The Kindergarten in American Education* (New York, 1923), 60.

113. Addams, *Twenty Years*, 83–84; Davis, *American Heroine*, 67–68; A. Hoffer, "The Social Settlement and the Kindergarten," National Education Association, *Address and Proceedings* (1895): 514–26.

114. Hoffer, "The Social Settlement and the Kindergarten," 518–19; Wade, *Graham Taylor,* 162; Davis, *Spearheads,* 44–45; Wandewalker, *The Kindergarten,* 107, 112; B. L. Pierce, *A History of Chicago, 1871–1893* (New York, 1957), 3: 383; Woods and Kennedy, eds., *Handbook of Settlements,* 37–80.

115. Submission of Elizabeth Harrison to the Harper Commission, Harper Commission, *Report,* 194; E. Harrison, *A Study of Child Nature from the Kindergarten Standpoint* (Chicago, 1895), 10. See also S. Rothman, *Woman's Proper Place* (New York, 1978), 103. For a contemporary statement of such a view from a feminist highly critical of mothering, see D. Dinnerstein, *The Mermaid and the Minotaur* (New York, 1977), esp. chs. 3, 8.

116. N. Vandewalker, "The Kindergarten in the Chicago School System," *Kindergarten Magazine* 9 (May 1897): 679.

117. *Chicago Tribune,* June 1, 1881; May 13, 1882; Pierce, *History of Chicago,* 3: 383.

118. Chicago Board of Education, *38th Annual Report, 1892,* 56–57; *39th Annual Report, 1893,* 41–43.

119. Idem, *40th Annual Report, 1894,* 63–65.

120. Idem, *41st Annual Report, 1895,* 144; *42nd Annual Report, 1897,* 47; *44th Annual Report, 1898,* 51; *45th Annual Report, 1899,* 134–35; *55th Annual Report, 1909,* 142–43; Drozier, "Kindergarten Movement," 358. See also the *Report of the Educational Commission of the City of Chicago* (Chicago, 1899), 95–97.

121. Chicago Board of Education, *60th Annual Report, 1914,* 215; *48th Annual Report, 1902,* 63–64; *Chicago Chronicle,* July 10, 1902; Chicago Board of Education, *51st Annual Report, 1905,* 129; G. M. Clippinger, "A Chicago Public School Kindergarten," *Kindergarten Magazine* 11 (1900–1901): 485–89.

122. Chicago Board of Education, *6th Annual Report, 1861,* 27; *18th Annual Report, 1872,* 12, 15. On the introduction of manual training, see chapter 4, below.

123. J. M. Rice, *The Public School System of the United States* (New York, 1893), 170, 171, 172, 173, 174, 175.

124. *Chicago Tribune,* April 20 and April 26, 1893. Many years later, Leonard Ayres recalled with sardonic humor the response of the National Education Association's leadership to Rice's charges: "The educators who discussed his findings and those who reviewed them in the educational press united in denouncing as foolish, reprehensible and from every point of view indefensible, the effort to discover anything about the value of the teaching of spelling by finding out whether or not children could spell." *17th Yearbook of the National Society for the Study of Education* (1918), 2: 11.

125. *Chicago Evening Post,* August 12, 1894; Chicago Board of Education, *Annual Report, 1894,* 55–61; J. F. Eberhart, "An Historical Sketch of the Cook County Normal School," *Chicago Schools Journal* 18 (January–June 1936); G. H. Gaston, "The Chicago Normal School," *Chicago Schools Journal* 6, 6 (February, 1924): 210–13. The label, the "new education" apparently dates from 1882 when J. R. Buchanan, a physician, lecturer, and educator, published a book he called *The New Education* (Boston, 1882). Cremin dates the beginning of the "progressive movement in American education" with the publication of Rice's articles in *The Forum* in 1892–93. L. A. Cremin, *The Transformation of the School* (New York, 1961), ch. 1.

126. C. F. Addams, *The New Departure in the Common Schools of Quincy* (Boston, 1879); idem, "Scientific Common School Education," *Harpers New*

Monthly Magazine 61 (October 1888): 934–42; A. D. Mayo, "The New Education and Colonel Parker," *Journal of Education* 18 (1883): 84–85; F. W. Parker, "The Quincy Method," in United States Bureau of Education, *Report of the Commissioner of Education for the Year 1902* (Washington, D.C., 1903), 237–423; M. F. Washburner, "Colonel Francis W. Parker: The Man and Educational Reformer," in *Francis Wayland Parker: His Life and Educational Reform Work,* souvenir issue in honor of the silver anniversary of the Quincy Movement (New York, 1900); F. W. Parker Papers, University of Chicago; Cremin, *The Transformation of the School,* 128–30; M. Curti, *The Social Ideas of American Educators* (Totowa, N.J., 1935), ch. 11; R. F. Tostberg, "Educational Ferment in Chicago, 1883–1904" (Ph.D. dissertation, University of Wisconsin, 1960), chs. 3, 4, 5.

127. F. W. Parker, *Talks on Pedagogics: An Outline of the Theory of Concentration* (New York, 1894), 3, 23–24, 434, 383 (emphasis in the original).

128. F. W. Parker, "An Account of the Work of the Cook County and Chicago Normal School from 1883 to 1899," U.S. Commissioner of Education, *Report, 1901–1902* (Washington, D.C., 1903), 249, 252–53; idem, *Talks on Pedagogics,* 25–46, 344, 377–82; idem, "Application of Child Study in the School," National Education Association, *Addresses and Proceedings* (1895): 425; idem, "Principles of Correlation," *School Journal* 62 (March 2, 1901): 217–19; idem, "An Account of the Work," 254.

129. Parker, "An Account of the Work," 249; idem, *Talks on Pedagogics,* 51–52, 118–19, 161, 173–79, 362, 378–82.

130. Parker, *Talks on Pedagogics,* 390, 408, 439, 401–10, 448; idem, "Discussion of German Methods of Using the Mother Tongue," National Education Association, *Addresses and Proceedings* (1894): 483; idem, "The School of the Future," National Education Association, *Addresses and Proceedings* (1891): 85–86; J. Cambell, *Colonel Francis W. Parker, The Children's Crusader* (New York, 1967), 170; F. T. Cook, "Colonel Francis W. Parker: His Influence on Education," *Chicago Schools Journal* 19, 7/8 (March–April 1938): 151. Parker's political views were not unusually conservative for his day, but he was decidedly less progressive on most issues than either Dewey or Addams. He was an outspoken opponent of strikes, unions, and socialism; he was a fervent supporter of George Pullman and his experiment in paternalism; he supported the hanging of the Haymarket martyrs; he sanctioned segregated schools and vocational education for blacks; he was an ardent supporter of the move to separate education from municipal politics; and he opposed collective bargaining by teachers. For a general discussion of Parker's politics, see Cambell, ch. 11 and Curti, *The Social Ideas of American Educators,* 385–95.

131. Cited in Cremin, *The Transformation of the School,* 129.

132. Cited by R. McCaul, "Dewey's Chicago," *School Review* (Summer 1959): 273–74.

133. J. Dewey, *The School and Society* (Chicago, 1900), 31.

134. K. C. Mayhew and A. C. Edwards, eds., *The Dewey School* (New York, 1966); A. C. Wirth, *John Dewey as Educator* (New York, 1966); Cremin, *The Transformation of the School,* chs. 4, 5; Curti, *The Social Ideas of American Educators,* ch. 15.

135. Dewey, *The School and Society,* 8–13.

136. Dewey, cited in Mayhew and Edwards, *The Dewey School,* 16.

137. Ibid., 23; J. Dewey, *My Pedagogic Creed* (Washington, D.C., 1929).

But of "these two sides, the psychological is the basis. The child's own instincts and powers furnish the material and give the starting point for all education." Indeed, "the only true education comes through the stimulation of the child's powers by the demands of the social situations in which he finds himself" (*My Pedagogic Creed*, 1).

138. Dewey, *The School and Society*, 34. Years later, when a number of avant-garde advocates of the pedagogical revolution not unexpectedly took Dewey's works at face value, Dewey felt obliged to sharply reprimand them for their excessive pediocentrism. "Such a method," he wrote, "is really stupid. For it attempts the impossible, which is always stupid; and it misconceives the conditions of independent thinking" (J. Dewey et al., *Art and Education* [Merion, Pa., 1947], 37); J. Dewey, "How Much Freedom in New Schools, *New Republic* 63 (July 9, 1930): 204–6; *Experience and Education* (London, 1963), ch. 5. For a discussion, see Cremin, *The Transformation of the School*, 234–35; C. Karier, *Man, Society and Education* (Chicago, 1968), 235–40.

139. Dewey, *My Pedagogic Creed*, 7, 1, 4; idem, *Democracy and Education* (New York, 1964), 76; Mayhew and Edwards, *The Dewey School*, 413. There have been few propositions in recent educational theory as controversial as Dewey's identification of the goal of education as growth. It has often been suggested that Dewey intended the use of the language of growth to describe the goals of education as metaphorical. This is incorrect. Dewey was not indulging in the use of a biological metaphor: he meant to *define* education as growth, not to compare it to growth. "When it is said that education is development, everything depends upon *how* development is conceived," he wrote in a much-quoted passage of *Democracy and Education*. "Our net conclusion is that life is development, and that developing, growing, is life. Translated into its educational equivalents, that means: (i) that the educational process has no end beyond itself; it is its own end; and (ii) the educational process is one of continual reorganizing, reconstructing, transforming" (*Democracy and Education*, 49–50). Dewey's most elaborate discussion of education as growth is contained in chapters 4 and 5 of *Democracy and Education*, although chapter 3 of *Experience and Education* is also important.

140. Dewey, *The School and Society*, 132–34; see also 19–29. The role of "occupations" at the Laboratory School and something of the theoretical rationale for their use is discussed at length in Mayhew and Edwards, *The Dewey School*, pt. 2 and app. 2; Cremin, *The Transformation of the School*, 135–42; and Wirth, *John Dewey as Educator*, chs. 7, 9, app.

141. Dewey, *The School and Society*, 14; idem, *My Pedagogic Creed*, 3. The influence of Jane Addams and the example of Hull House is particularly obvious at this point in Dewey's thought. The school, he came to believe, like the settlement, could be a force for both community and democracy. Discussing his views before an audience of the National Education Association (NEA) in 1902, Dewey explained, "I suppose whenever we are framing our ideals of the school as a social center, what we think of is particularly the better class of social settlements. What we want is to see the school, every public school, doing something of the same sort of work that is now done by a settlement or two scattered at wide distances through the city" (Dewey, "The School as a Social Center," NEA, *Addresses and Proceedings* (1902): 381.

142. Dewey, *The School and Society*, 13, 15, 16–17. Dewey never forgot these lessons he learned at the Laboratory School. In subsequent writings—partic-

ularly *Interest and Effort in Education* (1913) and *Democracy and Education*
(1916)—he wrote at length on the relationship between interest and discipline,
although he wrote his first essay on the topic in 1895 (a year before he established
the Laboratory School) for the National Herbart Society.

143. Mayhew and Edwards, *The Dewey School*, 32.

144. Dewey, *The School and Society*, 7, 14, 24–27; *Democracy and Education*,
87–88; Mayhew and Edwards, *The Dewey School*, 164. See also Dewey's "The
Situation as Regards the Course of Study," National Education Association, *Address and Proceedings* (1901): 345. Dewey's attack on traditional epistemological
dualisms is presented in *Reconstruction in Philosophy* (New York, 1920), esp. chs.
3, 4, 5, and 6; and in *The Quest for Certainty* (New York, 1964), esp. chs. 1, 2, 3.
Democracy and Education, chs. 7, 19, 20, provides a theory of the social structure
of traditional epistemological dualisms and their educational consequences.

145. John and Evelyn Dewey, *The Schools of Tomorrow* (New York, 1962),
168; Dewey, *The School and Society*, 29; J. Dewey, "The Need of an Industrial
Education in an Industrial Democracy," *Proceedings of the Second Pan American
Scientific Congress*, sec. 4, pt. 1 (Washington, D.C., 1917), 222.

146. Dewey, *The School and Society*, 24, 133, 19. Similar claims that Dewey
made about the ability of practical activities to make work meaningful have recently been made by proponents of career education.

147. Dewey, *My Pedagogic Creed*, 9, 11; Mayhew and Edwards, *The Dewey
School*, 436. "The ultimate social ideal was the transformation of society through a
new, socially minded individualism."

148. *Chicago Teachers Federation Bulletin*, May 6, 1904.

149. As a diminutive seventeen year old, Ella Flagg Young started teaching
"cowboys" on the southern outskirts of the city in 1862; later, she became a
demonstration teacher in the Cook County Normal School, a high school teacher,
an elementary school principal, an assistant superintendent of education, a student
of Dewey's at the University of Chicago, for a while supervisor of instruction at
the Laboratory School, a professor at the University of Chicago, principal of the
Chicago Normal School, and in 1909, superintendent of Schools. See J. T.
McManis, *Ella Flagg Young and a Half-century of the Chicago Public Schools* (Chicago, 1916).

150. E. F. Young, *Isolation in the Schools* (Chicago, 1901).

151. Cited by D. Tyack and E. Hansot, *Managers of the Virtue* (Standford,
1982), 326.

152. Dewey's theory of reflective thinking is systematically developed in his
How We Think (New York, 1910). Chapters 11 and 12 of *Democracy and Education*
summarize his position six years later. For a general review of the different approaches within the developmentalist perspective, see L. Kohlberg and R. Mayer,
"Development as the Aim of Education," *Harvard Educational Review* 42, 4 (November 1972): 449–96. E. Durkheim has some interesting comments on the
developmentalist perspective in *Education and Sociology* (Glencoe, 1956), 115. In
particular, he emphasizes the psychologizing of pedagogy reflected in the triumph
of developmentalist perspective in pedagogical theory.

153. W. C. Payne, "The Trend of the Elementary School," *Educational Bi-Monthly* (1908–09): 151, 155.

154. In the first year of publication of the *Educational Bi-Monthly*
(1906–07), the following articles appeared on the "dynamic factor": "Geography:

A Dynamic Factor in Education"; "The Herbartian Formal Steps in the Light of Dynamic Pedagogy"; "Nature Study as a Dynamic Factor in Education"; "The Dynamic Factor in Education"; "Dynamic Elements in Kindergarten Education"; "Dynamic Factors in Geography"; "From the Static to the Dynamic"; "Crisis as a Dynamic Factor"; "Dynamic Factors in Music."

155. Chicago Board of Education, *56th Annual Report, 1910*, 85; *Chicago Record Herald*, October 9, 1910, 8; *Educational Bi-Monthly* 10 (1915–16): 35–46.

156. Chicago Board of Education, *60th Annual Report, 1914*, 177.

157. See, for example, the following issues of the *Chicago Schools Journal*: vol. 2: September 1919, October 1919, December 1919, June 1920; vol. 3: October 1920; vol. 4: October 1921; vol. 5: October 1922, November 1922; vol. 6: November 1923; vol. 7: 1924–25; vol. 11: 1928–29. For a discussion of Kilpatrick's project method, see Cremin, *The Transformation of the School*, 215–24.

158. *Report of the Survey of the Schools of Chicago* (New York, 1932), vol. 2: 120; see also, 115–19, 121–33; vol. 3: 23–28, 66ff.

159. On the character and development of a distinctively bourgeois pedagogy of competitive evaluation and grading, grounded in possessive individualist assumptions about the individual and society, see P. Aries, *Centuries of Childhood* (Harmondsworth, Middlesex, 1973), pt. 2; E. Durkheim, *The Evolution of Educational Thought in France* (Boston, 1977), pt. 2; R. Dreeben, *On What Is Learned in School* (Reading, Mass., 1968), ch. 5; P. Jackson, *Life in Classrooms* (New York, 1968), ch. 1; J. Henry, *Culture Against Man* (New York, 1965), ch. 8; J. Goodlad, *A Place Called School* (New York, 1984), chs. 4, 7; T. Parsons, "The School Class as a Social System: Some of Its Functions in American Society," *Harvard Educational Review* 29 (Fall 1959): 297–318; R. W. Connell, D. J. Ashendon, S. Kessler, G. W. Dorsett, *Making the Difference* (Sydney, 1982), ch. 3.

160. *Survey*, 2: 120–21.

161. *Chicago Tribune*, August 12, 1896; McCaul, "Dewey's Chicago," 262ff.; Chicago Board of Education, *45th Annual Report, 1899*, 27–28, 29–79; F. G. Bruner, "The Testing of Children for Mental Efficiency," National Education Association, *Addresses and Proceedings* (1912): 111; Chicago Board of Education, *55th Annual Report, 1909*, 163–68, 18.

162. B. Bellingham, "The 'Unspeakable Blessing': Street Children, Rhetoric and the Social Organization of Misery in Early Industrial Capitalism," *Politics and Society* (forthcoming, Fall 1984).

163. P. Gay, ed., *John Locke On Education* (New York, 1964), 28, 29, 35, 37, 49. In the famous chapter "What Sort of Despotism Democratic Nations Have to Fear" in his *Democracy in America*, Alexis de Tocqueville, noting the passion of Americans for "individualism," "democracy," and "equality," suggested that they were peculiarly liable to an "administrative depotism" that would keep them in "perpetual childhood" (*Democracy in America*, ed. J. P. Mayer [New York, 1969], 2: 693, 692).

CHAPTER THREE: *The Limits of Reform*

1. U. Sinclair, *The Jungle* (New York, 1906).

2. The concept of "remaking" is borrowed from G. Jones, "Working Class Culture and Working Class Politics in London, 1870–1900: Notes on the Remak-

ing of a Working Class," *Journal of Social History* 7, 4 (Summer 1974): 460–508. See also the discussion of class formation in the preface, above.

3. Julia Wrigley's study of "class politics and public schools" suffers from, among other things, the assumption that organized labor constitutes the working class, the assumption that "class" analysis in education is exhausted by analyses of overt political conflicts over curriculum, control, and pedagogy, and the further assumption that "class politics" happens when organized labor and organized capital divide over an issue. See J. Wrigley, *Class Politics and Public Schools: Chicago, 1900–1950* (New Brunswick, 1982), chs. 1, 3.

4. *Chicago Tribune*, January 12, 1874; E. C. Bogart and C. M. Thompson, *The Industrial State, 1870–1893* (Springfield, Ill., 1920), 440, 446.

5. Bogart and Thompson, *The Industrial State*, 449.

6. Testimony of P. H. McLogan, *Report of the Committee of the Senate Upon the Relations Between Labor and Capital* (Washington, D.C., 1885), 1: 582.

7. Chicago Federation of Labor, *A Report on Public School Fads* (Chicago, n.d.), 7. From a copy at the Chicago Historical Society.

8. Illinois State Federation of Labor, *Proceedings, 1924*, 49–51.

9. Morgan, "Statement re Foundation of the Free Education League," folder 6, 1–2, Morgan Collection, University of Illinois, Urbana; idem, "How to Educate the Working Child," an address to the State Teachers Association of Wisconsin, Milwaukee, December 27, 1905, in folder 11, Morgan Collection, University of Illinois, Urbana; idem, "A Statement" to the members of the Committee of 100 established by the Civic Federation of Chicago, folder 6, 1, the Morgan Collection; idem, "Education," folder 6, Morgan Collection.

10. E. Staley, *History of the Illinois State Federation of Labor* (Chicago, 1930), 7, 297–98; ISFL, *Proceedings, 1920*, 215; idem, *Proceedings, 1921*, 351; idem, *Proceedings, 1923*, 53–54, 277, 419–91; idem, *Proceedings, 1928*, 93; idem, *Proceedings, 1930*, 160; idem, *Report of Committee on Schools* 7, in Victor Olander papers, box 148, Chicago Historical Society; E. R. Beckner, *A History of Labor Legislation in Illinois* (Chicago, 1929), 180.

11. Chicago Board of Education, *Proceedings, 1892–1893*, 325.

12. *Chicago Tribune*, January 13, 1893; February 7, 12, 18, 19, 23, 25, 26, 28, 1893. See also, *Chicago Evening Post*, January 21, 1893; *Chicago Daily News*, January 6, 1893.

13. Chicago Board of Educaton, *Proceedings, 1892–1893*, 335.

14. "The Public Schools: Their Condition, and Changes Advocated by the *Tribune, Post, Herald, News*, and *Journal*," folder 6, the Morgan Collection, University of Illinois, Urbana.

15. *InterOcean*, March 12, 1893, carried a full account of the meeting. See also *Chicago Tribune*, March 12, 1893. Samuel Gompers, P. J. McGuire, and G. E. McNeill of the AFL sent letters or telegrams of support to Morgan. Further support came from a meeting of six hundred to seven hundred German Americans in Chicago, the *Illinois Staats Zeitung, The Graphic*, and from Rabbi Stolz.

16. "He Is for the Fads," *InterOcean*, March 20, 1893; untitled manuscript on the working class, folder 31, in the Morgan Collection, University of Illinois, Urbana.

17. Chicago Federation of Labor, *Public School Fads*, 4, 5, 6, 8.

18. Illinois Bureau of Labor Statistics, *Second Biennial Report, 1882*, 288–95.

19. Ibid., *Report, 1884*, 135–391, esp. 257–58.

20. U.S. Immigration Commission, *Reports* (Washington, D.C., 1911), 26–27: 314; M. F. Byington, *Homestead: The Household of a Mill Town* (New York, 1910).

21. U.S. Department of Labor, *Ninth Special Report of the Commissioner of Labor. The Italians in Chicago: A Social and Economic Study* (Washington, D.C., 1897), 29–30.

22. J. A. Mayer, "Private Charities in Chicago from 1871 to 1915," (Ph.D. dissertation, University of Minnesota, 1978), 459, 461.

23. C. J. Bushnell, "Some Social Aspects of the Chicago Stockyards," *American Journal of Sociology* 4, 4 (January 1902): 458.

24. Idem, "Some Social Aspects of the Chicago Stockyards," ch. 2; idem, "The Stockyard Community at Chicago," *American Journal of Sociology* 7, 4 (November 1901): 313.

25. J. C. Kennedy et al., *Wages and Family Budgets in the Chicago Stockyards District* (Chicago, 1914), 14, 64.

26. For example, less than 7 percent of the Italian unemployed studied by the U.S. Department of Labor in 1895–96 relied totally on charity for survival. Of the upward of two hundred thousand men thrown out of work by the depression of 1893–94, only twenty thousand applied to the Central Relief Associatoin for aid, and only then after they had been out of work, on average, for five months. For details, see U.S. Department of Labor, *Ninth Special Report*, 29–30; *United States Industrial Commission Reports* 14 (1900): 165–66.

27. It is extremely difficult to judge the actual number of children at work in Chicago. The 1888 school census estimated that of the 199,631 children of school age in Chicago, only 89,578 (44.8 percent) were enrolled in public schools. A further 40,000 approximately (20 percent) were enrolled in parochial and denominational schools, 6,612 (3.3 percent) in other private schools, 7,802 (3.9 percent) in business colleges, leaving almost 60,000 (30.0 percent) children of school age not in school. It is impossible to say how many of these were at work, although presumably most were. It is not until 1903, when state law required children fourteen and over who left school to work to get an "age and school certificate," that it is possible to get some sense of the proportions involved. The following year, some 14,287 certificates were issued in Chicago. Ten years later, at the time of the 1914 school census, 14,854 work certificates were issued, representing 16.7 percent of the fourteen to sixteen age cohort. In 1919–20, 27,806 work certificates were issued, but six years later, the figure had dropped to 8,310. For further details, see Chicago Board of Education, *34th Annual Report, 1888*, 38–39; E. Abbott and S. Breckinridge, *Truancy and Non-attendance in the Chicago Schools* (New York, 1970), 307; M. F. Stone, "Child Labor in Chicago," *Chicago Schools Journal* 10, 2 (1927–28): 71.

28. Testimony of P. H. McLogan, *The Relations Between Labor and Capital*, 1: 575.

29. IBLS, *Report, 1884*, 269–70, 302, 359, 371.

30. Immigration Commission, *Reports*, 26–27: 318.

31. Ibid., 315–16, 319, 292.

32. E. L. Talbert, "Opportunities in School and Industry for Children of the Stockyards District," in *Readings in Vocational Guidance*, ed. M. Bloomfield (Boston, 1915), 403–5.

33. L. Montgomery, "The American Girl in the Stockyards District," in *Readings in Vocational Guidance,* ed. Bloomfield, 455, 473.

34. H. M. Todd, "Why Children Work, The Children's Answer," *McClure's Magazine* 40, 6 (April 1913), 69. Florence Kelley tells a similar story in *Hull House Maps and Papers:* "A typical example is the experience of a cloakmaker who began work at his machine in this yard at the age of fourteen years, and was found, after twenty years of temperate life and faithful work, living in a rear basement with four of his children apparently dying of pneumonia, at the close of a winter during which they had had, for weeks together, no food but bread and water, and had been four days without bread. The visiting nurse had two of the children removed to a hospital, and nursed the other two safely through their illness, feeding the entire family nearly four months. Place after place was found for the father; but he was too feeble to be of value to any sweater, and was constantly told that he was not worth the room he took up. A place being found for him in charge of an elevator, he could not stand; and two competent physicians, after a careful examination, agreed that he was suffering from old age. Twenty years at a machine had made him an old man at thirty-four" (Residents in Hull House, *Hull House Maps and Papers* [Boston, 1895], 37).

35. Todd, "Why Children Work," 69.

36. IBLS, *17th* Annual Report, 1914, 8; F. L. McCluer, "Living Conditions Among Wage Earning Families in 41 Blocks in Chicago, 1923" (Ph.D. dissertation, University of Chicago, 1928), 255–57.

37. G. H. Britton, *An Intensive Study of the Causes of Truancy in Eight Public Schools Including a Home Investigation of Eight Hundred Truant Children* (Chicago, 1906), 7–8.

38. Ibid., 12–13, 30–31.

39. Ibid., 31, 33.

40. Abbott and Breckinridge, *Truancy and Non-attendance,* 125, 129, 136.

41. Bodine to Olander, in Victor Olander Papers, box 8, Chicago Historical Society. Bodine also wrote elsewhere, "Poverty is one of the greatest foes of school attendance, and the cause of truancy in the majority of instances" (Chicago Board of Education, *65th Annual Report, 1909,* 173).

42. *Workingmans Advocate,* June 27–July 4, 1874. See also the issues of July 14, 1867, and August 29, 1868.

43. The relationship between home ownership and working-class culture and politics is discussed by Stephen Thernstrom in his *Poverty and Progress: Social Mobility in a Nineteenth Century City* (New York, 1972), chs. 5, 6, 7.

44. IBLS, *Second Biennial Report, 1882,* 288.

45. Derived from computer files on the 1900 census created for "The Organization of Work, Schools and Family Life in Philadelphia, 1838–1930" (University of Pennsylvania, Philadelphia), Michael Katz, principal investigator.

46. Montgomery, "The American Girl in the Stockyards District," 455–56.

47. The decline of boarding and lodging evident in these figures is intriguing. For Progressive reformers opposed the "lodger evil" and "overcrowding" and propagated the ideal of the lodger-free private household. It is unlikely that the privatization of the family resulted from the appeals of Progressive reformers, but its links with the creation of twentieth-century American family-centered and consumerist culture are tantalizing. Chicago census figures for 1930 suggest an

association between home ownership and privatization: The percentage of home-owners who took in boarders and lodgers was appreciably lower than the percentage of "tenant families" who did so. See U.S. Bureau of the Census, *15th Census, 1930. Population,* 6: 361. For further discussions of boarding and lodging, see J. Modell and T. Hareven, "Urbanization and the Malleable Household: An Examination of Boarding and Lodging in American Families," *Journal of Marriage and the Family* 35, 3 (August 1973): 467–79; B. Laslett, "The Family as a Public and Private Institution: An Historical Perspective," *Journal of Marriage and the Family* 35, 3 (August 1973): 480–92. On the private family and consumer culture, see S. Ewen, *Captains of Consciousness* (New York, 1976); on domestic architecture and privacy in Chicago, see G. Wright, *Moralism and the Model Home: Domestic Architecture and Cultural Conflict in Chicago, 1873–1913* (Chicago, 1980).

48. Both Katz and Perlman argue that one of the principal arguments of an earlier paper of mine ("Education and the Making of the Chicago Working Class, 1880–1930," *History of Education Quarterly* 18, 3 [Fall 1978], 227–70), that child labor contributed to the high levels of home ownership among the Chicago working class, rests upon spurious ecological associations derived from aggregate data. My data is clearly aggregate but neither the empirical results nor the arguments of Katz and Perlman convince me that my argument is unsound. First, my argument linked family income, child labor, and home ownership; the analyses of Katz and Perlman link father's occupation, school attendance, and home ownership. Head's occupation is not a good measure of head's income, let alone of family income; school attendance is not a good indirect measure of child labor, for as Katz and Dewey have noted elsewhere, school attendance among working-class children was not continuous but sporadically punctuated by bouts of child labor.

Second, their empirical results are quite consistent with my argument that child labor and home ownership are positively related. Katz, for example, found that among white families with male children thirteen and fourteen years old and freely owning or paying off a mortgage, 75 percent and 67 percent respectively of the children attended school in 1900. The percentage of thirteen- and fourteen-year-olds attending school from families who did not own their homes was far lower—47 percent. Among foreign-born thirteen- and fourteen-year-old male children, 69 percent and 68 percent of the children from families freely owning or paying off a mortgage attended school, while only 46 percent of thirteen- and fourteen-year-old foreign-born male children from families renting their homes attended school. In a multiple classification analysis of school attendance of thirteen- and fourteen-year-old males, Katz found that the beta for property ownership was easily the highest of all factors included in the model (place of birth, head's occupation, ownership of property, boarders and lodgers, head's literacy, family size, and head's employment record). In effect, all of Katz's results are perfectly consistent with my argument that *both* child labor and school attendance are associated with home ownership: The fact that school attendance and home ownership are strongly related by no means precludes a strong association between child labor and home ownership. (See M. Katz, "School Attendance in Philadelphia, 1850–1900," working paper, Organization of Schools, Work and Family Life in Philadelphia, 1838–1920 project, University of Pennsylvania, Philadelphia, December 1982, Tables 3B, 4A, 19A).

Third, Perlman admits that his measure of home ownership does not rule out the possibility that parents sent their children to work until the family had sufficient money saved to make a down payment on a home.

A good deal . . . hinges on when ownership was attained and how. If the process was completed before a particular child reached the age of 12 or 14, the struggle for ownership would not have involved sending him to work, and he might well have remained in school. Among families who did not own, on the other hand, many were probably struggling to purchase a home. In such families, the desire for home ownership might well have encouraged a resort to child labor. Perhaps, then, one should assume that the positive correlation between ownership and schooling . . . reflects the fact that homeowners no longer had to sacrifice for ownership, whereas a large proportion of non-owners, struggling to purchase a home were sending their children to work.

Indeed, some data he reports is consistent with such a conclusion: The children thirteen to sixteen years of age of fathers purchasing a home through mortgage payments were more than twice as likely to be at school than the children of non-owners (who presumably were at work, many of them to make possible a down payment at some later date), a relationship that held (indeed, was strengthened) when occupation and ethnicity were controlled. (See A. J. Perlmann, "Education and the Social Structure of an American City" [Ph.D. dissertation, Harvard University, 1980], II: 76).

49. U.S. Bureau of the Census, *15th Census, 1930. Population,* 6: 361. Among families with native-born heads with at least one parent of foreign parentage, the percentage was slightly lower (9.1 percent).

50. U.S. Bureau of the Census, *14th Census, 1920. Population,* 4: 801; idem, *15 Census, 1930. Abstract,* 383.

51. The Chicago Commission on Race Relations, *The Negro in Chicago* (Chicago, 1922), 205 and chs. 1, 2, 3, 5. See also C. S. Drake and H. B. Cayton, *Black Metropolis* (New York, 1945), ch. 8, esp. 178–80; and A. Spear, *Black Chicago* (Chicago, 1967), chs. 1, 11. The protective associations were by no means working-class organizations: They were often led (as in Hyde Park) by wealthy residents.

52. The Chicago Commission on Race Relations, *The Negro in Chicago,* chs. 1, 5, 11.

53. Todd, "Why Children Work," 74.

54. Immigration Commission, *Reports,* 29: 61, 92, 98.

55. L. F. Merrill, "A Report Concerning the Plans of 596 Children on Leaving Eighth Grade," *The Chicago Schools Journal* 5 (1922–23): 155. (Emphasis added.)

56. W. Thomas and F. Znaniecki, *The Polish Peasant in Europe and America* (Boston, 1920), 5: 46; *New World,* April 14, 1900; J. W. Sanders, *The Education of an Urban Minority* (New York, 1977), 57.

57. Sanders, *The Education of an Urban Minority,* ch. 4; T. M. Mulkerns, *Holy Family Parish* (Chicago, 1923); J. J. McGovern, "The Catholic Church in Chicago," *Souvenir of the Silver Jubilee* (Chicago, 1891); J. J. Thompson, *The Archdiocese of Chicago: Antecedents and Development* (Des Plaines, 1920); G. Garraghan, *The Catholic Church in Chicago, 1673–1871* (Chicago, 1921); C. J. Kirk-

fleet, *The Life of Patrick Augustine Feehan* (Chicago, 1922); P. Roberts, *The Problem of Americanization* (New York, 1920), 7, 12, 15, 20–21; H. Nelli, *Italians in Chicago* (New York, 1970), 181–98.

58. Thomas and Znaniecki, *The Polish Peasant*, 2: 364–65; J. Bodnar, "Materialism and Mortality: Slavic-American Immigrants and Education, 1890–1940," *The Journal of Ethnic Studies* 3, 4 (Winter 1976): 11.

59. S. J. Palickar, "The Slovaks of Chicago: With General Information on the Race and the Distribution of the Same," *Illinois Catholic Historical Review* 4, 2 (1921): 187, 194, 188.

60. See J. Bodnar, "Immigration and Modernization: The Case of Slavic Peasants in Industrial America," *Journal of Social History* 10, 1 (Fall 1976): 58; see also, P. Fox, *The Poles in America* (New York, 1922), 78; *Zogoda,* July 19, 1893; Bodnar, "Immigration," 50.

61. J. P. Grzemski, "Thrift Among the Poles," in *Poles of Chicago, 1837–1937* (Chicago, 1937), 184. Another estimate put the number of Polish *controlled* building and loan associations in 1928 at 115. See L. Magierski, "Polish American Activities in Chicago, 1919–1939" (M.A. thesis, University of Illinois, 1946), 23. For the Czech building and loan associations, see J. P. Reichman, *Czechoslovaks of Chicago: Contributions to a History of a National Group* (Chicago, 1937), 8–14.

62. Auditor of Public Accounts of Building, Loan and Homestead Associations of the State of Illinois, *Thirteenth Annual Report, 1904,* viii, ix.

63. E. Abbott and S. Breckinridge, *The Delinquent Child and the Home* (New York, 1970), 304.

64. Dziennik Zwiazkowy, May 25, 1909.

65. Ibid., June 16, 1909.

66. *Narod Polski,* June 23, 1909.

67. *Dziennik Zwiazkowy,* September 8, 1910.

68. Ibid., August 30, 1911.

69. Ibid., June 29, 1917.

70. *Polonia,* August 23, 1919.

71. *Przebudzenie,* November 6, 1927.

72. *Denni Hlastel,* September 11, 1915.

73. *Chicago Record Herald,* article cited by Sanders, *The Education of an Urban Minority,* 61; *Dziennik Zwiazkowy,* September 5, 1914.

74. *Dziennik Chicagoski,* May 27, 1904.

75. Thomas and Znaniecki, *The Polish Peasant in America,* 50.

76. This conceptualization of ethnic cultures in part parallels the notion of "emergent ethnicity" suggested by Ericksen, Yancey, and Juliani, but it reconceptualizes the notion in terms of class culture. See, W. L. Yancey, E. P. Ericksen, and R. N. Juliani, "Emergent Ethnicity: A Review and Reformation," *American Sociological Review* 41 (June 1976): 391–403. See also, K. N. Conzen, "Immigrants, Immigrant Neighborhoods, and Ethnic Identity: Historical Issues," *Journal of American History* 66, 3 (December 1979): 603–15.

77. Helen Day, cited in H. W. Zorbaugh, *The Gold Coast and the Slum: A Sociological Study of Chicago's Near North Side* (Chicago, 1929), 162–63. See also R. Vecoli, "Contadini in Chicago: A Critique of the Uprooted," *The Journal of American History* 51 (December 1964): 405–6.

78. Vecoli, "Contadini," 408.

79. L. Covello, *The Social Background of the Italio-American School Child* (Leiden, 1967), 274.

80. U.S. Commissioner of Labor, *Ninth Special Report. The Italians in Chicago, 1897,* 37.

81. L. F. Merrill, "A Report Concerning the Plans of 596 Children on Leaving Eighth Grade," *The Chicago Schools Journal* 5 (1922–23): 156.

82. G. Schiavo, *The Italians in Chicago: A Study in Americanization* (Chicago, 1928), 68.

83. Unhappily for the historian, Chicago's Jews have not produced the narrative histories and autobiographies that New York Jews, for instance, have. See Irving Howe's brilliant *Work of Our Fathers* (New York, 1976); Alfred Kazin, *A Walker in the City* (New York, 1951); Moses Rischin, *The Promised City: New York Jews, 1879–1914* (Cambridge, 1962); and John Higham, *Send These to Me* (New York, 1975). For Chicago's Jews see Phillip Bregstone's *Chicago and Its Jews* (Chicago, 1923); Louis Wirth, *The Ghetto* (Chicago, 1928); E. Mazur, "Jewish Chicago: From Diversity to Community," in *The Ethnic Frontier,* ed. M. Holli and P. Jones (Grand Rapids, 1977), 264–91; H. L. Meites, *History of the Jews of Chicago* (Chicago, 1924); and E. Rosenthal, "Accumulation Without Assimilation? The Jewish Community of Chicago, Illinois," *American Journal of Sociology* 66 (November 1960): 275–88.

84. Wirth, *The Ghetto,* 54.

85. Ibid., 91. As early as 1891, the Jewish press in Chicago positively evaluated the compulsory education law in Illinois. "The highest objective of the law is: send your children to school, take them off the streets, and if possible, take them out of the stores, shops and factories" (*The Reform Advocate,* February 20, 1891).

86. *Daily Jewish Courier,* March 18, 1914.

87. Ibid., September 4, 1916.

88. Ibid., March 18, 1914.

89. *Jewish Forward,* June 25, 1924.

90. See, for example, reports in the *Jewish Forward,* May 22 and June 15, 1924, June 8, 1928; *Daily Jewish Courier,* May 2, May 20, June 7, 1912; July 3, 1917; May 12, 1922; April 25, 1923; July 3, September 2, September 22, 1927; February 9, 1928; *Reform Advocate,* May 22, 1891; July 1, 1911; August 27, 1927; *Chicago Jewish Chronicle,* June 15, 1928; December 9, 1933; L. Wirth, "Culture Conflicts in the Immigrant Family" (Ph.D. dissertation, University of Chicago, 1925), 93.

91. Merrill, "A Report," 156.

92. Cited in M. Olneck and M. Lazerson, "The School Achievement of Immigrant Children, 1900–1930," *History of Education Quarterly* 14 (Winter 1974): 473.

93. On the ethnic differentiation of voluntary associations and saloons, see R. E. Roberts, "Ethnic Groups," in *Chicago Lutheran Planning Society,* ed. W. Kloetzle, vol. 1, pt. 2 (Chicago, 1963), 7, 9, 13, 15, 16, 21; Thomas and Znaniecki, 5: 38–46; Palickar, 188; E. C. Moore, "The Social Value of the Saloon," *American Journal of Sociology* 31 1 (1897): 8; idem, "Social Aspects of the Saloon in Great Cities—Chicago," in *Economic Aspects of the Liquor Problem,* ed. J. Koren (Boston, 1899); J. F. George, "The Saloon Question in Chicago," *Economic Studies* 2 (1897): 77; Bushnell, "Social Aspects of Chicago Stockyards," 305; R. Calkins, *Substitutes for the Saloon,* 2d ed., rev. (Boston, 1919), 9;

R. Melendy, "The Saloon in Chicago, I," *American Journal of Sociology* 6, 3 (1900): 293–94; idem, "The Saloon in Chicago, II," *American Journal of Sociology* 6, 4 (1901): 454. See also, P. Duis, "The Saloon in a Changing Chicago," *Chicago History*, Winter 1975–76, 220; W. T. Stead, *If Christ Came to Chicago* (Chicago, 1895), pt. 2, ch. 1. In a recent study of saloons in Chicago, Perry Duis wrote that what is significant about saloons "is the role that ethnic traditions played in the development of the saloon as a public place, for the ubiquity and adaptability that brought barrooms into so many varied social situations also made it an important part of almost every neighborhood. This could happen because each group modified the saloon to satisfy its own demands and used it for its own purposes. As a result, there was really no such thing as 'the saloon,' but rather, there were as many different kinds of saloons as there were neighborhoods" (Duis, "The Saloon and the Public City: Chicago and Boston, 1880–1920" [Ph.D. dissertation, University of Chicago, 1975], 591–92).

94. The distinction between "structural" and "cultural" embourgeoisement is a reworking of Milton Gordon's distinction between "cultural" and "structural" assimilation, although the meanings of Gordon's terms are quite different from mine. Gordon argues that immigrants in America have not been, by and large, structurally assimilated through intermarriage and the like, while they have been culturally assimilated (with respect to social behavior and language). See M. Gordon, *Assimilation in American Life* (New York, 1964).

95. As Addams pointed out, in exchange for votes at election, Powers gave coal to his constituents to stave off the bitter wind and cold, furnished bonds for ward residents charged with crimes, distributed food baskets or turkeys at Christmas, presents at weddings and christenings, supported church bazaars, sponsored ward dances, parades, and picnics, attended funerals, secured loans, and interceded with authorities to help his constituents get licenses and avoid fines, and secured jobs for those unemployed. At one time, Powers allegedly had twenty-six hundred people on the public payroll in a ward that contained only nine thousand registered voters. In return for these services, Powers asked for, and got, according to Jane Addams, "a sense of loyalty, a standing-by the man who is good to you, who understands you, and who gets you out of trouble." The fact that many politicians made a fat living out of politics bothered the immigrants not in the least. Jane Addams eventually realized that Johnny Powers "isn't elected because he is dishonest," but "because he is a friendly visitor." "An Italian laborer wants a 'job' more than anything else," she concluded, "and quite simply votes for the man who promises him one." See Jane Addams, "Why the Ward Boss Rules," *Outlook* 58 (April 2, 1898): 879; see also idem, "Ethical Survivals in Municipal Corruption," *International Journal of Ethics* 8 (April 1898): 289; idem, *Democracy and Social Ethics*, 239, 262–63; A. Davis, "Jane Addams vs. the Ward Boss," *Illinois State Historical Society Journal* 53 (1960): 256–57; H. Gosnell, *Machine Politics: Chicago Model* (Chicago, 1968), 39, 54, 73–74; J. Tarr, *A Study in Boss Politics: William Lorrimer of Chicago* (Urbana, 1971), 72, 373; Nelli, *Italians in Chicago*, 94–95.

CHAPTER FOUR: *The Triumph of Vocationalism*

1. Chicago Board of Education, *23rd Annual Report, 1877*, 1, 51–53, 55–56, 63–65.

2. Ibid., *30th Annual Report, 1884*, 52. See also idem, *33rd Annual Report, 1887*, 77.

3. During the 1840s and 1850s, common school reformers, most notably Horace Mann in his *Fifth Annual Report* in 1841, tried to persuade businessmen to support the common schools because the schools taught habits of industry and subordination desired in a good worker and would teach students to have proper regard for "the rights of person, property and character." In 1848 Mann also argued that education "beyond the power of diffusing old wealth . . . has the prerogative of creating new. It is a thousand times more lucrative than fraud; and adds a thousand fold more to a nation's resources than the most successful conquests; . . . education creates or develops new treasures" (cited in L. Cremin, ed., *The Republic and the School* [New York, 1957], 53, 88). Such claims differed from the kind of reforms introduced during the Progressive Era. Common school reformers merely argued that the common school had economic consequences of value to businessmen and to the nation at large; they did not try to justify the common schools, however, in these terms. They merely wished to persuade (Cremin describes Mann's Fifth Annual Report as "a masterful piece of salesmanship") businessmen of the valuable economic consequences of common schools. Reformers during the Progressive Era, however, explicitly justified their reforms in economic terms and rejected the specific political principle on which common school reformers had justified the common schools. Moreover, common school reformers made no attempt to vocationalize the common school's curriculum or pedagogy as the reformers of the Progressive Era did.

4. See, K. L. Kann, "Working Class Culture and the Labor Movement in Nineteenth Century Chicago" (Ph.D. dissertation, University of California, Berkeley, 1977), ch. 1.

5. S. B. Warner, *The Urban Wilderness* (New York, 1972), 93; R. Edwards, *Contested Terrain: The Transformation of the Workplace in the Twentieth Century* (New York, 1979), 28.

6. Warner, *The Urban Wilderness*, 93; Edwards, *Contested Terrain*, 23, 25, 27–28, 29, 43.

7. Derived from U.S. Bureau of the Census, *Fourteenth Census. Compendium for Illinois*, 171 (figures exclude Chicago Heights). See also, *Fifteenth Census, 1930. Manufacturing, 1929*, 3: 142, for statistics describing trends in Illinois between 1909 and 1929.

8. The best recent discussion of forms of labor control is Edwards, *Contested Terrain*.

9. E. Poole, *Giants Gone: Men Who Made Chicago* (New York, 1943), 94; W. T. Hutchinson, *Cyrus Hall McCormick*, 2 vols. (New York, 1930–35), 2: 485–87, 695–97; Kann, "Working Class Culture," 47; R. Ozanne, *A Century of Labor Management Relations at McCormick and International Harvester* (Madison, 1967), 3–28.

10. Testimony of the Reverend H. Newton, *Report of the Committee of Senate upon the Relations Between Labor and Capital* (Washington, D.C., 1885), 2: 549, 552. For a discussion of bureaucratic modes of control, see Edwards, *Contested Terrain*, ch. 8. Edwards seems to believe that bureaucratic control developed after World War II, but as Chandler has pointed out, it was common in large corporations by the late nineteenth century.

11. A. Chandler, *The Visible Hand: The Managerial Revolution in American Business* (Cambridge, Mass., 1977), 406–9.

12. C. W. Mills, *White Collar* (New York, 1956), 205–6. See also S. Aronwitz, *False Promises* (New York, 1974), ch. 6; M. Davies, "Women's Place Is

at the Typewriter: The Feminization of the Clerical Labor Force," *Radical America* 8, 4 (1974); H. Braverman, *Labor and Monopoly Capital* (New York, 1974), chs. 15, 16.

13. G. L. Coyle, "Women in the Clerical Occupations," *Annals of the American Academy of Political and Social Science* 143 (May 1929): 185.

14. F. J. Roethlisberger and W. I. Dickson, *Management and the Worker* (Cambridge, Mass., 1939), 10, 361–62.

15. Based on a comparison of the following industries for 1890 and 1930: agricultural implements, billiard tables, awnings and tents, blacksmithing, books, boots and shoes, bread, bricks and tiles, brass, brooms, carpeting, carriages and wagons, cars (railroad), men's clothing, women's clothing, drugs, electrical appliances, flour milling, food preparation, foundry and machine shop, furniture, gas, hardware, iron and steel, iron work, lamps, leather, liquors, lithographing, lumber, oil, oleomargarine, looking glass, mattresses, marble and stonework, masonry, musical instruments, paints, printing and publishing, saddlery, shipbuilding, slaughtering, soap, tinware, tobacco, type foundry, wire work. See the U.S. Bureau of the Census, *Eleventh Census, 1890. Compendium of the Eleventh Census,* 768–75; idem, *Fourteenth Census. Manufactures,* 9: 359–61; idem, *Fifteenth Census, 1930. Manufacturing, 1929,* 3: 158–59.

16. R. C. Edwards, M. Reich, D. M. Gordon, eds., *Labor Market Segmentation* (Lexington, Mass., 1975), ch. 1.

17. C. J. Bushnell, "Some Social Aspects of the Chicago Stock Yards," *American Journal of Sociology* 7, 2 (September 1901): 165–66.

18. D. Montgomery, "Workers' Control of Machine Production in the Nineteenth Century," *Labor History* 17, 4 (Fall 1976): 487.

19. Ibid.; A. Dawley, *Class and Community: The Industrial Revolution in Lynn, Massachusetts* (Cambridge, Mass., 1976), ch. 1, 23; B. Laurie, *Class and Culture* (Philadelphia, 1980), ch. 1; S. Hirsch, *Roots of the American Working Class* (Philadelphia, 1978), chs. 1, 2, 3; Braverman, *Labor and Monopoly Capital,* chs. 1–10; K. Stone, "The Origins of Job Structures in the Steel Industry," in *Labor Market Segmentation,* ed. Edwards, Reich, Gordon, ch. 2; D. Brody, *Steelworkers in America* (New York, 1960); N. Ware, *Labor in Modern Industrial Society* (New York, 1968); S. Giedon, *Mechanization Takes Command* (New York, 1969).

20. Economic historians have long debated the sources of America's high level of technological innovation during the nineteenth and twentieth centuries. The most popular hypothesis—the impact of labor scarcity specifically and the pecularities of America's factor supply conditions generally—was first systematically outlined by H. J. Habakkuk, *American and British Technology in the Nineteenth Century* (Cambridge, 1967), ch. 4; for recent restatements of the hypothesis, see P. A. David, *Technical Choice, Innovation and Economic Growth* (Cambridge, Mass., 1975), ch. 1; N. Rosenberg, *Technology and American Economic Growth* (New York, 1972); E. Mansfield, *Technological Change* (New York, 1971). While the general influence of factor supply conditions should not be discounted entirely, if one examines concrete processes of technological innovation, two other factors seem more salient: (1) class competition between capitalists for markets, which forces them to innovate in order to lower per unit costs and increase their input-output ratios (productivity), and (2) class conflict with labor over the nature and control of the labor process, since unless capital controlled the labor process it could not innovate when it needed—or desired—to.

21. Derived from the U.S. Bureau of the Census, *Tenth Census of the United*

States, 1880. Compendium of the Tenth Census, 146, 1,051; idem, *Fourteenth Census, 1920. Manufacturers,* 9; 359–65. The price index used to calculate 1920 prices was derived from series F 1-5 price index, "Gross National Product, Total and Per Capita, in Current and 1958 Prices: 1869 to 1970," in U.S. Department of Commerce, *Historical Statistics of the United States* (Washington, D.C., 1975), pt. 1, F 1-9. The same industries were used as listed in note 15.

22. Taylorism, strictly speaking, involved three principles: the reduction of the opportunity for the worker to exercise skill; separation of conception and execution; and the use of this monopoly of knowledge to control each step of the labor process. In effect, it was a "science of management" of the labor process, although in the hands of Hugo Munsterberg, Ethon Mayo, and the human relations school of industrial psychology, it also developed into a "science of control" of the labor force. It is very difficult to know how widely scientific management in either guise was adopted—the evidence suggests the greater popularity of the science of control. See Braverman, *Labor and Monopoly Capital,* pt. 1; S. Haber, *Efficiency and Uplift* (Chicago, 1964); L. Baritz, *Servants of Power* (New York, 1965); M. Burgwoy, "Toward a Marxist Theory of the Labor Process: Braverman and Beyond," *Politics and Society* 8, 3–4 (1978): 279–82; and D. Nelson, *Managers and Workers: Origins of the New Factory System in the United States, 1880–1920* (Madison, 1975); Edwards, *Contested Terrain.*

23. *Chicago Tribune,* March 26, 1890, 3.

24. H. Leech and J. C. Carroll, *Armour and His Times* (New York, 1938), ch. 1.

25. D. Brody, *The Butcher Workman: A Study of Unionization* (Cambridge, Mass., 1964), 15.

26. H. D. Call to F. Morrison, February 20, 1899, AFC Papers, Washington, D.C., cited in W. Tuttle, "Labor Conflict and Racial Violence: The Black Worker in Chicago, 1894–1919," *Labor History* 10 (Summer 1969): 412.

27. J. R. Commons, "Labor Conditions in Meat Packing and the Recent Strike," *Quarterly Journal of Economics* 19 (November 1904): 3–4. See also, H. E. Wilson, *Mary McDowell, Neighbor* (Chicago, 1940), 73–74.

28. Illinois Bureau of Labor Statistics (hereafter IBLS), *Report, 1892,* 362–63. See also F. Kelley, "The Sweating System," in *Hull House Maps and Papers* (New York, 1970), 27–45; N. M. Auten, "Some Phases of the Sweating System in the Garment Trades in Chicago," *American Journal of Sociology* 6 (July–May, 1900–01): 602–45.

29. R. R. Albertson, "The Decay of Apprenticeship and Corporation Schools," *Charities and Commons* 19 (October 1907): 815.

30. U.S. Bureau of Labor, *Conditions of Entrance to the Principal Trades,* by W. E. Weyl and A. M. Sakolski, bulletin no. 67, November 1906 (Washington, D.C., 1907), 686.

31. R. J. Myers, *The Economic Aspects of the Production of Men's Clothing* (Chicago, 1937), 12.

32. IBLS, *Report, 1892,* 385–86, 388.

33. For details, see G. Wright, *Moralism and the Model Home: Domestic Architecture and Cultural Conflict in Chicago, 1873–1913* (Chicago, 1980), 174–75.

34. Testimony of P. H. McLogan, *Report of the Senate Committee upon the Relations Between Labor and Capital* (Washington, D.C., 1885), 1: 568.

35. Federal Trade Commission, *Report on the Agricultural Implement and Machine Industry* (Washington, D.C., 1938), 105.

36. M. L. Stecker, "The Founders, The Molders, and the Molding Machine," in *Trade Unionism and Labor Problems*, ed. J. R. Commons (Boston, 1921), 434.

37. Ozanne, *A Century of Labor*, 26–27.

38. Ibid., 27–28, 69, 181, 242.

39. Bureau of Labor, *Conditions of Entrance to the Principal Trades*, 738–39.

40. M. L. Stecker, "The Founders, The Molders, and the Molding Machine," in *Trade Unionism and Labor Problems*, ed. J. R. Commons (Boston, 1921), 438, 435, 437, 441, 451, 455.

41. Ibid., 455.

42. Federal Trade Commission, *Report on the Agricultural Implement and Machine Industry*, 18; Stecker, "The Founders," 453–54.

43. J. Fitch, *The Steel Worker* (New York, 1968), 139–41.

44. U.S. Labor Bureau, *Report on Conditions of Employment in the Iron and Steel Industry in the United States* (Washington, D.C., 1913), 3: 109.

45. Ibid., 81. See also, J. C. Kennedy, *Wages and Family Budgets in the Chicago Stockyards District* (Chicago, 1914), 50–57; J. M. Gillette, *Culture Agencies of a Typical Manufacturing Group: South Chicago* (Chicago, 1901), 27–31.

46. P. Douglas, "American Apprenticeship and Industrial Education," *Columbia University Studies in History, Economics, and Public Law* 92, 2 (1921): 114–16.

47. Ibid., 111, 113–14, 117–19. But while it may have been true that in the 1920s repairmen were highly skilled, subsequent evidence suggests that shortly thereafter even these occupations were subject to the process of "deskilling." James R. Bright's extensive research in the 1960s led him to assert that "automation had reduced the skill requirements of the operating work force, and occasionally of the entire factory force, including the maintenance organization." He found that while in many cases maintenance requirements demanded new skills, there were a significant number of counter-examples, which raised strong doubts as to whether even repairmen, who in any case are always a very small proportion of a factory labor force, needed higher skills. So even the "labor aristocrat," the most highly skilled worker in the new labor process, has been deprived of most of the skill that craftsmen once possessed.

Unlike the skilled artisan possessing control over access to the trade and work practice, the labor aristocrat, stripped of craft control, was transformed into a relatively highly paid pacesetter for semiskilled and unskilled workers, for example, as the floorman and splitter in the meatpacking industry, the cutter in the clothing industry, or as repairmen, foremen, and sub-bosses. The existence of this small group—skilled workers, without control of the labor process and lacking the generalized knowledge of the overall production process that skilled workers previously possessed—was testimony to the effectiveness of capitalism in destroying the skill levels of the craft production process. See J. R. Bright, "The Relationship of Increasing Automation and Skill Requirements," in National Commission on Technology, Automation, and Economic Progress, *The Employment Impact of Technological Change* (Washington, D.C., 1966), 11–208; and Braverman, *Labor and Monopoly Capital*, ch. 9.

48. Figures for 1880 based on U.S. Bureau of the Census, *Tenth Census, 1880. Population*, 1: 870; for 1930, E. H. Bernett, "The Chicago Labor Force, 1910–1940" (Ph.D. dissertation, University of Chicago, 1949), app. E1, E2.

49. F. Tannenbaum, *The Labor Movement* (New York, 1921), 59–60.

50. Testimony of J. C. Kennedy, Commission on Industrial Relations, *Industrial Relations* (Washington, D.C., 1916), 4: 3, 479.

51. J. C. Kennedy, *Wages and Family Budgets*, 6.

52. Bureau of Labor, *Conditions of Entrance into the Principal Trades*, 692.

53. Fitch, *The Steel Worker;* see also, Stone, "The Origins of Job Structures in the Steel Industry"; Brody, *Steelworkers in America*, 31–32.

54. T. Veblen, *Theory of Business Enterprise* (New York, 1904), 308.

55. A. D. Dean, *The Worker and the State: A Study of Education for Industrial Workers* (New York, 1910), 166, 168.

56. Testimony of Horace Eaton, *Industrial Relations*, 1: 363.

57. Testimony of J. G. Shedd, *Industrial Relations*, 4: 3,375.

58. Douglas, "American Apprenticeship and Industrial Education"; J. Kett, *Rites of Passage* (New York, 1977), ch. 6.

59. Douglas, "American Apprenticeship and Industrial Education," 116.

60. Bureau of Labor, *Conditions of Entrance into the Principal Trades*, 707–8. For a similar analysis, see Dean, *The Worker and the State*, 167–68.

61. Chicago Board of Education *23rd Annual Report, 1877*, 1, 51–53, 55–56, 63–66; *25th Annual Report, 1879*.

62. Citizens Association of Chicago, *Report, 1881*, 17.

63. *Chicago Tribune*, May 1, 1915, June 5, 1912, July 10 and October 25, 1881; C. H. Ham, *Manual Training: The Solution of Social and Industrial Problems* (New York, 1886), 340.

64. Chicago Board of Education, *28th Annual Report, 1882*, 21–23.

65. Chicago Board of Education, *29th Annual Report, 1883*, 29, 46; *27th Annual Report, 1881*, 27; *29th Annual Report, 1883*, 27; *28th Annual Report, 1882*, 51; *29th Annual Report, 1883*, 32; *28th Annual Report, 1882*, 21–23; *29th Annual Report, 1883*, 29; and *31st Annual Report, 1885*, 28.

66. C. H. Ham, *Manual Training: The Solution of Social and Industrial Problems* (New York, 1886), 340; *Chicago Tribune*, March 27, 1882. The board of trustees of the school consisted of E. W. Blatchford, R. T. Crane, Marshall Field, William Fuller, John Creror, John Doane, N. K. Fairbank, Edison Keith, and George Pullman.

67. Report of the Commission on Industrial Education made to the legislature of Pennsylvania, Harrisburg, 1889, 89. Emphasis in the original.

68. Chicago Board of Education, *21st Annual Report, 1885*, 29–30, 64–66; *29th Annual Report, 1883*, 58–60; *Proceedings*, March 10, 1886, 127; ibid., June 2, 1886, 179; ibid., 180; and *32nd Annual Report, 1886*, 57, 7, 18, 21; *33rd Annual Report, 1887*, 25–26.

69. Chicago Board of Education, *34th Annual Report, 1888*, 79–80; *36th Annual Report, 1890*, 52; *37th Annual Report, 1891*, 123; *38th Annual Report, 1892*, 51. For a further example of the "people's demand" theory, see *40th Annual Report, 1894*, 18.

70. Idem, *37th Annual Report, 1891*, 123–26; see also *38th Annual Report, 1892*, 52, 164–67; *39th Annual Report, 1893*, 120–22; *40th Annual Report, 1894*, 42–44.

71. Idem, *34th Annual Report, 1888*, 84–85, 80–81; *35th Annual Report, 1889*, 50.

72. Idem, *33rd Annual Report, 1887*, 25–26.

73. Ibid., 26, 29, 27, 30–31, 39–41, 85; idem, *34th Annual Report, 1888*, 23–25, 27, 39–41.

74. Chicago Board of Education, *38th Annual Report, 1892*, 58; *44th Annual Report, 1898*, 60; *40th Annual Report, 1894*, 41.

75. Crane was not the only capitalist actively to support manual training. In 1893 the *Chicago Evening Post*, owned at that time by John R. Walsh, equipped a room for manual training in the Jones School. In 1896, Cyrus McCormick, who, according to Superintendent Lane, "has become greatly interested in the extension of this part of our educational work," equipped the Hammond School in the industrial southwest portion of the city, enabling manual training classes to be taught to boys from Hammond, Lawndale, Farragut, and the Howland Schools. And in 1914 George Pullman replicated the establishment of the CMTS by establishing, in the township of Pullman at a cost of $1.25 million, an independent manual training high school having seven departments: cabinetmaking, foundry, patternmaking, blacksmithing, and machine- and toolmaking. For further details, see Chicago Board of Education, *Proceedings*, July 9, 1902, to June 24, 1903, 265; *Proceedings*, July 1, 1908, to July 7, 1909, 562; and *InterOcean*, January 9, 1912, 1. In 1906 Crane offered to help the CMTS financially by purchasing on its behalf necessary tools, benches, machines, etc. See, *Chicago Record Herald*, January 7, 1906, 8; Chicago Board of Education, *51st Annual Report, 1896*, 68–69; *Chicago Tribune*, February 18, 1914, 15.

76. Chicago Board of Education, *41st Annual Report, 1895*, 228–30, 66–68.

77. Idem, *43rd Annual Report, 1897*, 17–18, 55; *44th Annual Report, 1898*, 63; *47th Annual Report, 1901*, 16, 103–4; *51st Annual Report, 1905*, 120; *55th Annual Report, 1909*, 145.

78. Idem, *50th Annual Report, 1904*, 23, 113–15.

79. Idem, *55th Annual Report, 1909*, 18.

80. Idem, *39th Annual Report, 1892*, 53; *Proceedings*, July 6, 1892, to July 5, 1893, 444; *44th Annual Report, 1898*, 56–57; *59th Annual Report, 1913*, 227–30; *65th Annual Report, 1919*, 29–32; *Chicago Record*, May 13, 1898, 8; and August 6, 1898, 4.

81. H. S. Tibbits, "The Progress and Aims of Domestic Science in the Public Schools of Chicago," National Education Association, *Addresses and Proceedings* (1901): 258; Chicago Board of Education, *65th Annual Report, 1919*, 29–32; Survey of the Schools of Chicago, G. D. Strayer, Director, *Report* (New York, 1932), 3: 223.

82. Chicago Board of Education, *56th Annual Report, 1910*, 84; *57th Annual Report, 1911*, 93; *58th Annual Report, 1912*, 162–63.

83. Idem, *57th Annual Report, 1911*, 93; Gillette, *Culture Agencies*, 45; Tibbits, "Domestic Science," 259.

84. Idem, *26th Annual Report, 1881*, 29; *31st Annual Report, 1885*, 30.

85. Idem, *40th Annual Report, 1894*, 43; *42nd Annual Report, 1886*, 28–32; *43rd Annual Report, 1897*, 19–20; *44th Annual Report, 1898*, 22–26.

86. Idem, *45th Annual Report, 1899*, 17–19, 146–47, 165–66; Educational Commission of the City of Chicago, W. R. Harper, Chairman, *Report* (Chicago, 1899), 107–11, 204–17. C. H. Thurber, "Is the Present High School Course a Satisfactory Preparation for Business? If Not, How Should it be Modified?" National Education Association, *Addresses and Proceedings* (1897): 808–18. Jane Addams came to a similar conclusion about the businessmen's attitude toward education. What the businessmen wanted, she paraphrased, was for the schools to "teach the children to write legibly, and to figure accurately and quickly; to acquire

habits of punctuality and order; to be prompt to obey and not question why; and you will fit them to make their way in the world as I have made mine" (J. Addams, *Democracy and Social Ethics* [New York, 1920], 191.

87. Chicago Board of Education, *46th Annual Report, 1900,* 206; *47th Annual Report, 1901,* 82–83; *48th Annual Report, 1902,* 49–50; *50th Annual Report, 1904,* 22–23; *Chicago Record,* February 2, 1901, 72; *Chicago Record Herald,* November 11, 1908, 6; Chicago Board of Education, *55th Annual Report, 1909,* 21; *Chicago Record Herald,* December 2, 1909; P. Sola, "Plutocrats, Pedagogues and Plebes: Business Influences on Vocational Education and Extracurricular Activities in the Chicago High Schools, 1899–1925." (Ph.D. dissertation, University of Illinois, 1972), 128–29.

88. Chicago Board of Education, *56th Annual Report, 1910,* 8.

89. Essentially, in advocating and securing the introduction of a differentiated education, reformers succeeded in institutionalizing a stratified system of education consistent with liberal conceptions of equal opportunity and a market-based class system.

90. Chicago Board of Education, *27th Annual Report, 1881,* 27; *Chicago Record,* September 29, 1900, 4.

91. Chicago Board of Education, *57th Annual Report, 1911,* 24; *54th Annual Report, 1908,* 288; R. E. Blount, "Pupils Lost from Ninth Grade," *Educational Bi-Monthly* 2, 4 (1908): 369.

92. Chicago Association of Commerce, *Industrial and Commercial Education in Relation to Conditions in the City of Chicago* (Chicago, 1909), 4–6, 9; "Professional Comment on the Subject Matter of Chicago's Problem of Industrial Education," *Chicago Commerce,* December 24, 1909, 18. In its "Professional Comment," the association acknowledged that "the parents of this pamphlet are the Board of Education and the Association of Commerce" (17). The association made detailed plans for the distribution of the report. Some ten thousand copies were made and distributed to each member of the association; to the superintendent of schools, assistant and district superintendents, every supervisor, and each member of the board of education; to the mayor and every member of city council; to the principal of every private school in the city; to the public libraries; to the presidents of every college and university, and each settlement house; to the daily, weekly, and monthly press, and twenty-five periodicals published outside the city; and to thirty leading citizens.

Clearly, the association did not take its responsibilities lightly. Nor did it cease to do so. In 1914 it established an elaborate system of Civic Industrial Clubs in Chicago's high schools, gave considerable publicity to Edwin Cooley's findings on vocational education in Europe (gathered by Cooley on a trip to Europe funded by the Commercial Club), strongly supported the efforts of the Commercial Club to introduce a dual system of vocational education in Illinois—the Cooley Bill controversy—and took a leading role in the introduction of vocational guidance into Chicago's schools. For a detailed account of the Civic Industrial Clubs, see Sola, "Plutocrats, Pedagogues and Plebes," ch. 6; for the association's efforts to publicize Cooley's investigations, see "Edwin G. Cooley, Investigator for Commercial Club on German Industrial Training," *Chicago Commerce,* October 6, 1911, 18–22; and "Edwin G. Cooley Explains His Foreign Mission for Chicago Boy Who is Not Given Best Start in Public School," *Chicago Commerce,* June 17, 1910, 27–32.

93. City Club of Chicago, *A Report on Vocational Training in Chicago and in Other Cities* (Chicago, 1912), v–vi. For a similar analysis of the report, see P. Violas, *Training of the Urban Working Class* (Chicago, 1978), 2–3, 29–30, 31–32, ch. 6.

94. City Club, *Report*, 4; see also 32, 6, 7, 8, 10.

95. *The Bulletin*, November 16, 1906, 12–13; "How Europe's Commercial Nations Extend Foreign Trade" *(London Times)*, in *Chicago Commerce*, March 27, 1908, 11–22.

96. "Industrial Education—Industrial Supremacy," *Chicago Commerce*, January 24, 1908, 3, 8, 21–22, 23; "Ways and Means Committee Considers Commercial Education," *Chicago Commerce*, April 17, 1908, 1; "Ways and Means Committee Hears Philosophy and Practice of Industrial Education," *Chicago Commerce*, September 25, 1908, 9–10.

97. E. G. Cooley, "Industrial Education: Report on Investigation of Industrial Education in Europe," The Commercial Club of Chicago, *Year-Book, 1911–1912*, 96, 135; "Edwin G. Cooley, Investigator for Commercial Club on German Industrial Training," 18–22. Cooley's full analyses are contained in his *Some Continuation Schools of Europe* (Chicago, 1912).

98. T. W. Robinson, "The Need of Industrial Education in our Public Schools," National Education Association, *Addresses and Proceedings* (1910): 369–73. Three years later, Robinson published a pamphlet in which he elaborated on these ideas, "The Need of Vocational Education" (Chicago, 1913), 7–8.

99. City Club of Chicago, *A Report on Vocational Training*, 46–47, 65.

100. Ibid., 258, 259, 260, 261, 262, 263.

101. Ibid., 14.

102. Ibid., 98, 41.

103. Ibid., 7–8. Later in the report, the committee differentiated between manual training and vocational education in this manner: "A distinction is made throughout this report between manual training and industrial training, in the sense that the latter aims primarily and definitely at preparation for industrial vocations, whereas the former aims at the general education of the individual, through the hand, whatever his vocation is to be. . . . The term industrial training, however, is reserved for those courses which lay definite hold upon the vocational motive of pupils, which give more time to handwork than manual training courses give, and which sooner or later provide specialized and intensive training for industrial pursuits" (28).

Likewise, in the draft of a vocational bill that was designed to serve as an alternative to the Cooley Bill, the City Club defined vocational education as "any instruction, the controlling purpose of which is to fit for profitable employment" (Chicago City Club, *Bulletin*, 1912, 377).

104. City Club of Chicago, *A Report on Vocational Training*, 7, 14.

105. W. B. Owen, "The Educational Value of the High School Commercial Course," National Education Association, *Addresses and Proceedings* (1912): 105 (emphasis in the original). See also J. T. McManis, "Psychology of Industrial Courses in Sixth, Seventh, and Eight Grades," *Educational Bi-Monthly* 10, 2 (December 1915): 99; E. G. Cooley, "The Gospel of Work," National Education Association, *Addresses and Proceedings* (1901): 199–201; J. L. Stockton, "The Project, Work, and Democracy," *American Schools Journal* 5 (1972–73): 186; C. A. Prosser and C. R. Allen, *Vocational Education in a Democracy* (New York,

1925), 194–97; and for a survey of these changes nationally, see Violas, *Training*, ch. 7.

106. F. M. Leavitt, *Examples of Industrial Education* (Boston, 1912), 1–2. See also his "Some Sociological Phases of the Movement for Industrial Education," National Education Association, *Addresses and Proceedings* (1912): 921–26; and "Vocational Education for Illinois," *City Club Bulletin*, May 18, 1915, 105. Leavitt by this time had succeeded Mead as chairman of the City Club's committee on schools. Other educators in Chicago developed similar arguments. Rufus Hitch, a district superintendent, emphasized the importance of vocational education to "wage earners"; two other district superintendents, G. E. English and W. C. Dodge, did likewise. Helen Todd, a factory inspector, emphasized the tyranny of teachers over children as a critical factor propelling children out of schools. See Chicago Board of Education, *58th Annual Report, 1915,* 83; and H. M. Todd, "Why Children Work: The Children's Answer," *McClure's Magazine* 40, 6 (April 1913): 75–76.

107. W. S. McKinney, "A Partial Forecast of the Report of Committee on Research Standardization and Correlation," National Education Association, *Addresses and Proceedings* (1912): 1,034. See also, G. H. Mead, "Industrial Education, the Working Man, and the School," *The Elementary School Teacher* (March 1909): 370–72; S. R. Smith, "The Cosmopolitan High School," *The Elementary School Teacher* 8, 10 (1908): 606; Cooley, "The Adjustment of the School System," 5–7; Chicago Board of Education, *55th Annual Report, 1909,* 18–20; idem, *57th Annual Report, 1911,* 25; idem *58th Annual Report, 1912,* 19, 109; idem, *59th Annual Report, 1913,* 112–33; idem, *61st Annual Report, 1915,* 85. At the annual conferences of the NEA throughout the first decade of the century, delegates heard similar sentiments time and again. See, for example, C. F. Warner, "Education for the Trades in America—What Can Technical High Schools Do for It?" (1901): 665–73; A. S. Draper, "The Adaptation of the Schools to Industry and Efficiency" (1908): 65–78; "Report of the Committee on the Place of Industries in Public Education" (1910): 652–777; L. D. Harvey (president's address), "The Need, Scope, and Character of Industrial Education in the Public School System" (1909): 49–70; C. C. Pearse, "The City Trade School—An Important Instrumentality for Improving the Vocational Need of the City Child" (1912): 411–16; F. D. Cramshaw, "Needed Changes in Industrial Arts" (1912): 932–34; C. G. Pearse, "Vocational Education and the Labor Problem" (1915): 828–32.

Finally, during the 1920s and 1930s in Chicago, the marriage of individual differences and vocational education was celebrated anew every year. For the 1920s, for example, see "Equality of Opportunity for Education," *Chicago Schools Journal* 5 (1922–23): 385–88; and from the same journal, F. W. Weck, "The Elimination of Waste in Education" 7 (1924–25): 201–3; R. H. Rodgers, "How Can Vocational Schools Provide for Individual Differences?" 7 (1924–25): 208–13; A. I. Stoddard, "Adaptation of Individualized Instruction to a Small High School System" 8 (1925–26): 87–91; F. L. Gjesdahl, "Type Adjustments to Individualized Instruction" 8 (1925–26): 96–99; and J. H. Henery, "Individual Advancement and Instruction under Chicago Conditions" 8 (1925–26): 100–103.

108. Chicago Board of Education, *41st Annual Report, 1895.* See also W. B. Owen, "The Educational Value of the High School Commercial Course," National Education Association, *Addresses and Proceedings* (1912): 1,051–56.

109. E. G. Cooley, "Continuation of Schools," National Education Association, *Addresses and Proceedings* (1912): 1,206; idem, "Professor Dewey's Criticism of the Chicago Commercial Club and Its Vocational Educational Bill," *Vocational Education* 3 (September 1913): 25; idem, "Public School Education in Morals," *Educational Bi-Monthly* 1 (1906–07): 80–81. So impressed was Cooley with the importance of the habit of industry in particular that he believed that while "slavery was wrong . . . whatever else it did or did not do, it compelled the acquisition of habits of industry in the slaves and marked a step in advance over the previous condition of savagery." Indeed, Cooley's only criticism of slavery was that "the slave did his own work from fear of punishment and not from a desire to do something for his own sake." Cooley likened children to "savages" and believed both needed "to be trained to habits of industry" or "systematic and thorough going habits of work" in preparation for life in modern civilization.

110. Commercial Club of Chicago, *Year Book, 1911–1912,* 278; Robinson, "The Need of Vocational Education," 10. See also his contribution to a book produced by the Commercial Club, *The Merchants Club of Chicago, 1895–1906* (Chicago, 1922), 118. See also H. E. Miles's, of the National Association of Manufacturers, discussion of industrial education in the National Education Association, *Addresses and Proceedings* (1912): 964; and A. J. Todd, "The Public and the Consumer," National Society for Vocational Education, *Bulletin*, no. 32, 1920, 9, 13. In order to demonstrate the economic advantages of vocational training to Chicago's youth, the City Club's committee went to considerable trouble to collect statistics that purportedly demonstrated the economic value of vocational education. The idea, of course, was not new; in 1887 President Allan Story articulated an early prototype of the theory of human capital in attempting to find a justification for manual training: "The remedy for the condition of the poor and destitute lies in training their brains together with their hands" he observed. "Skilled hands and trained brains increase the capacity of the individual to earn—to add to the wealth of himself and the State." Likewise in 1909, the Association of Commerce in its report on *Industrial and Commercial Education* provided statistics that compared the earning power of different grades of labor as a means of providing the economic advantages to the individual of industrial education. The City Club, in its report, cited statistics indicating, for example, that workers with only on-the-job training received sixteen dollars a week at age twenty-one, whereas workers of the same age with trade school training received twenty dollars a week. Nor was this the last effort to demonstrate the "economic efficiency from the point of view of the individual" of industrial education. At the 1912 NEA convention, two papers were given on the economic rewards of industrial education; in 1915 Theodore Robinson, vice-president of Illinois Steel and a leading figure in the education committee of the Commercial Club, estimated that four years in practical training in agriculture or the trades would increase the earning power of individuals by twenty cents a day, or $1.5 million for the nation as a whole; in 1917, a bulletin published by the U.S. Bureau of Education counted over 120 studies that had attempted to document the "money value of education"; and in 1920 Valentina Denton, a teacher at Parker High School, attempted to prove that the fact that the average weekly salary of a group of Parker High girl graduates had increased between 1915–16 and 1920 was a consequence of the girls having taken shorthand while at school. See City Club of Chicago, *A Report on Vocational Training,* 232 (see also 233–37); Pearse, "The City Trade School,"

415; J. H. Beveridge, "Efficiency in the Business Department of the High School," National Education Association, *Addresses and Proceedings* (1912): 1,037–43; Commercial Club of Chicago, *Year-Book, 1914–1915,* 199; A. C. Ellis, *The Money Value of Education,* Bulletin No. 22, Bureau of Education (Washington, D.C., 1917); V. J. Denton, "The Value of Shorthand to Parker High School Graduates of 1915 and 1916," *The Chicago Schools Journal* 3 (1920–21): 78–80.

111. C. B. Connelley, "Citizenship in Industrial Education," National Education Association, *Addresses and Proceedings* (1912): 900, 906.

112. F. M. Leavitt, "Some Sociological Phases of the Movement for Industrial Education," National Education Association, *Addresses and Proceedings, 1912,* 922, 925; "Edwin G. Cooley, Investigator for Commercial Club on German Industrial Training," 19; E. G. Cooley, *Vocational Education in Europe* (Chicago, 1912), 329.

113. Addams, *Democracy and Social Ethics,* 185–89, 193, 195.

114. Ibid., 203; idem, *The Spirit of Youth and the City Streets* (New York, 1909), 126–27; idem, "Social Education of the Industrial Democracy," *Charities and Commons,* June 30, 1900, 2.

115. J. Adams, *Twenty Years* (New York, 1910), 172–77; idem, *Democracy and Social Ethics,* 213, 219; idem, *The Spirit of Youth,* 126–27. The difficulty of this approach to industrial education was that it was, at the very least, as she herself realized, "a difficult idealization." More accurately, it was self-defeating. She could hardly insist, on the one hand, that machines and the organization of work *caused* worker alienation, and, on the other, expect that "socialized education" alone could eliminate it. The source of this difficulty was that her analysis of the sources of worker alienation placed her in a double bind, since she could hardly support a radical restructuring of the labor process. To do that would entail class conflict, and class conflict was the enemy of social democracy. Out of this fear, she pulled back from the implications of her own analysis and chose instead an educational strategy that dealt, even on her own account, with symptoms, not causes. In a very real sense, Addams's approach to industrial education represented a triumph of liberal ideology over indignation and compassion. For further discussion, see C. Lasch, *The New Radicalism in America* (New York, 1965), 13–14; idem, *The Social Thought of Jane Addams* (New York, 1965), 106; A. Davis, *American Heroine* (New York, 1973), 154–55.

116. Chicago Board of Education, *57th Annual Report, 1911,* 24–25, 88; *58th Annual Report, 1912,* 19.

117. City Club, *A Report on Vocational Training,* 108.

118. Chicago Board of Education, *60th Annual Report, 1914,* 308–11.

119. Idem, *61st Annual Report, 1915,* 85.

120. Idem, *59th Annual Report, 1913,* 247–70.

121. R. W. Kelly, *Training Industrial Workers* (New York, 1920), 94.

122. City Club, *A Report on Vocational Training,* 83–84; Leavitt, *Examples,* 156–57, 171–73; Chicago Board of Education, *59th Annual Report, 1913,* 259; Survey of the Schools of Chicago, *Report,* 3, 208.

123. Chicago Board of Education, *58th Annual Report, 1912,* 107, 82.

124. Idem, *57th Annual Report, 1911,* 90.

125. City Club, *A Report on Vocational Training,* 85, 89, 93, 94.

126. Chicago Board of Education, *58th Annual Report, 1912,* 119–23, 109–12, 163, 249.

127. Idem, *59th Annual Report, 1913,* 254–57.

128. Ibid., 247.

129. Idem, *60th Annual Report, 1914,* 333; see also, *61st Annual Report, 1915,* 122–23.

130. "New Educational Plan," *Chicago Commerce,* June 28, 1912, 6.

131. *Chicago Record Herald,* June 21, 1912, 5; June 24, 1912, 8; "Review of the Week," *Chicago Commerce,* September 6, 1912, 1; "Committee on Commercial Courses," *Chicago Commerce,* September 20, 1912, 10.

132. "Association Aids Board of Education to Plan Improvements in Commercial Training in High Schools," *Chicago Commerce,* October 23, 1912, 1, 34; *Chicago Record Herald,* October 25, 1912, 3.

133. *Chicago Record Herald,* October 26, 1912, 6; City Club, *A Report on Vocational Training,* 239–40, 91–112. See also M. C. Lyons, "An Argument for Business English," *Educational Bi-Monthly* 7, 2 (December 1912): 108–11.

134. Chicago Board of Education, *59th Annual Report, 1913,* 272; *60th Annual Report, 1914,* 324–25, 329–30.

135. W. Bachrach, "High School Course in Selling and Advertising," *Chicago Schools Journal* 4, 10 (June 1922): 31–39; Chicago Board of Education, *61st Annual Report, 1915,* 128–29; "Committee on High Schools," *Chicago Commerce,* January 2, 1914, 16; "Commerce in Public Schools," *Chicago Commerce,* January 23, 1914, 28; "Improved Commercial Education," *Chicago Commerce,* February 7, 1913, 7; Chicago Board of Education, *64th Annual Report, 1918,* 149, 64.

136. Survey of the Schools of Chicago, *Report 3,* 221–22.

137. Chicago Board of Education, *59th Annual Report, 1913,* 249, 259–60; idem, *60th Annual Report, 1914,* 32–33; *Chicago Schools Journal* 1 (September 1918): 23; F. M. Leavitt and E. Brown, *Prevocational Education in the Public Schools* (Boston, 1915), 23, ch. 5.

138. W. Hodges, "A Year of Prevocational Work," *Educational Bi-Monthly* 7, 3 (February 1913): 195, 197.

139. E. G. Cooley, "The Adjustment of the School System," 1–11; G. Kerschensteiner, *Education for Citizenship,* trans. A. J. Pressland (Chicago, 1911); Cooley's role in persuading Kerschensteiner to visit the U.S. was described by Cooley in the Commercial Club *Year-book, 1911–1912,* 96.

140. Commercial Club of Chicago, *Year-book, 1911–1912,* 95–136, 176–77, 276–78, 311. The membership of the Commercial Club, established originally in 1877 as a small private social club for businessmen with "conspicuous success" in business, was composed almost exclusively of the founders and top executives of Chicago's largest and leading industrial and commercial organizations: the Swifts, Armours, McCormicks, Fields, Donnelleys, Cranes, and Reynoldses of Chicago's capitalist class. Its education committee in 1911–12 was composed of Theodore Robinson, first vice-president of Illinois Steel Company; Edward B. Butler, president of Butler Brothers; Edward Carry, first vice-president and general manager of the American Car and Foundry Company; Clayton Mark, vice-president of National Malleable Castings Company; Bernard Sunny, president of Chicago Telephone Company; Frederic Upham, president of the City Fuel Company; and Charles Wacker, a leading figure in real estate. No educators belonged to the committee, or indeed, the club.

141. Ibid.

142. Idem, *1912–1913,* 147–56.

143. Ibid., 148; The Commercial Club of Chicago, *Vocational Schools for Illinois*, 3–6; The Commercial Club of Chicago, *Year-book, 1914–1915*, 254; J. M. Beck, "Chicago Newspapers and the Public Schools, 1890–1920" (Ph.D. dissertation, University of Chicago, 1953), 287–92.

144. *City Club Bulletin* 5 (December 4, 1912): 373–77; G. H. Mead, "The Larger Educational Bearings of Vocational Guidance," in *Readings in Vocational Guidance*, ed. M. Bloomfield (Boston, 1915), 46.

145. *Chicago Record Herald*, January 16, 1913, 3; February 18, 1913, 4; May 12, 1913, 3; Chicago Board of Education, *59th Annual Report, 1913*, 112–15.

146. *Chicago Record Herald*, December 1, 1912, 7; December 28, 1912, 1; February 20, 1913, 2; "Elementary Manual Training Club," *Chicago Principals Club Reporter* 11 (October 1912): 9–12; Chicago Board of Education, *59th Annual Report, 1913*, 258.

147. *Chicago Record Herald*, November 10, 1912, 5.

148. Ibid., April 2 and June 16, 1913; *Chicago Tribune*, June 16, 1913.

149. *The Chicago Record Herald*, November 10, 1912; J. N. Rathnau, "The Cooley Vocational Education Bill, 1912–1917," (Ph.D. dissertation, University of Chicago, 1973), 249–50; *Chicago Record Herald*, April 2 and June 16, 1913; *Chicago Tribune*, January 4 and June 16, 1913; *Champaign News*, September 26, 1912; the *Illinois State Journal* 3, 8, and May 18, 1912; *Chicago Tribune*, October 6 and December 29, 1912.

150. Quoted by City Club of Chicago, *A Report on Vocational Education*, 74–75.

151. Ibid., 76, 77–79.

152. Illinois State Federation of Labor, *Report of the Committee on Vocational Education, 1914*, 12–13, 14–15, 6, 7; idem, *Proceedings, 1914*, 45–54.

153. Idem, *Report of the Committee on Vocational Guidance*, 6.

154. Ibid., 9–10.

155. Idem, *Proceedings, 1915*, 72–74; *Weekly Newsletter*, May 8, 1915; ibid., May 15, 1915.

156. J. Dewey, "An Undemocratic Proposal," *Vocational Education* 11 (1913): 374–77. The following year, 1914, almost identical arguments were forwarded by William Bagley, professor of education at the University of Illinois, in an address to the Chicago division of the Illinois State Teachers Association and published in the *Education Bi-Monthly*. Indeed, Bagley's arguments were almost carbon replicas of Dewey's, even to the order in which the arguments were presented. See W. Bagley, "The Unit versus the Dual System of Vocational Education," *Educational Bi-Monthly* 9 (February 1915): 191–99.

157. Commercial Club, *Year-book, 1918–1919*, 362, 367.

158. See E. Abbott and S. Breckinridge, *Truancy and Non-attendance in the Chicago Schools* (New York, 1970), App. 7, 455. See also U.S. Department of Labor, "Vocational Guidance and Junior Placement," *U.S. Children's Bureau Publication No. 149* (Washington, D.C., 1915), 155; S. Breckinridge and E. Abbott, *Finding Employment for Children Who Leave the Grade Schools To Go to Work* (Chicago, 1911), 7–11.

159. Breckinridge and Abbott, *Finding Employment*, 10. See also, J. B. Davis, "Vocational Guidance, A Function of the Public School," *Educational Bi-Monthly* 6 (1911–12): 206–17.

160. Abbott and Breckinridge, *Truancy*, 457–65.

161. Chicago Board of Education, *59th Annual Report, 1912,* 22–23.

162. Abbott and Breckinridge, *Truancy,* 458, 459; Chicago Board of Education, *59th Annual Report, 1913,* 204–8, 269–70; Chicago Association of Commerce, *Minutes of the Executive Committee Meeting of July 12, 1912,* 226–27; Chicago Association of Commerce, *Annual Report of 1912,* 58; Chicago Board of Education, *59th Annual Report, 1913,* 204.

163. "Vocational Guidance and the Association's New Department of Civic Service," *Chicago Commerce,* November 29, 1912, 12; "Vocational Guidance and Delinquency," *Chicago Commerce,* May 9, 1913, 30–31. See also, "Vocational Guidance and Parents," *Chicago Commerce,* November 14, 1913, 4; "What Shall I Do?" *Chicago Commerce,* November 6, 1914, 14; Chicago Association of Commerce, *Annual Report of 1913,* 62.

164. E. L. Talbert, "Opportunities in School and Industry for Children of the Stockyards District," in *Readings in Vocational Guidance,* ed. Bloomfield, 396–453; L. Montgomery, "The American Girl in the Stockyards District," in Bloomfield, 454–84; A. Davis, "Occupations and Industries Open to Children Between Fourteen and Sixteen Years of Age," in Bloomfield, 542–56.

165. "Corrective Forces at Work in Chicago on the Educational and Industrial Problem of 'Hiring and Firing,' " *Chicago Commerce,* May 22, 1914, 7–11; Chicago Board of Education, *60th Annual Report, 1914,* 351, 343, 341, 352.

166. Chicago Association of Commerce, *Annual Report of 1915,* 65; "Association's Service to Vocational Guidance and Need and Prospect of Establishment of Bureau by Chicago Board of Education," *Chicago Commerce,* December 31, 1915, 37; "On Recommendations of Committee of Education Executive Committee Will Request Chicago Board of Education to Found Vocational Guidance Bureau," *Chicago Commerce,* November 19, 1915, 8–10; "Committee on Education," *Chicago Commerce,* January 28, 1916, 4; Abbott and Breckinridge, *Truancy,* 460; Chicago Association of Commerce, *Annual Report of 1916,* 58.

167. Chicago Board of Education, Bureau of Vocational Guidance, *Report, 1916,* 6.

168. Idem, *65th Annual Report, 1919,* 95. See also, "The Vocational Bureau and the Child Labor Law," *Chicago Schools Journal* 1 (1919): 15–16; U.S. Children's Bureau, "Vocational Guidance," 157, 183; A. W. Walz, "Vocational Education and the Vocational Guidance Bureau," *Chicago Schools Journal* 7 (1924–25): 161–67.

169. M. Hall, "Mental Tests," *Educational Bi-Monthly* 9 (1914–15): 66–78.

170. "Questions and Answers," *Chicago Schools Journal* 3 (1920–21): 248; R. H. Bracewell, "Segregation in Ability Groups as a Means of Taking into Account Individual Differences," *Chicago Schools Journal* 4 (1921–22): 94–95; "Questions and Answers," 149; D. Geyer, "Can We Depend upon the Results of Group Intelligence Tests?" *Chicago Schools Journal* 4 (1921–22): 203–10, 245–53; W. D. Scott, "Intelligence Tests for Prospective Freshmen," *Chicago Schools Journal* 4 (1921–22): 321–24; "Shall We Classify Pupils by Intelligence Tests?" *Chicago Schools Journal* 5 (1922–23): 35; M. Ross, "The Use of Intelligence Tests in Our Schools," *Chicago Schools Journal* 5 (1922–23): 152–53; see "Recent Publications in the Field of Measurement," *Chicago Schools Journal* 6 (1923–24): 364–73; F. F. Keaner, "A Mental Ability Test in First Year High School," *Chicago Schools Journal* 6 (1923–24): 374–77; P. J. Carlin, "A Short History of Intelligence Tests,"

Chicago Schools Journal 5 (1922–23): 378–82; A. O. Rape, "What Mental Tests Mean to the Classroom Teacher," *Chicago Schools Journal* 7 (1924–25): 18–19; E. Everett, "Mental Measurement in the Kindergarten," *Chicago Schools Journal* 7 (1924–25): 96–98; *Research Bulletin No. 1*, Bureau of Standards and Statistics, Division of Instructional Research, quoted in *Illinois State Federation of Labor Weekly Newsletter*, July 26, 1924, 1.

171. E. Freeman, "Sorting Students," *Educational Review* 68 (November 1924), 169–71.

172. Keaner, "A Mental Ability Test," 374–77; Weck, "The Elimination of Waste in Education," 177–79; U.S. Bureau of Education, *City School Leaflet No. 22*, 1926; Survey of the Schools, *Report 2*, 108, 194–95.

173. *Weekly Newsletter*, June 26, 1924.

174. Ibid. Olander had some reason to utilize the Hindu caste metaphor as a way of explaining the meritocratic system. On several occasions he referred to a statement by G. B. Cutten, president of Colgate University, that had lauded the virtues of a meritocratic society in terms of the Hindu caste system. Reprinted in *American Federation of Labor Weekly News Service*, November 7, 1925, from a copy in the Victor A. Olander Collection, box 2, Chicago Historical Society.

175. ISFL, *Weekly Newsletter*, July 26, 1924.

176. J. F. Gonnelly, "Development of the Junior High School in Chicago," *Chicago Schools Journal* 12 (1929): 46; Chicago Board of Education, *64th Annual Report, 1918*, 9; idem, *Proceedings*, July 11, 1923, to June 25, 1924, 1,266–67; M. Herrick, *The Chicago Schools* (Beverly Hills, 1971), 145–47. Meanwhile, the *Chicago Schools Journal* (the official journal of the board) published a steady stream of articles favorable to the junior high school idea. See, for example, J. D. Eisenhauer, "The Junior High School as an Aid in Individual Pupil Adjustment," *Chicago Schools Journal* 6, 5 (1924): 166; and from the same journal, B. Laughlin, "The Junior High School: Its Essential Features and Growth" 6, 7 (1924): 250; W. R. Hatfield, "Junior High Schools in Chicago," 6, 7 (1924): 252; W. T. McCoy, "Individual Differences in Junior High School," 12, 3 (1929): 89–91.

177. *New Majority*, May 31, June 7, 1924; G. S. Counts, *School and Society in Chicago* (New York, 1928), 170–72, 194, 198. Both Counts and Philip Curoe dismiss the Chicago Federation of Labor and the Illinois State Federation of Labor's rejection of the junior high school. Counts simply asserts that the representatives of labor "were fundamentally mistaken in their estimate of this movement" (177). He provides no arguments for this bald assertion. Curoe argues that labor in Chicago was either "not familiar with or does not accept the statements of purposes of the junior high school" which were "available from the responsible leaders of the movement" (160). He cites as evidence of these statements of purpose a study of Professor Briggs, which suggested that 60 of the 266 cases investigated introduced junior high schools "to provide educational opportunity."

178. Counts, *School and Society*, 194; *City Club Bulletin*, June 16, 1924, 99–100.

179. *Weekly Newsletter*, July 5, 1924; *New Majority*, July 5, 1924, July 12, 1924.

180. *Weekly Newsletter*, July 26, 1924.

181. *New Majority*, July 26, 1924.

182. *Weekly Newsletter*, July 26, 1924.

183. Counts, *School and Society*, 194–95. See also the *Jewish Forward*, May 22, 1924.

184. ISFL, *Weekly Newsletter,* June 28, 1924.

185. *City Club Bulletin,* October 6, 1924, 111.

186. Survey of the Schools of Chicago, *Report 2,* 8, 51, 148, 151.

187. "News of Chicago Schools," *Chicago Schools Journal* 7 (1924–25): 107.

188. Quoted in Survey of the Schools of Chicago, *Report 2,* 175–76.

189. "News of Chicago Schools," 108–9; Survey of the Schools of Chicago, *Report 2,* 52, 176–77.

190. *Junior High Schools in Theory and Practice,* Chicago Board of Education Handbook 2, 1931, 6; Hatfield, "Junior High Schools in Chicago," 253; Survey of the Schools of Chicago, *Report 3,* 224–25.

191. "Excerpts From Reports of Representatives of the South End Public School Association on Visits to Junior High Schools in Chicago," May 2, 1927, Victor Olander Files, box 10, Chicago Historical Association.

192. Ibid.

193. Ibid., May 6, 1927.

194. Ibid., May 9, 1927; May 13, 1927.

195. Ibid., February 20, 1928 (box 16).

CHAPTER FIVE: *Centralization and the Transformation of Public Education*

1. *Report of the Educational Commission of the City of Chicago* (Chicago, 1899), (Hereafter referred to as the Harper Report); R. L. Reid, "The Professionalization of Public School Teachers: The Chicago Experience, 1895–1920" (Ph.D. dissertation, Northwestern University, 1968), 46.

2. The Harper Report covered twenty main topics: the organization of the board of education; the business management of the board; the system of school supervision; the examination, appointment, and promotion of teachers; the elementary schools; the high schools; the normal school; special studies; resident commissioners; textbooks; the evening schools and free lecture system; vacation schools and school playgrounds; ungraded rooms and schools; the compulsory attendance law and parental school; teacher compulsory attendance law and parental school; teachers' institute and library; school faculties and councils; the school census; school accommodations; teaching citizenship; and school buildings and architecture. The quotes are from p. 14.

3. Nicholas Murray Butler, for instance, praised the Harper Report as "at once the most complete and most illuminating document on the organization and administration of the school system of a large American city that has ever been published. It may be commended to students of educational administration at home and abroad as representative of the broadest knowledge, the highest skill, and the wisest experience that America has to contribute to the discussion and understanding of this important subject (*Educational Review* 17 [March 1899]: 261–86).

4. David Tyack argues that "the administrative progressives" represented one wing of "progressivism" in education that "constituted a political-educational movement with an elitist philosophy and constituency. They tried to transfer control of urban education to a centralized board and expert superintendent under a corporate model of governance." Tyack also argues that the administrative progressives also took the lead in "differentiating the structure and fulfilling the goals of social efficiency and social control," and concludes that "they were primarily

concerned with organizational behavior and the linkage of school and external control, with aggregate goals rather than individual development" (D. Tyack, *The One Best System* [Cambridge, Mass., 1974], 196). In general, our argument is similar although not identical to Tyack's. In particular, we do not include "social control" among the objectives of the "administrative progressives," we argue that the objectives of the administrative progressives were successfully implemented through the combined efforts of a coalition of businessmen and "administrative progressives," we emphasize the links between administrative progressivism in education and administrative progressivism generally as a key component of political progressivism discussed in chapter 1, and we do not believe that the administrative structure the administrative progressives imposed was modeled entirely on corporate industry. The conflict between the board and the CTF has been analyzed in several works: Reid, "The Professionalization of Public School Teachers"; M. Murphy, "From Artisan to Semi-Professional: White Collar Unionism Among Chicago Public School Teachers, 1870–1930" (Ph.D. dissertation, University of California, Davis, 1981); S. Diner, *A City and Its Universities: Public Policy in Chicago, 1892–1919* (Chapel Hill, 1980), ch. 5; C. W. Collins, "Schoolmen, Schoolma'ams, and School Boards: The Struggle for Power in Urban School Systems in the Progressive Era" (Ed.D. dissertation, Harvard University, 1976); M. Herrick, *The Chicago Schools* (Beverly Hills, 1971), ch. 5; J. Wrigley, *Class Politics and Public Schools: Chicago, 1900–1910* (New Brunswick, 1982), chs. 4, 5.

5. For details, see Herrick, *The Chicago Schools*, 96–97; Murphy, "From Artisan to Semi-Professional," ch. 1; Collins, "Schoolmen, Schoolma'ams, and School Boards," 157–61. The papers of the CTF are held by the Chicago Historical Society.

6. *Chicago Record*, March 20, 1899; Reid, "Professionalization," 57; Haley, *Autobiography*, 216.

7. *CTF Bulletin*, March 6, 1903; *Chicago Tribune*, February 19, 1899; M. Murphy, "Margaret A. Haley and the Chicago Teachers Federation, 1897–1917" (M.A. thesis, San Jose State University, 1974), 8.

8. *Chicago Tribune*, May 8, 1899.

9. *Chicago Tribune*, June 19, 1899.

10. *Chicago Tribune*, February 28, 1899; Reid, "Professionalization," 57.

11. *Chicago Tribune*, July 15, 1899.

12. *Chicago Tribune*, September 29, 1899.

13. *Chicago Tribune*, November 4, 1899.

14. *Chicago Tribune*, November 10–11, 1899.

15. *Chicago Tribune*, December 28, 1899; February 10, 1900.

16. Andrew Draper, "Common School Problems of Chicago," address delivered at a citizens meeting under the auspices of the Commission of One Hundred of the Civic Federation of Chicago, December 1, 1900, 30.

17. *Chicago Tribune*, May 20, 1900; June 10, 1900; June 11, 1900.

18. Chicago Board of Education, *27th Annual Report, 1881*, 21; idem, *36th Annual Report, 1890*, 16; idem, *47th Annual Report, 1901*, 99–102; Reid, "Professionalization," 75–76; Murphy, "From Artisan to Semi-Professional," 92.

19. *Chicago Tribune*, October 4, 1900; T. A. DeWesse, "Two Years Progress in the Chicago Public Schools," *Educational Review* 24 (November 1902): 324–28; Reid, *"Professionalization," 72–73*.

20. Chicago Board of Education, *48th Annual Report, 1902*, 11–12; *Chicago Tribune*, July 3 and July 6, 1902.

21. Chicago Board of Education, *48th Annual Report, 1902,* 13; H. E. Dewey, "School Administration in Chicago, 1890 to 1920," *School Board Journal,* February 1938, 42.

22. *CTF Bulletin,* September 1, 1902.

23. Cooley's antipull campaign received a wide press. Ten feature stories on "school shake-ups" were reported in 1903, four in 1904, and ten in 1905, and when Cooley was having greatest difficulty with the board in 1906, twenty-one such articles appeared in the *Tribune.* One board member openly accused Cooley of using the list (*Chicago Tribune,* January 1, 1905), and another accused Cooley of abusing "pull" by publishing names selectively and "intriguing to keep himself in power" (*Chicago Tribune,* April 11, 1905). The *Tribune* used the issue to portray teachers as corrupt boodlers in headlines such as "Teachers Want Pull" (*Chicago Tribune,* January 30, 1906). See also, *Chicago Tribune,* November 14, 1902; March 29, 1904; June 10, 1904; February 11, 1905; September 3, 1905; January 9, 1907.

24. Chicago Board of Education, *48th Annual Report, 1902,* 11–12; *49th Annual Report, 1903,* 52–56; C. D. Lowry, "Genesis of a School," Chicago Literary Club, February 28, 1944, Newberry Library; DeWesse, "Two Years Progress," 336; Chicago Board of Education, *Bulletins,* 1904–08; Murphy, "From Artisan to Semi-Professional," 54–59.

25. Reid, "Professionalization," 84–85; Collins, "Schoolmen, School-ma'ams, and School Boards," 209–10.

26. M. A. Haley, "Comments on the New Education Bill," *CTF Bulletin,* January 23, 1903, 1; see also January 16, 1903, 1–2; March 13, 1903.

27. *CTF Bulletin,* January 23, 1903.

28. Ibid.

29. For details of the tax case, see M. Murphy, "Taxation and Social Conflict: Teacher Unionism and Public School Finance in Chicago, 1898–1934," *Journal of the Illinois State Historical Society* 74, 4 (Winter 1981): 242–49.

30. *CTF Bulletin,* March 6, 1903; M. Haley, "Why Teachers Should Organize," National Education Organization, *Addresses and Proceedings* (1904): 145–52; "Organization Among Teachers," *Chicago Teachers Federation Bulletin* 1 (June 27, 1902).

31. Wayne Urban asserts that "The CTF lost . . . an undetermined but large number of its total membership through resignations." We found no evidence to support the inference that a "large" fraction of the membership resigned. See Urban, *Why Teachers Organized* (Detroit, 1982), 82.

32. Haley, "Why Teachers Should Organize," 150–51; Reid, "Professionalization," 82–83.

33. *Chicago Record Herald,* July 22, 1907; "Resolutions Adopted by Chicago Federation of Labor at Mass Meeting on School Situation, December 2, 1906," *CTF Bulletin,* December 7, 1906. See also, Chicago Merchants Club, *Public Schools and Their Administration* (Chicago, 1906); C. Merriam, "The Chicago Charter Convention," *American Political Science Review* 2, 1 (November 1907): 1–14; Reid, "Professionalization," 129, 138; Murphy, "From Artisan to Semi-Professional," ch. 2.

34. *Chicago Tribune,* August 23, 1904; J. Addams, *Twenty Years* (New York, 1910), 231; Murphy, "From Artisan to Semi-Professional," ch. 6; Reid, "Professionalization," 99–106. Dunne was elected on a reform ticket that emphasized municipal ownership and "democratization," much to the dismay of Clayton Mark

and the board of education but to the delight of the CTF. During the mayoral campaign the CTF came under a barrage of criticism—particularly from the business community, Clayton Mark, and the Reverend Rufus White, a member of the board of education and the Civic Federation's education committee—for its affiliation with the CFL and its involvement in political affairs. Reid, 100–104.

35. Addams, *Twenty Years*, 234.

36. Ibid., 331; Murphy, "From Artisan to Semi-Professional," 122–29; Reid, "Professionalization," 108, 111–12; A. Davis, *American Heroine* (New York, 1973), 132–34. The clash between Haley and Addams is quite revealing of the major differences between the two women. Addams viewed her role—as she did in most situations—to be that of arbitrator and compromiser, traditional roles for women, only transplanted into the social arena. Addams had a morbid fear of class consciousness and saw no need for it; Haley, on the other hand, did not shrink from calling a spade a spade. Of the two women, Haley seems much the stronger, incisive, and forceful. See Murphy, ch. 3; *Chicago Tribune*, June 21, 1906; and Collins, "Schoolmen, Schoolma'ams, and School Boards," 295–96.

37. E. Ritter, "Some Needs of the Schools," *CTF Bulletin*, March 15, 1907, 2–3; Reid, "Professionalization," 115–16.

38. Chicago Board of Education, "Special Report on the Promotional Examination and Secret Marking of Teachers," *Proceedings, 1906*, 18–22; *CTF Bulletin*, November 16, 1906, 1–3; December 14, 1906, 2–7. For further details, see Collins, "Schoolmen, Schoolma'ams, and School Boards," 223–34; Reid, "Professionalization," 116–17.

39. Chicago Board of Education, *Proceedings*, January 16, 1907, 760–62; *CTF Bulletin*, January 4, 1907, 1; January 18, 1907.

40. Murphy, "From Artisan to Semi-Professional," ch. 3; Reid, "Professionalization," 117–28.

41. *Chicago Tribune*, October 10, 1906; Addams, *Twenty Years*, 337.

42. Chicago Merchants Club, *Public Schools and Their Administration*, 40; *Chicago Chronicle*, December 9, 1906.

43. Shortly after his election, Busse and his cabinet were wined and dined by seventy-five "representative" businessmen at the Atlantic Club. The Chicago Association of Commerce bulletin remarked that "it was a meeting auspicious of the new era now dawning in the civic history of the city. It was a conference of the new municipal authorities with cities business interests, and its effect upon a participant was inspirational. No partisan note was sounded to check the growing hope that it is possible to conduct the municipal business of Chicago as if it were a vast institution in trade or manufacture" (*Chicago Association of Commerce Bulletin*, April 26, 1907, 10). The new members of the board appointed by Busse were all businessmen or professionals: One was the president of a large corporation; one had been president of the board at the time the *Tribune* had been granted its infamous lease; one the head of a large firm of real estate operators; one a president of a big coal company; one a vice-president of a steel company. See *Chicago Tribune*, June 26, 1907; *CTF Bulletin*, June 25, 1907; G. S. Counts, *School and Society in Chicago* (New York, 1928), 248–49; Reid, "Professionalization," 134.

44. Chicago Board of Education, *Proceedings*, July 3, 1907, 6, 30; Reid, "Professionalization," 135.

45. Reid, "Professionalization," 138–39.

46. E. F. Young, *Isolation in the Schools* (Chicago, 1901), 6–11.

47. J. T. McManis, *Ella Flagg Young and a Half-Century of the Chicago Public Schools* (Chicago, 1916), 180–84; Chicago Board of Education, *Proceedings,* July 30, 1909, 66; Reid, "Professionalization," 140–42; Herrick, *The Chicago Schools,* 114–22; J. K. Smith, *Ella Flagg Young: Portrait of a Leader* (Ames, Iowa, 1979); R. V. Donatelli, "Two Contributions of Ella Flagg Young to the Educational Enterprise" (Ph.D. dissertation, University of Chicago, 1971).

48. McManis, *Ella Flagg Young,* 163; Donatelli, "Two Contributions," 359–60; Smith, *Ella Flagg Young,* 214.

49. In 1912 Alfred Urion, president of the school board and corporation counsel for Armour and Company, requested Mrs. Young to persuade teachers to accept greater school board representation on the pension board. William Rothmann, in particular, wished to gain appointment to the pension board. There can be little doubt that Urion and Rothmann wished to use the pension board as a means of controlling the activities of the CTF or to use it as a source of investment funds. As Armour corporation counsel, Urion was, at the time, defending Armour against the tax suit brought against Armour (and nineteen other companies) by the CTF. Rothmann's law partner was the president of the Board of Review, named in the tax suit for its failure to properly assess the corporations. Margaret Haley believed also that Rothmann had kept all the interest from a police pension fund that he had formerly supervised. M. Haley, "Alderman Kennedy's Four Points," *Margaret A. Haley's Bulletin,* October 21, 1915; Smith, *Ella Flagg Young,* 188; Wrigley, *Class Politics and Public Schools,* 125–26.

50. Smith, *Ella Flagg Young,* 187; Wrigley, *Class Politics and Public Schools,* 128.

51. Smith, *Ella Flagg Young,* 196–206; Wrigley, *Class Politics and Public Schools,* 128–29.

52. Smith, *Ella Flagg Young,* 193.

53. Herrick, *The Chicago Schools,* 124–25; Reid, "Professionalization," 156–58; *Chicago Tribune,* throughout July 1915.

54. *Chicago Tribune,* August 24, 1915; Herrick, 122–24.

55. J. Loeb, stenographic report of address, February 2, 1917, Chicago Teachers Federation Collection, Chicago Historical Society; *Chicago Tribune,* April 10, 1916.

56. Stenographic report of Jacob Loeb's testimony before the Baldwin Commission, Chicago Teachers Federation Collection, Chicago Historical Society.

57. Cited by B. Rinehart, "Mr. Gompers and the Teachers," *Changing Education* 1, 7 (Summer 1966): 15. Speaking before the NEA in 1916, Loeb denounced the CTF's affiliation with organized labor as unethical and unprofessional and urged that businessmen with their commitment to economy and efficiency be placed in charge of school systems. See J. Loeb, "The Businessman and the Public Service," NEA, *Addresses and Proceedings* (1916): 354. Freeland Stecker, a Chicago high school teacher, elected the first secretary of the American Federation of Teachers in 1916, believed the Loeb Rule was aimed at the CTF "not merely because it was the oldest of the teachers unions and had more members, but because it had full-time officials, and intricate political connections." The CTF, moreover, "became the vanguard of the backyard rebellion against the centralization of authority at a time when Chicago was very much in the national educational spotlight. At the turn of the century, Chicago seemed to be the political

national laboratory of school affairs, or so, at least, it was frequently expressed. However, the effort to regiment the Chicago schools for the benefit of spectator city school systems was not an entire success. For example, the Chicago Teachers' Federation had become a militant organization, reflecting the spirit of the Irish who were predominant among elementary teachers, and evolving the best leadership the school world had known. Catharine Goggin and Margaret Haley, with an able staff, had turned many a trick, proved themselves the equals of City Hall and Board of Education politicians and had won the support of thousands of teachers, and a growing admiration throughout the land" (Stecker, "The First Ten Years of the American Federation of Teachers" [1946], Arthur Elder Collection, Archives of Labor History, Wayne State University; Murphy, "Battleground," 121).

58. CFL, "Verbatim Report of a Meeting Held Under the Auspices of the Chicago Federation of Labor . . . ," September 8, 1915, CTF Papers, Chicago Historical Society; Herrick, *The Chicago Schools*, 123.

59. Letters of protest to the governor of Illinois signed by Fitzpatrick and Nochels of the CFL, Walker and Olander of the ISFL, and Flood of the AFL. See CFL, minutes of meeting of September 5, 1915, 6–11, and the minutes of the meeting of October 17, 1915, 7, John Fitzpatrick, Papers Chicago Historical Society; ISFL, "Report of the Committee on Schools," *34th Annual Proceedings of the Illinois State Federation of Labor,* October 16, 1916, 4–5. Many individual unions also adopted resolutions condemning the Loeb Rule: for details, see Wrigley, *Class Politics and Public Schools,* 132.

60. *Margaret A. Haley's Bulletin,* September 23, 1915, 1.

61. Chicago Board of Education, *Proceedings,* September 29, 1915, 885–86.

62. George H. Mead to board of education in behalf of the City Club of Chicago, June 13, 1916, CTF Papers, Chicago Historical Society; M. McDowell to board of education, June 12, 1916, CTF Papers.

63. CTF, "Report of a Public Demonstration Held at the Auditorium on Saturday, June 17, 1916 . . . ," CTF Papers, Chicago Historical Society.

64. Reid, "Professionalization," 175–86.

65. Carl Scholz (president of the PSL) to Harry Judson, November 20, 1916, President's Papers, Special Collections, University of Chicago Library.

66. The Buck Bill was the outcome of an investigation by the city council's committee on schools, fire, police, and Civil Service in 1916. The investigation— suggested by Haley to Buck—called on a large number of "educational experts" including William Maxwell, Leonard Ayres, Charles Judd, and Frank Spaulding, who advocated "efficiency" and administrative professionalization. They were not sympathetic to "democracy in schools," but they did support tenure for teachers, the primary goals of the CTF in those beleaguered days.

67. Reid, "Professionalization," 186–89; Herrick, *The Chicago Schools,* 132–34; *Public Education Association of Chicago Bulletin,* nos. 1–4 (1917); "Four Discussions of School Problems in Chicago," *City Club Bulletin* 10 (March 27, 1917); "Otis Law Has Never Had a Fair Trial, Says Shannon," *City Club Bulletin* (February 27, 1928): 1.

68. *Public Education Association of Chicago Bulletin,* no. 1 (n.d.): 4, 5. The PEA also published three other bulletins supporting the Otis Bill.

69. Herrick, *The Chicago Schools,* 135; Reid, "Professionalization," 191.

70. Herrick, *The Chicago Schools,* 134–37; Reid, "Professionalization," 159–94; *Chicago Tribune,* April 20, 1917; Murphy, "From Artisan to Semi-Professional," 1–2.

71. For the history of these events, see Reid, "Professionalization," 193–200; and Herrick, *The Chicago Schools,* 137–43.

72. Herrick, *The Chicago Schools,* 154–57; William McAndrew to Charles H. Judd, January 29, 1930, C. H. Judd Papers, Special Collections, University of Chicago Library.

73. "Superintendent Lets the Cat Out of the Bag: From the News Columns," *Margaret A. Haley's Bulletin,* May 15, 1927, 246, 255. Reprinted from the *Chicago Daily Journal,* April 18, 1927.

74. Herrick, *The Chicago Schools,* 150–54; Chicago Board of Education, report of the superintendent, 1924, 10; idem, 1926, 31–36.

75. Herrick, *The Chicago Schools,* 154–57; William McAndrew, "Official Notice," *Chicago Schools Journal* 8 (1925–26): 182–83; idem, "The Principal," *Chicago Schools Journal* (November, 1924): 81–85. Margaret Haley complained that McAndrew's "daily demands for reports, graphs, statistics, tests in so-called fundamental subjects, records of civic services by the children to which teachers were required to certify," represented "an intensely sharpened system of supervision and inspection that harrasses principals, teachers and pupils alike" (Margaret Haley, "What's Wrong in Our Schools: Veteran Teacher Gives Views," *Chicago Daily News,* January 7, 1928).

76. William McAndrew, "Speaking to This and That," *Chicago Schools Journal* 8 (December 1925): 121–44; "Association of Commerce Representatives Visit Schools: Superintendent of Schools Extends Invitation," *Margaret A. Haley's Bulletin,* June 25, 1925, 74.

77. Chicago Board of Education, *Citizens Sampling Day: Chicago Public Schools* (Chicago, 1926); William McAndrew to Charles H. Judd, May 20, 1926, C. H. Judd Papers, Special Collections, University of Chicago Library.

78. CFL, *Federation News,* June 12, 1926.

79. Herrick, *The Chicago Schools,* 166; L. Wendt and H. Kogan, *Big Bill of Chicago* (Indianapolis, 1953), ch. 24; W. H. Stuart, *The Twenty Incredible Years* (Chicago, 1935), 255–91; Wrigley, *Class Politics and Public Schools,* 188–95.

80. Herrick, *The Chicago Schools,* 166; Counts, *School and Society,* 227; Joint Committee on Public School Affairs, *Educational Extension and Community Centers; Recommendation and Report Based on a Survey of 76 Chicago Schools,* January 16, 1924, Chicago Historical Society; *New York Times,* November 4, 1927.

81. Counts, *School and Society,* 49–50, 60.

82. For a general discussion of these issues, see R. Dreeben, *On What Is Learned in School* (Reading, Mass., 1968), and "American Schooling: Patterns and Processes of Stability and Change," in *Stability and Social Change,* ed. B. Barber and A. Inkeles (Boston, 1971), 83–119.

83. See W. Waller, *The Sociology of Teaching* (New York, 1932). My formulation differs slightly from Waller's: Waller believed that school bureaucracies were primarily dominative because of the need to contain student-staff conflict and to mediate local community demands upon teachers. The Chicago example suggests that concern over labor productivity and the need to prevent coalitions rather than isolating teachers from political pressures was more salient. See also R. Edwards, *Contested Terrain: The Transformation of Work in Twentieth Century*

America (New York, 1979), 16–22, ch. 8; W. Heydebrand, "Organizational Contradictions in Public Bureaucracies: Toward a Marxian Theory of Organizations," *The Sociological Quarterly* 18 (Winter 1977): 83–107; and H. Gintis, "The Nature of the Labor Exchange and the Theory of Capitalist Production," *Review of Radical Political Economics* 8, 2 (Summer 1976).

Cherry Collins has, in a suggestive application of Amitai Etzioni's typology of organizational affiliations, pointed out that the administrative progressives "wanted the relationship between superintendent and the school board to rest on normative-moral considerations only (that is, those appropriate to professionals) but wanted the relationship of superintendent and grade teacher to be remunerative—calculative (associated with strictly material considerations in employer-employee relationships). The . . . teachers, on the other hand, wanted the whole system to operate by normative-moral compliance" ("Schoolmen, Schoolma'ams and School Boards," 285). She recognizes, however, that Etzioni's typology fails to appreciate the fact that professional aspirations were not limited to an official acknowledgement of the authenticity of the professional organizational position, but also included a demand for autonomy—based on their scientific training—and power. Moreover, Etzioni's typology does not provide an account of the mechanism of change in the structure of decision-making within the organization. Collins recognizes this also and uses Cyert and March's coalition theory of organizational decision-making to fill in the lacuna. While their model heads in the right direction, more useful are the accounts provided by Heydebrand, Benson, Gintis, and Edwards.

84. R. E. Callahan, *Education and the Cult of Efficiency: A Study of the Social Forces That Have Shaped the Administration of the Public Schools* (Chicago, 1962), ch. 3.

85. The distinction between control and coordination is drawn from Edwards, *Contested Terrain*, 16–22. It is also central to the argument of Wolf Heydebrand's "Organizational Contradictions," and J. K. Benson's "Organization: A Dialectical View," *Administrative Science Quarterly*, March 22, 1977, 1–21. The genesis of the distinction, however, rests ultimately in the long theoretical attack upon the Weberian model of bureaucracy, a history described by C. Perrow in his *Complex Organizations* (Glenview, Ill., 1972).

86. In only the most brazen example, the board leased property on the corner of Dearborn and Madison to the *Chicago Tribune* for thirty thousand dollars a year, about half of its actual leasing value, and then rented back some office space to the board for thirty-one thousand dollars! The president of the board of education, a member of the committee on school fund property, was at the time the *Tribune*'s general attorney. For the history of the board's continuing fiscal crisis, see Herrick, *Two Chicago Schools*, 75–79, 99–106, and Murphy, "Taxation and Social Conflict," 252–60.

87. The most useful study of the endeavor to create a science of educational administration is Callahan, *Education and the Cult of Efficiency*, ch. 8. At the University of Chicago, for example, the number of courses offered in educational administration increased from two in 1915 to fifteen in 1917 (Callahan, 199). A nationally prominent educator at the University of Chicago, Charles Judd, was anything but shy in advocating meritomatic expertise as the preeminent form of social authority. Judd wanted to generate "a movement to abolish school boards" in order to ensure "the simplification of government" and "reliance upon experts" (L. Cremin, *The Transformation of the School* [New York, 1961], 138–39). An

excellent theoretical analysis of the importance of an adequate cognitive base for professionalization is outlined by M. S. Larson in *Rise of Professionalism* (Berkeley, 1977).

88. On the "collective mobility" aspect of professionalization, see Larson, *Rise of Professionalism*, pt. 2. Edwin Cooley is a case in point. Cooley's national reputation as an administrator was built on the foundation (Margaret Haley considered it to be built on the backs of Chicago's teachers) of the merit "promotional" scheme. Within two years of announcing the scheme, Cooley had been made head of the NEA's prestigious department of superintendents; in 1905 he was admitted to the National Council of Education, and finally, in 1907, he became president of the NEA. Despite the misleading thrust of the point, Robert Wiebe's suggestion that the "heart of progressivism was the ambition of the new middle class to fulfill its destiny by bureaucratic means" is not without its relevance (R. Wiebe, *The Search For Order* [New York, 1967], 166).

89. For further details of the influence of Dewey and Parker, see chapter 2, and Reid, "Professionalization," 27–33; Collins, "Schoolmen, Schoolma'ams, and School Boards," 169–70; R. E. Tostberg, "Educational Ferment in Chicago, 1883–1904" (Ph.D. dissertation, University of Wisconsin, 1960); and R. McCaul, "Dewey's Chicago," *School Review* (Summer 1959).

90. Haley, "Why Teachers Should Organize," 146; M. Haley to Stella Crothers, September 10, 1905, in Murphy, "Battleground," 104.

91. See M. Murphy, "Progress of the Poverty of Philosophy: Two Generations of Labor Reform Politics: Michael and Margaret Haley," paper presented to the Knights of Labor Conference, Newberry Library, May 1979, 56.

92. For details of the involvement of the CTF in the municipal ownership movement, see Reid, "Professionalization," 91–94; Collins, "Schoolmen, Schoolma'ams, and School Boards," 214–17.

93. On Haley's involvement in the women's suffrage movement, see W. Urban, *Why Teachers Organized* (Detroit, 1982), 77–80. Urban stresses Haley's use of arguments that appealed to women's economic or material interests.

94. The motto, interestingly enough, of the AFT was "Democracy in Education: Education for Democracy." Its largest local was Local No. 1, the Chicago Teachers Federation. Reid, "Professionalization, 246–55; Collins, "Schoolmen, Schoolma'ams, and School Boards," 266–73.

95. Reid, "Professionalization," 201–45; Collins, "Schoolmen, Schoolma'ams, and School Boards," 241–66; Murphy, "From Artisan to Semi-Professional," 328–36.

96. Wayne Urban, for example, describes the CTF in these terms and argues that the pursuit of such political objectives as women's suffrage and affiliation with organized labor were "part of their pursuit of economic benefits" (Urban, *Why Teachers Organized,* 68). Neither of these claims, we think, are supportable. Two oversights explain Urban's difficulties: a failure to examine the history of the CTF in the context of the political battles over centralization, and a failure to approach the history of the CTF from the perspective of class formation. Urban's study fails to advance beyond the conceptual limits and theoretical conclusions of the Commons school of labor history.

97. Both Reid, and his mentor, Robert Wiebe, explain the behavior of the CTF as an expression of the process of professionalization. Reid, "Professionalization," ch. 7; Wiebe, *The Search for Order,* 120.

98. The original table for this information appears in Marjorie Murphy,

"From Artisan to Semi-Profesional," 106. This is a study of Chicago public school teachers and clerical workers in 1880 and 1900. Each teacher and clerk, of which there were 1,275 and 709 respectively, had a record of socioeconomic background collected from the 1880 and 1900 United States census using a cluster sample of six of sixteen reels for 1880 and ten of fifty-two reels for 1900. A cross-tabulation of clerks and teachers by the occupational rank of fathers (using S. Thernstrom's model) for 1880 produced a table with five degrees of freedom; Cramers V = .24; Contingency Coefficient = .23 with a total of 229 cases in 1880; for 1900, there were five degrees of freedom with Cramers V = .34; Contingency Coefficient = .32.

CHAPTER SIX: *Conclusion*

1. L. Cremin, *The Transformation of the School* (New York, 1961), viii.
2. In a review of the historiography of the Progressive Era, Rodgers concluded that "those who called themselves progressives did not share a common creed or a string of common values" but that they did possess "an ability to draw on three distinct clusters of ideas—the distinct social languages—to articulate their discontents and their social visions": the rhetoric of antimonopolism, the language of social bonding, and the language of social efficiency. "Together," he suggests, "they formed not an ideology but the surroundings of available rhetoric and ideas—akin to the surrounding structures of politics and power—within which progressives launched their crusades, recruited their partisans, and did their work" (D. P. Rodgers, "In Search of Progressivism," in *The Promise of American History: Progress and Prospects,* ed. S. I. Kutler and S. N. Katz [Baltimore, 1982], 123).
3. Cremin, *The Transformation of the School,* viii.
4. R. Wiebe, *The Search for Order* (New York, 1967), ch. 5; M. White, *Social Thought in America: The Revolt Against Formalism* (Boston, 1957).
5. J. Addams, *Democracy and Social Ethics* (New York, 1920), 2–3, 4, 6–7, 8, 11–12.
    Several historians have recently commented on the significance of languages of "social bonding" and "interdependence" in Progressive social thought. See, in particular, Rodgers, "In Search of Progressivism," 124–25; T. Haskell, *The Emergence of Professional Social Science: The American Social Science Association and the Nineteenth Century Crisis of Authority* (Urbana, 1977), esp. ch. 11; M. Furner, *Advocacy and Objectivity: A Crisis in the Professionalization of American Social Science, 1865–1905* (Lexington, 1975); J. B. Quandt, *From the Small Town to the Great Community: The Social Thought of Progressive Intellectuals* (New Brunswick, 1970); H. and J. R. Schwendinger, *The Sociologists of the Chair: A Radical Analysis of the Formative Years of North American Sociology (1883–1922)* (New York, 1974); H. Purcell, *The Crisis of Democratic Theory* (Lexington, 1973), pts. 1 and 2; and M. Katz, *Poverty and Policy in American History* (New York, 1983), pt. 4.
6. G. H. Mead, *The Philosophy of the Present,* ed. A. E. Murphy (Chicago, 1932); idem, *Mind, Self and Society,* ed. C. W. Morris (Chicago, 1934); idem, "The Social Settlement: Its Basis and Function," *University of Chicago Record* 12 (April 1926): 109; idem, "Philanthropy from the Point of View of Ethics," in *Intelligent Philanthropy,* ed. E. Faris (Chicago, 1930), 146.

7. J. Dewey, *Freedom and Culture* (New York, 1939), 23; idem, *Reconstruction in Philosophy* (Boston, 1957), 188, 190.

8. Dewey, *Reconstruction in Philosophy*, 200. See also idem, *Democracy and Education* (New York, 1964), 4–5, 99; idem, "Classes, Groups and Masses," in *Intelligence in the Modern World: John Dewey's Philosophy*, ed. J. Ratner (New York, 1939), 435; idem, *The Public and Its Problems* (New York, 1927), 191.

9. Dewey, *The Public and Its Problems*, 148; idem, *Democracy and Education*, 87.

10. Idem, *Liberalism and Social Action* (New York, 1935), 71; idem, "Educators and the Class Struggle," in *Intelligence in the Modern World*, ed. Ratner, 442.

11. Dewey, *The Public and Its Problems*, 153, 184. See also idem, *Individualism Old and New* (New York, 1962), 83.

12. H. W. Schneider, *A History of American Philosophy* (New York, 1946), 556–68. For a more general view, see T. Lowi, *The End of Liberalism* (New York, 1969), ch. 1.

13. Other intellectual habits of the Progressives are described in M. White, *Social Thought in America: The Revolt Against Formalism* (Boston, 1957), and Haskell, *The Emergence of Professional Social Science*, esp. ch. 11.

14. H. Adams, *The Education of Henry Adams* (Boston, 1961), 343–44. Rodgers's conclusion, "Progressive politics—fragmented, fluid, and issue-focused—was, in short part of the major, lasting shift in the rules of the political game," essentially restates Adams's conclusion. Rodgers, "In Search of Progressivism," 116. See also, W. D. Burnham, *Critical Elections and the Mainsprings of American Politics* (New York, 1970), chs. 4–5.

INDEX

Abbott, Edith, 75, 112–13, 181
Abbott, Grace, 64, 75, 210
Adams, Henry, 235
Addams, Jane: anti-vice campaign, 72; appointment to Board of Education, 204; campaign for Progressive Party in 1912 election, 30; on charity and friendly visiting, 33; Chicago Civic Federation and, 31, 37; on Chicago unemployment (1893), 21; on child labor and education, 52, 54; on class conflict and the separation of the classes, 26, 35, 36, 37, 232–33; *Democracy and Social Ethics*, 26, 233; on female suffrage, 28–29; founding of Hull House, 25–26; on juvenile delinquency, 64, 66, 67–69; kindergartens and, 80; opposes Loeb Rule, 210, 219, 220; playgrounds and, 70, 71; on vocational education, 166–67
"Administrative progressives," 195, 216–17
Allswang, John, xix, 76–77
Altgeld, John Peter (Governor): anti-Clevelandism, 23, 24; arbitration, 35–36; child labor agitation, 53; elected Governor, 19; Pullman Strike, 23
Americanization, 59, 82
American Railroad Union, 21–22
Anderson, Eric, 79–80
Anderson, Perry, xiii, xvi
Andrews, Benjamin (Superintendent): appointed Superintendent of Schools, 195, 196; policies, 158, 197–98
"Années Terrible," 17, 235

Anti-vice campaign, 72–75
Arbitration, 35–37
Armour Mission, 13

Bailyn, Bernard, xxi
Bellingham, Bruce, 94
Blacks: housing discrimination, 122; race riots (1919), 122
Bluthardt, T. J., 58
Bodine, William, 113–14
Boodling: extent of, 38; Progressive opposition to, 37–39, 43
Boyer, Paul, 77–78
Bowles, Samuel, xii
Brace, Charles Loring, 63
Braverman, Harry, 143
Breckinridge, Sophonisba: on housing, 75; on juvenile delinquincy, 64; on truancy, 112–13; and vocational guidance, 181
Britton, G. H., 110–11
Bryan, William Jennings: election of 1896, 24–25
Buenker, John, 77
Burnham, Daniel, 72
Bushnell, Charles, 142
Business leaders: covenant with Democratic Party, 44–45; opposition to civic reform, 43–44; relationship to civic corruption, 37–38; support centralization of School Board, 196, 198, 201, 206–7, 217–19; support civic reform, 31–32, 35, 37–38, 39–43

Busse, Frederick (Mayor), 7, 206–8
Butler, Nicholas Murray, 198, 206

Callahan, Raymond, 216
Cameron, Andrew, 5
Capitalism. *See* Class analysis; Class
    formation; "Great Transformation";
    Market Revolution
Catholicism: and protestantism, 12; school
    system, 125–27, 131
Centralization: centralization of school
    administration, 198, 200–201, 214–17,
    226–27; municipal reform, 37–38, 39,
    40–42; opposition to centralization of
    school administration, 196–97, 201–2,
    203, 205–6, 207, 220–21, 225–26. *See
    also* Chicago Board of Education;
    Chicago Teachers' Federation
Central Relief Association, 32
Central Trade Union, 8
Cermak, Anton (Mayor), 44, 45
Charity Organization Society of Chicago,
    15–17, 47–48
Charity reform, 15–17, 32–33
"Charity relation," Jane Addams on, 33
Charter, for home rule, 40–43
Chicago: economic growth, 1–2, 139–40;
    immigration, 3; labor force and
    population growth, 2–3, 149
Chicago Association of Commerce: and
    Cooley Plan, 175; and vocational
    education, 161–62, 171–72; and
    vocational guidance, 182–84; *Chicago
    Association of Commerce Bulletin,* 161
Chicago Bar Association, 62
Chicago Bible Institute, 13
Chicago Board of Education: Busse Board,
    206–8; centralization, 198, 200–201,
    203, 205–6, 207, 214–17, 226–27; child
    labor policy, 54–55, 56, 57–58; class
    composition of Board, 214–15;
    compulsory education policy, 59–60;
    Dunne Board, 204–6; finances,
    200–201, 217; junior high schools, 187,
    188, 190, 191; kindergartens, 81–82;
    manual training, 152–53, 154, 155–56;
    mental testing, 185–86; pedagogical

Chicago Board of Education (*continued*)
    innovations, 82–83, 91–93; vocational
    education, 156–58, 167–74; vocational
    guidance, 182–84
Chicago Bureau of Public Efficiency, 41–42
Chicago Central Labor Council, 197
Chicago Charter Convention (1904), 40
Chicago City Council: boodling and
    reform, 38–39
Chicago City Missionary Society, 13
Chicago Civic Federation: anti-corruption
    campaign, 37–39, 42–43; centralization
    of municipal administration, 39–40, 42;
    and child labor legislation, 54; and city
    charter, 40; and Commission of One
    Hundred, 198; and Cooley Bill, 175; and
    creation, 31; on depression of 1893, 21;
    and educational centralization, 198, 200,
    217, 219; and Harper Bill, 195, 196,
    197, 217; and Municipal Voters League,
    37, 38; prosopography, 47; and public
    utilities, 43; and Pullman Strike, 35; and
    regulation of trusts, 43
Chicago Civil Service Commission, 39
Chicago Civil Service Reform League, 39
Chicago Commission on Race Relations,
    122
Chicago Evangelization Society, 13
Chicago Federation of Labor: and Cooley
    Bill, 177–78; and education, 98, 100;
    and educational centralization, 196, 197,
    201, 209, 225–26; opposes Harper
    Commission proposals, 196, 197;
    opposes Loeb Rule, 209, 225
Chicago Froebel Association, 80
Chicago Herald, 22
Chicago Joint Club Committee, 74, 75
Chicago Kindergarten Club, 80
Chicago Labor League, 97
Chicago Law and Order League, 74
Chicago Manual Training School
    Association, 153
Chicago middle class. *See* Middle Class
Chicago Missionary Society, 12
Chicago Normal School, 83
Chicago Parks Commission, 69–70
Chicago Plan Commission, 72
Chicago Real Estate Board, 75

Chicago Relief and Aid Society, 15–16

Chicago Relief Association, 15–16

Chicago Society for Social Hygiene, 74, 75

Chicago Teachers' Federation: class
    formation and, 222–25, 226; declining
    power, 211, 223–25, 226; founding,
    110, 195, 196; historiography, 222–23;
    joins Chicago Federation of Labor,
    202–3; litigation against tax evaders,
    202, 203; and the Loeb Rule, 209–10;
    opposes centralization, 195, 201–2,
    220–21; opposes city charter convention
    proposals, 203; opposes Cooley Plan,
    177; opposes Cooley's promotions
    policies, 199–200, 220; opposes Harper
    Bill, 195, 196; supports administrative
    decentralization and teachers councils,
    220–21; supports Edward Dunne,
    203–204; supports social democracy,
    201–3, 221–22

Chicago Trades and Labor Assembly, 8

Chicago Tribune: on alcohol, 11; on anti-
    vice campaign, 73; on compulsory
    education, 59; on fads and frills in the
    schools, 99; on the founding of Hull
    House, 25; on the growing separation of
    classes, 3; on practical training, 152, 206;
    on 1877 strike, 6; on 1894 strike, 22

Chicago Vice Commission, 47, 74–75,
    78–79

Chicago Women's Club, 48, 61

Chicago working class. *See* Working class

Chicago Worlds' Fair, 71–72

Child-centered pedagogy, 82–93

Child labor: extent of, 52, 53, 55–57; and
    family economy, 105–22; legislation and,
    53–55; opposition to legislation, 56

Child saving campaigns: anti-vice, 74–75;
    child labor legislation, 53–55;
    compulsory education legislation, 57–60;
    curriculum, 87, 152–67; ideology,
    28–29, 51–52, 77–79; 83–84, 89;
    juvenile court and probation, 60–65;
    kindergartens, 79–82; and the Market
    Revolution, xii, 51–52, 93–95, 228–29;
    pedagogy, 82–91; playgrounds, 68–71

Child Study Department, 92–93

Church attendance, 14–15

Church Federation, 74

Citizens' Association of Chicago:
    educational reform, 59, 152; on 1877
    strike, 6

Citizenship: education and, 58–60, 82;
    vocationalism and, 165–66

Citizens' League for Law and Order, 11

Citizens' League for the Suppression of the
    Sale of Liquor to Minors, 11

City Club of Chicago: *A Report on
    Vocational Training in Chicago and in
    Other Cities* (1911), 160–61, 162–65; on
    centralization, 211; and junior high
    schools, 188, 190; opposes Loeb Rule,
    210; vocational education and, 160–61,
    162–65, 171, 176

Class analysis, xiii–xx, 195, 230–31. *See also*
    Class formation

Class conflict. *See* Classes, separation of

Classes, separation of and origins of
    Progressive reform: Jane Addams on, 26,
    27, 29, 33, 166–67; arbitration and,
    35–37; William Jennings Bryan on,
    24–25; charity relation and, 33; Charity
    Organization Society on, 16–17;
    Chicago Civic Federation and, 32;
    Chicago Tribune on, 3; child saving and,
    51–52; citizenship and, 58–60, 82, 154,
    165–66; John Commons on, 9;
    evangelical Protestants and, 11, 12–13;
    friendly visiting and, 17, 32, 35; Charles
    Henderson on, 16; Gareth Stedman
    Jones on, 17; Henry Demarest Lloyd on,
    19; P. H. McLogan on, 7; pedagogy
    and, 85, 88–89; playgrounds and, 71;
    Populists on, 18; professional casework
    and, 35; Progressive reform and, xii,
    xxiv, 3, 26–27, 31, 32, 35–37, 46,
    48–50, 51–52, 88–89, 93–94, 228,
    231–32; Pullman Strike and, 21–23;
    radical republicanism and, 5, 7, 98–99,
    101, 186–87, 188–89; Social Gospel
    and, 17; William T. Stead on, 17; welfare
    and, 6–62; Frederick Wines on, 17; work
    relations and, 7, 140–42. *See also* Class
    formation; Social Democracy

Class formation: *Chicago Tribune* on, 3;
    class conflict and, xv, xvi, 49–50; defined,

Class formation (*continued*)
xiv–xviii, xx; educational administration and, 216–17, 226; home ownership and, 114–22, 136–37; making of the Chicago middle class, 46–50, 224–25, 231–32, the Market Revolution and, xiii, xvi, xviii, 25, 46–50; Progressive reform and, 46–50, 224–25, 231–32; remaking of the Chiago working class, 96–97, 136–37, 231; school attendance and, 123–37; social insurance and, 123–37; teachers and, 222–26; Robert Wiebe on, 48–49, 95, 232. *See also* Classes, separation of
Cleveland, Grover, 23, 24
Clothing industry, 145–46
"Commerce and virtue," dialectic of: in 18th century thought, xxi–xxiii; in 19th century reform, xxi–xxiv; in Progressive reform, xxiv, 49–50, 52, 94, 193, 235
Commercial Club of Chicago: anti-vice campaign, 73; city planning, 72; Cooley Plan, 175, 181; and law and order, 10; vocational education, 159–60, 162, 175
Commercial education, 157–58, 163–64, 170, 171–73
Commission of One Hundred, 198
Committee of Fifteen, 47, 45, 78–79
Commons, John, 9, 144–45
Compulsory education, 57–60
"Conference Bill" (1913), 177
Congress on Industrial Conciliation and Arbitration, 35
Connell, Robert W., xii, xvi–xvii, xviii–xix
Cook County Progressive Committee, 30
Cooley, Edwin (Superintendent): appointment of teachers, 198–99, 215; centralization, 200–201; promotions policy, 199, 200, 206, 215; vocational education, 162, 165–66, 175
Cooley Bill, 176, 193
Cooley Plan: opposition to, 176–81; principles of, 175–76; support for, 175–176
Couglin, John, 38
Council of Trade and Labor Unions of Chicago, 97
Counts, George, xi–xii, 189
Covello, Leonard, 132–33

Crane, Richard, 153, 155–56
Cremin, Lawrence, xii–xiii, 228–29
Curriculum reform. *See* Dewey, John; Manual training; Vocational education; Vocationalism
Curtis, Henry, 71
Czech immigrants and education, 128–32

Dawley, Allan, xii
Dean, Arthur, 151
DeBey, Cornelia, 204, 205–6
Debs, Eugene, 21, 22
Delinquency: Jane Addams on, 66, 67–69; Chicago Juvenile Court, 60–65
Democracy, 155. *See also* Radical republicanism; Social democracy
Democratic Party: Altgeld versus Cleveland, 23, 24; Cermak-Kelley machine, 45
Depression of the 1890s, 20–21
de Tocqueville, Alexis, xxiv
Dewey, John: Cooley Bill and, 180; Laboratory School, 85–88; *School and Society*, xi; social theory, 233–34
Diner, Stephen, 48
Domestic feminism, 28–29
Douglas, Paul, 149, 151
Dunne, Edward (Mayor), 203–4

Easley, Ralph, 32
Education. *See* Americanization; Centralization; Chicago Board of Education; Child saving campaigns; Citizenship; Class formation; Commercial education; Compulsory education; "Great Transformation"; Kindergartens; Manual training; Market Revolution; Pedagogy; Progressive education; Vocational education; Vocationalism; Working class
Educational Commission of the City of Chicago. *See* "Harper Commission"
"Edward's Law," 57–58
Eight-hour day, 5, 9–10
Ela, John, 39–40
Embourgeoisement, 135–36
Environmentalism, 63, 77–78
Evangelism, 12–15

"Fads and frills" controversey, 99–100
Family economy: child labor, 103–114;
home ownership, 114–22; income,
101–4; school attendance, 123–36; and
social insurance, 33–34. *See also* Class
formation; Working class
Farmer Labor Party, 19–20, 23–24
Female suffrage. *See* Domestic feminism
Field, Marshall, 6, 153
Fitzpatrick, John, 210, 213
"Fourteen to sixteen problem," 159–61
Freeman, Frank, 185
Froebel Society, 80

Gage, Lyman, 31–32, 38–39, 43, 49
General Managers' Association, 22
Germans, in Chicago, 3
Giddens, Anthony, xiii, xviii
"Gilded Age" reform, 4, 11–17, 48, 66, 77
Gintis, Herbert, xiii
Glenn, John M., 56
Goggin, Catherine, 196
Gompers, Samuel, 210
Gosnell, Harold F., 45
Goss, C. F., 14
"Great Transformation": definition, xviii,
xx–xxi, 1; and Progressive education, xii,
192–93, 226–27, 230–32, 235; and
Progressive reform, xii, 50, 228, 230–32,
235. *See also* Market Revolution;
Progressive education; Progressive
reform; Structuration
"Great Upheaval," 5–6
Gutman, Herbert, xiii

Haley, Margaret: on Jane Addams, 204;
centralization and, 196, 201–2; on
decentralized administration, 89,
220–23; and Knights of Labor, 222–24;
and social democracy, 221–22; and tax
evasion by Chicago corporations, 202.
See also Chicago Teachers' Federation
Ham, Charles, 153
Hamilton, Thomas, xxi, xxiii
Harper, William Rainey, 194, 195
"Harper Bill," 195, 196–97, 217
"Harper Commission," 69, 158, 194–95
Harrison, Carter, Jr. (Mayor), 29–40, 54,
69, 194, 207, 208

Harrison, Elizabeth, 81
Hawthorne factory, 141
Haymarket riot, 9–10, 12, 13
Hays, Samuel P., 48
Henderson, Charles: on city planning,
66–67; on urban conditions, 67; on
welfare, 16, 33, 34
Hofstadter, Richard, xix, 48
Home ownership. *See* Family economy
Housing reform, 75–76
Howe, Samuel Gridley, 63
Howland, George (Superintendent),
138–39, 154
Hull House: activities, 26–30; child labor
and, 52–53, 55; foundation, 25–26; and
immigrants, 26–28; kindergartens and,
80–81; playgrounds and, 67–68, 69;
vocational education, 27, 166–67. *See
also* Addams, Jane; Settlement houses
Hurley, Timothy, 61, 62

Illinois Anti-Saloon League, 76–77
Illinois Bureau of Labor Statistics, 5, 8, 9,
102, 103, 110, 114–115, 145
Illinois Childrens Home and Aid Society,
60
Illinois Immigrants' Protective League, 47,
74, 75
Illinois Manufacturers' Association: and
child labor, 56; and teacher unionism,
210, 216, 218
Illinois State Board of Arbitration, 35–36
Illinois State Board of Charities, 61–62
Illinois State Federation of Labor: and
"fads and frills" controversy, 99–101;
opposes child labor, 97–99; opposes
intelligence testing, 186–87; populism
and, 19; supports compulsory education,
97, 98–99, 101; vocational education
and, 177–80. *See also* Olander, Victor
Illinois State Progressive Committee, 30
Illinois Vigilance Association, 74
Immigrants: Americanization in the
schools, 82; home ownership, 114–22;
income levels, 101–4; and religion,
125–27; school attendance, 123–26
Immigration, 2–3
Incomes, 101–4

Industrial and Commercial Education in Relation to Conditions in the City of Chicago (Chicago Association of Commerce), 159–60
Industrialization. *See* Manufacturing; Market Revolution
Intelligence testing: introduction into Chicago schools, 185–86; opposition to, 186–87
International Harvester, 140, 147–48
International Working Peoples' Association, 8, 10, 96
Irish, 126
Irving, Terry, xiii

Jacksonian Democracy, xxii, xxiii–xxiv
Jefferson, Thomas, xxi, xxiii
Jensen, Richard, xiii
Jews, and education, 133–35
Johnson, Richard, xiii
Jones, Gareth Stedman, 16–17
Junior high schools: curriculum and pedagogy, 191–92; introduction of, 187–88; opposition to, 187–91
Juvenile courts: agitation for, 60–63; procedures, 62, 64–65; significance, 62, 63, 64, 65
Juvenile Protection League, 67, 74, 75

Karier, Clarence, xiii
Katz, Michael, xiii, 120, 125
Kelley, Florence: and child labor, 53–57; housing reform, 66; and social reform, 37
Kelsey, Carl, 60–61
Kennedy, John C., 150
Kilpatrick, William Heard, 91
Kindergartens, 79–82
Kleppner, Paul, xix
Knights of Labor, 8–9, 18, 23, 223
Kolko, Gabriel, 45
Kramnick, Isaac, xxi

Labor. *See* Chicago Federation of Labor; Illinois Federation of Labor; Trade unions; Unemployment; Working class
Laboratory School, 85–89
Labor-Populist alliance, 19–20, 23–24
Lane, Albert C. (Superintendent), 57, 83, 156, 158

Laurie, Bruce, xiii
Law and order campaigns, 4, 6, 10, 11
Law and Order League, 6, 11
Lazerson, Marvin, xiii
Leavitt, Frank, 165
Lehr and Wehr Verein, 7
Liberalism: in Jacksonian America, xxii, xxiii–xxiv; "Lockean Moment," 46–50, 94–95; Lockean tenets, xxi; and republican liberalism, xxi–xxiv, 46, 50, 94–95. *See also* "Commerce and virtue"
Lloyd, Henry Demerest, 19–20, 24, 99
Locke, John, 95
"Lockean Moment," 46–50, 94–95
Loeb, Jacob, 208, 201, 211, 218
Loeb Rule, 208–10, 225–26

McAndrew, William (Superintendent): appointed superintendent, 211; close relations with businessmen, 212–13; dismissed by Mayor Thompson, 213–14; introduces Citizens Sampling Day, 213; supports centralization, 211–12, 215; supports intelligence testing, 185–86; supports junior high schools, 187, 188
McCluer, F. C., 110
McCormick, Cyrus, 140
McDowell, Mary, 30, 37, 80, 210
Machine politics, 38–39, 42, 44–45, 73
McLogan, P. H., 7, 98, 103, 146–47
Madison, John, xxi
Mann, Horace, 51
Manual training: business demand for, 152–53, 154, 158; introduced into Chicago schools, 152–53, 154, 158
Manufacturing: employment patterns, 139–40, 141, 149; growth of, 1–3; labor process, 142–52. *See also* "Great Transformation"; Market Revolution; Mechanization; Specialization
Mark, Clayton, 175
Mark-Cooley Bill, 201, 217–18, 219
Market Revolution: and child labor, 55, 56–57, 58–59; and child saving, 52, 58–60, 93–95; defined, xi, xii, 1; and economic growth, 1–3, 139–52; and juvenile delinquency, 66, 67–69; and pedagogy, 84–85, 87, 88–89, 92–94, 191–92; and Progressive reform, xxiv, 46–50, 60, 93–95, 226–27, 228–32,

Market Revolution (*continued*) 235; and vice, 73–74; and vocationalism, 139, 152, 181, 184, 192–93, 194–95. *See also* Progressive education; Progressive reform; "Great Transformation"

Marx, Karl, 143

Mayer, John, 102, 104

Mead, George Herbert: advocate of vocational education, 160; member of City Club of Chicago, 47; opposes Cooley Plan, 176; opposes Loeb Rule, 210, 220; social theory, 233, 234

Meat packing industry, 144, 150

Mechanization: effects of, 149–52; extent of, 143–50

Mental testing. *See* Intelligence testing

Merchants' Club of Chicago: and city planning, 72; civic reform and, 40; and educational centralization, 200, 206, 217; playgrounds and, 69, 70

Merriam, Charles, 40, 41–42, 177, 210, 220

Merrill, L. F., 124, 133

Merritt Conspiracy Law, 10

Metal trades, 147–48

Methodism, 11

Middle class: making of Chicago middle class and Progressive reform, 10–17, 46–49, 52, 93–95, 216–17, 231–32. *See also* Class formation; Progressive reform

Mills, C. Wright, 141

Monopolies. *See* Lloyd, Henry Demarest; Manufacturing; Trusts

Montgomery, David, 142

Montgomery, Louise, 109, 117

Moody, Dwight, 12, 13, 14, 80

Moody Bible Institute, 13

Morgan, Thomas: on education, 98–100; labor-farmer alliance, 19, 20; social problems in Chicago, 31

Mothers' pensions, 33–34

Mowry, George, xix

Municipal Voters' League, 37–39, 47

National American Woman Suffrage Association, 29

National Association for the Advancement of Colored People, 29

National Association of City Planning, 29

National Child Labor Committee, 29

National Conference of Charities and Corrections, 29

National Consumers' League, 29

National Education Association, 29

National Farmers' Alliance, 29

National Housing Association, 29

National Playground Association, 71

National Progressive Committee, 30

National Progressive Service, 30

National Woman's Trade Union League, 30

Newton, Huber (Rev.), 140–41

New York Times, 6

Norris, Frank, 2

Olander, Victor: and I.Q. testing, 186–87; and junior high school, 188–90; and Loeb Rule, 210; and vocational education, 179–80. *See also* Illinois State Federation of Labor

Olney, Richard, 7

Otis Bill (1917), 210–11

Paine, Thomas, xxiii. *See also* Radical republicanism

Parens patriae, 62–63

Parker, Francis, applauds John Dewey, 85; appointed to Cook County Normal School, 83; child saving and social reform, 83–84; "new education," 83; views on democracy, 84–85

Parks, 69–70

Patronage in teacher appointments, 198–99

Pedagogy: Chicago Board of Education policy, 82–83, 91–93; competitive individualism, 84–85; developmentalism, 90–91; John Dewey, 85–89; "fads and frills" controversey, 99–100; learn by doing, 164–65, 169, 170, 172, 174, 191–92; Joseph Rice Mayer, 82–83; Francis Parker, 83–84

Peoples' Party, 18–19, 23–24. *See also* Labor-Populist alliance

Perlman, Joel, 120, 125

Pickard, Josiah (Superintendent), 138, 152

Platt, Anthony, 65
Playgrounds, 69–71
Pocock, J. G. A., xxi, xxii–xxxiii
Polanyi, Karl, xviii
Polish immigrants and education, 5,
    128–32
Political capitalism, 45
Populism, 17–19, 23–24. *See also* Peoples'
    Party
Post, Louis, 204, 205
Poverty, 101–104
Probation, 63–65
Producer ideology. *See* Radical
    republicanism
Progressive education: administrative
    centralization, ch. 5; and child labor
    legislation, 53–55; compulsory education
    legislation, 57–60; curriculum, 87,
    152–67; historiography, xii–xiii,
    228–30; ideology, 28–29, 51–52,
    77–79, 83–84, 89; junior high schools,
    187–92; juvenile court and probation,
    60–65; kindergartens, 79–82; and the
    market revolution, xii, 51–52, 93–95,
    228–29; mental testing, 185–87;
    pedagogy, 82–91; playgrounds, 68–71;
    vocational education and, 154–55, 156,
    158–61, 165, 166–67, 174, 192–93;
    vocational guidance, 181–84. *See also*
    Child saving campaigns; Progressive
    reform
Progressive Party, 305
Progressive reform: child saving and,
    51–52, 60, 93–95; civic reform and,
    37–46; class formation and, 46–49,
    216–17, 224–25, 230–32; effect on
    Chicago working class, 34, 96–97,
    136–37, 231; Prohibition, 76–77;
    relationship to the Market Revolution
    and the "Great Transformation," xii, xxiv,
    3, 17–25, 26–27, 31, 32, 35–37, 46–50,
    51–52, 88–89, 93–95, 226–27, 228–29,
    230–32; relationship to republicanism
    and liberalism, 46, 50; settlement houses,
    27–30, 47; social theory and, 232–34.
    See also Arbitration; Centralization;
    Charity reform; Chicago Civic
    Federation; Child saving campaigns;
    Hull House; Market Revolution;

Progressive reform (*continued*)
    Municipal Voters' League; Progressive
    education
Prohibition, 76–77. *See also* Temperance
    movement
Prostitution, campaigns against, 73–75
Protestantism, 11–15, 73, 74
Public Education Association, 210, 211
Public School League, 210
Pullman, George, 4, 6–7
Pullman Strike (1894), 21–22
Putnam, Alice, 79–80

Radical republicanism, 5, 7, 98, 101,
    186–87, 188–89. *See also* Lloyd, Henry
    Demarest; Olander, Victor; Paine,
    Thomas
Rainwater, Clarence, 70
Republicanism, xxi, xxii. *See also* Liberalism
Rice, Joseph Mayer, 82–83
Riis, Jacob, 69
Ritter, Emil, 204, 205
Robins, Margaret, 30
Robins, Raymond, 30
Robinson, Theodore W., 162, 175, 207,
    218, 219
Rockefeller, John D., 194
Rodgers, Daniel, 229
Roe, Clifford, 73–74, 75
Roethlisberger, F. J., 141
Roosevelt, Theodore, 25
Rosenwald, Julius, 44
Ross, E. A., 79
Rothmann, William, 208

Saloons, 76–77. *See also* Temperance
    movement
Schneider, Herbert, 234
School attendance: compulsory education
    and, 57–60; family economy and,
    123–36. *See also* Class formation;
    Working class
Scientific management: and educational
    administration, 194–95, 198, 199–201,
    211–13, 215; in the workplace, 143,
    144. *See also* Social efficiency
Searchlight, 20
Settlement houses, 25, 27–30, 47
Sherman Anti-Trust Act, 43

Sinclair, Upton, 96
Skills. *See* Manufacturing
Slavic immigrants and education, 128–32
Slums, 53, 66. *See also* Housing reform
Small, Albion, 38, 46
Social control, historiography of, xii, 52, 65, 77–79, 95, 135, 229–30
Social democracy: Jane Addams on, 26, 29, 232–33; John Dewey on, 88–89, 233–34; Margaret Haley and, 221–22; Francis Parker on, 85; Progressive reform and, xx, 232–33. *See also* Classes, separation of and origins of Progressive reform; Progressive education; Radical republicanism
Social efficiency: and administrative centralization, 38, 40–41, 194–95, 198, 199–201, 211–13, 215, 229; and junior high schools, 187; and Market Revolution and Progressive reform, xx, 138–39, 192–93, 229–30; and mental testing, 185; and reorganization of the labor process, 143, 152; and vocational education, 159, 161–62, 229. *See also* Centralization; Progressive education; Progressive reform; Scientific management; Vocationalism
Social insurance, 33–35
Socialist Labor Party, 8
Social justice and Progressive reform, xx, 26, 27, 29, 30, 39, 50, 51–52, 229, 232. *See also* Progressive education
Social Science Directory, 34–35
Specialization, effects of, 144–52
Spring, Joel, xviii
Starr, Ellen Gates, 25, 28
State Federation of Womens' Clubs, 55
Stead, William T.: juvenile offenders, 60; support for Hull House, 31; on urban conditions, 31, 66, 71
Steel industry, 148–49, 150–51
Steffens, Lincoln, 39, 43–44
Stone, Katherine, 143
Story, Alan, 155
Strayer, George, 91
Strikes: 1877, 5–6; 1894, 21–23; eight-hour movement and Haymarket, 8–10; incidence (1881–1900), 4. *See also* Class formation; Classes, separation of

Structuration, xviii, xx, 135–36, 230–31. *See also* Class analysis; Connell, R. W.; Giddens, Anthony; "Great Transformation"; Market Revolution
Sunday schools, 13
Survey of the Schools of Chicago, 91–92

Talbot, Ernest, 109
Taylor, Graham: and arbitration, 37; on class conflict, 36; on the depression of 1893, 21; and municipal reform, 37; and playgrounds, 70
Teachers. *See* Chicago Teachers' Federation
Teachers councils, 201–2, 205–6, 207–8, 220–21
Temperance movement, 11, 73, 76–77
Thomas, W. B., 131
Thompson, Edward P., xiii, xiv–xviii
Thompson, William Hale (Mayor), 44, 210, 211, 213–14
Thurber, Charles, 158
Thurston, Henry, 64
Todd, Helen, 109–110, 123
Trade unions. *See* Chicago Federation of Labor; Illinois State Federation of Labor; Strikes
Truancy, 110–13
Trusts, 19, 43
Turner, George Kibbe, 73
Tyack, David, xiii, 195

Unemployed Relief System, 20
Unemployment (1893), 20
Union League, 10
United Societes for Local Self-Government, 76–77
United States Commissioner of Labor, 133
United States Immigration Commission, 105–109, 115–17, 119
United States Industrial Relations Commission, 37

Vanderwalker, Nellie, 81
Vice. *See* Anti-vice campaign
Violas, Paul, xiii
"Virtue and commerce." *See* "Commerce and virtue"
Vocational education: 155–58, 167–74; link to Market Revolution, xii, 139, 174,

Vocational education (*continued*) 192–93, 232; organized labor's attitude toward, 177–79; prevocational education, 173–74; relationship to administrative centralization, 218–19. *See also* Commercial education; Cooley Bill; Cooley Plan; Crane, Robert; Manual training; Vocationalism

Vocational guidance, 181–84

Vocationalism, 154–55, 156, 158–61, 165, 174, 192–93. *See also* Addams, Jane; Chicago Association of Commerce; City Club of Chicago; Commercial Club of Chicago; Cooley Bill; Cooley Plan; Market Revolution; Progressive education; Social efficiency; Vocational education

Walker, Edwin, 23

Walker, John, 98

Waller, Willard, 215–16

Weaver, General, 19

Welfare. *See* Social insurance

Weyl, Walter, 146, 147–48, 150, 151

Whig ideology, xxii, 50–51, 154

White, Morton, xx, 232

Wiebe, Robert, 48–49, 95, 232

Wilentz, Sean, xii, xiii

Wines, Frederick, 17

Women's Christian Temperance Union, 74

Workers Compensation, 33–34

Working class: class formation in 19th century, 5–6, 7–8, 9–10; class reformation after Pullman Strike, 23, 45, 97, 122, 135–37; family economy of, 34, 103–22; and home ownership, 114–22; impact of Progressive reform, 34, 96–97, 136–37, 231; and school attendance, 123–36. *See also* Class formation

Workingman's Advocate, 5

Working Man's Party of Illinois, 97

Wood, Gordon, xxi

Wrigley, Julia, xix

Yerkes, Charles T., 38, 42

Young, Ella Flagg (Superintendent): appointed to Chicago Normal School, 204; appointed superintendent, 207–8; opposes Cooley Plan, 176–77; opposes Loeb Rule, 211; supports vocational education, 157, 171, 172

Young Mans Christian Association, 11